CHALLENGING HISTORY

BRITAIN IN THE NINETEENTH CENTURY

HOWARD MARTIN

WITHDRAWN FROM
Thomas Rotherham
College
Learning Resources

D0487322

941.081 MAR

Thomas Nelson and Sons Ltd
Nelson House Mayfield Road
Walton-on-Thames Surrey
KT12 5PL UK

Thomas Nelson Australia
102 Dodds Street
South Melbourne
Victoria 3205 Australia

Nelson Canada
1120 Birchmount Road
Scarborough Ontario
M1K 5G4 Canada

All rights reserved. No part of this publication may be
reproduced, copied or transmitted save with written
permission or in accordance with the provisions of the
Copyright, Design and Patents Act 1988, or under the
terms of any licence permitting limited copying issued
by the Copyright Licensing Agency, 90 Tottenham
Court Road, London W1P 9HE.

Any person who does any unauthorised act in relation
to this publication may be liable to a criminal
prosecution and civil claims for damages.

Printed in United Kingdom by Ebenezer Baylis and
Son Ltd.

© Howard Martin 1996

Acquisitions: Roda Morrison, Steve Berry
Administration: Jenny Goode
First published by Thomas Nelson and Sons Ltd 1996   Design: Multiplex Techniques
                                                          Editorial: Nick Brock
ITP Thomas Nelson is an International   Marketing: Jane Lewis
     Thomson Publishing Company   Production: Liam Reardon
ITP is used under licence

ISBN 0-17-435062-7
NPN 9 8 7 6 5 4 3 2 1

ACKNOWLEDGEMENTS

ANN RONAN: 2 (bottom), 3, 4 (top & bottom), 9, 16 (top & bottom), 80 (bottom), 107, 114, 130, 139, 144, 150, 153 (top & bottom), 157, 162 (bottom), 163, 167 (top), 172, 174, 184 (top & bottom), 190 (top & bottom), 196, 199 (left & right), 218, 226, 229, 239 (left & right), 241, 243 (top & bottom), 244, 254, 257, 258, 260, 263, 264 (top & bottom), 265, 266 (left & right), 273, 274 (top left & bottom), 280, 281, 282, 283, 284, 285, 286, 287, 295, 297, 300, 305, 307, 308, 311, 314 (top), 315, 319, 321, 323, 327, 334, 344, 348, 354, 357, 361 (top & bottom), 378, 380 (top), 382, 390 (bottom right), 403.

CLWYD RECORD OFFICE: 275 (right).

FOTOMAS INDEX: 31, 33, 34 (top & bottom), 48, 49, 97.

HULTON GETTY COLLECTION: 2 (top), 53, 70, 73, 80 (top), 88, 105, 107, 118, 142, 164, 170, 190 (middle), 202, 208 (left & right), 222, 223, 236, 246, 247, 294, 304, 337, 349, 370 (top), 373, 375, 386 (bottom), 390 (top), 396, 397, 405, 406.

IMAGE SELECT: 245, 358, 390 (bottom left).

MANSELL: 7 (top & bottom), 28, 43, 65, 66, 67, 68, 81, 91, 94, 148, 162 (top).

MARY EVANS PICTURE LIBRARY: 186, 195, 209, 213, 306, 314 (bottom), 331, 364, 369 (top & bottom), 370 (bottom), 398.

NELSON PRINT: 29, 44, 47, 79, 99, 100 (top & bottom), 154, 180, 274 (top right).

OXFORD PHOTOGRAPHIC ARCHIVES: 275 (left).

POPPERFOTO: 380 (bottom), 391.

ROYAL ARCHIVES, WINDSOR CASTLE: 173.

TRADE UNION CONGRESS LIBRARY: 167 (bottom).

Contents

Editor's Preface

This book offers you the challenge of history. It encourages you to engage with the past in a creative and personal way; it also presents you with the many challenges which the past provides for present-day students. It demands a rigorous and scholarly approach. In return, we expect that you will increase your understanding, improve your skills, and develop a personal involvement in historical study.

The challenge is presented to you through the different components of each chapter:

Preview   Each chapter begins with a presentation which is designed to arouse your interest, and alert you to one or more of the major themes of the chapter.

Text   The text demands an active response from you. The book has been carefully written, designed and fully illustrated to develop your learning and understanding. Photographs, artwork, cartoons, statistical tables, maps, graphs are among the many visual images that reinforce the quality of the text.

Examining evidence   These sections present a wide variety of Historical sources, both primary and secondary. They encourage you to analyse the opinions of others, to assess the reliability of evidence, and to formulate and test your own personal views.

Focus   Focus sections zoom in on, and highlight, particular events, people and issues of the period. They are designed to enable you to see these more clearly and to find your way through the complexity of historical problems.

Talking Points   They are scattered widely throughout the book. By talking and listening, we can all learn about the major issues which translate the past into the present. In doing so, we question our own perceptions, test out our ideas and widen our range of interests.

Questions   Throughout the chapters, questions encourage you to consider what you see and read. They invite your personal response and encourage you to share it verbally with your fellow students, and in writing with your teachers.

Review   Each chapter contains an exercise, often a formal essay or question, which enables you to revise the learning and understanding of the whole chapter. You will find supporting ideas and structures to help you to formulate your answer.

This book offers you many experiences of History. It opens up to you the thoughts and feelings of contemporaries; it classifies the distinctive nature of your period; it places people, events and issues in the context of the flow of History. Just as important, it invites and encourages you to formulate your own personal insights and opinions in a living and developing debate. The challenge of History is essential to the vitality and well-being of the modern world.

J.A.P. Jones

General Editor

1 Background to a Century of Change

PREVIEW

Precursors of the Future

Source A

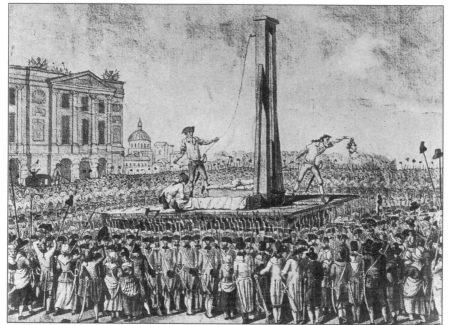

WHEN THE FRENCH REVOLUTION BEGAN IN 1789 MOST BRITISH POLITICIANS WELCOMED IT AS EVIDENCE THAT THE FRENCH WERE AT LAST MOVING TOWARDS A CONSTITUTIONAL MONARCHY. THE EXECUTION OF LOUIS XVI IN 1792 CHANGED THAT. REVOLUTIONARY IDEAS BECAME DANGEROUS THREATS TO STABILITY ON THE CONTINENT AND IN BRITAIN.

Source B

INDUSTRIALISATION CREATED NEW WORKING CONDITIONS AND NEW SOCIAL CLASSES.

Source C

British Population (millions)			
1751	7.00	1861	23.19
1801	10.69	1871	26.16
1811	12.15	1881	29.79
1821	14.21	1891	33.12
1831	16.37	1901	37.09
1841	18.55	1911	40.89
1851	20.88		

BRITAIN'S POPULATION (EXCLUDING IRELAND) QUADRUPLED BETWEEN 1801 AND 1911. WHAT POTENTIAL PROBLEMS DOES THIS RATE OF INCREASE POSE?

Source D

THE GROWTH OF CITIES, AND THE PROSPECT OF IMPROVED ECONOMIC CONDITIONS, ATTRACTED PEOPLE FROM THE SURROUNDING COUNTRYSIDE.

A political revolution, an industrial revolution, a demographic revolution and an urban revolution – all had their impact on the political and social development of the nineteenth century.

1 Consider the effects of the execution of Louis XVI and of the upheavals in France on the attitudes of the British ruling elite.
2 The factory and the industrial town: for contemporaries they created wonder and alarm in equal proportions. Why?

The Political Consequences of the French Revolution

WILLIAM PITT THE YOUNGER HAD BEEN PRIME MINISTER SINCE 1783. PITT BUILT HIS AUTHORITY ON THE KING'S CONFIDENCE NOT ON A PARTY FOLLOWING. HE ALWAYS CLAIMED TO BE AN INDEPENDENT WHIG. THERE WERE ONLY ABOUT 50 MPS IN HIS PERSONAL FOLLOWING, HIS COMMONS MAJORITY DEPENDING ON THE COURT AND OFFICIAL GROUP AND THE INDEPENDENT COUNTRY GENTLEMEN. BETWEEN 1784 AND 1790 HE RE-ORGANISED THE NATIONAL FINANCES, REFORMED ADMINISTRATION AND BEGAN THE FREEING OF TRADE FROM UNNECESSARY RESTRICTIONS THAT WAS TO BE EXTENDED BY HIS TORY SUCCESSORS AND POLITICAL HEIRS IN THE 1820S.

CHARLES JAMES FOX WAS LEADER OF THE OPPOSITION WHIGS. HE RESENTED HIS DISMISSAL FROM OFFICE BY THE KING IN 1783 AND REPLACEMENT BY PITT. BY 1789 HE HAD ACQUIRED A REPUTATION FOR UNPRINCIPLED OPPOSITION MOTIVATED BY A DISLIKE OF PITT RATHER THAN A THOROUGH APPRECIATION OF GOVERNMENT POLICIES. HE HAD A FOLLOWING OF ABOUT 130 MPS IN THE HOUSE OF COMMONS.

Party labels are a problem at the end of the eighteenth century. The Whigs were the dominant political group and conflict was between different Whig factions rather than distinct parties. The Tory label was avoided because of its association with rebellion and subservience to monarchy. By the 1780s the main difference between the Whig groups was over the prerogatives and powers of the Crown. George III preferred Pitt to Fox because the latter insisted that Parliament should nominate ministers, not the King. Late eighteenth century politics has been called a two-party game with only one party name.

Unattached MPs prided themselves on their independence, although they could usually be relied upon to support the King's Ministers. There was still a substantial number of these Members in 1815, the fiction of independence not disappearing until the passage of the Reform Act in 1832 ushered in a more clear-cut two party system.

It was believed that the British constitutional monarchy and the freedoms and liberties of the people were the consequence of the Glorious Revolution when James II had been forced to abdicate by William of Orange (William III).

Charles Grey, with other younger Whigs, formed the Society of the Friends of the People to give the reformers aristocratic leadership. As Lord Grey, Whig Prime Minister 1830–34, he piloted the Reform Act through parliament, 1831–32.

The Whig and Tory parties of the early nineteenth centuries emerged from the political reaction to the French Revolution and the radical ideas it stimulated. British politicians initially viewed events in France with some condescension – at last the French were going to acquire a constitutional monarchy on the British model. Although Edmund Burke, a Foxite Whig, published his attack on the Revolution in 1790 *(Reflections on the Revolution in France)* few took his predictions of regicide, expropriation of property, and eventual military dictatorship seriously. The declaration of the French Republic in 1792, the execution of Louis XVI, the beginning of the 'Terror' in 1793, and the expansionist intentions of the republican government revealed that the French Revolution was very different from the Glorious Revolution of 1688 with which it had been compared.

Whilst Fox pressed Pitt to recognise the French Republic some members of his opposition Whig group were becoming alarmed. When the French National Convention offered assistance to any peoples struggling for their freedom, and then declared war on Britain in February 1793 the more conservative led by the Duke of Portland began to look for an alliance with Pitt.

In July 1794 Portland entered a coalition government with Pitt. His group wanted an energetic prosecution of the war and firm repression of the radical reformers at home. For the next twenty years the propertied elite rallied behind the government fearful of the consequences for internal order and stability of the revolutionary ideas permeating from France. Defence of Monarchy, Church and national institutions became a patriotic duty.

By 1807 the term Tory was being used in some constituencies to describe candidates who defended the royal prerogative, supported the privileges of the Church of England, encouraged patriotic feeling and believed that radical dissent should be forcibly suppressed. Pitt had resigned in 1801 and his coalition had broken up. In 1812 Lord Liverpool's government brought all the Pittite elements back together. Backbenchers called it 'Tory'. By 1815 Ministers accepted the label and most MPs could be assigned to either the Whig or Tory parties.

By 1815 the Whigs probably numbered about 150 MPs but they were a demoralised and poorly led group. Apart from the 'Ministry of all the Talents' (1806–7), in which Fox had served as Foreign Secretary until his death in 1806, they had been out of office since 1783. All the young men of ability and ambition had gravitated into the Pittite circle where political careers could be made. Whig prospects looked bleak as the Liverpool government basked in the glory of having finally defeated France and destroyed Napoleon.

TALKING POINT

Between 1783 and 1812 fifty two different individuals held cabinet office, of whom only twelve were commoners (five of these were eventually elevated to the peerage). Nine of Liverpool's 1812 cabinet had sat in Pitt's second cabinet (1804–6), most had started their ministerial career under him. What does this suggest about:
– the nature of government in the early nineteenth century,
– the long term influence of Pitt,
– the benefits of a restricted pool of ministerial talent?

1.1 The Unreformed Electoral System

Source B

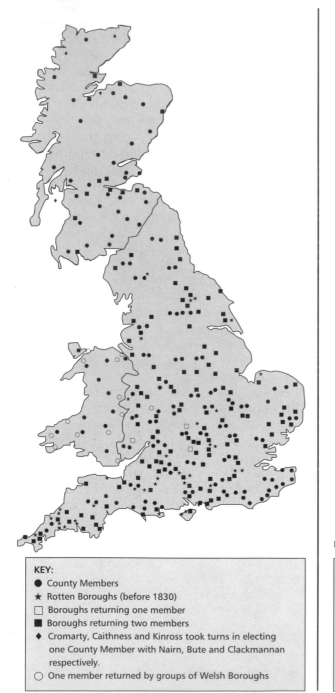

The Distribution of Borough Seats, England, 1830. It is clear that there was great inequality of representation throughout the country at this time.

In England and Wales in 1831, 366,250 adult males were entitled to vote out of 3,463,795 (11 per cent). The population of England and Wales in 1831 was 14, 019, 000.

8 MPs covered the London area – 4 for the City, 2 for Westminster, 2 for Middlesex. London' population was 1,907,000.

Map labels: Tynemouth, Newcastle, Sunderland, York, Bradford, Leeds, Preston, Halifax, Hull, Blackburn, Oldham, Wigan, Salford, Bolton, Stockport, Liverpool, Manchester, Macclesfield, Chester, Sheffield, Stoke, Nottingham, Wolverhampton, Derby, Shrewsbury, Leicester, Norwich, Dudley, Great Yarmouth, Coventry, Birmingham, Cambridge, Ipswich, Oxford, Bristol, Bath, LONDON, Portsmouth, Brighton, Exeter, Plymouth

KEY:
- ● County Members
- ★ Rotten Boroughs (before 1830)
- ☐ Boroughs returning one member
- ■ Boroughs returning two members
- ◆ Cromarty, Caithness and Kinross took turns in electing one County Member with Nairn, Bute and Clackmannan respectively.
- ◯ One member returned by groups of Welsh Boroughs

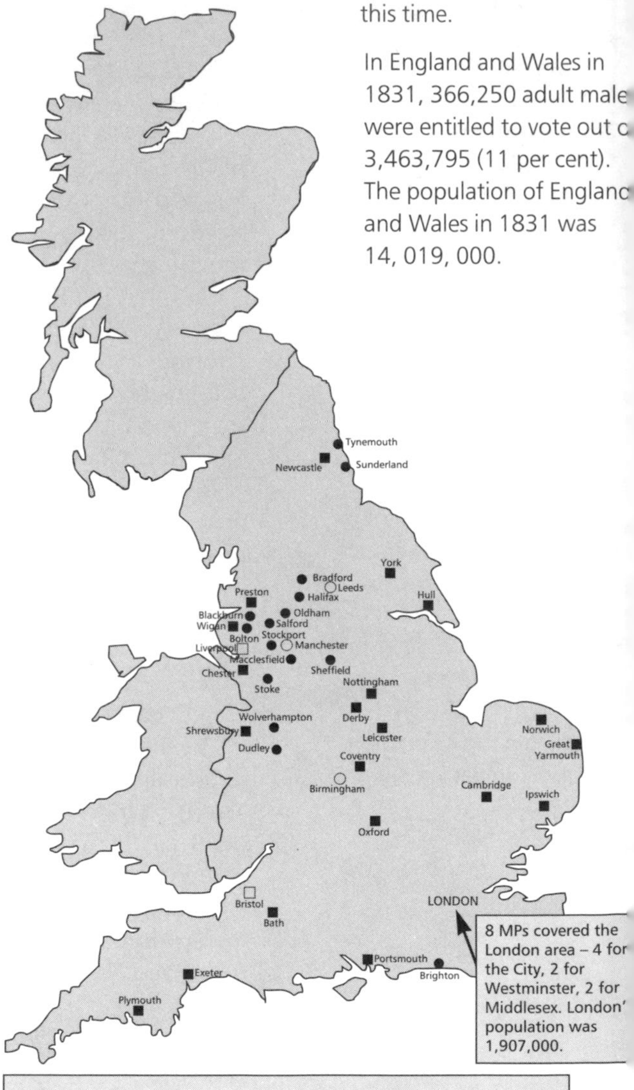

KEY:
- ● Towns with 20,000+ population which did not return MPs.
- ■ Towns with 20,000+ population which did return MPs
- ◯ Manchester – Towns with 100,000 which did not return MPs
- ☐ Liverpool – Towns with 100,000+ which did have MPs

Source C

VOTING WAS IN PUBLIC ON THE HUSTINGS. ELECTORS HAD TO PROVIDE EVIDENCE OF THEIR QUALIFICATION BEFORE VOTING. LEGISLATION IN 1785 LIMITED THE POLL TO A MAXIMUM OF FIFTEEN DAYS. THERE WAS NO SECRET BALLOT AND THE POLL BOOKS WERE AVAILABLE FOR INSPECTION.

Source D

DUNWICH, OLD SARUM AND BRAMBER WERE THREE FAMOUS EXAMPLES OF ROTTEN BOROUGHS, IMPORTANT CENTRES IN THE MIDDLE AGES THAT HAD DECAYED SO THAT THE 'OWNER' HAD COMPLETE CONTROL. GATTON, WITH ONLY SIX HOUSES IN THE BOROUGH, WAS SOLD FOR £180,000 IN 1830.

Source A

	England	Scotland	Ireland	Wales
Country Seats	82	30	64	12
Borough Seats	403	15	35	12
University Seats	4	–	1	–
Totals	489	45	100	24=658

THE COMPOSITION OF THE UNREFORMED HOUSE OF COMMONS, 1830.

Source E

Elections could be very rough affairs.

On entering the town the horses were taken from Sir Charles's carriage, and he was drawn in by the populace. When arrived at the bottom of the High Street, the cavalcade was met by Mr Evans's friends on their return from canvass; a tumult in consequence ensued, and several windows of the Stag and Pheasant Inn, (the rendezvous of Sir Charles's committee) were broken; a child was killed during the affray – and some persons seriously injured; but peace was restored during the night.

Leicester Journal, **26 May 1826**.

	No. of contests	Constituencies	%
1812	57	243	23.46
	20		
1818	93	243	38.27
1820	73	243	30.04
1826	88	243	36.21
1830	83	243	34.16
1831	75	243	30.86

CONTESTED ELECTIONS IN ENGLAND.

QUESTIONS

1 Why were there so few contested elections?

2 Referring to the evidence in this Focus section, put together the reformer's case against the early nineteenth century electoral system.

Industrialisation and Urbanisation

THE DEVELOPMENT OF THE FACTORY SYSTEM SAW A CHANGE IN THE SIZE AND STRUCTURE OF CITIES.

The growth of towns

It was a town of red brick that would have been red if the smoke and ashes had allowed it; but as matters stood it was a town of unnatural red and black like the painted face of a savage. It was a town of machinery and tall chimneys, out of which interminable serpents of smoke trailed themselves for ever and ever, and never got uncoiled. It had a black canal in it, and a river that ran purple with ill-smelling dye, and vast piles of buildings full of windows where there was a rattling and a trembling all day long, and where the piston of the steam engine worked monotonously up and down like the head of an elephant in a state of melancholy madness.

Charles Dickens' description of Coketown appeared in *Hard Times* in 1854. He was not the only Victorian novelist to be fascinated by the Victorian city and its social problems, but how typical were scenes like this by 1850?

Towns of all kinds increased in population. In 1801 only London had more than 100,000 people; by 1851 there were ten towns of this size. In 1851 the Census recorded that more people lived in towns than in the countryside. London grew from 959,000 in 1801 to 2,362,000 in 1851. Manchester from 75,000 to 303,000, Bradford from 13,000 to 104,000. The textile towns in Lancashire, Yorkshire and Scotland attracted migrants because of the opportunities for employment they offered. Metal-working centres in the Black Country around Birmingham experienced the same process. Ports, and in particular Liverpool which grew from 82,000 in 1801 to 376,000 fifty years later, expanded as trade increased. Commercial and industrial centres were only exceptional in the rapidity of their growth. Administrative centres like Chester and York almost doubled their populations in fifty years. Brighton's inhabitants increased tenfold between 1801 and 1851. Appalling living conditions were not confined to the industrial towns – all growing towns had their slums with large proportions of the population living in squalor.

Few contemporaries shared Robert Vaughan's optimism:

Our age is pre-eminently the age of great cities.

If any nation is to be lost or saved by the character of its great cities, our own is that nation.

Robert Vaughan, *The Age of Great Cities*, 1843.

Alexis de Tocqueville recorded Manchester's squalor and ceaseless activity, ending on a note of wonder and admiration:

From this foul drain the greatest stream of human industry flows out to fertilise the whole world. From this filthy sewer pure gold flows. Here humanity attains its most complete development and its most brutish; here civilisation makes its miracles, and civilised man is turned back almost into a savage.

Alexis de Tocqueville, *Journeys to England and Ireland*, 1835.

Cooke Taylor, a defender of the factory system, had more misgivings:

... as a stranger passes through the masses of human beings which have accumulated round the mills he cannot contemplate these crowded hives without feelings of anxiety and apprehension amounting almost to dismay. The population is hourly increasing in breadth and strength. It is an aggregate of masses, our conception of which clothe themselves in terms which express something portentous and fearful.

W. Cooke Taylor, *Notes of a Tour in the Manufacturing District of Lancashire*, 1844.

Peter Gaskeell (*Artisans and Machinery*, 1836) was concerned at the 'brutalising agency' of slum living, the destruction of 'all notions of sexual decency and domestic chastity.' Friedrich Engels deplored the segregation of the classes in Manchester that meant its middle class inhabitants were totally ignorant of the lives of their employees. The 'Religious Census' of 1851 only proved what many had feared – that the churches had failed to evangelise the inner cities and provide moral and religious discipline. Political protests and trade union activities suggested that social control had collapsed, that the deferential society was under threat. There was more to fear than to welcome in an urban society.

Industrialisation

The Industrial Revolution was a long evolutionary process. Despite the attention they received from Parliamentary Committees of Inquiry, Royal Commissions and in the writings of travellers and investigators the employee in a cotton mill was not a typical early nineteenth-century worker.

The factory system emerged in the eighteenth century within the framework of a dynamic small-producer framework. It took until the early nineteenth century in one industry, cotton textiles, for it to become the dominant form of organisation. In many other industries the rise of the factory system was a long drawn-out affair taking until the mid- to late nineteenth century.

M. Berg, *The Age of Manufactures 1700-1820*, 2nd edn, 1994.

Even in the textile industry most firms operated on a small scale. In 1841 43 per cent of Lancashire cotton concerns employed fewer than 100 workers; only 9 per cent employed more than 500. Before the 1830s the technology was relatively cheap to install and small producers could take advantage of the small steam engines, spinning mules, power looms and efficient water power systems that were available. In 1851 91 per cent of woollen mills and 63 per cent of worsted mills employed fewer than 50 hands. The contrasts between large and small scale were just as great in coalmining and ironmaking. In the North East in 1830 the average colliery workforce was 300, for the country as a whole it was 80. Similarly the iron industry contained a few celebrated large firms in South Wales and Scotland – over 2000 were employed at the Carron Works in 1814, 6000 at Dowlais in 1842 – but most concerns were much smaller.

What developments can be seen from this chart?

Source A

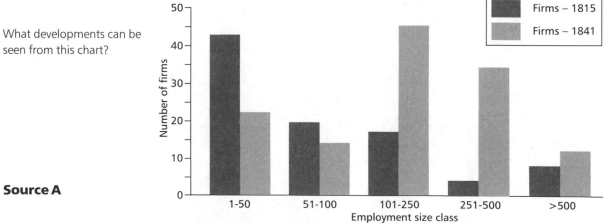

EMPLOYMENT SIZE CLASSES IN THE COTTON INDUSTRY, MANCHESTER 1815 AND 1841.

The 1851 Census revealed that 1,296,000 were employed in the textile industries, 572,000 in metal manufacture and 394,000 in mining. The largest labour force, over 2,000,000, was still employed in agriculture whilst domestic service occupied well over 1,000,000 females. Only 14 per cent of the total workforce was in textiles, with perhaps 25 per cent in occupations that had been directly affected by the changes in employment, technology, organisation or transport.

The cotton mills made an impact because they were new and because for the first time large numbers of workers, particularly women and children, were employed in one building. Abuses were easier to target and practices that had been tolerated in family controlled domestic work situations became unacceptable. By 1850 textile workers were the most protected with hours of work set by Act of Parliament. In this, too, they were untypical.

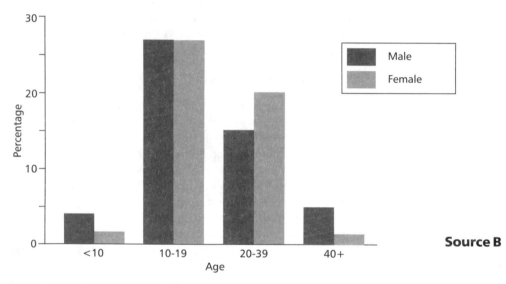

Source B

COMPOSITION OF THE WORKFORCE BY AGE AND GENDER IN THE COTTON INDUSTRY, 1833.

The key advantage of the factory for the employer was the control he had over the workforce. Those workers who entered the factory system had to change their attitudes to work and leisure. Timekeeping and routine were essential for the mill's profitability hence the fines for lateness at work, for inattention to detail and to task. In one mill in 1830, for example, 'Any person found from the necessary place of work, except for necessary purposes, or talking with anyone out of their own Ally, will be fined 2d for each offence.' By the 1830s, however, cotton mills were increasingly paying piece-rate wages to encourage discipline and concentration rather than controlling the workforce through fines.

Examining the Evidence

What Happened to the Standard of Living?

The effect of the Industrial Revolution on the standard of living of the working class has long been at the centre of historical debate. Evidence suggests a close correlation between the 'bad years' and political agitation and discontent. Solving the 'Condition of England' question was a major concern of politicians in the 1840s and contemporary commentators provided dramatic evidence of the decline in living standards in the industrial towns.

The Optimists

One of the merits of the factory system was that it offered regularity of employment and hence greater stability of consumption. During the period 1790–1830 factory production increased rapidly. A greater proportion of people came to benefit from it both as producers and as consumers. The fall in the price of textiles reduced the price of clothing. Boots began to take the place of clogs, and hats replaced shawls ... and after 1820 such things as tea and coffee and sugar fell in price substantially.

T .S. Ashton, 'The Standard of Living of Workers in England, 1790–1830' in A.J. Taylor (ed.), *The Standard of Living in Britain in the Industrial Revolution,* 1975.

unquestionably the amount and variety of food consumed increased between 1800 and 1850.

R.M. Harwell, 'The Rising Standard of Living in England, 1800–1850' in A.J. Taylor (ed.), op. cit.

The Pessimists

It is altogether likely that living standards improved over much of the eighteenth century. It is not improbable that, sometime soon after the onset of the Industrial Revolution ... they ceased to improve and declined. Perhaps the middle 1790s, the period of Speenhamland and shortages, mark the turning point. At the other end, the middle 1840s certainly mark a turning point.

E.J. Hobsbawm, 'The British Standard of Living 1790–1850' in A. J. Taylor (ed.), op.cit.

In fifty years of the Industrial Revolution the working-class share of the national product had almost certainly fallen relative to the share of the property-owning and professional classes. The 'average' working man remained very close to subsistence level at a time when he was surrounded by the evidence of the increase of national wealth, much of it transparently the product of his own labour. In psychological terms, this felt very much like a decline in standards. His own share in the 'benefits of economic progress' consisted of more potatoes, a few articles of cotton clothing for his family, soap and candles, some tea and sugar

E.P. Thompson, *The Making of the English Working Class,* 1963.

Talking Point

Hobsbawm and Thompson were both Marxists. To what extent is their 'pessimist' opinion a reflection of their own political views?

---

1   Compare the 'optimist' and the 'pessimist' positions in the debate.

Optimists	Pessimists
Prices did rise during the war years to 1815 but for many the rise in real wages was greater.	Unrestricted capitalism led to a deterioration in living standards.
Despite bad years there was fuller employment.	Price rises were not matched by wage rises.
Consumption of luxury items increased.	The death rate rose in the period 1810s–1840s.
Prices stabilised after 1815. Life expectancy increased	Frequent cyclical slumps caused unemployment and poverty.
Majority shared in the increasing prosperity.	In the early 1840s at least 10 per cent of the population were paupers.

2 Review the evidence above and show how the different sources can be used to support either the optimists or the pessimists.

Source C

	% price changes		% wage changes
1788/92 – 1809/15	+74.1	1788/92– 1810/14	+63.1
1809/15 – 1820/26	−29.3	1810/14– 1820/24	−10.6
1820/26 – 1846/50	−16.4	1820/24– 1846/50	+0.4

AVERAGE INDICES OF PRICE AND WAGE MOVEMENTS, 1788–1850.

3 What of value can be learnt from these wage and price indices?

Source D

	s.	d.
1800	25	0
1810	19	6
1820	9	0
1830	5	6

WAGES: A BOLTON HANDLOOM WEAVER, PER WEEK.

What do these statistics tell us about 'real wages'?

Real wages: the spending value of the wage earned. If prices fall and the wage remains static the real wage has increased. If prices increase and the wage falls behind then the real wage has decreased, because it purchases less.

Indices of wages must be used carefully. They do not allow for regional variations. Also, being based on the weekly wage there is no allowance for the hours worked, periods of unemployment, payments made in kind or the support given to a family's income by the wife's and the children's employments. Similar problems surround price indices.

Explain the significant increase in wages in Lancashire and Northumberland by 1794–5 and the increase in Buckinghamshire and Norfolk by 1845.

Source E

	1767–70		1794–5		1833–45	
	s.	d.	s.	d.	s.	d.
Buckinghamshire	8	0	7	4	9	10
Norfolk	8	0	8	1	10	7
Dorset	6	9	8	3	7	10
Lancashire	6	6	10	1	12	5
Northumberland	6	0	10	3	11	9

WAGES: AGRICULTURAL LABOURERS, PER WEEK.

Why does Hobsbawm cite these statistics as evidence for the pessimist case? His critics argue that Smithfield was not the only London meat market, pork and bacon was most widely consumed by the working class and that by the 1840s meat slaughtered elsewhere was reaching London by rail.

Source F

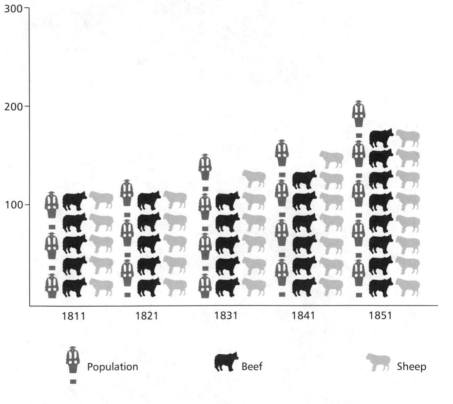

NUMBER OF CATTLE AND SHEEP KILLED AT THE SMITHFIELD MEAT MARKET, LONDON, 1801–1851.

TALKING POINT

How could the growth of the railway system contribute to an improving urban standard of living from the 1840s?

Source G

THE PESSIMIST INTERPRETATION LAYS STRESS ON THE DECLINING QUALITY OF LIFE IN THE INDUSTRIAL TOWNS. THEIR CRITICS HAVE ARGUED THAT MIGRANTS FROM RURAL AREAS AND SMALL TOWNS ACCEPTED THE ENVIRONMENTAL DETERIORATION AND THE ROUTINES AND DISCIPLINES OF FACTORY WORK AS A SMALL PRICE TO PAY FOR THE HIGHER CITY WAGES.

Source H

PATERNALISTIC EMPLOYERS LIKE THE GREGS AT STYAL AND CADBURYS AT BOURNEVILLE (ABOVE) BUILT GOOD QUALITY COTTAGES FOR THEIR EMPLOYEES. WAGES WERE MUCH LOWER THAN IN MANCHESTER AND BIRMINGHAM BUT THE LABOUR FORCE WAS REMARKABLY STABLE, SUGGESTING THAT CONSIDERATIONS OTHER THAN WAGES DID INFLUENCE DECISIONS.

Source I

	Manchester	Leeds	Liverpool	Rutland	Wilts
Professional persons and gentry and their families	38	44	35	52	50
Tradesmen and their families (includes farmers in Rutland and Wiltshire)	20	27	22	41	48
Mechanics, labourers and their families	17	19	15	38	33

AVERAGE AGE OF DEATH IN RURAL AND URBAN AREAS IN THE 1840S.

Source J

A description of the cottage and circumstances of John Ridgway, collier, of Poynton, a Cheshire mining village. He was married with six children, the eldest, a girl aged 13 living away from home as a domestic servant. The cottage was newly built.

having at its front a small flower-plot and behind a garden laid out for growing potatoes, cabbages, peas and other vegetables there was also a shippon and a pigstye. The cottage consists of two rooms below and two above, very clean and well whitewhashed. In the front sitting-room was a good iron fire-grate with oven, and grates were also in the back-room and in the front-room above. In the sitting-room was a chest of mahogany drawers, a good eight-day clock in mahogany case, six rush-bottomed chairs, a child's cradle, three tables, a bird and cage, a mahogany corner-cupboard well filled with glass and crockery, a gun, a good oak sofa with loose cushion, several small pictures, with fender, chimney ornaments. In the kitchen were a number of washing-mugs, with milk-basins and small churn, a table-stool, and shelf with bread, butter, &c; upstairs were two beds, with good clean bedding, with three chairs and a small table.

He can earn on average 22s. per week; works eight hours per day; he buys his flour by the load of 14 score and bakes their own bread has not had more than 2s. worth of butchers' meat per month; buys half a pig from his wife's father, which they cure and make into bacon; they keep a cow, which keeps them in butter and milk. He is a member of Odd Fellows' Society, to which he pays 1s. 8d. per month, and in case of sickness receives 10s. per week from the society. He has built this house himself with money saved from his earnings, and cost about £80.

'Report of the Royal Commission on Children's Employment in Mines', 1842.

4 War, government policies, population increase, economic change all affected the working class standard of living 1790–1850. Research and comment on their effects, assessing the significance of each.

Essay Starting from the evidence in this section, prepare an essay plan: to what extent did the living standards of industrial workers decline in the first half of the nineteenth century?

EXAMINING THE EVIDENCE
The Roots of the Radical Tradition

Source A

Thomas Paine published *The Rights of Man* in 1791. It was a reply to Edmund Burke's denunciation of events in France in his *Reflections on the Revolution in France. The Rights of Man* became the principal text for the political societies which began organising themselves in Britain from the end of 1792. Paine continued to inspire radical reformers into the Chartist period. Part II, which appeared in 1792, sold 200,000 copies in its cheap edition.

> ... men are all of one degree, and consequently that all men are born equal, and with equal natural rights ...
>
> Man did not enter into society to become worse than he was before, not to have fewer rights than he had before, but to have those rights better secured.
>
> Though it might be proved that the system of Government now called NEW is the most ancient in principle of all that have existed, being founded on the original inherent Rights of Man; yet, as tyranny and the sword have suspended the exercise of those rights for many centuries past, it serves better the purpose of distinction to call it the new than to claim the right of calling it the old.
>
> The first general distinction between these two systems is that the one now called old is hereditary, either in whole or in part; and the new is entirely representative.
>
> All hereditary government is in its nature tyranny. An heritable crown, or an heritable throne ... have no other significant explanation than that mankind are heritable property. To inherit a Government, is to inherit the people, as if they were flocks and herds.
>
> Hereditary succession ... puts [monarch] in the most ridiculous light, by presenting it as an office which any child or idiot may fill. It requires some talents to be a common mechanic; but to be a King requires only the animal figure of man – a sort of breathing automaton.
>
> T. Paine, *The Rights of Man*, Vol. I 1791, Vol. II 1792.

Source B

The Resolutions of the London Corresponding Society, 2 April 1792.
Man as an individual is entitled to liberty...

> As a member of society the preservation of that liberty becomes his indispensable duty.
>
> When he associated he gave up certain rights, in order to secure the possession of the remainder;

TALKING POINT

Given all the difficulties and differences is it possible to assume a single standard of living in this period? If not, does the concept have any value?

Paine had been a propagandist for American independence, was elected to the French Convention in 1792 but fled to the United States in 1794 to escape the Terror.

The London Corresponding Society, 1792, was the leading radical political society in London. Its intention was to open links with similar provincial societies. Total membership peaked at about 3000 in 1795, with about 1500 active in the branches.

TALKING POINT

Compare the demands, arguments and methods of the LCS with those of the radical reformers 1815–20, and of the Chartists (pages 158–159).

TALKING POINT

The pessimists blame the Industrial Revolution for the declining standard of living, but the Industrial Revolution coincided with an unprecedented increase in population. Discuss what would have happened if there had been no economic growth, and consider the view that industrialisation saved Britain from a demographic crisis.

But, he voluntarily yielded up only as much as was necessary for the common good:

He still preserved a right of sharing the government of his country; – without it no man can, with truth call himself free.

Resolved, – That every individual has a right to share in the government of that society of which he is a member ...

Resolved, – That it is no less the right than the duty of every Citizen, to keep a watchful eye on the government of his country; that the laws, by being multiplied, do not degenerate into oppression, and that those who are entrusted with the government, do not substitute private interest for public advantage.

Resolved, – That the people of Great Britain are not effectually represented in Parliament.

Resolved, – That in consequence of a partial, unequal, and therefore inadequate representation, together with the corrupt method in which representatives are elected; oppressive taxes, unjust laws, restrictions of liberty, and wasting the public money have ensued.

Resolved, – That the only remedy for those evils is a fair, equal and impartial representation of the People in Parliament.

Resolved, – That a fair, equal, and impartial representation of the People in parliament can never take place until all partial privileges are abolished.

Resolved, – That this Society to express their Abhorrence of tumults and violence, and that, as they aim at reform, not anarchy, but reason, firmness, and unanimity, are the only arms they themselves will employ, or persuade their Fellow Citizens to exert against Abuse of Power.

Minute Book of the London Corresponding Society, 2 April 1792.

---

1 There are references in these sources to political concepts and ideas. Using the sources, and your wider knowledge, explain what is meant by: man's natural rights, and his rights as a member of society, hereditary succession, representative government, universal suffrage, annual parliaments, parliamentary reform.
2 Consult sources A and B. How do they help to explain the Home Office's alarm about Paine and his writings?
3 In what senses could sources A and B be interpreted as potentially revolutionary documents and the LCS a revolutionary society?

Focus

1.2 A Question of Class

Eighteenth century writers referred to the 'lower orders' and the 'middling ranks'; by the early nineteenth century the terms 'working class' and 'middle class' were appearing.

Industrialisation, with its imposition of new ways of working, the discipline and routine of the factory and a changed relationship between employer and employee, helped to give birth to a new class society. The ideals of the French Revolution contributed to the emergence of a more politically aware working class. Recognising the valuable qualities of the manufacturing and commercial middle class the aristocratic ruling elite extended the franchise to them in 1832 isolating the working class. Chartism was that class's response to their exclusion from the power and to their exploitation by the employing middle class.

This is a simplistic view. The roots of class are far more complex than this suggests and it is difficult to define homogeneous middle and working classes. Class terminology also implies conflict, an appreciation of common interests which differ sufficiently from those of other groups in society to create a distinct identity. It could be argued that this does not emerge until the end of the nineteenth century and the beginning of the twentieth with the developments that eventually led to the formation of the Labour Party.

Talking Point

The terminology of class is a convenient device used by historians. What is its value, and what are its dangers?

The Contemporary Perspective

Source A
We are daily advancing towards the state in which there are but two classes of men – masters and abject dependants.

William Cobbett in *Political Register*, **15 March 1806.**

Source B
I see two classes dependent on each other in every possible way, yet each evidently regarding the interests of the other as opposed to their own; I never lived in a place before where there were two sets of people always running each other down.

Elizabeth Gaskell, *North and South*, **1855.**

Source C
The middle class have more in common with every other nation of the world than with their own workers who live on their own doorsteps. The workers differ from the middle class in speech, in thoughts and ideas, in customs, morals, politics and religion

F. Engels, *The Condition of the Working Class in England,* **1958 edn.**

Source D
A resolution passed at a mass meeting of workers in Oldham.

Labour is the source of all property; and without a surplus of labour has been performed and of property produced no accumulation of property can take place _ the primary object of all legislation ought to be to secure for the labourer the entire fruit of his labour _ the various classes of capitalists have the power of making and administering the laws which is almost uniformly done for their own benefit _. Until the [working people] lay their hands and hearts together their condition (bad as it is) will grow gradually worse till they are actually slaves or worked out of existence.

Northern Star, **18 March 1838.**

---

1 To what extent do sources A, B, C and D suggest the existence of a growing working class consciousness?

Historians and Class

Source E

In the years between 1780 and 1832 most English working people came to feel an identity of interests as between themselves, and as against their rulers and employers. This ruling class was itself much divided, and in fact only gained in cohesion over the same years because certain antagonisms were resolved in the face of an insurgent working class. Thus the working-class presence was, in 1832, the most significant factor in British political life.

    ...the final definition of this class consciousness was, in large part, the consequence of the response to working-class strength of the middle class. The line was drawn, with extreme care, in the franchise qualifications of 1832.

E.P. Thompson, *The Making of the English Working Class,* **1963.**

Source F

    The essence of class is not merely antagonism towards another class or classes but organised antagonism with a nationwide appeal to all members of one broad social level. By this definition the working class almost sprang into existence with the Parliamentary Reform movement of 1816–19.

    H. Perkin, *The Origins of Modern English Society,* **1969.**

Perkin argues that eighteenth century society was divided into vertical interest groups and that it was the breakdown of this system which led to the birth of class. Class conflict, however, centred around three class ideals, the aristocratic, the entrepreneurial and the working class. By the mid-nineteenth century the middle class entrepreneurial ideal had become dominant.

Source G

    'Working class' is anachronistic in implying a stage in class formation and consciousness which had hardly been reached even by 1815. Its plural 'working classes', allows for differentiation and even hierarchy among the lower orders but still reflects nineteenth-century rather than eighteenth-century usage. In a book spanning the years 1750 to 1850, the present writer opted for 'labouring classes'. It is still my preference.

    J.G. Rule, *Albion's People: English Society 1714–1815,* **1992.**

Source H

    Class consciousness was a transparent veil which could be thrown over, but could not conceal, the immense variety of working organisation and experiences in nineteenth-century Britain. Class is too crude and too misleading a concept to encompass them.

    E.J. Evans, *The Forging of the Modern State,* **1983.**

Source I

    As with that other contemporary concept, the middle class, the existence of the idea of the working class as an article of faith for deeply committed individuals in that day and later need not be doubted. If it is realised that entities such as the middle class and the working class represent a mode of thought rather than an objective representation of social realities, it may be possible to avoid the conceptual straitjacket which thinking in broad class terms often entails.

    N. McCord, *British History 1815–1906,* **1991.**

Talking Point

What conditions are necessary for broad based class action and conflict?
In the early nineteenth century:
agricultural labourers and domestic servants were the largest occupational groups;
most people lived in small locally orientated communities;
communications were poor;
literacy was limited.
Are these sufficient reasons for the assuming that broad class-based conflict was unlikely?

---

2 For what reasons do both Thompson and Perkin (sources E and F) feel that a working class consciousness had emerged by the early nineteenth century.

3 How do sources G, H and I cast doubt on the use of class as a concept in the early nineteenth century: why might it be misleading?

4 'Working class' and 'middle class' are convenient labels for the historian, but they are no more than labels in the first half of the nineteenth century. Discuss this view with reference to all the sources in this Focus and your broader understanding of the period to 1850.

REVIEW

The most remarkable thing about the far-reaching economic and social changes known as the Industrial Revolution was the fact that they occurred without any accompanying political revolution.

I. Thomis, *Responses to Industrialisation*, 1976.

1 Summarise the challenges to the old society under these three headings:
   political
   economic
   social

2 Assess the strength of the challenge to justify Thomis's use of the phrase 'most remarkable'.

3 Return to this Review after you have completed the next seven chapters. In what ways, and with what success, had the governing elite responded to and overcome the challenges of political, economic and social change?

2 Surviving the Post-war Crisis, 1815–20

PREVIEW

A repressive regime? The Tories 1815–20

Source A

THIS CARTOON WAS PUBLISHED IN 1817. WHY ARE GOVERNMENT MINISTERS LORDS CASTLEREAGH AND ELDON STANDING ON A DISMANTLED PRINTING PRESS? WHAT HAS HAPPENED TO LIBERTY? WHY? WHAT 'EVIDENCE' DO YOU THINK IS HIDDEN IN ELDON'S LARGE SACK? WHO, AND WHAT ELSE IS SHOWN AGAINST LIBERTY? THE FIGURES ON THE HILL ARE JOHN BULL, SURROUNDED BY THE REFORMERS COCHRANE, BURDETT, HUNT AND COBBETT. WHY IS JOHN BULL WEEPING?

Source B

Extract from 'The Mask of Anarchy' written by Shelley in 1819 after hearing reports of the Peterloo Massacre in Manchester.

As I lay asleep in Italy
There came a voice from over the Sea,
And with great power it forth led me
To walk in the visions of Poesy.

I met Murder on the way -
He had a mask like Castlereagh -
Very smooth he looked, yet grim;
Seven blood-hounds followed him:

All were fat; and well they might
Be in admirable plight,
For one by one, and two by two,
He tossed them human hearts to chew
Which from his wide cloak he drew.

Next came Fraud, and he had on,
like Eldon, an ermined gown;
His big tears, for he wept well,
Turned to mill-stones as they fell.

And the little children, who
Round his feet played to and fro,
Thinking every tear a gem,
Had their brains knocked out by them.

Clothes with the Bible, as with light,
And the shadows of the night,
Like Sidmouth, next Hypocrisy
On a crocodile rode by.

And many more Destructions played
In this ghastly masquerade,
All disguised, even to the eyes,
Like Bishops, lawyers, peers, or spies.

Last came Anarchy: he rode
On a white horse, splashed with blood;
He was pale even to the lips,
Like Death in the Apocalypse.

And he wore a kingly crown;
And in his grasp a sceptre shone;
On his brow the mark I saw -
'I AM GOD, AND KING, AND LAW!'

DEATH or LIBERTY! or Britannia & the Virtues of the Constitution in danger of Violation from the gr.t Political Libertine, Radical Reform.

THIS CARTOON APPEARED IN 1819.

1 What do sources A and B suggest about the policies of the government between 1815 and 1819? Try to refer to each source in your answer.

2 Give examples of the ways in which Shelley shows his detestation of the ministers he refers to, explaining his use of the words 'Murder', 'Fraud' and 'Hypocrisy'. Who, or what, is 'Anarchy'?

3 How does source C justify the fears of anti-reformers?

4 Both cartoons were drawn by George Cruikshank. Do the messages contradict each other? If so, how does this affect their value as historical evidence?

2.1 The Men in Power – Lord Liverpool's Cabinet

Castlereagh, Eldon and Sidmouth were the ministers held responsible for the government's unpopular policies. Read the following summaries of their political careers, and that of Lord Liverpool the Prime Minister. List all the things that they have in common and the ways in which their backgrounds and careers differed. What was their main qualification for ministerial office at this difficult time? What experience and knowledge do you think they all lacked? These biographical sketches are based on entries in the *Dictionary of National Biography*.

ADDINGTON, Henry, 1st VISCOUNT SIDMOUTH (1757–1844) – son of a doctor who owned a moderate family estate in Oxfordshire. Educated at Winchester and Brasenose College, Oxford. Taking his BA in 1778 he became a lawyer. A friend of William Pitt, he entered Parliament in 1784 as MP for Devizes where his brother-in-law had influence over the electors. 1789 elected Speaker of the House of Commons, largely thanks to support received from Pitt. He needed the salary of £6,000 p.a., and held the post until 1800. He was always trusted by the country gentlemen in the Commons because of his strong religious views. 1801–3 he was Prime Minister and Chancellor of the Exchequer. 1805 created Viscount Sidmouth and entered Pitt's

JENKINSON, Robert Banks, 2nd EARL OF LIVERPOOL (1770–1828) – eldest son of Charles Jenkinson who groomed him for a political career. Family was long established on estate in Oxfordshire. Educated at Charterhouse and Christ Church College, Oxford. Spent three years on the Grand Tour of Europe before entering Parliament for Appleby in 1790 with the influence of Sir James Lowther. Given a minor government post by Pitt in 1793, he was almost continually in office until 1827. 1801 appointed Foreign Secretary by Addington; raised to the peerage as Baron Hawkesbury in 1803; Home Secretary 1804–6, 1807–9. Succeeded his father as Earl of Liverpool 1808. Foreign Secretary and later Secretary for War 1809-12. Became Prime Minister after the assassination of Spencer Perceval in 1812.

cabinet as Lord President of the Council. 1806–7 served in the coalition 'Ministry of all the Talents'. 1812 appointed Lord President of the Council by Spencer Perceval, and then Home Secretary under Liverpool.

SCOTT, John, 1st EARL OF ELDON (1751–1838) – third son of William Scott, a successful Newcastle-upon-Tyne businessman and merchant. Educated at Newcastle Grammar School and University College, Oxford; BA in 1770, MA in 1773. Married Elizabeth Surtees, daughter of a wealthy Newcastle banker, 1772. Member of the Middle Temple, 1773; called to the bar 1776. Returned as MP for Weobley in 1783, under the patronage of Lord Weymouth; represented this borough until 1796 when he was returned for Boroughbridge, a seat owned by the Duke of Newcastle. 1788 appointed Solicitor-General, 1793 promoted to Attorney-General, 1799 appointed Lord Chief Justice of the Common Pleas and created Baron Eldon. He had already purchased a large estate in Co. Durham. In 1801 he became Lord Chancellor, a post he was to hold until 1827 except for a short gap 1806–7.

STEWART, Robert, 2nd MARQUIS OF LONDONDERRY (1769–1822) – better known as Viscount Castlereagh. Second son of Robert Stewart, 1st Marquis of Londonderry. Family owned extensive estates in County Down and was influential in Irish politics. Educated at St. John's College, Cambridge. Went on the Grand Tour. 1790 he entered the Irish Parliament after a contest for one of the County Down seats which cost £60,000 and nearly ruined his family. In 1794 he married the youngest daughter of the second earl of Buckinghamshire. 1797 he was appointed Pitt's Chief Secretary for Ireland, and was responsible for getting the Act of Union through the Irish Parliament in 1801. Entered the House of Commons 1801. 1802 appointed President of the Board of Control with a Cabinet seat; Secretary for War 1805–6, 1807–9. Resigned in 1809 after quarrelling and fighting a duel with George Canning, the Foreign Secretary. 1812 entered Perceval's cabinet as Foreign Secretary, combining that post with the Leadership of the House of Commons when Liverpool became premier.

A Prime Minister's problems

Liverpool became Prime Minister in 1812, less through his own abilities than the reluctance of abler colleagues to serve under each other. Within three years he had consolidated his position as the leader of the government that had at last won the war, retaining the premiership until ill-health forced his resignation in 1827. This long premiership was a tribute to his mediatory skills. Politicians who held sharply differing opinions on crucial issues, and whose personal rivalries were intense, collaborated under his leadership. Disraeli dismissed him unfairly as the 'Arch Mediocrity who presided rather than ruled over the Cabinet of Mediocrities', but for the Duke of Wellington, who entered the cabinet in 1818, he was 'a very superior man, like a tender plant'. Other contemporaries noted his underlying sensitivity and nervousness. Liverpool took a broad view of his role -' the first minister is necessarily at the head of every department when important business is concerned', he wrote. He positively encouraged the initiation of new economic policies after 1820, and Robert Peel, Home Secretary 1822–27, wrote gratefully of Liverpool's support for his legal and prison reforms.

In 1815 only four cabinet ministers were MPs; the rest sat with the Prime Minister in the House of Lords. Castlereagh, Leader of the House of Commons as well as Foreign Secretary, was the government's chief spokesman in the Commons. His colleagues were uninspiring speakers and debaters; the strain he experienced was immense. In 1816 Liverpool strengthened his front bench team by persuading George Canning, who had refused to serve under him in 1812, and was Castlereagh's great personal rival, to enter the cabinet as President of the Board of Control.

Castlereagh became Marquis of Londonderry in 1821. Since this was an Irish peerage which did not confer a seat in the House of Lords, he continued to sit in the House of Commons. Lord Palmerston, MP 1807–65, Prime Minister 1855–58, 1859–65, was another Irish peer whose political career was passed in the Commons.

When the Prime Minister was a peer in the House of Lords it was essential that the Leader of the House of Commons was a capable politician. For some the Leadership of the House was a stepping stone to the premiership itself. Canning, Russell, Peel, Gladstone, Disraeli and Balfour all made this move.

GEORGE CANNING (1770–1827) WAS ANOTHER OF PITT'S PROTÉGÉS. AN MP AT 23, HE ENTERED POLITICS VIA ETON, CHRIST CHURCH, OXFORD AND A POCKET BOROUGH FOUND FOR HIM BY PITT. BY 1796 HE WAS A JUNIOR MINISTER, EVENTUALLY ENTERING THE CABINET AS FOREIGN SECRETARY IN 1807. TWO YEARS LATER HE FOUGHT HIS DUEL WITH CASTLEREAGH AND WAS COMPELLED TO RESIGN. A COMBINATION OF OBVIOUS AMBITION, ARROGANCE AND A CAUSTIC WIT MADE HIM THE MOST DISTRUSTED AND DISLIKED POLITICIAN OF HIS TIME AMONGST THE RULING ÉLITE. HIS LACK OF AN ARISTOCRATIC BACKGROUND, AND SCANDAL SURROUNDING HIS MOTHER'S PERSONAL LIFE, PRESENTED SNOBBISH ENEMIES WITH ANOTHER WEAPON. NEVERTHELESS, HIS ABILITIES MADE HIM INDISPENSABLE TO HIS FRIEND LIVERPOOL, DESPITE THE ANTAGONISMS HE AROUSED. CANNING WAS, PERHAPS, THE ONLY MINISTER WHO CONSCIOUSLY SOUGHT, AND GAINED, PUBLIC POPULARITY. THIS, TOO, EARNED HIM THE DISAPPROVAL OF THE POLITICAL WORLD, BUT THE MERCHANTS OF LIVERPOOL ELECTED HIM AS THEIR MP IN 1812.

The Duke of Wellington brought his own immense prestige as Europe's leading general into the Cabinet in 1818, but he was a reluctant politician. Liverpool had to accept the Duke's condition that his duty to the country would come before duty to the Party.

The Catholic question is dealt with in Chapter 3.

United in their opposition to all forms of parliamentary reform, ministers held differing views on Catholic emancipation. Castlereagh was among the ministers who supported Pitt's proposal that the Irish Act of Union should be accompanied by legislation to free Roman Catholics from the civil disadvantages imposed on them in the seventeenth century. Confronted by the adamant opposition of George III, who feared that any concession would undermine the Protestant nature of the constitution and force him to break his coronation oath, Pitt resigned the premiership in 1801 and was followed out of office by Castlereagh. Nevertheless, the Tories continued to regard Catholic emancipation as an 'open question' and it did not become a divisive issue until the resignation of Liverpool and the appointment of Canning, a strong supporter of the Catholic cause, as premier in 1827.

THE DOCTOR.
" At his last gasp—as if with opium drugg'd."

DERRY-DOWN TRIANGLE.
" He that sold his country."

THE SPOUTER OF FROTH.
" With merry descants on a nation's woes—
There is a public mischief in his mirth."

THE GUILTY TRIO.
" Great skill have they in *palmistry*, and more
To conjure clean away the gold they touch,
Conveying worthless dross into its place;
Loud when they beg, dumb only when they steal.
  *   *   *
———————— Dream after dream ensues!
And still they dream, that they shall still succeed,
And still are disappointed."

This is THE DOCTOR
    of *Circular* fame,
A Driv'ller, a Bigot, a Knave
    without shame:

And *that's* DERRY DOWN TRIANGLE
    by name,
From the Land of mis-rule,
    and half-hanging, and flame:
And *that* is THE SPOUTER OF FROTH
    BY THE HOUR,
The worthless colleague
    of their infamous power:
Who dubb'd *him* ' the Doctor'
    whom now he calls ' brother,'
And, to get at his Place,
    took a shot at the other;
Who haunts their *Bad House*,
    a base living to earn,
By playing Jack-pudding, and Ruffian,
    in turn;
Who bullies, for those
    whom he bullied before;
Their *Flash*-man, their Bravo,
    a son of a ———— ;
The hate of the People,
    all tatter'd and torn,
Who curse the day
    wherein they were born,
On account of Taxation
    too great to be borne,
And pray for relief
    from night to morn;

'THE HOUSE THAT JACK BUILT' WAS PUBLISHED IN 1819 AFTER PETERLOO. THIS EXTRACT ATTACKS SIDMOUTH, 'THE DOCTOR'; CASTLEREAGH, 'DERRY DOWN TRIANGLE'; AND CANNING, 'THE SPOUTER OF FROTH'. WHAT IS THEIR BAD HOUSE? WHY DID THE RADICALS PICK ON THESE THREE MINISTERS; WHO IS MOST ABUSED, AND, FROM THE EVIDENCE, WHY?

Adjusting to Peacetime conditions – Protection and Taxation

> The restoration of general peace, though it may relieve the country from great difficulties, does not make the government more easy to be conducted in the House of Commons.
>
> Liverpool to Wellington, January 1815.

> The truth is the country at this moment is peace mad. Many of our best friends think of nothing but reduction of taxes and low establishments.
>
> Liverpool to Castlereagh, February 1815.

Explain the 'great difficulties', 'our best friends', and 'low establishments'.

Liverpool's anxieties were compounded by Castlereagh's absence at the peace negotiations in Vienna. His prestige and experience were needed in the Commons to control Members eager to return the country to their perception of normal peacetime conditions.

In fact, ministers were soon to be confronted by problems they could never have anticipated, and for which they were ill-prepared. Their entire political experience had been formed in the reaction to the French Revolution and the almost continuous war since 1793. There had been little serious opposition at home since 1812 when the last outbreak of working class discontent, Luddism, had been suppressed. In Parliament the Whig opposition had been non-existent. The revival of trade and an improving economic situation boded well, and the government had the prestige of having won the war.

As Liverpool feared, the demand for a significant reduction in the level of wartime taxation was immediate. By 1815 there was also an increasingly strident demand from farmers and landowners for protection from foreign competition. Whig politicians looked forward to being able to harass ministers on a whole mass of issues, confident of the support of independent MPs and of middle class opinion outside Parliament.

Napoleon's escape from his exile on the Mediterranean island of Elba postponed the taxation crisis for twelve months but ministers had to respond to the clamour for agricultural protection.

1 The Corn Laws

Farmers and landowners feared the effect of renewed imports of continental grain on prices once wartime restrictions were lifted. During the war, marginal land had been taken into cultivation at great cost and farmers had enjoyed prosperity and high prices, landlords had increased rents, and loans had been contracted at high wartime interest rates. Protection would save many who farmed the poorer soils from bankruptcy. The government was willing to acquiesce.

Agriculture was still the greatest national industry and employer of labour, facts which alone justified special treatment. For Liverpool, however, other concerns provided a clear political argument in favour of protection:

What point is Liverpool making?

I am satisfied ... that such a price is desirable, for the purpose of giving a proper stimulus to the agriculture of the country; and, if the measure should be adopted, I do not despair of the United Kingdom being able to feed itself in the course of a few years, except in very bad seasons ... If one quarter of the wheat land of the kingdom was thrown out of cultivation, no foreign supply could possible make up the deficiency in the quality of food.

Corn Laws, 1815

1 Import of foreign grain prohibited until the price of home grown wheat reached 80 shillings (£4) a quarter ton.

2 Colonial wheat was to be allowed in when the price reached 67 shillings.

3 Corn dealers were permitted to warehouse supplies at the ports for release when the price was right.

Ministerial good intentions, Liverpool's promise that 'The great object was the interest of the consumer. The present measure ... would render grain cheaper instead of dearer.' and assertions that protected farmers would increase production, were unacceptable to many. Radicals and manufacturers condemned a measure they claimed would cause famine, whilst the London mob chased Ministers through the streets and broke their windows. Ministers were accused of putting the needs of the landed interest before those of the rest of society. The Corn Laws were added to the list of abuses and oppressions for which they were held responsible.

The Blessings of Peace or the Curse of the Corn Bill.

TALKING POINT

Who were the 'landed interest'? If it encompassed all those who depended on agriculture for their living, then the largest group within this category would have been agricultural labourers. In what sense could the Corn Laws be called 'class legislation'?

CONTRAST THIS VIEW OF THE CORN LAWS WITH LIVERPOOL'S. HOW DO THEY DIFFER?

The Corn Laws passed through the Commons with large majorities. The Whig opposition, supposedly the friends of the people, found themselves in an ambivalent position. Many landowning Whig MPs voted for the measure. Historians with widely differing political perspectives have agreed that the Corn Laws were 'one of the most naked pieces of class legislation in English history' (Lord Blake, *The Conservative Party from Peel to Churchill* (1970)), a scheme 'to maintain prices by exploiting the political strength of the landed interest.' (E.J. Hobsbawm and G. Rude, *Captain Swing* (1973)).

ANNUAL AVERAGE PRICE OF BRITISH WHEAT PER QUARTER, 1810–24

1 How many years between 1815 and 1824 was the import of wheat allowed under the Corn Laws?

2 Using these figures, explain why you think the Corn Laws disappointed the farmers.

3 By 1820 farmers were again putting pressure on the government – what would they expect, and why?

4 From your reading of the rest of this chapter, what connection is there between the events from 1816 to 1819 and these prices? What might be the effect of the price change after 1820, and how might this influence government policy?

2 Income Tax

More serious for Ministers than the popular hostility to the Corn Laws were the consequences of their defeat over income tax in the following year. An assault on the high level of taxation was expected, but government could not afford a return to pre-war levels. An army of occupation had to be maintained in France, an expanding Empire entailed additional military and administrative costs, and the greatly increased National Debt had to be serviced. The proposed tax reductions did not, however, satisfy a parliamentary opposition sustained by a vigorous campaign by property owners. The Whigs exploited the issue, reckoning that they would be able to defeat Ministers and gain some much needed popularity.

Ministers complacently hoped to scrape through with a majority. In the event about 80 of their usual supporters voted with the opposition and there were many abstentions. The income tax was abolished, and the government now found itself with an income of £12 million and expenditure of £30 million. They had to resort to borrowing, which they had hoped to avoid, and to increasing the indirect taxes on items of everyday consumption. Antagonisms were increased, and a sense of grievance created which reformers like Hunt and Cobbett (see Focus 2.2, page 34) could exploit.

Income tax had been introduced by William Pitt as a wartime emergency measure in 1798, with the understanding that it would cease once the war ended.

OVERTAXED, JOHN BULL GROANS UNDER THE WEIGHT OF THOSE HE SUPPORTS. WHICH MONARCH SITS ON THE THRONE, AND WHO IS ON THE ISLAND SURROUNDED BY THE FLEET?

THE BRITISH ATLAS, or John Bull supporting the Peace Establishment.

Cuts in government expenditure were essential, and were expected by both independent MPs, spurred on by the Whigs, and the reformers outside parliament. Military personnel was pruned, ships laid up, the extravagances of the Prince Regent curtailed and the civil list reduced. Ministers had outflanked the Whigs by their willingness to economise, but by 1818 this process was threatening the continued efficiency of government and ministerial control of the House of Commons. A more imaginative approach was desperately needed to solve the severe financial crisis which the government faced.

2.2 William Cobbett and Henry Hunt - opinion makers

Henry 'Orator' Hunt

Born 1772; prosperous farming background in Wiltshire. His political activism developed after falling out with country society. Imprisoned, 1810, for attacking a gamekeeper; shared a cell with Cobbett. Contested Bristol as radical candidate, 1813.

> Why do these two seem surprising leaders for a reform movement centred on London and the industrial districts of the North and Midlands?

HUNT AS OTHERS SAW HIM - THE REVOLUTIONARY; HIS ASSOCIATES INCLUDE THISTLEWOOD, WATSON AND PRESTON WHO WERE ACQUITTED OF TREASON CHARGES AFTER THE SPA FIELDS MEETING OF 2 DECEMBER 1816. *BLACK DWARF* WAS A RADICAL NEWSHEET. WHAT REFERENCES TO THE FRENCH REVOLUTION ARE THERE?

William Cobbett

Born 1763 son of small farmer and innkeeper. Always believed that rural life was the best. Served in the army; went to France 1792; emigrated to USA 1793. Defended English policy towards France and attacked Tom Paine in his daily newspaper *Porcupine's Gazette*; returned to England in 1800. Began to publish the *Weekly Register*, 1802, supporting the Tory government. Became a reformer and was imprisoned, 1810, for his campaign against flogging in the army.

TALKING POINT

What value are political cartoons to historians?

FEARING PROSECUTION, COBBETT FLED TO THE UNITED STATES IN 1817, RETURNING TWO YEARS LATER BRINGING THE BONES OF TOM PAINE. PAINE HAD SETTLED IN THE UNITED STATES AFTER THE PUBLICATION OF THE *RIGHTS OF MAN* IN 1792. HIS BOOK WAS ESSENTIAL READING FOR THE REFORMERS.

The Power of the Press

At this time the writings of William Cobbett suddenly became of great authority; they were read on nearly every cottage hearth in the manufacturing districts ... Their influence was speedily visible; he directed his readers to the true cause of their sufferings - misgovernment; and to its proper corrective - parliamentary reform. Riots soon became scarce ... Cobbett's books were printed in a cheap form; the labourers read them, and thenceforward became deliberate and systematic in their proceedings.

Samuel Bamford, *Passages in the Life of a Radical*, 1841.

Cobbett became influential after his decision to publish the leading articles from his *Weekly Political Register* in pamphlet form, thus escaping the newspaper stamp duty which put the *Political Register* out of the reach of individual working men. Cobbett's periodicals preached a simple message:

As it is the labour of those who toil which makes a country abound in resources, so it is the same class of men, who must by their arms, secure its safety and uphold its fame ...
As to the *cause* of our present miseries, it is the *enormous amount of the taxes*, which the government compels us to pay for the support of its army, its placement, its pensioners, etc. and for the payment of the interest of its debt ...
The *remedy*... consists wholly and solely of such a *reform* in the Commons ... as shall give to every payer of *direct taxes* a vote at elections, and as shall cause the members to be *elected annually* ...

'The Address to the Journeymen and Labourers', number 18, 2 November 1816.

And the message reached a massive audience:

The effects of No.18 were prodigious. It occupied the conversation of all the acting men in the kingdom. The whole town was a buzz. The labouring classes of people seemed as if they had never heard a word of politics before ... In town and country, there were, in two months, more than two hundred thousand of this one Number printed and sold; and this, too, in spite of all the means which the Government, the Church, the Military and Naval Half-Pay, and all the innumerable swarms of Tax-Gatherers and Tax-Eaters, were able to do to check the circulation.

The Autobiography of William Cobbett

The Power of the Platform

Hunt, on the other hand, was the great orator of his age, reaching his audience from the hustings. Standing over six feet tall, 'Orator' Hunt was an impressive sight when in full flow:

His eyes were blue or light grey - not very clear nor quick, but rather heavy; except ... when he was excited in speaking; at which times they seemed to distend and protrude; and if he worked himself furious ... they became blood-streaked, and almost started from their sockets. Then it was that the expression of his lips was to be observed - the kind smile was exchanged for the curl of scorn, or the curse of indignation. His voice was bellowing; his face swollen and flushed; his gripped hand beat as if it were to pulverise; and his whole manner gave token of a painful energy, struggling for utterance.

Samuel Bamford, *Passages in the Life of a Radical*, 1841.

Revolutionaries?

Hunt and Cobbett both aimed at the reform of Parliament, advancing this cause by constitutional methods. Cobbett had high opinions of his ability to promote this peaceful reformism:

I proved to them that the riots must make matters worse. And the effect. the wonderful effect was, that all riot and disposition to riot ceased throughout the kingdom, though the misery of the people had been increasing all the while.

Cobbett on his 'Letter to the Luddites', 1816.

Hunt, however, thought that force might eventually have to be resorted to:

He well knew what ought to be done in such a crisis. He knew the superiority of mental over physical force; nor would he counsel a resort to the latter till the former had been found ineffectual. Before physical force was applied to, it was their duty to petition, to remonstrate, to call aloud for timely reformation ... Those who resisted the just demands of the people were the real friends of confusion and bloodshed; but if the fatal day should be destined to arrive ... he should not be found concealed behind a counter, or sheltering himself in the rear.

Report of Hunt at the Spa Fields meeting, 2 December 1816.

Both men preferred open action to secret plotting, and Hunt revelled in the occasion of great public meetings. Cobbett warned his readers 'to have nothing to do with any *Political Clubs*, and secret *Cabals*, any *correspondencies*, but to trust to *individual exertions* and *open meetings*'.

Leadership Potential?

This preference for 'individual exertions' and dislike of political scheming meant that for all their popular influence, neither Cobbett nor Hunt ever became closely involved with a political organisation.

Many years ago ... I set out as a sort of self-dependent politician. My opinions were my own. I dashed at all prejudices. I scorned to follow any body in matters of opinion.

William Cobbett.

Hunt says his mode of action is to dash at good points, and care for no one; that he will mix with no committee, or any party, he will act by himself; that he does not intend to front anyone, but cares not who is offended ... he is a very pretty sample of an ignorant, turbulent, mischief-making fellow.

Francis Place, a letter to John Mill snr, 1816.

QUESTIONS

1   Comment on the way in which the cartoonists treat Hunt and Cobbett. What are they trying to achieve, and how far do they succeed?

2   Cobbett claimed that the 1817 legislation against seditious publications was directly aimed at him. In 1820 the authorities successfully convicted Hunt after his arrest at Manchester in 1819. From the evidence you have seen, how justified were the fears of the authorities?

3   Historians suggest that both men played an important part in the political education of the working class. To what extent does this evidence support that conclusion?

Time of Troubles

1816 was a bad year.

> Of the state of the country I cannot report favourably. The distress is extreme, the indications of a disposition to disturbance less general than might have been expected. But it is to the autumn and winter that I look with anxiety.

> Sidmouth to his brother, 24 July 1816.

The Home Secretary had good reason for his concern. In the spring East Anglian farm labourers rioted against food shortages, high prices, low wages, low poor relief allowances and the use of threshing machines by farmers. Five men were executed, but their protest did not have wider political objectives, being one of the last major attempts at what has been described as 'collective bargaining by riot'. Elsewhere, there were renewed outbreaks of machine breaking in the East Midlands, and food riots and other disturbances reported from all parts of the country.

Economic problems and the prospect of a bad harvest aggravated the situation. The expected post-war trade boom had not materialised. Instead British exports slumped as the re-opening of European markets stimulated competition. In Shropshire, in South Wales and in the shipyards of the South Coast the cancellation of government wartime contracts caused immediate unemployment. In Shropshire alone, 7000 men were idle. As conditions worsened on the coal fields, Midlands colliers organised marches to London, pushing barrows of coal to draw attention to their plight. The influx of 300,000 discharged soldiers and sailors onto the labour market added to the difficulties. As wheat prices rose towards 100 shillings a quarter, Sidmouth looked to the future with some foreboding:

> We must expect a trying winter, and it will be fortunate if the Military establishment which was pronounced to be too large for the constitution of the country shall be sufficient to preserve its internal tranquillity.

> Sidmouth to Lord Sheffield, 1 November 1816.

Under the influence of Cobbett, Hunt and Major John Cartwright working class discontent caused by distress began to take an increasingly political direction. In 1812 Cartwright had made the first of three tours through the industrial districts encouraging his audiences to petition for reform of Parliament. Active in the reform movement since the late eighteenth century, he was convinced that only a mass popular movement could force ministers and MPs to give way. In this political climate, Hampden Clubs, inspired by Cartwright, started up throughout the country, providing a forum for the discussion of parliamentary reform, and spreading these ideas among working people.

> One of these clubs was established in 1816, at the small town of Middleton, near Manchester ... The Club prospered; the number of members increased; the funds raised by contribution of a penny a

week, became more than sufficient for all our out-goings; and taking a bold step we soon rented a chapel ... and there we held our meetings on the evenings of Monday and Saturday ...

Resolutions were passed declaratory of the right of every male to vote, who paid taxes; that males of eighteen should be eligible to vote; that parliaments should be elected annually; that no pensioners or placement should sit in parliament; that every twenty thousand of inhabitants should send a member to the house of commons; and that talent, and virtue, were the only qualifications necessary.

Samuel Bamford, *Passages in the Life of a Radical,* 1841.

TALKING POINT

Consider the practicality of this programme for a society in which the largest working group were agricultural labourers, illiteracy was widespread, most people lived in small self-contained communities, and communications were rudimentary.

At the end of 1816 the clubs prepared to send delegates to a London convention. Meanwhile, Hunt had made his mark at the great Spa Fields meeting of 15th November, where he was the only prominent reform leader to join the revolutionary gathering. Unfortunately for the reform movement, he failed to dissuade Arthur Thistlewood and John Watson from using the second meeting on 2 December as an opportunity to launch a ramshackle attack on the Tower of London. Hunt was not involved in the conspiracy but the government tried to implicate him.

When the Hampden Club Convention assembled, its members rejected the moderate proposals of Cobbett and adopted Hunt's full universal suffrage programme, coupled with a mass petitioning of Parliament. Cobbett withdrew, and the radical MP Sir Francis Burdett refused to become involved. Ministerial alarm was intensified when a window of the Prince Regent's coach was shattered as he was driven to open the 1817 session of Parliament.

Whilst the reformers held mass-meetings and prepared their petitions, both Houses of Parliament appointed Committees of Secrecy to examine the Home Office papers on the disturbances. Eventually over 700 petitions from 350 towns or villages were presented. They made little impression on MPs. Burdett's reform motion was lost by 265 votes to 77 and the Commons Committee of Secrecy found sufficient evidence to justify fears of a national revolutionary conspiracy centred on the Spa Fields meetings and riot. Alarmed, the government pushed three measures through Parliament:

1 Suspension of Habeas Corpus for six months.
2 The Seditious Meetings Act – restricted freedom to hold public meetings.
3 Incitement to Mutiny was made a hanging offence.

The legislation was effective. Cobbett fled to the United States and Bamford's local organisation broke up:

Personal liberty not being now secure from one hour to another, many leading reformers were induced to quit their homes, and seek concealment where they could obtain it ...

Our society ... became divided and dismayed; hundreds slunk home to their looms, and dared not come out, save like owls at nightfall, when they could perhaps steal through bye-paths or behind hedges, or down some clough, to hear the news at the next cottage ... Open meetings thus being suspended, secret ones ensued; they were originated at Manchester ... Sometimes they were termed 'benefit societies'; sometimes 'botanical meetings' ... but their real purpose ... was to carry into effect the night attack on Manchester.

Samuel Bamford, *Passages in the Life of a Radical,* 1841.

The Whigs, seen as the natural leaders of the reform cause, were silenced by the findings of the Committee of Secrecy. Shocked by the violence of the petitioning movement, Lord Grey wrote, 'I have now no hope of seeing a moderate and useful reform effected during my life, and we have to thank Major Cartwright, Mr Cobbett & Co principally for it.'

1817 – Continuing Unrest

With hopes for reform shattered, and Parliament appearing to be oblivious to calls for change, some reformers began to take their appeals direct to the Prince Regent. On 10 March 1817 several thousand weavers, each equipped with a blanket, assembled in St Peter's Fields, Manchester. They intended marching to London with petitions for the Prince Regent requesting measures to ease the depression in the cotton trade. However, the local magistrates, alarmed by reports that the march had insurrectionary aims, called in troops to break up the gathering. Most of the Blanketeers dispersed peacefully, but some had already set off and were arrested as they made their way south.

Others reacted to the government's clamp-down more violently. On the wet and dismal night of 9 June Jeremiah Brandreth led the ironworkers, stockingers and farm labourers of the Nottinghamshire and Derbyshire border around the village of Pentrich in a march on Nottingham. They had been led to believe that they were one small part of a general rising.

The rebels advanced, equipped with pikes and guns, but were met and dispersed by a group of 20 cavalrymen – fleeing without a shot being fired. Forty-eight men, including Brandreth, were captured and imprisoned. Brandreth and two others were executed and 14 transported.

The Pentrich rebels had gained their information about the non-existant nation-wide uprising from a spy called Mr Oliver who had been appointed by Sidmouth. Because there was no effective police force, the Home Office and local magistrates relied on spies and informers for intelligence about the activities of working class reformers. These spies were all too keen to feed their nervous employers with tales of plots and insurrection, and easily became agents provocateurs.

The Pentrich prisoners could not call on Oliver as a witness in court as 'provocation' could not be used as a defence. Therefore, the government got its convictions and made a public example of the rebels. However, elsewhere the revelations of spies' activities discredited government

THE BLACK DWARF WAS AN UNSTAMPED RADICAL NEWSPAPER SOLD BY STREET SELLERS TO AVOID THE NEWSPAPER STAMP DUTY. IT ASSUMED A HIGH LEVEL OF LITERACY AMONGST ITS READERS.

prosecutions. Both the Spa Fields conspirators and the Holme Valley insurgents were acquitted and London juries refused to convict the radical printers Wooler and Hone on charges of sedition and blasphemy.

Furthermore, the coverage of the Pentrich trial in the *Leeds Mercury* weakened the credibility of the government's case and shocked middle class liberal opinion. The Whigs did not sympathise with the working class radicals, but they could not resist the temptation of attacking Ministers on a popular issue. Although the government had a secure majority in the Commons their perceived political isolation from 'respectable opinion' contributed to the policy changes that can be detected after 1819.

Examining the evidence
'Mr Oliver'–
Sidmouth's spy and the Pentrich Rebellion

The Pentrich Rebellion raised a number of issues of public concern:
● The use of agents provocateurs by the authorities.
● The complicity of government in the 'manufacturing' of a crisis.
● The reality of the revolutionary threat, 1815–20.
The following sources shed some light on these issues by focusing on the role of Sidmouth's spy, Mr Oliver.

Responsibility – the Contemporary View

Source A
There prevails very generally in the country a strong and decided opinion that most of the events that have recently occurred in the country are to be attributed to the presence and active agitation of Mr Oliver. He is considered as the *main spring* from which every movement has taken its rise. All the mischievous in the country have considered themselves as subordinate members of a great leading body of revolutionists in London, as co-operating with that body for one general purpose, and in this view to be under its instructions and directions, communicated by some delegate appointed for the purpose. Had not then a person pretending to come from that body and for that purpose, made his appearance in the country, it is not assuming too much to say that probably no movement whatever would have occurred – it does not follow that a dangerous spirit could not have been found lurking in any breast, but that spirit would not have found its way into action ...

I am quite assured that the general opinion is that the mass of the people are sound, that the disaffected are few in number, and contemptible in description and consideration.

Lord Fitzwilliam to Lord Sidmouth, 17 June 1817.

Fitzwilliam, a leading Whig peer, was Lord Lieutenant of the West Riding of Yorkshire. In 1819 he was dismissed for attending the county meeting protesting against the Peterloo Massacre.

Source B
This is the work of Government and Oliver.

William Turner on the gallows, 9 November 1817.

Source C

Oliver drew towards London, leaving his victims successively in the traps that he had prepared for them ... The employers of Oliver might, in an hour, have put a total stop to those preparations, and have blown them to air ... [They] wished, not to prevent, but to produce those acts.

Cobbett's *Political Register,* 16 May 1818.

---

1 What do sources A, B and C agree on? What are the differences between them?
2 In the circumstances, why might Sidmouth find Fitzwilliam's letter embarrassing? Refer to the source in your answer.

Responsibility – the historian's view

Source D

There is no reason to suppose that Sidmouth deliberately employed Oliver for the diabolical purpose of fomenting an abortive rebellion, and this view was undoubtedly held at the time. The guilt of the Government was grave enough but it was not this. They took Oliver into their employment without knowing anything of his character ... Then came the disclosures of the *Leeds Mercury* ... When Brandreth and his fellow victims were on their trial the Government knew enough about Oliver to make them suspect that these foolish ranters had been drawn into their ludicrous escapade by the craft of the man who was receiving the money of the taxpayers and acting as their servant. The temptation to produce something that looked like a spontaneous disturbance was strong, for hitherto the life of the country had borne no resemblance to the pictures drawn by the Government in the House of Commons.

J.L. and B. Hammond, *The Skilled Labourer,* 1919.

Source E

Oliver ... seems never to have been capable of making up his mind whether he was an atomising agent or a bread-poultice ...

The parliamentary opposition and the Whig and Radical press set to work to prove that there would have been no sedition had not Oliver and Lord Sidmouth manufactured it. Historians of the same complexion ... have maintained that the outcry against Oliver the Spy was an expression of national indignation against a system ... of government by a reactionary gang of Tories. But 'system' was there none. Instead, a broken-down master-builder of dubious morals and low-grade intelligence, who offered his services as an informer, was casually employed on terms of 'payment-by-results'. Sidmouth's offence was that he employed Oliver ... indiscriminately ... He even omitted the elementary precaution of informing local magistrates, in any systematic fashion, that this casual 'tourist' was coming into their midst ... Worst of all Oliver went blundering into a situation which he did not understand.

R. J. White, *Waterloo to Peterloo*, 1957.

Source F

Oliver was not the only spy in the secret organisation. The magistrates in Lancashire and Nottingham were kept well briefed by their own local informers. But, at the same time, it is not true that the only instigators of revolution were spies. Bamford was visited ... not by Oliver, but by ... Thomas Bacon and Turner – both of whom were to be involved in the Pentridge Rising. Suggestions that Oliver was not a provocateur, or, alternatively, that if he was, he exceeded Sidmouth's instructions, cannot be sustained ... The Government wanted blood - not a holocaust, but enough to make an example ...

Persistent rumour suggested that Brandreth himself had been a Luddite – perhaps even a Luddite 'captain'... There is reason, then, to suppose that some of those involved were not dupes but experienced revolutionaries ... We may see the Pentridge rising as one of the first attempts in history to mount a wholly proletarian insurrection, without any middle-class support ... Even without Oliver's patent provocations, some kind of insurrection would probably have been attempted ... Indeed, in the Crown's view, not Oliver ... but Thomas Bacon who ... had travelled between Nottingham, Derby, Yorkshire, Lancashire and Birmingham, was the main instigator of rebellion.

E. P. Thompson, *The Making of the English Working Class,* 1963.

Source G

That groups of militants existed before Oliver appeared on the scene is quite clear; he did not create revolutionaries out of nothing, though he probably encouraged them both by what he said and what he did not say. Nor was he responsible for the notion of an armed insurrection, for that too had preceded Oliver, though he probably contributed more to the shaping and formulation of the insurrection that finally took place in June than he was ever prepared to admit. His connections with Brandreth are very tenuous and difficult to establish. A meeting between the two men has never been proved ... Whatever Oliver's actual words to the companies among whom he moved, he conveyed an impression, whether by his speeches or his silences, that revolution was going ahead throughout the country and was himself understood to be the sign that there was a national leadership in London which expected revolution and was prepared to give it direction.

M.I. Thomis and P. Holt, *Threats of Revolution in Britain 1789–1848,*1977.

---

1 To what extent do these historians differ in their views of the role of Oliver, Sidmouth and the government, and of the real danger of insurrection in 1817?
2 Using the evidence you have seen, why is it possible for historians to reach such a wide variety of conflicting interpretations?
3 'Every detail of the story illustrates the weakness of the revolutionary organisation, and the lack of an experienced leadership.' (E.P. Thompson).
Explain this statement, and, using these sources and wider knowledge, assess how close the country was to insurrection and revolution during this period.

COBBETT POINTED OUT THE DIFFICULTY OF 'AGITATING' A MAN ON A 'FULL STOMACH'. IT IS SIMPLISTIC TO EXPLAIN POLITICAL DISCONTENT IN THESE TERMS ALONE BUT THE GRAPH SUGGESTS THAT THERE WAS SOME TRUTH IN HIS ASSERTION.

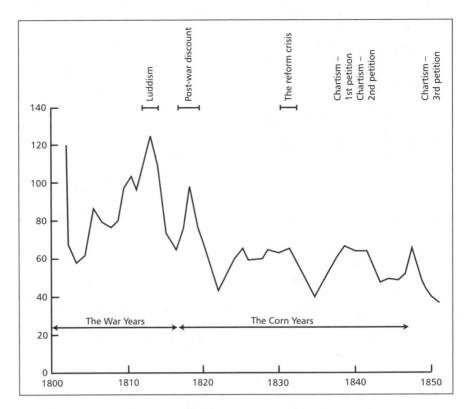

Peterloo and the Six Acts

PETERLOO OFFERED A PROPAGANDA BONUS FOR THE RADICALS. COMMENT ON THE WAYS IN WHICH BOTH CRUIKSHANK IN THIS CARTOON AND WILLIAM HONE IN HIS SATIRICAL VERSE 'THE HOUSE THAT JACK BUILT' TURN THE INCIDENT TO POLITICAL ADVANTAGE.

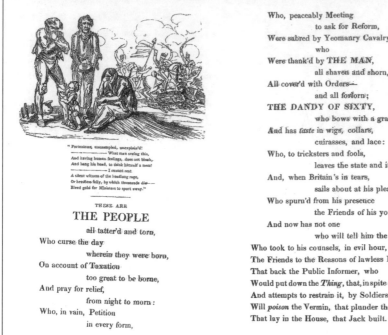

" Portentous, unexampled, unexplain'd!
————————— What man seeing this,
And having human feelings, does not blush,
And hang his head, to think himself a man?
————————— I cannot rest.
A silent victim of the headlong rage,
Or heedless folly, by which thousands die——
Bleed gold for Ministers to sport away."

THESE ARE

THE PEOPLE

all tatter'd and torn,
Who curse the day
            wherein they were born,
On account of Taxation
            too great to be borne,
And pray for relief,
            from night to morn :
Who, in vain, Petition
            in every form,

Who, peaceably Meeting
            to ask for Reform,
Were sabred by Yeomanry Cavalry,
            who
Were thank'd by THE MAN,
            all shaven and shorn,
All cover'd with Orders—
            and all forlorn;
THE DANDY OF SIXTY,
            who bows with a grace,
And has *taste* in wigs, collars,
            cuirasses, and lace :
Who, to tricksters and fools,
            leaves the state and its treasure,
And, when Britain's in tears,
            sails about at his pleasure :
Who spurn'd from his presence
            the Friends of his youth,
And now has not one
            who will tell him the truth ;
Who took to his counsels, in evil hour,
The Friends to the Reasons of lawless Power,
That back the Public Informer, who
Would put down the *Thing*, that, in spite of new Acts,
And attempts to restrain it, by Soldiers or Tax,
Will *poison* the Vermin, that plunder the Wealth,
That lay in the House, that Jack built.

IDENTIFY 'THE DANDY OF SIXTY', 'THE FRIENDS OF HIS YOUTH', 'THE FRIENDS TO THE REASONS OF LAWLESS POWER' IN THE EXTRACT FROM 'THE HOUSE THAT JACK BUILT'. THE 'THING' WAS THE PRINTING PRESS – WHY WOULD THAT 'POISON' THE VERMIN'?

Following the economic problems and social unrest of 1815–16, the early months of 1817 saw a pattern emerge of an improving economy and a decline in public discontent. However, despite these trends, the darkest moment of the struggle between the authorities and the radical protest movement was still to come.

Once the suspension of Habeas Corpus and the restrictions on public meetings came to an end, the radicals cautiously re-emerged. Although the Thistlewood group continued its conspiratorial activities in London, in the provinces the approach of Cartwright, Cobbett and Hunt – the mass public meeting – was followed. In January 1819 Hunt launched a new campaign to by-pass Parliament by adopting Remonstrances to be presented directly to the Prince Regent. In July a London mass meeting resolved that the Acts of an unrepresentative Parliament could have no authority after 1 January 1820, whilst in Birmingham Sir Charles Wolseley was elected as 'legislatorial attorney' for the unrepresented community. When a similar 'election' was proposed for Manchester the local magistrates were able to ban the meeting. The Manchester organisers took legal advice and dropped the election, but rescheduled the meeting for 16 August. 'Orator' Hunt was to be the principal speaker.

Apprehension gripped the local magistrates. Their nerves had been frayed during the long cotton spinners' strike of 1818, and a recent inflammatory speech made by Wolesley in Stockport made matters worse. Now their informers and police officers reported that groups were drilling on the moors. Hunt's promised appearance at St. Peter's Fields on 16 August seemed to signify that an insurrection was imminent.

Samuel Bamford was involved in organising the mass meeting. His record of the event explains the drilling on the moors:

We had frequently been taunted by the press, with our ragged, dirty appearence ... and the moblike crowds in which our numbers were mustered; and we determined ... that we should disarm the bitterness of our political opponents by a display of cleanliness, sobriety, and decorum.

Samuel Bamford, *Passages in the Life of a Radical*, 1841.

This was the spirit of Cobbett rather than training for an insurrection. Since large numbers were expected, there had to be a high level of organisation. Routes to be followed by columns from neighbouring towns were laid down. Banners were prepared. People looked forward to a day out.

Archibald Prentice, editor of the radical *Manchester Times*, observed the scene at St Peter's Fields:

It seemed to be a gala day with the country people who were mostly dressed in their best and brought with them their wives, and I saw boys and girls taking their father's hand in the procession ... At length Hunt made his appearance ... he was received with enthusiastic applause; the waving of flags; the blowing of trumpets; and the playing of music ... I heard the sound of a horn, and immediately the Manchester Yeomanry appeared ...

Their sabres glistened in the air, and on they went, direct for the hustings ... As the cavalry approached the dense mass of people, they used their utmost efforts to escape: but so closely were they pressed in opposite directions by the soldiers, the special constables, the position of the hustings, and their own immense numbers, that immediate escape was impossible.

Hunt was seized and taken away. Bamford describes the scene:

In ten minutes the field was an open and almost deserted space ... The hustings remained, with a few broken or hewed flag-staves erect, and a torn or gashed banner or two drooping; whilst over the whole field were strewed caps, bonnets, hats, shawls, and shoes, and other parts of male and female dress: trampled, torn and bloody. The yeomanry had dismounted – some were easing their horses' girths, others adjusting their acoutrements; and some were wiping their sabres. Several mounds of human beings still remained where they had fallen, crushed down and smothered. Some of these were still groaning – others with staring eyes, were gasping for breath, and others would never breathe more.

Eleven were killed and over 400 injured.

Together with speakers on the hustings had been reporters from *The Times*, *The Leeds Mercury* and other leading newspapers. This meant that 'Peterloo', as it came to be known, was given maximum press coverage. Government ministers felt they had no other option than to stand by the actions of the magistrates. If magistrates did not feel confident of government support then they would be reluctant to take difficult independent decisions. A formal message of thanks was sent from the Prince Regent, but not all ministers were convinced of the soundness of their actions. Writing to Canning, Liverpool reflected on the ministerial dilemma:

TALKING POINT

Discuss the reasons why Peterloo is often seen as the representative event of this period.

When I say that the proceedings of the magistrates ... were justifiable, you will understand me as not by any means deciding that the course which they pursued on that occasion was in all parts prudent ... but, whatever judgement might be formed in this respect, being satisfied that they were substantially right, there remained no alternative but to support them.

Warning of the revolutionary nature of the situation in the north, Sidmouth pressed for an early recall of Parliament. Liverpool's reluctance to agree is sufficient to cast doubt on any possibility of the massacre having been planned, as is the absence of eight cabinet ministers on the continent. Immune to the wilder assertions of his Home Secretary and of Eldon, Liverpool was able to write reassuringly to Canning:

The accounts of the proceedings at Manchester will of course have reached you, and will probably have in some degree alarmed you. To enable you to judge, however, fairly of the actual state of things, I must begin with acquainting you that, if certain manufacturing districts are excepted, that is Lancashire, part of Cheshire, the West Riding of Yorkshire, some parts of the central counties which are contiguous, and likewise Glasgow and Paisley and their neighbourhood, I have never known the country in general, since the conclusion of the war, and I believe I might say since I have been in Parliament, in a more prosperous situation. I include in this statement the metropolis, where the reformers have been able to do nothing because they have no distress nor practical grievance to work upon.

The Radicals' response to Peterloo was a rash of public demonstrations. Recrimination and abuse from this quarter did not disturb Liverpool but, more seriously, during September the Whigs slowly began to take up Peterloo to launch a renewed assault on the Tory government. Reluctantly at first, and then with increasing eagerness, Whig politicians attended urban public meetings and organised a series of county meetings. The government could not acquiesce to the growing clamour for a committee of inquiry and the decision to recall Parliament on 23 November was a political response to pressure from the Whigs rather than the action of a Cabinet alarmed by the state of the country.

Most MPs accepted the ministerial view that a few agitators were systematically destroying 'all respect for established authority and ancient institutions' (Liverpool, see Review below), that freedom of the press was being abused to defame Church and State, and that organised public meetings were enabling demagogues to acquire an undue influence via intimidation and inflammatory speeches. Ministers were able to present wide-ranging evidence to justify a new batch of repressive measures - measures which provided a retrospective justification of the Manchester magistrates. This legislation became the notorious Six Acts. The Whigs were outflanked. Fearful for property, anxious for stability, they appeared to be inconsistent, and the independent country gentlemen found the arguments of ministers far more persuasive. Only 150 votes could be mustered on the Whig motion for a parliamentary committee of inquiry.

Notorious at the time, and since, the Six Acts were in fact comparatively mild in their impact. The main purpose was to quell the anxieties and

---

The Six Acts, 1819

1 An Act giving magistrates emergency powers to search houses for weapons

2 An Act to prevent all but the smallest public meetings

3 An Act to prevent delays by the accused in blasphemy and treason trials

4 An Act to prevent evasions of newspaper stamp duty

5 An Act to enable magistrates to seize and destroy seditious and blasphemous publications

6 An Act forbidding unauthorised military training

excitement raised by the large public demonstrations, but they were singularly ineffective in controlling the outpourings of the radical press. The restriction on public meetings was not renewed when its provisions expired the following year.

TALKING POINT

In this radical condemnation of the Six Acts, Castlereagh perches like a bird of prey on his victim. Comment on the interpretation of the Six Acts in the cartoon. This government's repressive reputation is based on what it did in 1817 and 1819. Compared to other regimes you have studied, how justified is that reputation?

Poor John Bull – The Free Born Englishman – Deprived of his Seven Senses By the Six New Acts!

EXAMINING THE EVIDENCE

Peterloo – some modern assessments

Source A

Peterloo, as the evidence of the Home Office shows, was never desired or precipitated by the Liverpool Ministry as a bloody repressive gesture for keeping down the lower orders. If the Manchester magistrates had followed the spirit of Home Office policy there would never have been a 'massacre'.

D. Read, *Peterloo: the Massacre and its Background*, 1958.

Source B

We shall probably never be able to determine with certainty whether or not Liverpool and Sidmouth were parties to the decision to disperse the meeting with force ... If the Government was unprepared for the news of Peterloo, no authorities have ever acted so vigorously to make themselves accomplices after the fact ... If the Peterloo decision was unpremeditated, it would appear to have been the signal for which the Government was waiting.

E. P. Thompson, *The Making of the English Working Class*, 1963.

Source C

No evidence of the ministerial or Home Office plot to initiate the events of the 16th has been established, and the tragic events of 'Peterloo' probably owed far more to the incompetence of the magistrates and the Manchester and Salford Yeomanry than to premeditated action.

J. Stevenson, *Popular Disturbances in England, 1700–1870*, 1979.

Source D

Peterloo was a blunder, it was hardly a massacre.

N. Gash, *Aristocracy and People*, 1979.

1 Compare and contrast these assessments of Peterloo.

2 Discuss the factors which lead historians to have different views of a widely reported event like Peterloo.

The Cato Street Conspiracy and the end of the troubles

A MAY DAY GARLAND for 1820.

In February 1820 the Cato Street Conspiracy to assassinate the entire Cabinet was exposed. Arthur Thistlewood and four of his colleagues were executed, although the infiltration of the group by a government spy did earn them some sympathy. Hopes that a nationwide rising was imminent, as in 1817, led to isolated outbreaks in Glasgow and the Barnsley area at the beginning of April, but there were no organisational links between London and the provinces, and these proved to be the last flickerings of the old insurrectionary and violent response to discontent.

MINISTERS DANCE AROUND THE SEVERED HEADS OF THE CATO STREET CONSPIRATORS, BUT THE SPY EDWARDS PLAYS THE TUNE.

Hunt and his associates, including Bamford, had been convicted in March. Sentenced to two and a half years, Hunt was incarcerated in Ilchester gaol, but he had the satisfaction of knowing that the constitutional approach to reform, and open organisation which excluded spies, had entered the mainstream of working class radicalism. 'It was', as the historian R. J. White has written, 'a case of conversion to Cartwright and Cobbett.'

After 1819 the worst that ministers faced was popular hostility and abuse during their reluctant attempt to provide George IV with a divorce from his estranged wife, Queen Caroline. With their leaders imprisoned, working class reformers were in no position to challenge the forces of law and order, whilst the economic revival contributed to a re-appraisal of priorities.

'Which is the Dirtiest ....'

RADICAL SYMPATHY WAS WITH CAROLINE, AND THE WHIGS EXPLOITED THE POPULAR MOOD FOR THEIR OWN POLITICAL PURPOSES, VIGOROUSLY AND SUCCESSFULLY OPPOSING THE GOVERNMENT'S ATTEMPT TO GET THE DIVORCE LEGISLATION THROUGH THE LORDS. BOTH GEORGE AND CAROLINE HAD SCANDALOUS REPUTATIONS, AND THE MASSES ENJOYED THIS PUBLIC WASHING OF ROYAL 'DIRTY LINEN.'

Review

The post-war crisis – a question of responsibility

In a letter to Lord Grenville, 14 November 1819, Liverpool outlined the causes of the crisis facing the country.

> Though it cannot be denied that the great increase of our manufacturing population, the dependence of the great part of that population on foreign demand, and the refinements in machinery (which enable manufacturers to perform that work in weeks which formerly occupied months, and which lead consequently to extravagant wages at one time, and to low and inadequate ones at another), have recently subjected, and must in the nature of things subject this country to evils with which in the same degree we were formerly unacquainted; yet all these circumstances would not have accounted for the present state of the public mind in certain parts of the country, if the events of the French Revolution had not directed the attention of the lower orders of the community, and those immediately above them, to political considerations; had not shaken all respect for established authority and ancient institutions; and had not familiarised mankind with a system of organisation which had been justly represented to be as ingenious and appropriate to its purpose as any invention in mechanics.

Consider this list of factors which historians suggest contributed to the crisis:

Reference to chapter 1 will help with this Review.

- The impact of industrialisation
- The Corn Laws
- Bad harvests and rising food prices
- Growth of class consciousness
- Influential radical leaders
- Effects of urbanisation
- Population growth
- Abolition of income tax
- Reduction of government's military expenditure
- Post-war economic depression
- Repressive policies
- Provocative use of spies and informers
- Unrepresentative electoral system
- Excessive burden of indirect taxation
- Ministers' concern with maintaining law and order
- Government's failure to deal with consequences of economic depression
- Effects of the French Revolution

1 Some of these factors were outside the government's control; some, it could be argued, they were responsible for. Divide the factors into these two categories. Explain the choices you have made.

2 Some of these factors created the conditions for discontent, others were immediate causes of unrest, others perhaps explain the motives of those involved. Now make three lists putting the factors into these new categories. Once again, be prepared to justify your choices. Are there any links between the two sets of lists?

3 Is it possible to pinpoint any one of the immediate causes of unrest as the most important catalyst in provoking the crisis? Explain your answer with reference to the events of the period 1815–20.

4 Liverpool picks out two main causes of the public discontent and agitation. What are they, and how can his emphasis on these two be explained? What value can be put on his assessment?

5 **Essay:**
   How far was Lord Liverpool's government directly responsible for the popular unrest of the years from 1815 to 1820?

3 The End of the Old Constitution, 1820–30

PREVIEW

The failure of Liberal Toryism?

Source A

The cause of reform has made great progress ... almost the whole press, and all public meetings, are loud for reform, and ... on our side of the question ... nothing is spoken or written to oppose the torrent of the reformers ... We should not give an inch to parliamentary reform ... I said in general that no one could guess what the consequences of reform would be. I should have said its eventual consequences, for the first step or two seem plain enough – the day which reforms the House of Commons, dissolves the House of Lords, and overturns the Church. Beyond that I cannot venture to guess.

J. W. Croker to Robert Peel, February 1822.

Source B

Peel considers a revolution at no great distance – not a bloody one and perhaps not one leading to a republic, but one utterly subversive of the aristocracy and of the present system of carrying on the government. He thinks we may get on quite as well after this change as before; but he considers it inevitable.

Record of a conversation with Robert Peel in 1824.

Source C

Lord John Russell had become the most persistent parliamentary reformer in the House of Commons.
The very last time [Russell] had mentioned the question [parliamentary reform] in the course of the last session, he had declared that would be the last occasion of his doing so. And why had he made that declaration? Because he found a great lukewarmness on the subject throughout the country.

Lord John Russell in the House of Commons, 3 May 1827.

Source D

Two years ago I thought Reform of Parliament almost hopeless. I now believe it to be certain and approaching. The longer delayed, the more it will be radical.

Sir Robert Heron, Whig backbencher, at the end of 1830.

Using the evidence of these sources briefly comment on the apparent success, and eventual failure, of the Tory administrations, 1822–30.

The Reformers' Attack on the Old Rotten Tree; or, the Foul Nests of the Cormorants in Danger.

LORD GREY LOOKS ON AS WHIG MINISTERS CHOP AT THE ROTTEN TREE OF THE CONSTITUTION WHICH IS BEING SHORED UP BY THE ANTI-REFORMERS, INCLUDING PEEL AND WELLINGTON.

Tory government in crisis

Truck payments were made in tokens which could only be redeemed at shops approved by the employer. Employers benefited, workers felt cheated. The Act made this illegal. Peel's Factory Act attempted to protect children employed in cotton mills.

Despite its reactionary reputation, the Liverpool ministry had never been entirely negative although its ameliorative measures were weak and ineffective. These included limited attempts to encourage emigration and some support for local public works through the Poor Employment Act in 1817. Workers' interests were protected by the Truck Act of 1817, whilst, in 1819, Liverpool gave his personal support to Peel's Factory Bill. The Church Building Act (1818) aimed to counter Nonconformist religion and radical political ideas by strengthening the Church of England in the new urban areas.

Ministers believed that public discontent was the result of economic distress being exploited by a few agitators. Their response was to grant emergency powers to local magistrates to deal with the threat of violence and to maintain law and order.

Although ministers subscribed to laissez faire economic theories, their record suggests that a pragmatic approach was being adopted and that some tentative reform and intervention to deal with economic and social problems was possible.

Their biggest economic problem was created by the abolition of income tax in 1816 and the strident opposition demands for cuts in expenditure. Tax revenue after 1815 was still three times higher than it had been before the war, but over £55 million went to service the national debt and pay army and naval pensions. In 1818 only £18 million was required for 'normal' government expenditure but there was a deficit of £13 million financed by borrowing. The revenue crisis had to be resolved before effective government became impossible.

Liverpool knew that if the traditional forms of aristocratic government were to be preserved, the support of 'the rational part of the community' had to be won and retained. Concessions would have to be made to win that sympathy and to demonstrate that the old order could respond to the needs of an industrialising society with its new classes and interests.

Thus, at the start of the 1820s, these were the major issues facing the Liverpool government:

- Unemployment and a depressed economy
- High taxation
- Future of the Corn Laws
- Demands for parliamentary reform
- Complaints against repressive policies
- Catholic and Nonconformist emancipation
- Corruption – patronage and sinecures
- Need for 'new blood' in the Cabinet to strengthen the Ministry in the Commons
- Pressure to lessen the restrictions on trade (free trade)

The 'Liberal Tories' – Myth or Reality?

Long standing weaknesses in the House of Commons were emphasised by the Government's defeat on the royal divorce and by Canning's resignation at the end of 1820. The following year Liverpool successfully recruited the Grenvillite Whig faction to the government side, gaining perhaps an extra 12 votes. His attempt to get Peel into the Cabinet stumbled on Peel's reluctance to accept the India Office in succession to Canning and on Castlereagh's unwillingness to see significant promotion for an able young rival.

Canning was the great difficulty. Liverpool would have liked him back, but George IV had been incensed by his opposition to the divorce and suspected that Canning had been one of his wife's many lovers. If, as the Whigs hoped, Canning's bitterness persuaded him to oppose ministers, then the government would be in real trouble. By the end of 1821 he had been bought off with the promise of the lucrative Governor Generalship of India, and Sidmouth's decision to relinquish the Home Office opened the way for Peel to enter the Cabinet in a senior position. All these calculations and expectations were overturned in August 1822 when a disturbed and depressed Castlereagh committed suicide.

TALKING POINT

Discuss the nature of the issues facing ministers suggesting where concessions were possible and where compromise was unlikely. Prepare a report from your findings, basing your comments and proposals on your knowledge of the period and of the political views and intentions of ministers.

Sir Robert Peel (1788–1850) was born near Bury, son of a wealthy Lancashire mill owner and factory reformer. Educated at Harrow and Oxford, his father purchased him a parliamentary seat on his 21st birthday. Junior office followed in 1810. Peel was appointed Chief Secretary for Ireland in 1812.

In succession to Castlereagh, Peel would have made a suitable Leader of the House, and was acceptable to the King, but Canning was the only possible candidate for the Foreign Office, and he demanded Castlereagh's full inheritance. Liverpool had to wrestle with the King's hostility, but it was Wellington, despite his personal aversion to Canning, who finally overcame royal opposition. With Canning came Frederick Robinson, replacing Vansittart at the Exchequer, and Huskisson as the new President of the Board of Trade, although he did not get the Cabinet status he craved until 1823. The reconstructed ministry now possessed a formidable front bench team in the House of Commons.

Until recently, historians wrote about the 'new men' of 1822, and dated the government's change of direction from their appointments. However, all four had previously served the Liverpool ministry. Peel had been Chief Secretary for Ireland 1812–18 and had chaired the influential Bullion Committee of 1819; Canning, in the Cabinet 1816–20, had supported all the repressive measures of those years; Huskisson had influenced economic policy from minor office, whilst Robinson was promoted from the Presidency of the Board of Trade.

To all appearances the government was stronger, and Canning's leadership made it more assertive in the Commons, but the unity that had existed since 1815 was broken. Canning's constant restlessness, 'perpetually doing and undoing', engendered uncertainty. His personal manner had made him many powerful enemies. Wellington dismissed him as a 'charlatan parvenu', and deplored his popularisation of foreign policy. As early as 1823 George IV was worrying about Canning's close relationship with the Prime Minister:

> The King dreaded his admission into the Cabinet from the fear he had lest his influence should be great with you. The King now thinks that those fears have been realised ... He would far rather make Canning his Prime Minister rather than continue to have the conviction that the real power is already vested in him, while the name alone remains with you.
>
> Charles Arbuthnot to Lord Liverpool, 7 October 1823.

In fact, as the Cabinet split into pro- and anti-Canning factions, Liverpool's mediatory powers were more in demand, and his pre-eminence was never challenged. When Burdett's Catholic emancipation motion won a Commons majority in 1825 (Peel was the only minister to oppose it), but was defeated in the Lords, Canning threatened to break the unwritten convention and raise the issue in Cabinet. Only Liverpool's warnings of the possible consequences persuaded him to refrain from doing so.

Focus

3.1 How 'Liberal' were the Liberal Tories?

1 New Economic Policies – Freer Trade

Trade expansion to be encouraged as an employment policy to reduce discontent.
Wallace prepares, 1821 and 1822; Huskisson gets the credit.

Duty reductions 1824, 1825
— Industry gets cheaper raw materials
— Exchequer benefits from increased trade and customs revenues

Reciprocity Act 1823
— Board of Trade can negotiate mutually advantageous trade treaties with other countries
— Navigation Laws relaxed
— Colonial suppliers encouraged with preferential duties
— The Corn Laws appear increasingly vulnerable.
Was the government trying to forge a new alliance with the City and industry to the detriment of agriculture?

Responding to new challenges – planning for change

1 1819 Peel chairs the parliamentary committee (the Bullion Committee) which recommends the resumption of cash payments by the Bank of England. These had been stopped as wartime emergency measure by Pitt in 1797. This is viewed as the final step in the return to normality after the war. Return to the gold standard completed in 1822. Exporters benefit but agriculturists suffer from the re-valuation.

2 1819 New budgetary policy initiated, which would balance the budget and create a surplus.

3 1819 Opposition motions to reduce the number of offences punishable by death carried against the government. Home Office officials begin to prepare for reform.

4 May 1820 Liverpool speaks favourably of free trade in a Lords debate. Thomas Wallace, Vice-president of the Board of Trade begins to plan for a change in economic policy.

2 Financial Policy

Vansittart's successful budgets since 1819 provide the surpluses for Robinson's tax cuts of 1823 and for Huskisson's duty reductions. 'Prosperity' Robinson given credit for tax cuts of about £12 million.

3 Peel at the Home Office

a. Rationalisation of the criminal law in response to the reformers. Number of capital offences, reduced to make the law enforceable.

b. Prison Reform Acts, 1823 and 1824, make prisons more humane and set common standards.

c.   Peel's concern to prevent crime thwarted by suspicion of his police proposals until 1829: metropolitan police force established.

4 Trade Unions

1824 Repeal of the Combination Acts ('not a government measure)
1825 Trade Union Act gives unions the legal right to exist whilst restricting freedom to picket.

> 'Men who ... have no property except their manual skill and strength, ought to be allowed to confer together, if they think fit, for the purpose of determining at what rate they will sell their property.'
> - Robert Peel.

5 Joint Stock Bank Act

(1826), paves the way for a major change in the banking system: Henceforth only the Bank of England can issue bank notes, and joint stock banks can be established. This measure instils confidence by ending note issuing by the small family-owned country banks, blamed for the financial crisis 1825–26.

822 The 'New Men' appointed Peel, Canning, Huskisson, obinson. Do they deserve all the redit for the new policies?

The return to prosperity was an essential pre-condition for change.
Rising employment and falling prices saw a decline in public discontent.

> 'Great Britain was never in such a state of internal welfare and content as at present.'
>
> Lord Liverpool, 1823.

erpool and Liberal Toryism

1822 – 1827

Maintaining Tory principles in Church and State

1 The Catholic Question

1821 Plunkett's pro-Catholic motion is the first to be passed in the Commons since 1813. The House of Lords maintains its traditional opposition.

1825 Peel is the only Cabinet minister in the Commons to vote against Burdett's successful motion. Both he and Liverpool contemplate resignation. Canning willing to break the Cabinet moratorium on the issue.

Events in Ireland keep emancipation at the forefront of politics.

2 Parliamentary Reform

> 'Can we resist – I mean not next session or the session after that – but can we resist for seven years Reform in Parliament?'
>
> Peel, 1820.

Commons votes the disenfranchisement of Grampound, and for its seats to go to Leeds. The House of Lords compromised, and the seats go to Yorkshire.

Lord John Russell gets 164 votes for his reform Bill, but the Cabinet remains united in its opposition.

Prosperity killed the demand for reform, and in 1827 Russell conceded that there was a public lack of interest in reform 'attributable to the improvement which had taken place in the manner of conducting the government.'

3 The Corn Laws

1819–23 were bad years for farmers. They blamed the deflationary effect of the Currency Act (1819), and sought increased protection, tax cuts and cheaper money. Government now wanted to persue a cheap food policy as a key to maintaining of public order. Huskisson managed the parliamentary select committees, 1821 and 1822, in the government's favour. Ministers wished to review the Corn Laws and abandon the self-sufficiency policy. During the economic crisis 1825–26 the Corn Laws were suspended, and Huskisson was planning a new Corn Law in 1826. 'The Agricultural is not the only interest in Great Britain.'

Lord Liverpool, 1822.

> 'in truth the real opposition of the present day sit behind the Treasury Bench; and it is by the stupid old Tory party ... that the progress of the Government in every improvement which they are attempting is thwarted and impeded.'
>
> Lord Palmerston, 1826.

Examining the evidence

Was 1822 a turning point?

The reforms made ministers respected and popular, at least with the commercial middle classes. In 1826 the *Manchester Guardian* noted that it did not know 'by whom, among the present race of public men, their places might advantageously be supplied.' Sources A, B and C suggest that a different assessment might have been made at the beginning of the decade.

Comment on the significance of this remark appearing in the *Manchester Guardian*.

Source A

The low periodical press has everywhere done more mischief than many are disposed to admit. I can trace it among our yeomanry in the Country. They despise the Whigs; but they are no longer what they were ten years ago in their attachment to the old Tory interests and principles which are prevalent in the Nobility and Gentry

3 July 1818.

Be assured that the feeling is strong in the Country, that we have not done enough' ... The old Remark that a Ministry enjoying the cordial good will of the Sovereign is best for War, but unfitted for Peace, and especially with the present Sovereign, is making way among many well-meaning people, notwithstanding all their other apprehensions of the possible consequences of not supporting the present Administration.

9 July 1818.

Letters written by William Huskisson to Lord Liverpool after the 1818 General Election in which government supporters lost ground.

Source B

Do not you think that the tone of England – of that great compound of folly, weakness, prejudice, wrong feeling, right feeling, obstinacy, and newspaper paragraphs, which is called public opinion – is more liberal – to use an odious but intelligible phrase – than the policy of the Government? Do not you think there is a feeling, becoming daily general and more confirmed – that is, independent of the pressure of taxation, or any immediate cause – in favour of some undefined change in the mode of governing the country?

Robert Peel to John Wilson Croker, 23 March 1820.

Source C

Ministers who had gained a considerable degree of credit for their conduct of the war, had lost it almost entirely by the occurrences of the peace.

Anon, *A Political View of the Times; or a Dispassionate Enquiry into the Manners and Conduct of the Ministry and Opposition*, 1821.

1 Using your wider knowledge of the period, discuss the validity of the comment made in source C.
2 Explain the 'apprehensions' Huskisson was referring to in source A as the 'possible consequences of not supporting the present Administration'.
3 Consult all three sources.
a To what extent do A and B support the opinion expressed in C?
b Compare the assessments of the government's problem made in sources A and B.

The significance of Castlereagh's death

Source D

There are some now who ... cannot remember without emotion, what they saw and heard that day. They could not know how the calamity of one man ... could penetrate the recesses of the world, not as a calamity, but as a ray of hope in the midst of thickest darkness.

Harriet Martineau, *A History of the Thirty Years Peace, 1816–1846, vol. 1*, 1848.

Source E

The death of Lord Londonderry [Castlereagh], at the early age of fifty-one, was one of the most important events in the history of the present century ... The effects of his death on the home politics of this country were revolutionary. His decease was not the mere death of a man: it gave the deathblow to a system. Tory government, in the old fashioned sense of the phrase, ceased with Lord Londonderry ... it was impossible to foresee that a complete revolution in foreign and domestic politics would result from the reconstruction of a Tory Cabinet ...

Lord Liverpool was not the originator of ... policy. During the first ten years of his Ministry, Castlereagh was the guiding spirit who inspired his measures. During the last four years of his Ministry, Canning was, to all intents and purposes, Prime Minister. During the shorter period Lord Liverpool kept order among his colleagues, composed their quarrels, and oiled the wheels to make it possible for the machinery of government to work.

S. Walpole, *History of England from the Conclusion of the Great War in 1815*, 1878.

Source F

The suicide of Castlereagh in 1822 did not break up the Tory government; it marked the end of the old Toryism because the leadership of the House of Commons passed to Canning ... Within a short time Canning gave a new tone to the administration ... he ... realised that the Tory party could check the reform movement only by showing that they could pass improving measures of an administrative kind, and were not occupied merely with the maintenance of abuses.

Sir Llewellyn Woodward, *The Age of Reform, 1815–1870*, 1938, 2nd edn, 1962.

Source G

In fact, Liverpool's administration was neither reactionary nor suddenly reformist in 1822 ... An awareness of the importance of 'respectable' opinion not formally represented in the institutions of the state characterised every notable transaction of the government. It encouraged its steady pursuit of economical reform and partly explained the interest it acquired in legal reform; it helped to ensure that the enquiry into the currency question would achieve serious results; it, more than anything else, brought about the decision to destroy the bill of pains and penalties against Queen Caroline ...; it both made capitulation to the agriculturists impossible and gave representations in favour of 'freer' trade their maximum effect. The ministers knew well that the old order's chances of survival were greatly reduced if once the new forces arising in society found little or nothing to admire in it; and therefore that how they, as the foremost representatives of the ruling class, used their power was of more than passing importance...

Mainly the Tory governments of the period after Waterloo were held back by their desire to present reforms which would have the widest possible acceptance. They feared above all the division of society into competing classes or interests, the destruction of the confidence which had formerly subsisted between the nation at large and the ruling class and between the ruling class and the Crown ... Ideally, reform preserved what was of value and did nothing to disturb the nation's confidence in aristocratic government.

J. E. Cookson, *Lord Liverpool's Administration, 1815–1822*, 1975.

Source H

What overshadowed much historical judgement was the fact that the Liverpool system broke down permanently within a few years of his death ... Like many ... regimes in their decline, it was a reforming administration; and ... its reforms seemed afterwards to have been too limited in scope and too late in execution. Liverpool sought by parsimonious government and enlightened economic policy to demonstrate the continuing value of the traditional institutions of the state. In the event all he was able to do was to postpone for a few years those organic constitutional changes which the altered circumstances of British society rendered inevitable ...

It is easy to forget that having won the war, Liverpool also won the peace. The work of the 1820s laid the foundations of that great liberal free-trade revolution in financial and commercial policy which was carried on by Peel in the 1840s and consolidated by Gladstone in the 1850s and 1860s ... the Whig decade of constitutional reform ... becomes a mere interlude in the continuity of economic policy between Liverpool and Peel ... The fiscal and financial policies of the latter years of the Liverpool administration were in effect prototypes of those put into force by Peel twenty years later ...

Liverpool clearly ranks as one of the great though unacknowledged architects of the liberal, free-trade Victorian state, second only to Peel in importance.

N. Gash, *Lord Liverpool*, 1984.

Source I

Despite recent attempts at rehabilitation, little in Liverpool's career suggests a Prime Minister of other than modest capabilities. His strength was his capacity for survival, a capacity buttressed by the willingness of innately more able men to serve under him rather than under any abler rivals to themselves.

E. J. Evans, *The Forging of the Modern State,* 1983.

Historians are formed by the period in which they write. Liverpool's reputation suffered because nineteenth century historians viewed theirs as an enlightened century in which liberal democracy, free trade and religious freedom prevailed. The Whigs of 1830, and Peel, were the heroes. In the late twentieth century, historians have challenged earlier interpretations of this period, and looked for continuities rather than sudden changes. Referring to sources D, E, F, G, H and I, discuss the validity of this view, and comment on the changing interpretations the sources contain.

1a With reference to sources A and G, and to your own knowledge, what is meant by:
'Our yeomanry in the country' (source A);
'respectable opinion not formally represented in the institutions of the state' (source G).
b How successful were the Liberal Tories in satisfying the interests of these two groups after 1822; why was it difficult to secure the full support of both groups?
2 Consult sources D, E, F and G. In what ways do Walpole and Woodward differ from Cookson in their interpretation of the change that took place in 1822. How do they agree on its purpose?
3 With reference to extracts H and I, and your wider knowledge, comment on and compare the different views of Liverpool's political achievement.
4 'At bottom Liverpool's policy was a social policy designed to close the gap between the state and society and to allay discontent by spreading prosperity. It was also a conservative policy, designed to blunt radical attacks on the constitution, by demonstrating that the aristocratic system was capable of producing an administration that looked to national needs and worked to national ends.'
N. Gash, *Aristocracy and People: Britain 1815–1865*, 1979.
Using these sources and your wider knowledge discuss this comment on the Liberal Tories.
5 Essay:
To what extent did the reconstruction of Liverpool's Cabinet between 1821 and 1823 lead to a new direction in Tory policy?

The path to Reform – the break-up of the old Tory Party

The Canningite interlude, 1827

On Saturday 17 February Lord Liverpool was found unconscious on the floor of his study. Although it was six weeks before his wife formally delivered his resignation to George IV, it was clear that his political career had come to an end. The immediate effect of Liverpool's collapse was to throw the political world into turmoil. The events of the next three years served to emphasise the extent to which Cabinet unity and a sense of common purpose had depended on Liverpool's skilful leadership.

The obvious successor, in terms of experience, seniority and ability, was Canning. Nevertheless, it was the beginning of April before he received the royal commission to form an administration. In the interim attempts were made to hold the government together by keeping him out of the premiership. He was disliked and distrusted by many, others, like the Duke of Wellington, had been alarmed by his policies as Foreign Secretary and Peel was unwilling to continue as Home Secretary under a pro-Catholic premier. Once Canning began to build his Cabinet the extent of the rift in Tory ranks became apparent. Forty-one senior and junior ministers rejected his approaches.

> At bottom, as it became increasingly evident, it was not merely Protestant feeling but a general dislike of Canning's foreign policy, and more fundamental still, a deep distrust of the man himself, that was responsible for the dramatic rupture of Liverpool's Cabinet.
>
> N. Gash, *Mr Secretary Peel,* 1961.

Canning had to turn to the Whigs. Despite the opposition of Lord Grey, who shared the general aristocratic antipathy to him, some were prepared to accept office on Canning's terms. To satisfy the King, Catholic emancipation had to remain an open question in Cabinet, and parliamentary reform was temporarily abandoned. Grey called it an unprincipled agreement, but when Canning first met the Commons as premier he had the support of moderate Tories and of the bulk of Whig MPs. It was not a strong government, but it was a cross-party ministry of the centre and survival seemed possible.

The 1827 session went smoothly enough, although Huskisson's new Corn Bill had to be withdrawn following a severe mangling from Wellington and the Tories in the Lords. Time was running out, however. Whilst attending the Duke of York's funeral at the beginning of the year Canning had caught a chill. He never really recovered and died on 9 August.

Robinson was elevated to the peerage as Lord Goderich to lead the Lords for Canning.

The King turned to Lord Goderich. Perhaps the King wanted a minister he could dominate. Certainly he did not want the only alternative, a ministry headed by Wellington and Peel. Unfortunately, Goderich lacked the political acumen of either Canning or Liverpool, a quality which was badly needed to control and guide the coalition he had inherited. 'Never surely', wrote Huskisson, 'was there a man at the head of affairs so weak, undecided, and utterly helpless!' Prevented from strengthening the ministry by the King's hostility to introducing more Whigs, intrigued against by his own colleagues, and bullied by the monarch, Goderich resigned before meeting Parliament in January 1828.

The Wellington premiership

Reluctantly the King turned to Wellington and Peel. Peel, as Home Secretary and Leader of the House of Commons, had a clear aim:

> My view is to re-unite the old Party which was in existence when Lord Liverpool's calamity befell him. I cannot undertake the business in the House of Commons without more assistance than the mere Tory party, as it is called, would afford me.
>
> Sir Robert Peel to Julia Peel, 10 January 1828.

Some accommodation with Huskisson and the other Canningites was imperative for effective management of the Commons. Huskisson, an outstanding expert on trade and finance, but shy, indecisive and

The other Canningites were Lord Dudley, Lord Palmerston and Charles Grant. William Lamb remained Chief Secretary for Ireland outside the Cabinet.

unpopular with the Tory backbenchers, was the main obstacle to reunion, but after a week of negotiations he joined the Cabinet with three other Canningites. There were no places for the Whigs, nor did they expect any; Eldon, on the extreme right, was also not approached.

Despite appearances the old Liverpool party had not been rebuilt. The political changes had torn apart the old governing group. Bitterness and distrust lay just below the surface. When the new Cabinet dined together for the first time Ellenborough noted that 'the courtesy was that of men who had just fought a duel.' Wellington lacked the politician's touch needed to heal the wounds. He possessed many qualities as an experienced diplomat and administrator, and was a man prepared to push through unpopular measures if he thought them necessary; but he was indifferent to public opinion and remote from parliamentary life. His military background had accustomed him to obedience from subordinates and he found distasteful the constant arguments in Cabinet, and what he felt to be unreasonable demands from the Canningites. He scorned Peel's attempt to play a mediatory role:

> The truth is that Peel is afraid of the Opposition, his colleagues and his supporters. He is afraid to place himself on the high ground. He never fixes his mind on any good principle to be held in discussion; nor on any principle at all till he gets into the House of Commons; and then he seeks for one which he thinks will be safe.
>
> Wellington to Mrs Arbuthnot, 5 April 1828.

Wellington, however, did not face Peel's task of managing a House of Commons in which there was no guaranteed government majority. Thus, it was Peel who had to accept the humiliation of adopting as government policy Russell's motion to repeal the Test and Corporation Acts as they affected Nonconformists, a measure he had initially opposed. This development had wider implications because of the demands from Ireland for Catholic emancipation.

In Cabinet Peel smoothed over disagreement between Wellington and Huskisson on the Corn Bill. Canningite opposition and threats of resignation irritated him but he accepted a compromise and a new sliding scale of duties. Peel's political skill did not go unobserved:

> Peel is so right headed and liberal and so up to the opinions and the feelings of the times, that he smoothes difficulties which might otherwise be insurmountable.
>
> Lord Palmerston to Lady Cowper, 25 March 1828.

However, even Peel could not prevent the final breach. The boroughs of East Retford and Penryn were to be disfranchised for corruption. The Canningites wanted the seats to go to Manchester and Birmingham, but the Duke of Wellington wanted them to be absorbed by the counties of Cornwall and Nottinghamshire. A compromise, allocating the Penryn seats to Birmingham, and the others to Nottinghamshire, was voted down in the House of Lords. Huskisson abstained on the East Retford vote in the Commons. Exasperated by Huskisson's critical attitude in the Cabinet room and convinced that there was a systematic policy to force Canningite opinions on everybody else, Wellington seized on his letter of explanation as one of resignation. By the end of May Huskisson's colleagues had followed him out of office.

This made Peel's task more difficult but he did at least face a divided opposition. More seriously, the resignations led directly to a crisis in Ireland which meant that the Catholic question could no longer be ignored.

The path to Reform – Catholic emancipation

The Corporation Act (1661) and the Test Act (1672) imposed religious tests on all public officeholders, effectively excluding all Roman Catholics and Protestant Nonconformists, although annual indemnity acts had freed the latter from this restriction since 1715. The small, and relatively insignificant, English membership of the Roman Catholic church did not present a problem. The Irish Catholic majority made emancipation a serious issue, threatening both the Protestant character of the constitution and the continuance of the union between Britain and Ireland.

The Act of Union (1800), following the disastrous United Irishmen's rising of 1798, had been Pitt's response to the threat of revolution and French intervention in Irish affairs. Ireland's own parliament was abolished, and subsequently 100 Irish MPs were returned to the United Kingdom Parliament. The savage penal laws imposed on the Catholic majority at the end of the seventeenth century had gradually been removed, and after 1800 Catholics could vote in parliamentary elections, although the requirements of the Test Act made it impossible for them to become MPs or to hold office. Pitt failed to persuade George III to agree to emancipation, though Pitt recognised that without it the Union he had created was extremely fragile.

Amongst the Tories a small but powerful group favoured emancipation, and in 1812 the Liverpool Cabinet agreed that Ministers could speak and vote according to their consciences on this issue. The Whigs were proud of their consistent support for religious and civil liberty, as Grey stated, writing to Lord Holland in 1820, 'To Catholic Emancipation I consider myself so pledged that I could not come in [to government] without it.' He was quick to condemn those Whigs who compromised their principles to join Canning in 1827.

In 1812, 1821 and 1825 Catholic Relief proposals were carried in the House of Commons, only to be overturned in the House of Lords. Some limited exploitation of popular prejudices in the 1826 General Election gained about thirteen seats for the anti-Catholics. A pro-Catholic motion in 1827 was consequently lost by six votes. With an evenly balanced House of Commons, a hostile Crown and House of Lords, and a divided Cabinet, only a major crisis in Ireland could force a conclusion to this debate.

3.2 Aspects of the Irish Problem

Ireland's Population

Date	Population (m)	% Change
1801	5.22	—
1811	5.96	+14.2
1821	6.80	+14.1
1831	7.77	+14.3
1841	8.20	+5.5
1851	6.51	−20.6
1861	5.79	−11.1
1871	5.40	− 6.7
1881	5.15	− 4.6
1891	4.68	− 9.1
1901	4.45	− 4.9
1911	4.38	− 1.6

Compare these statistics with those for the rest of the British Isles on page 3. What differences are there, and how can they be explained?

Irish Poverty and Irish Land

COTTAGE, OR CABIN.

Population pressures aggravated poverty in rural Ireland. During the eighteenth century landlords and farmers had increased the acreage used for grain production to supply the English market. Conditions in Ireland are better suited to livestock farming, however, and the collapse of grain prices after 1815 threatened ruin. Progressive landlords began to consolidate holdings to make them big enough to be viable as livestock farms. Tenants had no legal protection, no security of tenure, and no compensation for any improvements they might have made, although the economic, moral, and physical pressures against landlords and against new and incoming tenants, made many hesitate.

The potato had been the peasantry's staple diet since the mid-eighteenth century. Requiring minimal cultivation, a small plot could produce enough to feed a family. Dependence on one food source was to prove disastrous. Landlords, however, encouraged the sub-division of holdings as peasants cultivating a small plot of potatoes would have most of their time available for working on the landlord's labour-intensive arable farms.

Size of Holdings in 1845

Size of Holding	% of tenancies
1 to 5 acres	24
5 to 15 acres	40
over 15 acres	36

In 1841 70 per cent of the rural population was landless or depended on inadequate holdings of less than 5 acres. Over 135,000 tenants had less than an acre. Very few had more than 30 acres. These are national figures and in the western counties the situation was much worse.

Protestant Ascendancy

Over 80 per cent of the population was Catholic, but the Irish administration did not officially recognise their Church. The Church of Ireland was Protestant, Anglican and supported by the state; everyone, Catholic or Protestant, paid tithes to its parish clergy. However, its membership was small as the dominant form of Protestantism was the Nonconformist Presbyterian Church.

The Test Act ensured that all members of the Irish administration, from the Lord Lieutenant and the Chief Secretary down to the humblest clerk, were Protestants. Magistrates were exclusively Protestant, although Peel, as Chief Secretary and Home Secretary, tried to keep the most bigoted off the bench, and to curb the activities of the Orange Societies:

> The more I think upon the subject the more I am convinced that even the most loyal associations in Ireland for political purposes are dangerous engines ... There are many phrases applied to the Association of Orangemen which are of much too military a character to suit my taste. Regiments and Colonels and Captains, etc., do not sound well to my ear when applied to societies not under the control of Government.

TALKING POINT

The Irish Catholic middle class, the Catholic gentry and the peasantry all had different grievances against the system and the Union. Suggest what these might have been, and why co-operation between them was unlikely.

THE IRISH LANDOWNER SEEMED TO LEAD AN IDYLLIC EXISTENCE WITH HIS STATUS PROTECTED BY THE MECHANISM OF PROTESTANT ASCENDANCY

Rural Violence

A general insurrection prevailed in the South of Ireland where the civil power had ceased to have any authority, and was incapable of offering protection: the movements of the insurgents had assumed so serious an aspect that it was deemed prudent to concentrate the troops, to call in small detachments, and to withdraw safeguards from the houses of the gentry, and most persons who could afford to quit their homes had fled to the towns for safety.

Lord Bantry reporting the situation in 1822.

In a large part of Ireland there is still less security of person and property than in any other part of Europe, except perhaps the wildest districts of Calabria and Greece.

Cornewall Lewis, *Local Disturbances in Ireland* (1836).

Lawlessness was endemic. Secret societies, like the Ribbonmen and the Whiteboys, terrified witnesses into silence. Their violence was social rather than political, directed against landlords and the hated tithe payment. The authorities were often powerless to respond, and dealt harshly with any lawbreakers they were able to apprehend. Peel's reaction, as Chief Secretary, was to improve policing arrangements. In 1814 his Peace Preservation Act paved the way for the creation of the Irish Constabulary.

DEPENDENCE ON THE POTATO MEANT FREQUENT LOCAL SHORTAGES AND FAMINES. THE CARTOON DEPICTS ANOTHER OF THE CHARGES AGAINST THE ABSENTEE ANGLO-IRISH LANDLORDS.

The path to Reform – Daniel O'Connell and the Catholic Association

See how all the people turn to look after him ... they like to see him walking so bravely along, with his broad shoulders and his full breast; and 'tis thought he likes to be seen by them stepping out over the flags of Dublin, through thick and thin, friend and foe.

John Banim, *The Anglo-Irish of the Nineteenth Century*, 1828.

He loved organisations, bands, public shows, emotion, uniforms

R. F. Foster, *Modern Ireland, 1600–1972*, 1988.

DESCENDED FROM A CATHOLIC LANDOWNING FAMILY, O'CONNELL TRAINED FOR THE LAW AS THE ONLY PROFESSION IN WHICH IT WAS POSSIBLE FOR IRISH CATHOLICS TO COMPETE ON LEVEL TERMS WITH PROTESTANTS, THOUGH THE HIGHEST POSTS WERE CLOSED TO THEM. O'CONNELL WAS AN IMPOSING FIGURE – PHYSICALLY AND THROUGH HIS POWER AS AN ORATOR.

1 What impression do these extracts give of Daniel O'Connell?
2 Why might these characteristics make him a good leader of a mass movement?

O'Connell's fame in the law courts gave him the opportunity to seize the leadership of the Catholic movement. By the early twenties the emancipation campaign had become moribund. Since the Act of Union its support had mainly come from the Catholic middle class, but they lacked the energy to sustain it. O'Connell viewed emancipation as the essential first step to repeal of the Act of Union. In 1823, together with another Catholic lawyer Richard Shiel, he founded the Catholic Association.

Initially the Association struggled. Both men recognised the need to widen its appeal from the Catholic middle class to the mass of the Catholic peasantry, even if this meant taking up the tithe issue and other peasant grievances. In February 1824 O'Connell announced a scheme to collect subscriptions of 1d a month from the peasantry through the agency of their priests. Half the money was to be used for educational purposes in the parishes, the rest to create a fighting fund for emancipation and to finance action on other grievances. This subscription was known as the Catholic Rent.

A judicial attempt to silence O'Connell failed. The government reacted by making the Catholic Association illegal. Exploiting loopholes in the law, O'Connell formed the New Catholic Association and renewed collection of the Rent during 1826. His achievement was to bring the Catholic middle class, the peasantry and the Catholic Church in Ireland together into a mass movement for emancipation.

Was O'Connell really a revolutionary?

This had to be backed up by the implicit threat of mass disobedience, of a unilateral withdrawal of allegiance, even of a refusal to recognise the legitimacy of the state. O'Connell's achievement was to indicate this while maintaining a commitment to pacific principles: but it is unlikely that it could have been as effective without the ominous precedent of Whiteboyism and Ribbonism.

R.F. Foster, *Modern Ireland, 1600–1972*, 1988.

The Catholic Association

Source A

	£
1 Before banning of the Catholic Association, March 1825	
Founded May 1824 – Dec 1824	7,573
Jan 1825 – March 1825 (banned)	9,263
2 The New Catholic Rent	—
(re-formed) July 1826 – Dec 1826	5,680
Jan 1827– Dec 1827	2,900
Jan 1828 – Dec 1828	22,700
Jan 1829 – Feb 1829 (banned)	3,712
Grand Total	**51,828**

CATHOLIC RENT – AMOUNT COLLECTED

Source B

If we cannot get rid of the Catholic Association, we must look to civil war in Ireland sooner or later.

Wellington to Peel.

Source C

It is not concealed that whenever an election shall take place the people will be placed in opposition to their landlords and such members only returned as shall please the Association.

Henry Goulburn (Irish Chief Secretary) to Peel, 1824.

Source D

One penny each month, is your just due,
Collected by some faithful brother,
Then why should Patrick's friends refuse
In this grand plan to assist each other.

Extract from a ballad, 'The Catholic Rent or Catholic Freedom' (1824).

O'Connell's triumph

The 1826 General Election revealed the potential power of the Catholic Association. There was no organised campaign, but in Waterford the established Beresford family interest was decisively defeated to secure the return of a liberal Protestant landowner who was a member of the Catholic Association. Here, and in County Louth, the Catholic tenants deserted their landlords in droves. Leslie Foster, who just managed to hang on to second place in Co. Louth, sent Peel a graphic account of the intimidation and pressure used by the Association's supporters against him:

> **1** From the evidence of sources A and D:
>
> **a** What had O'Connell achieved by the end of 1824?
>
> **b** Why should this alarm the government?
>
> **2** What challenges did Wellington and Goulburn anticipate?

Now it is all over I hardly know what is to be the consequence. The landlords are exasperated to the utmost, the priests swaggering in their triumph, the tenantry sullen and insolent. Men who a month ago were all civility and submission now hardly suppress their curses when a gentleman passes by. The text of every village orator is, 'Boys you have put down three Lords. Stick to your priests, and you will carry all before you.

Leslie Foster to Peel, 8 July 1826.

Explain 'the priests swaggering in their triumph', and comment on Foster's tone and language.

A COMMENT ON THE DILEMMA FACING CATHOLIC 40-SHILLING FREEHOLDERS IN IRISH ELECTIONS.

With this warning it is perhaps surprising that Wellington promoted the Irish MP for Co. Clare, Vesey Fitzgerald, to the Presidency of the Board of Trade after the Canningite resignations. Fitzgerald was, however, a well respected landlord and an emancipationist. The Catholic Association, which had resolved to contest the seats held by all ministerial supporters, found it impossible to persuade a liberal Protestant to stand against him. The decision to nominate O'Connell was made as a last resort. The campaign was bitter with the priests and the landlords contesting the control of the 40-shilling freeholders, but the result was never really in doubt. When Fitzgerald finally withdrew from the poll he only had 982 votes to O'Connell's 2057.

MPs who accepted office had to seek re-election by their constituents.

As a Catholic O'Connell was not debarred from standing for Parliament, but he made it very clear during the campaign that he would refuse to take the anti-Catholic oath required when an MP took his seat. The government feared a major crisis : if O'Connell refused to take his seat, would civil war break out in Ireland? At the next General Election, would the Catholic Association repeat these tactics throughout Ireland?

Examining the Evidence

Catholic emancipation – High point of Liberal Toryism or pragmatic concession?

Source A

The Clare election was the dramatic flashpoint which finally tipped the balance on the side of the argument of political necessity against the hazards of toleration.

F. O'Farrall, *Catholic Emancipation: Daniel O'Connell and the Birth of Irish Democracy*, 1985.

Source B

The election, thank God, is over, and I do feel happy in its being terminated, notwithstanding its result.

I have polled all the gentry and all the fifty-pound freeholders – the gentry to a man.

Of others I have polled a few tenants of [illegible] only, my own, and not much besides that adhered to me in that way.

All the great interests broke down, and the desertion has been universal ...The conduct of the priests has passed all that you could picture to yourself.

The Sheriff declared the numbers to-night. To go on would have been idle. I have kept on for five days, and it was a hopeless contest from the first ... The Sheriff has made a special Return, and you will say a strange one; but it will force Parliament instantly to take it up. It states that I was proposed being a Protestant, as a fit person to represent the country in Parliament; that Mr O'Connell, a Roman Catholic, was also proposed; that he, O'Connell, had declared before the Sheriff that he was a Roman Catholic, and intended to continue a Roman Catholic...

For the degradation of the country I feel deeply and the organisation exhibited is so complete and so formidable that no man can contemplate without alarm what is to follow in this wretched country.

Vesey Fitzgerald to Robert Peel, 5 July 1828.

Mrs Arbuthnot was the Duke of Wellington's female companion from 1822. She faithfully recorded the events around her, and the political opinions he confided in her.

Source C

The Duke feels that this state of things cannot be allowed to continue; that government of Ireland is now in the hands of Mr. O'Connell, that the King cannot dissolve the Parliament because he would be sure to have the whole representation of Ireland in the hands of the demagogues of the Association; he cannot make an Irish member a Peer or give him an office because the same scenes would recur that took place in Clare; in fact, the

King's Government is paralysed and his representative brought into contempt by the state of the Catholic body, and, in order to obtain power from Parliament for putting an end to such a state of things he must devise some scheme by which, with safety to the Constitution and with due protection to the Protestant Establishment, he can remove the disabilities of the Catholics. It will be an arduous task but, if anybody can do it, he will.

The Journal of Mrs Arbuthnot, 29 July 1828.

Source D

Extracts from J. W. Croker's diary (1829)

31 January

Saw Peel. He announced to me his conversion to Catholic concession ... I was in great difficulty what to say to him. I was glad of the arrangement of the question, though it comes too late for any good; but I fear he will individually lose some of the public confidence.

2 February

Saw Peel, to whom I felt it to be due to say that the greatest surprise of the public was not so much the concession to the Catholics, as his consenting to be the mover of it.

5 February

Went to the House; the thing went off very flatly ... Peel only cheered by the Opposition, as Canning used to be in 1827.

9 February

Lowther is still very reluctant to stay in; he showed me a long explanatory letter which the Duke has written to the Duke of Rutland, and of which he had sent copies to the other grandees, and amongst the rest to Lord Lonsdale. Lord Lonsdale's answer was that he could not pledge himself. The Duke of Wellington's letter concludes by saying that, if the Duke of Rutland and the other great interests would not support him he would resign, for he would not be left at the mercy of the *rump* of the Whigs and Mr Canning.

4 March

The Ministers, that is the Chancellor, D of W, and Peel are gone down to Windsor to-day on a sudden summons which arrived very late last night. The King is in great perplexity about this Catholic question. He is, I have no doubt, sincerely distressed.

5 March

The Ministers came home last night *out of office*, but during the night more prudent counsels prevailed at Windsor, and a messenger arrived to-day with the King's acquiescence in the measure which, therefore, Peel will open this morning

The Croker Papers, ed. L. J. Jennings, 1884.

Burkeing the Constitution of England!!!!!

ONE VIEW OF CATHOLIC EMANCIPATION. RESEARCH THE MEANING OF 'BURKEING THE CONSTITUTION OF ENGLAND'.

Source F

Peel justifies his changed opinion

(i) The events of the Clare election, with the conviction that the same scenes would be enacted in nearly every county in Ireland if matters were to remain just as they have been for the last five or six years, convinced me that it was not safe for the Protestant interest in Ireland that they should remain so.

Peel to Colonel Yates, 18 February 1829.

(ii) I believe that the time has come when less danger is to be apprehended to the general interests of the empire and to the spiritual and moral welfare of the Protestant establishment, in attempting to adjust the Catholic question, than in allowing it to remain any longer in its present state ... I do not think it was an unnatural or unreasonable struggle. I resign it, in consequence of the conviction that it can be no longer advantageously maintained; from believing that there are not adequate materials or sufficient instruments for its effectual and permanent continuance. I yield, therefore, to a moral necessity which I cannot control, unwilling to push resistance to the point which might endanger the Establishments that I wish to defend.

Peel addressing the House of Commons, 5 March 1829.

---

1 With reference to these sources and your own knowledge, explain what is meant by the following phrases in the context of events 1828–29.
a 'all the great interests broke down' (source B)
b 'the organisation exhibited' (source B)
c 'The Sheriff has made a special Return' (source B)
d 'the King's Government is paralysed' (source C)
e 'he will individually lose some of the public confidence' (source D).
2 Consult sources B, C and D.
a Briefly discuss the connection between the three.
b Comment on Wellington's motives for dealing with Catholic emancipation.
3 Consult sources C and D. What evidence is there that Wellington and Peel faced opposition to their policy from Tory backbenchers, fellow ministers, and the King?
4 Study sources E and F. How effectively does Peel respond to the fears expressed in the cartoon?
5 Was the Catholic emancipation the high-point of Liberal Toryism, a generous concession, or a prudent, pragmatic response to a sudden difficulty? Explain your opinion by reference to the sources and your wider knowledge.

The emancipation legislation

Three measures made up the package:
- An Act banning the Catholic Association.
- The Emancipation Act, which removed all civil disabilities and enabled Roman Catholics to hold public office.
- The 40-shilling (£2) freeholders in Irish counties were disfranchised. The new £10 qualification, excluding the mass of the Catholic peasantry, was intended to protect the electoral interests of the Protestant landlords.

The path to Reform – the significance of emancipation

Ireland

> The law does nothing for us. We must save ourselves. We have a little land which we need for ourselves and our families to live on, and they drove us out of it. To whom should we address ourselves? We ask for work at eightpence a day and we are refused. To whom should we address ourselves? Emancipation has done nothing for us. Mr O'Connell and the rich Catholics go to Parliament. We die of starvation just the same.
>
> Peasant to a priest in de Tocqueville, *A Journey to England and Ireland.*

Fundamentally nothing had changed. Protestant ascendancy remained untouched and public office was closed to the Catholic middle class. In the countryside the peasants still feared famine and eviction, and contested the imposition of tithe payments. O'Connell ('the liberator')'s leadership of the nationalist movement was assured, but, despite Peel's fears the Church of Ireland, the Union and the Anglo-Irish landlord class were not immediately challenged.

Parties and personalities

The crisis finally destroyed what was left of the Liverpool anti-reform coalition, thus opening the door to parliamentary reform.

Both Peel and Wellington had acted pragmatically in the crisis. They knew that a dissolution of Parliament and a General Election on the issue would return an anti-Catholic majority to the Commons and create an impossible situation in Ireland. With no viable alternative available, they followed their perceptions of the national interest and of their role as the King's ministers.

The price they paid was unmitigated abuse from the Ultras. The Duchess of Richmond kept a number of stuffed rats in her drawing room, each named after a leading member of the government. Wellington felt compelled to challenge an abusive Earl of Winchelsea to a duel, in which Winchelsea was wounded. However, it was Peel, for so long the leader of the Protestants, who suffered most for his 'betrayal'. Detractors mocked him, saying that a new holy day had been added to the Catholic calendar – the 'conversion of St. Peel', and that 'Orange Peel' had become 'Lemon Peel'. His sense of honour persuaded him to seek re-election for his Oxford University seat. The country parsons made sure he was defeated. He then suffered the humiliation of being returned for Westbury under the influence of Sir Manassah Lopes, one of the most corrupt borough 'owners'.

Ultras: the extreme Protestant opponents of Peel and Wellington.

Oxford graduates had the vote in elections for the university seat. Many of these were clergymen.

If Peel can be criticised it is not for insincerity or lack of principle, although it seemed like that to his critics, but for clinging to an outdated position for too long. Professor Gash, always sympathetic to Peel, comments, 'Not lack of resistance, perhaps, so much as delay in accepting the inevitable was the gravamen of the charge against Peel' *(Mr Secretary Peel* (1961)).

The Ultras were determined to get their revenge. Seriously weakened in the Commons, Wellington's ministry could only survive as long as its opponents remained divided, or by bringing some of them in. Charles Arbuthnot summed up the situation for Peel as Parliament re-assembled in February 1830:

> The Ultra-Tories will never ... give us [their] Vote ... The Canning Party will only support us when they feel they have been previously committed to our line of conduct. The Whigs are behaving most shabbily ... with compliments in their mouths, they will try to destroy us because they see that they are not to be taken in as a body.

For the Whigs, with religious liberty granted, there was no alternative to taking up the reform question, especially as public opinion began to move in that direction during 1830.

Reform

> Catholic emancipation was the battering ram that broke down the old unreformed system.
>
> J. Cannon, *Parliamentary Reform 1640–1832*, 1973.

> After emancipation Reform was unavoidable.
>
> M. Brock, *The Great Reform Act*, 1973.

> Reform was not the culmination of a well-informed campaign of enquiry and planning, but the hurried and confused consequence of Emancipation.
>
> J.C.D. Clark, *English Society 1688–1832*, 1985.

Emancipation was the first great measure forced through Parliament by externally organised pressure. Radical reformers quickly appreciated the example they had been set. In May 1829 Thomas Attwood told his audience:

> By union, by organisation, by general contribution, by patriotic exertion, and by discretion, keeping always within the law and the constitution. These are the elements of Reform. By the peaceful combination of means like these the Irish people have lately obtained a glorious and bloodless victory.

Attwood sought O'Connell's advice when setting up the Birmingham Political Union the following year.

At the other end of the political spectrum some Ultras were converted to reform, arguing that a truly representative House of Commons would not have passed the Emancipation Act. Its success, they alleged, was due to the votes of MPs from the rotten boroughs. The unseemly sight of Peel's hurried return for Westbury merely underlined the corruption of the unreformed system.

Previous belief that the constitution was unchangeable had been destroyed. If the 40 shilling freeholder in Ireland could be disfranchised, then new voters could be enfranchised. Opponents of emancipation argued that the axe had been laid to the very root of the 1688 Protestant constitution, so a mere reform of Parliament was a very insignificant matter. Suddenly change and reform seemed to be on the political agenda.

REVIEW

The failure of Liberal Toryism?

This question opened the chapter. A superficial response might be that Liverpool and the traditionalists had failed. Catholic emancipation had been achieved, the anti-reform coalition shattered and parliamentary reform had returned to the political agenda. Nineteenth century historians, writing in the Whig tradition of history as progress from a lesser to the higher state of perfection, wrote of a Tory ministry that obstructed 'progress'. Its achievements were forgotten, Liverpool's political acumen belittled and its contribution to a successful resolution to the Reform Crisis ignored.

Source A

Historians study the process of change over time. Even in such a short period as 1815 to 1832 changes took place of critical importance in understanding the transition from what might be termed the 'old' world of hereditary privilege, localism, paternalism and protection to a 'new' order encompassing representation of interests, liberalisation, free trade and an increasing role for central government. The new order stressed economic growth as essential to feed and find employment for a population which was growing much more rapidly ... than ever before. It believed trade liberalisation to be the only way to secure growth. Industrialisation provided a greater diversity of wealth, not only in urban but also in rural society. A balance needed to be achieved between interests which would otherwise conflict. A more complex society required both more government and greater direction from the centre.

E. Evans, *Britain Before the Reform Act: Politics and Society 1815–1832*, 1989.

Source B

Adam Smith, 18th century economist and author of *The Wealth of Nations* (1776), setting out the principles of free trade; David Ricardo, early nineteenth century economist; Thomas Malthus, economist and social theorist, author of *Essay on the Principle of Population* (1798).

Liberal Toryism was not ... some self-evident creed to which the government arbitrarily turned in 1822 ... Continuity was the clue to the ministry's behaviour. As confidence grew and domestic dangers diminished, Liverpool felt it was realistic to give greater scope to presumptions which had been there from the beginning. The example of Pitt loomed larger than the theories of Smith, Ricardo and Malthus though such theories could be cited to give more articulate justification to policies which were thought practicable, profitable and safe...

Liverpool's achievement showed that traditionalism in politics could still accomplish much. Just as Pitt had demonstrated the vitality of traditional assumptions, so Liverpool had revived and renewed them by his mastery of men and events. But the fate of the Tory party after his death reveals the limits which must be placed on his achievement and the necessity to judge him by the standards of his own time ... Judged by the standards of their Age both Pitt and Liverpool were consummate politicians. They showed that the traditional system could survive the challenge of war, the threat of revolution and the impact of unprecedented social change. Yet each appeal to the familiar chain of belief and practice was marked by an openness to new developments which enabled transition to take place while continuity was preserved. When the final crisis of the old order came, with the struggle over the great Reform Bill, it was surmounted without any breach in historical continuity and in a fashion which, when compared with the French Revolution, was marked by courtesy and restraint. However vehemently they debated the issues or assailed each other ... the leading politicians of the time regarded their primary loyalty as being that which they owed to the constitution. Preserving the system was dear to both Tory and Whig. They were agreed on essentials. They disagreed over what was the best means of preserving the country's institutions and familiar liberties, not the desirability of such an objective ... Renovation, not innovation, was the most effective rallying cry for reformers.

J. W. Derry, *Politics in the Age of Fox, Pitt and Liverpool*, 1990.

TALKING POINT

In History there are few dramatic turning points. It is a constant process of adaptation to changing circumstance. Continuities have been more significant than sudden change. Consider the relevance of this view to any other period or periods of history you have studied.

1 To what extent, and how, did the Tory governments of 1815–30 positively contribute to the transition from the 'old world' to the 'new order'?
2 In what ways, and how successfully, did they hinder that transition?
3 'The arch-mediocrity'
   'The indispensable operator of the political machine'
   Refer back to the sources on Lord Liverpool pages 58–61. Then, using your wider knowledge and the assessments given in sources A and B above, decide which description best fits the abilities and achievements of Lord Liverpool, 1815–1830. Justify your choice.

4 The Triumph of Reform

PREVIEW

Reform – the driving force

Manufactures & Commerce support the Workmen they the Merchants & Masters who are the chief tax payers & thereby support The great tax eater Church-and-State.

MANUFACTURES &

COMMERCE

STATE OF THE NATION. "An over-true Tale"

IN 1829 BOTH 'MANUFACTURES' AND 'COMMERCE' WERE IN DEPRESSION. WHAT VIEW OF THE 'STATE OF THE NATION' IS THIS CARTOON FROM THAT YEAR CONVEYING? HOW DOES IT SUPPORT THE REFORM CAUSE? HOW MIGHT THE WORKMEN AND MASTERS DEPICTED DIFFER ABOUT THE SOLUTION?

THE BIRMINGHAM POLITICAL UNION APPARENTLY UNITED MIDDLE AND WORKING CLASS REFORMERS IN A COMMON PURPOSE. CONSIDER THE IMPACT OF MASS PUBLIC DEMONSTRATIONS LIKE THIS ON BOTH WHIG AND TORY POLITICIANS.

Reform – the unexpected issue?

The collapse of the anti-reform majority in the House of Commons following the emancipation crisis was an essential precondition for a successful outcome to any campaign for parliamentary reform. Other economic and political factors, however, contributed to a crisis which was eventually to be resolved by a Whig cabinet led by Lord Grey.

GREY'S PEDIGREE AS A REFORMER WAS UNCHALLENGEABLE. HE HAD BEEN A FOUNDER MEMBER OF THE SOCIETY OF THE FRIENDS OF THE PEOPLE IN 1792, HAD BRIEFLY BEEN FOREIGN SECRETARY 1806–7, BUT HAD BEEN IN OPPOSITION THROUGHOUT THE LONG TORY DOMINANCE. AS WHIG LEADER HE HAD BEEN ALOOF FROM PARLIAMENTARY BATTLES AND HAD GONE INTO RETIREMENT IN THE 1820S TO RE-EMERGE WHEN IT SEEMED THAT A REAL PUBLIC DEMAND FOR REFORM EXISTED IN 1830. HE PROVIDED THE WHIGS WITH A CREDIBLE ALTERNATIVE PREMIER TO THE DUKE OF WELLINGTON.

Depression and discontent

PSC: Do you conceive that the depression of trade in late years has had any effect in producing ... discontent?

WM: Very great.

PSC: Do you think the working classes of Staffordshire ever show political discontent so long as they are doing well in their particular trade?

WM: Not at all; you cannot get them to talk of politics so long as they are well employed.

William Mathews, Staffordshire iron manufacturer, giving evidence to a
Parliamentary Select Committee, 1832.

OMINOUSLY, FOR A LANDED RULING CLASS, THE AUTUMN OF 1830 WITNESSED THE OUTBREAK OF SERIOUS RIOTING BY FARM LABOURERS ACROSS THE SOUTH OF ENGLAND. THE 'SWING RIOTS' WERE ABOUT WAGES, TITHES AND POOR LAW ALLOWANCES, NOT POLITICS, BUT THEY HEIGHTENED THE SENSE OF CRISIS AND MENACE.

Industry had never really recovered from the 1826 collapse and for groups, like the Lancashire handloom weavers, facing technological unemployment, things were never to improve. A series of bad harvests compounded the crisis. In the north west John Doherty, who had unsuccessfully tried to organise the Manchester cotton spinners to protest against imposed wage cuts, founded a national cotton spinners' union and, in 1830, tried to bring all trades together in the National Association for the Protection of Labour. From all parts of the country came reports of strikes and disturbances.

Cobbett and Hunt, through their writings and speeches, were reviving the old reform debate, and in London a radical group meeting at the Rotunda in Blackfriars were preaching class warfare and wearing revolutionary emblems. In November 1829 the government cancelled George IV's state visit to the City of London because they felt his safety could not be guaranteed.

STATE OF THE COUNTRY.

The political unions

> To obtain by every just and legal means, such a REFORM in the COMMONS' HOUSE OF PARLIAMENT, as may ensure a REAL and EFFECTUAL REPRESENTATION OF THE LOWER AND MIDDLE CLASSES OF THE PEOPLE in that HOUSE.
>
> Report by the Birmingham Town's Meeting, 25 January 1830.

This was the objective of the Birmingham Political Union, a new factor in the political situation. Thomas Attwood, its leader, was a Birmingham banker and currency reformer who blamed the 1819 decision to resume cash payments for much of the economic dislocation. His analysis gained some support amongst the small manufacturers of the West Midlands metal industries. Although Attwood's politics were Tory, when the Commons rejected a Birmingham petition requesting currency reform in 1829 he turned to parliamentary reform as the only way forward. In January 1830 he proposed the formation of the Birmingham Political Union.

Political Unions appeared elsewhere, but Birmingham was the only place where the middle and working classes were embraced in the one organisation. With its many small workshops it was better suited to class co-operation; in Manchester mill owners' and mill workers' interests were too divergent for a united approach; in Leeds there were three separate reform organisations, whilst many working men were involved in the Ten Hours movement opposed by the liberal mill owners and their press organ, the *Leeds Mercury*.

Attwood's achievement was to ensure that the authorities never had any excuse to suppress the BPU. He insisted that its activities should be legal and constitutional. His argument linking distress to bad and unrepresentative government was familiar and plausible. Perhaps he was naive in assuming that a reformed Commons would be sympathetic to his financial ideas, but he deserves much of the credit for channelling the demand for reform into legitimate forms.

The emergence of Lord Grey

Until the beginning of 1830 Grey entertained hopes of being invited by Wellington to join the government. When it became clear that the premier had no intention of broadening his administration in a Whig direction Grey became increasingly critical of ministerial blindness to the revolutionary crisis he feared the country faced.

> I am afraid that the ministers are deceiving themselves very fatally as to the real situation in the country and the spirit that is rising in it ... The newspapers in their attacks upon the landowners have succeeded in destroying all respect for rank and station, and for the institutions of the government. Another year like the last and who can answer for the consequences.
>
> Grey to Edward Ellice, 2nd March 1830.

Grey was motivated by alarm at the increasing discontent, and evidence that the middle classes were apparently emerging to lead it through the political unions. Personal political ambition was not a significant factor for Grey. He believed that the inertia of the Wellington ministry had made it a

What was new about the purpose of the Birmingham Political Union? Why were Whig politicians like Grey alarmed by its appearance and possible role in a crisis?

danger to the country. Some reform, in Grey's opinion, had become essential to stave off a potentially revolutionary situation.

The changing political context

Neither the worsening situation in the country nor Grey's re-emergence really undermined the government's position, but when George IV died at the end of June 1830, the last major obstacle to a Whig government and a Grey premiership was removed. William IV did not share his brother's antipathy to the opposition politicians. Following the accession of the new King a General Election had to be held. Wellington hoped that a judicious use of government electoral influence would strengthen his position in the House of Commons. These calculations, and a concerted attack on the Canningites, went disastrously wrong.

> Not one man [was] elected in any contested place (except I believe Bristol) on ministerial principles. Whigs and Ultra Tories and radicals and reformers and economists were everywhere successful against those who stood on the government interest. I know this is not the light in which the treasury views the returns, but I see in them the seeds of the most troublesome and unmanageable Parliament since that of 1640 which overturned the monarchy and beheaded the monarch.
>
> John Wilson Croker, 1830.

Only 83 English constituencies (34%) were contested, but opinion was swinging against the government. Peel's two brothers and his brother-in-law were all defeated; he came in for the family seat of Tamworth. In Yorkshire the West Riding manufacturers and nonconformists achieved a great success by forcing the local Whig magnates to accept the popular radical lawyer Henry Brougham as one of the candidates for the county. Elsewhere there were attempts to overthrow aristocratic influence in smaller boroughs and in some counties.

The elections took place in July and August, too soon to be influenced by news of the successful and relatively bloodless revolution in France. Nevertheless, that event played its part in maintaining a high state of tension into the autumn as meetings were held to congratulate the French.

As the new Parliament assembled it was still not clear whether Wellington would be able to strengthen his ailing ministry by bringing in the Canningites. Huskisson's death in September 1830, and Palmerston's rejection of Wellington's advances unless they were coupled with the promise of a moderate measure of parliamentary reform, left Peel anticipating continuing difficulties in the House of Commons. Neither Wellington nor Peel were willing to abandon Party principles again so soon after Catholic emancipation.

Wellington finally sealed the government's fate. Stung by Grey's assertion that a reform measure was imperative, he denied the existence of a demand for change, declaring his confident belief in the soundness of the constitution. The premier did not appreciate the significance of his comments but they served to unite all the opponents of his government,

TALKING POINT

How might the report of revolution in France have influenced voters?

and on 15 November a majority voted against the ministry on a minor civil list issue. Peel was scarcely able to conceal his relief as the decision was taken to resign and avoid humiliation.

The Ultras had had their revenge. Over half of the new MPs returned in the elections for English constituencies voted against or abstained on the crucial civil list vote. Wellington had badly miscalculated, and where a better politician might have compromised and sought conciliation he had antagonised and failed to sense the direction of public opinion. William IV invited Grey to form a ministry, agreeing to his condition that he should be allowed to tackle the reform question.

The civil list was normally non-contentious. Any government which could not enact the sovereign's civil list had lost the confidence of the House.

Examining the Evidence

Historians and the reform crisis

Source A
Catholic emancipation was the battering ram that broke down the old unreformed system.

> J. Cannon, *Parliamentary Reform 1640–1832*, 1973.

Source B
What precipitated parliamentary reform was the coincidence of a cabinet crisis and the severe economic depression in the country.

> N. Gash, *Aristocracy and People*, 1979.

Source C
The essential success of the parliamentary Reform movement in the years 1830–2 lay in the effective mobilisation of public opinion in a situation of political excitement and flux

> D. Fraser in *Popular Movements 1830–1850*, 1970.

Source D
Parliamentary reform was enacted not primarily because of the strength of external pressure but because of the quite sudden weakening of the anti-reform majority in the Commons between 1827 and 1831.

> E. Evans in *History Sixth*, October 1988.

Source E
None of these abuses was new in the 1820s though some of them had not been practised hitherto on so large a scale. The system was increasingly in ill repute, not so much because it was growing more corrupt, but because more was known about its corruption. Incidents which might once have passed unnoticed were now familiar to every newspaper reader. Visitors flocked to Old Sarum to see the field and ancient earthwork which returned two members to Parliament. Moreover standards of public conduct were rising. It was no longer entirely acceptable that Leicester's charitable funds should be reserved almost exclusively for voters of sound views.

> M. Brock, *The Great Reform Act*, 1973.

1 Which sources give prominence to:
a political factors?
b economic and social factors?
c the extra-parliamentary agitation?
d public awareness and morality?
2 Despite their differences of emphasis, these interpretations all contribute
   to a total understanding of the reform crisis.
   Comment on this statement, making reference to the sources and your
   wider knowledge of the period.
3 Either on your own, or in group discussion, produce an explanation for
   the emergence of parliamentary reform as a viable issue by 1830.
   Consider long term factors, the motives of participants, and the
   immediate events of 1830. Complete the following grid:

	Factor		
	Long-term	Immediate	Motives
Political			
Economic			
Social			
Extra-parliamentary agitation			
Public morality			
Others			

4 Use the completed grid as preparation for this essay: Why had
   parliamentary reform become practical politics by the end of 1830, when
   it had appeared moribund in 1827?

PARLIAMENTARY REFORM –
CHRONOLOGY OF A CRISIS, 1830–1832

1830

15 November   Tory Government defeated in House of Commons.
16 November   Wellington resigns.
Grey's new cabinet is mainly aristocratic and Whig, but includes the Canningite Lords Palmerston, Melbourne, Goderich, and Charles Grant together with the Duke of Richmond, an Ultra Tory.
December   The drafting committee of four (Lord Durham, Lord John Russell, Sir James Graham, Lord Duncannon) begins its deliberations.

1831

1 March   Russell introduces the reform proposals to the Commons:
Redistribution:
1. Boroughs with fewer than 2,000 to lose both members.
2. Boroughs with 2–4,000 to lose one member.
3. Unrepresented towns with over 10,000 population to be enfranchised (11 to get two members, 21 to have one).
4. 26 counties to be divided into two two-member constituencies; Yorkshire Ridings each to have two members.
Franchise extension:
In counties, £10 copyholders and £50 long leaseholders to join 40 shilling freehold voters; £10 householder franchise for the boroughs.
23 March   Second reading of the Reform Bill carried by one vote.
20 April   Reform Bill defeated in committee (299 v. 291) a motion critical of the reduced number of English MPs (the reformed House would have had 62 fewer).
22 April   Parliament dissolved.
April – May   General Election – popular support for the Bill ensured Whig victory. Reform majority of about 130.
25 June   Second Reform Bill introduced.
Main change during Bill's passage through the Commons the Chandos Clause, an opposition amendment to enfranchise the £50 tenant at will in counties. Ministers oppose this amendment because it would increase land-lord influence in county elections.
22 September   Third reading carried 345 v. 236.
8 October   Second Reform Bill defeated by 41 on second reading in the Lords. During October there are serious disturbances in several areas.
12 December   Third Reform Bill presented to the Commons with redistribu-tion clauses amended to keep the new House the same size as the old. Some of the disfranchised boroughs are reprieved and more seats go to the industri-al areas. These moves are an attempt to win over Tory waverers in the Lords.

1832

24 March   Bill completes its passage through Commons.
14 April   Second reading carried in the Lords, 184 v. 175.
7 May   Lord Lyndhurst's wrecking amendment succeeds in committee.
9 May   William IV refuses to create sufficient peers to enable the Whigs to control the Lords – Lord Grey resigns.
10–15 May   The 'Days of May': Wellington attempts to form a ministry to bring in a moderate reform measure. Protest builds up in the country – has a revolutionary situation been created?
15 May   The King asks Grey to re-form his ministry.
18 May   Grey agrees on condition that the Bill should not be modified, and that the King would create extra Whig peers if necessary
4 June   Third reading carried in the Lords; Wellington and most Tory peers abstain, preferring to see the Bill pass than to lose control of the House of Lords.
7 June   Reform Act given royal assent.

Freeholders owned their property.
Copyholders held their property on the basis of old manorial records.
Long leaseholders were tenants holding property on several years' lease at a fixed rent.
The above groups were held to be free from landlords' influence.
Tenants at will held property on an annual lease, and were believed to be susceptible to electoral pressures from landlords.

As you read the following text, you will need to refer to the chronology to put events in context.

The popular movement and the crisis

It was the manner of its passing rather than its content or its immediate consequences which made men look back proudly to the struggles of the past and look forward hopefully to an 'age of reform'.

A. Briggs, *The Age of Improvement*, 1959.

Attwood's Birmingham Political Union was to be legal and peaceable in its tactics. This enabled it to attract and retain middle class support. It was this middle class demand for reform that influenced the Whigs, whether voiced through the Political Unions or through the increasingly influential provincial press represented by the *Manchester Guardian* and the *Leeds Mercury*. Certainly Grey used the growing pressure in the country to justify his Cabinet's policies to the King:

> The perilous question is that of Parliamentary Reform, and, as I approach it, the more I feel all its difficulty. With the universal feeling that prevails on this subject it is impossible to avoid doing something; and not to do enough to satisfy public expectations (I mean the satisfaction of the rational public) would be worse than to do nothing.

Lord Grey to William IV, 13 January 1831.

What does Grey mean by 'the rational public'?

Grey used the same argument three months later when, following the defeat of the Reform Bill, he requested the dissolution of Parliament :

> The Bill had been generally approved, public expectation had been raised high, and the effect of disappointment seemed greatly to be feared as likely to disturb the peace of the country. To prevent, therefore an agitation of so formidable a nature, your Majesty's servants felt themselves called upon humbly to advise your Majesty to dissolve the present Parliament.

Cabinet minute, 21 April 1831.

Grey got his dissolution and the subsequent elections revealed the full extent of the Bill's popularity.

William IV had never been firmly committed to his government's proposals, and the agitation in the country merely served to increase his nervousness. Reluctance to create the additional peers Grey wanted in the spring of 1832 (see chart) was partly the result of this anxiety and partly of reactionary pressure on him at Court. Nevertheless, the King recognised that some reform was essential; indeed, his insistence that Wellington should form a ministry which would bring in a moderate reform measure was one reason for the Duke's failure to form a government during the 'Days of May'.

The King's anxieties had been heightened by the reaction to the Lords' defeat of the Reform Bill in October 1831. London newspapers 'mourned' the event by appearing with black borders; in Birmingham the church bells tolled all night, and everywhere the role of the bishops, 21 of whom had voted against the Bill, came under attack. Riots broke out in Derby and Nottingham, where the Duke of Newcastle's home, Nottingham Castle, was burnt. These disturbances, however, paled into insignificance against the three days of disorder in Bristol, where the jails were thrown open, the Bishop's palace burnt down and houses and shops looted and set fire to.

TALKING POINT

Historians have debated the significance of the extra-parliamentary reform agitation between 1830 and 1832. After you have read this section, consider the extent to which the Whigs were responding to the perceived danger of a revolutionary threat.

However, the outbreaks were not connected and were outside the control of any political organisation. In general, they started as outbursts against anti-reformers – in Nottingham the Duke of Newcastle and in Bristol the noted anti-reform MP, Sir Charles Wetherell. The violence did not spread and was quickly quelled. Nevertheless, the middle class reformers were greatly alarmed by the unrest, and its threat to property, as was the government. Attwood claimed that the Unions guaranteed stability, and trouble had only occurred in places where there was no effective local organisation. There was talk of forming a National Guard to protect property, and in Birmingham the BPU considered plans for arming its members to defend themselves from the mob. Such schemes, however, could not be allowed by the government, and the BPU pulled back when faced by the threat of banning.

ORDER IS RESTORED IN BRISTOL. MISCALCULATION BY THE MILITARY AND LOCAL AUTHORITIES ALLOWED THE RIOTERS TO GAIN CONTROL OF THE CITY. COMMENT ON THE IMPRESSION CREATED BY THIS ILLUSTRATION.

It has been suggested that Attwood, Francis Place, who organised the London moderates, and Joseph Parkes, a Birmingham solicitor, were employing the 'language of menace', and that talk of arming middle class reformers fits into that pattern. John Roebuck, another radical reformer, later reported a conversation with a leading campaigner for reform:

We must frighten them ... No reality we can create will be sufficient for our purpose. We must work on Lord Grey's imagination. We must pretend to be frightened ourselves.

In the late autumn of 1831 there were fears that the Cabinet would reach a compromise with moderate Tories to get the Bill through the Lords. The Birmingham scheme could have been a calculated attempt to

Who does Grey mean when he writes of 'all the sound part of the community', and what can we learn about his attitude to the political unions from this extract?

remind ministers of the strength of the demand for the Reform Bill, and of the possible consequences of a retreat. Writing to the King, Grey pointed out that the power of the political unions rested on uncertainty:

On the other hand, if the question can be settled, all the sound part of the community would not only be separated from, but placed in direct opposition to, associations whose permanent existence every reasonable man must feel to be incompatible with the safety of the country. Under such circumstances these Unions could not long continue to exist, and all the real influence and power of society would be united with that of the Government in putting them down.

8 November 1831.

The modifications of the Third Reform Bill were welcomed by the reformers, but in the early weeks of 1832 popular interest was receding. From the North, Henry Hunt reported working class indifference towards a Bill that gave them nothing. Then the House of Lords decisively rejected the Bill, and public pressure had to make its final push.

It was estimated that 200,000 attended the BPU's public meeting on 7 May to urge the Lords to allow the Bill to pass. Their protest was irrelevant. The King refused to create the Whig peers needed for a Lords majority and so Grey resigned. In London Francis Place orchestrated public opposition to the Duke of Wellington. Joseph Parkes was his link in the Midlands. Throughout the country there were reports of arms being collected, and of pikes being manufactured. In Birmingham, Attwood's Union declared a willingness to take military action, and it advised members to refuse to pay direct taxes if the Duke formed a ministry. In London, Place recommended a run on the banks – 'to stop the Duke go for gold.' Even in Manchester middle and working class reformers dropped their history of antagonism to hold a joint protest meeting. What filled contemporaries with foreboding was the absence of disturbances – 'All seemed reserved for a tremendous explosion' (Sir Robert Heron, a Whig MP).

Was there a revolutionary crisis?

Whereas E.P. Thompson and Eric Hobsbawm have both suggested that May 1832 was the time when Britain came closest to revolution, M. Brock and J. Cannon in their studies of parliamentary reform have discounted the importance of the activities of the political unions and their organisers. In their view, political considerations were more significant. The King required Wellington to produce a moderate reform measure and this made Peel unwilling to join him. Without Peel, Wellington could not manage the Commons and he had to abandon his attempt to help the King. What mattered to Peel was not the state of public opinion, but his reputation as a politician and a man of principle and honesty. Public opinion played its part, but not in the 'Days of May'.

The King had been so thoroughly persuaded of the need for a comprehensive reform that he made it a sine qua non of any government – thus bolting the door to an anti-reform Tory ministry. This, in turn, made it impossible for Peel and his immediate allies to serve.

J. Cannon, *Parliamentary Reform 1640–1832*, 1973.

In the autumn of 1831 and in the 'Days of May' Britain was within an ace of a revolution.

E.P. Thompson

This period is probably the only one in modern history ... where something not unlike a revolutionary situation might have developed.

E.J. Hobsbawm

Despite their bravado, and later assertions that they would have lived up to their revolutionary claims, it is doubtful whether Place and Parkes could have led a united movement in the years before the railways made rapid communication possible. In London, Place was distrusted by the leaders of the more radical National Union of the Working Class, and the middle class leaders had little control over the working class reform unions across the country. Admittedly the authorities only had 11,000 troops available, of which 7,000 were in the London area, but the potential revolutionaries do not seem to have found an army officer prepared to lead them, and their claim that the soldiers would desert to the reformers was never tested. At a more practical level, the middle class had as much to fear from the uncertainty of revolution as the aristocracy. Both Parkes and Place were in contact with Whig ministers and doubtless fed them alarmist reports. This implies that the threat of revolution was a tactical ploy, a bluff, which neither hoped would be called.

> The expertise of Attwood and Place lay, not in military matters, but in the politics of agitation. Their calculations ... smelled more of politics than of powder and shot. They relied, not on the intrinsic strength of Attwood's army, but on the political impossibility of opening fire on it.
>
> M. Brock, *The Great Reform Act,* 1973.

More important was the myth of the 'Days of May'. Public opinion, it was believed, had forced Wellington to give way, and had kept the King and his ministers up to the mark. If public opinion could prevail in this way then it could do so again. Lord Grey's achievement was to show that the system could be changed without resort to violence and revolution, and to release the pressure that threatened the stability of nineteenth century society. In this sense the significance of the Act was largely psychological. As John Bright was to remark later, 'It was not a good Bill, but it was a great Bill when it passed.'

The Whigs – A conservative approach to reform?

The Reform Bill, when first unveiled by Russell, shocked people with its boldness. Its terms had alarmed some moderates in the Cabinet when revealed to them, now their supporters gasped with amazement. Edward Baines reported in the *Leeds Mercury* 'that the Reformers in this part of the kingdom are both surprised and delighted with the plan', whilst the Whig diarist Thomas Creevy noted 'It is its boldness that makes its success so certain.'

The sweeping nature of the proposals left Peel in an impossible position, although some Tories mistakenly believed that its very radicalism would lead to its early defeat:

> The Reform proposed is much more extensive than was expected. Parts of it were very absurd. There was no little laughter as they were detailed. The feeling in the Gallery was against it, as absurd.
>
> Lord Ellenborough's diary, 2 March 1831.

Lord Melbourne, the Home Secretary, was a reluctant reformer, but even he recognised the urgency of the situation: 'Do not make that measure which is safe, if adopted immediately, dangerous by delay.' Contemplating possible defeat in the Lords, Lord Holland noted in his diary that 'The loss of the Bill is civil war and revolution.'

1 Think about a revolution you have studied. What general factors created the revolutionary situation and contributed to a successful outcome?

2 Here are four conditions for a successful revolution:

- mass discontent
- a determined and dedicated leadership
- loss of nerve by the authorities
- the army joining the revolutionaries.

How far do they apply to the example you have discussed?

3 Now review the events of 1815–20, 1831–32. To what extent did a revolutionary situation really exist in Britain during these periods?

A MEMENTO OF THE GREAT PUBLIC QUESTION OF REFORM.
THE KING - 2. DUKE OF SUSSEX - LORDS - 3. JOHN RUSSELL - 4. GREY - 5. ALTHORPE - 6. BROUGHAM - 7. LANSDOWNE - 8. HOLLAND - 9. SIR F. BURDE
10. O'CONNELL - 11. HUME 12. STANLEY.
1. DUKE OF CUMBERLAND - 2. WELLINGTON 3. ELDON - 4. WETHERELL - 5. CROKER.
Designed and Engraved exclusively for the Bells New Weekly Messenger, and delivered Gratis. April 15. 1832.

THE WHIGS AND THEIR ALLIES SCATTER THE ANTI-REFORMERS IN THIS TRIBUTE, BUT DID THEY DESERVE SUCH ADULATION? WHAT WERE THEIR AIMS DURING THE CRISIS, AND HOW SUCCESSFULLY DID THEY ACHIEVE THEM?

Opponents suspected that the Cabinet was seeking political advantage from the changes they proposed. That would only have been human, and their overwhelming success in the 1832 election did seem to herald a long period of Whig government. If such had been their purpose, however, their 1841 election defeat was to show how much they had failed. The charge also implies a more systematic plan than Grey and his colleagues actually had.

There was much more to it than a simple removal of grievances. Grey consistently assured the King that success would bring allies to the aristocracy, that it was to be 'such a reform as might be effectual for the removal of what is most complained of without endangering the institutions of the country.'

These allies were to be the new middle class voters, of whom Grey wrote to a wavering Palmerston in October 1831:

> My information leads me to believe that the middle classes, who form the real and efficient mass of public opinion, and without whom the power of the gentry is nothing, are almost unanimous in this question [in favour of reform].

Grey's conservative reaction was not to respond to public opinion in general, however, but to appeal to 'responsible' elements in society, who were to be invited into the citadel to join the gentry in defending the constitution against democracy. Middle class grievances were to be met to split them from working class allies.

> The cabinet aimed to recast the system so as to restore its popularity among the middle class without weakening the facilities which it provided for the ruling few ... Their Bill was meant to end agitation and yet to leave the most important levers of power in aristocratic hands.
>
> M. Brock, *The Great Reform Act*, 1973.

The borough franchise was based on rateable values. The higher the figure, the more exclusive the electorate.

The Drafting Committee had originally linked the secret ballot to a £20 household franchise; this was rejected in Cabinet in favour of the more extensive £10 franchise. The initial proposal would have left some boroughs with tiny electorates. During the autumn of 1831 Russell tried to discover who the new voters would be. Edward Baines wrote from Leeds:

> canvassers stated unanimously, that the £10 qualification did not admit to the exercise of the elective franchise a single person who might not safely and wisely be enfranchised; that they were surprised to find how few comparatively would be allowed to vote ... It appeared that in the parts occupied chiefly by the working classes, not one householder in fifty would have a vote ... In the township of Holbeck, containing 11,000 inhabitants, chiefly of the working classes, but containing several mills, dye-houses, public houses and respectable dwellings, there are only 150 voters.

The Act was not a surrender to public opinion; it was a concession to one group in society to ensure stability and to safeguard the constitution and aristocratic power. It did not intend handing over power to the middle class, nor did it aim to create a new political system. The landed interest, as Russell told the Commons in 1837, had been given a preponderance through the additional county seats because 'a preponderance in favour of that interest tends to the stability of the general institutions of the country.'

That does not necessarily mean that ministers were deliberately separating urban and rural electorates, as the American historian Professor Moore has suggested, to consolidate and enhance the power of the landed interest, a process bolstered by the enfranchisement of the £50 tenants at will (the Chandos clause). That implies a surer initial strategy and greater agreement than ministers possessed.

In 1837 Grey commented that if he could have foreseen the changes since 1832 he would not have embarked on reform in 1830. Nevertheless, he had acted as a truly conservative statesman with an intuitive understanding of middle class attitudes and values.

This does not detract from the perceptiveness of Peel's criticisms during the reform debates. Despite Russell's assertion of its finality the Act paved the way for a peaceful progression to a more democratic system, and within 20 years Russell himself was preparing a new reform bill. A door had been opened which could not be shut. The lesson had been learnt that, judiciously applied, overwhelming public pressure could force the legislature to act.

Constitutionally, reform consolidated the authority of the House of Commons and hastened the diminution of the prerogatives of the Crown. As Peel forecast, a majority in the House of Commons now decided whom the monarch chose as premier, and in 1834 when William IV dismissed Melbourne and appointed Peel he was the last Prime Minister to be chosen in the old way. In 1835 the King had to take the Whigs back because Peel had failed to win a majority in the General Election

Examining the Evidence

Perspectives on reform

FOR

Source A

Grey's instruction to the Drafting Committee, December 1830, was to prepare:
> the outline of a measure ... large enough to satisfy public opinion and to afford sure ground of resistance to further innovation, yet so based on property, and on existing franchises and territorial divisions, as to run no risk of overthrowing the ... form of government.

What do these extracts suggest about Grey's motives, purposes and priorities?

Source B

The plan of Reform ... ought to be of such scope and description as to satisfy all reasonable demands, and remove at once and for ever, all rational grounds for complaint from the minds of the intelligent and independent portion of the community.

Report of the Drafting Committee, January 1831.

Source C

The principle of my reform is, to prevent the necessity for revolution .... There is no one more decided against annual parliaments, universal suffrage and the ballot than I am. My object is not to favour, but to put an end to such hopes and projects.

Grey in the House of Lords, November 1831.

Source D

IDENTIFY 'LORD JOHN' AND EXPLAIN WHY THE CARTOONIST IS CELEBRATING THE REFORM BILL.

REFORM! REFORM!! REFORM!!!

REFORM is become absolutely necessary — the Representation is corrupt — we have now Representatives of Green mounds, of Stone Walls, even of a Pig-sty, while many of our most populous manufacturing towns remain unrepresented

Lord John stalking over the Boroughmongers; or, the Rotten Representation in Danger. See Report of Speech House of Commons March 1, 1831

Source E

Ministers have thought ... that it would not be sufficient to bring forward a measure which should merely lope off some disgusting excrescences, or cure some notorious defects; but would still leave the battle to be fought again with renewed and strengthened discontent. They have thought that no half measures would be sufficient – that no trifling, no paltering, with so great a question could give stability to the Throne – authority to the Parliament – or satisfaction to the country ... The chief grievances of which the people complain are these;– First, the nomination of Members by individuals. Second, the Elections by close Corporations; third, the Expense of Elections ... It is my opinion ... that the whole measure will add to the constituency of the Commons House of Parliament, about half a million of Persons, and these all connected with the property of the country, having a valuable stake amongst us, and deeply interested in our institutions.... I think that those measures will produce a further benefit to the people, by the great incitement which it will occasion to industry and good conduct. For when a man finds that by industrious exertion, and by punctuality, he will entitle himself to a place in the list of voters, he will have an additional motive to improve his circumstances.... in adding to the constituency, we are providing for the moral as well as for the political improvement of the country.

Lord John Russell introducing the Reform Bill to the Commons, 1 March 1831.

Source F

Their principle is plain, rational and consistent. It is this, to admit the middle classes to a large and direct share in the representation, without any violent shock to the institutions of our country ... I oppose universal suffrage because I think it would produce a destructive revolution. I support this measure because I am sure that it is our best security against a revolution ... I support this measure as a measure of reform; but I support it still more as a measure of conservation. That we may exclude those whom it is necessary to exclude, we must admit those whom it may be safe to admit. At present we oppose the schemes of revolutionists with only one half, with only one quarter of our proper force. We say, and we say justly, that it is not by mere numbers, but by property and intelligence, that the nation ought to be governed. Yet, saying this, we exclude from all share in the government vast masses of property and intelligence, vast numbers of those who are most interested in preserving tranquillity and who know best how to preserve it. We do more. We drive over to the side of revolution those whom we shut out from power. Is this a time when the cause of law and order can spare one of its natural allies? Turn where we may ... the voice of great events is proclaiming to us, 'Reform, that you may preserve ... Save the greatest, and fairest, and most highly civilised community that ever existed, from calamities which may in a few days sweep away all the rich heritage of so many ages of wisdom and glory.'

Thomas Babington Macaulay in the House of Commons, 2 March 1831.

---

1 With reference to source E, and your wider knowledge, explain what is meant by:
a 'the nomination of Members by individuals'
b 'the Elections by close Corporations'
2 'A practical remedy for a felt grievance.' Comment on this view of the Reform Act, referring to sources A, B and E, and your wider knowledge of the Reform Act.
3 Compare the arguments used by Grey, Russell and Macaulay to justify reform, showing how the language and tone of their speeches reflects their different purposes and approaches.

AGAINST

Source G

It is the very absence of symmetry in our elective franchises which admits of the introduction to this House of classes so various ... opens the door to the admission here of all talents, and of all classes, and of all interests. How far under any other than the present circumstances, the rights of the distant dependencies, of the East Indies, of the West Indies, of the Colonies, of the great Corporations, of the commercial interests generally ... would find their just support in the House, I know not ... Under that system men of abilities are introduced to the House, without the necessity of mob patronage, or the profession of mob oratory ... In this way many of those who, (sitting for close or for rotten boroughs, as they have been this night designated ...) have constituted the chief ornaments of this House in the past and present age.

Tory MP Sir Robert Inglis in the House of Commons, 1 March 1831.

Inglis refers to the theory of 'virtual representation' which justified the anomalies of the unreformed electoral system because it enabled all interests to acquire some representation in the House of Commons.

Source H

It was proposed to enlarge that body [the electorate] by including in it men of limited information, of strong prejudices, of narrow and contracted views, such as shopkeepers and small attorneys. He begged, not to be misunderstood, he was not disparaging this class but, he did conceive that retired tradesmen inhabiting houses rated at £10, members of small clubs, and persons of that description; persons, he repeated, of narrow minds and bigoted views, who were now to be called in to counsel the nation, were not the best fitted to execute that important trust.

A report of Tory MP H. Twiss in the House of Commons, 2 March 1831.

Source I

While Calne, with 4,612 inhabitants, is to return two Members, Bolton, with 22,000 ... is to return but one; while Knaresborough, with 5,280 ... is to nominate two Members, Blackburn, with 22,000 ... is to be limited to one.

J. W. Croker on the redistribution proposals, House of Commons, 4 March 1831.

Source J

Peel on Reform:

i)   my belief is, that neither the monarchy nor the peerage can resist with effect the decrees of a House of Commons that is immediately obedient to every popular impulse, and that professes to speak the popular will; and that all the tendencies of such an assembly are towards the increase of its own power and the intolerance of an extrinsic control ... I was unwilling to open a door which I saw no prospect of being able to close

Sir Robert Peel in the House of Commons, 6 July 1831.

ii)   I will continue my opposition to the last, believing as I do, that this is the first step, not directly to a revolution, but to a series of changes which will affect the property, and totally change the character, of the mixed constitution of this country. I will oppose it to the last, convinced that though my opposition will be unavailing, it will not be fruitless, because the opposition made now will oppose a bar to further concessions hereafter. ... On this ground I take my stand, not opposed to a well-considered reform of any of our institutions which need reform, but opposed to this reform.

Sir Robert Peel in the House of Commons, 17 December 1831.

Source K

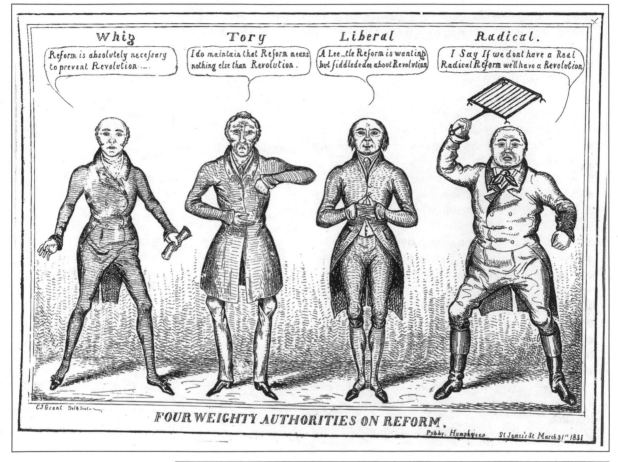

4 Discuss the reasons for opposing the Reform Bill raised in sources G, H, I and J.

5 Contrast the view of the middle class expressed in source G with those of Macaulay and Russell. Comment on the language Twiss uses.

6 How convincingly does Peel respond to the hopes of Grey in sources A and C, and to the vision of Macaulay in source F.

7 Professor Gash has suggested that whilst the Whigs were right to bring in reform, the Tories were proved correct in many of their pessimistic forecasts. Using these sources, and your wider knowledge of the nineteenth century, comment on this view.

8 Study the cartoon (source K). Use the other sources and your wider knowledge of the reform crisis to comment on the appropriateness of views attributed to Grey (the Whig), Wellington (the Tory) and Cobbett (the Radical).

The Great Reform Act, 1832
Redistribution of seats
- 56 boroughs were disfranchised.
- 30 boroughs lost one member.
- 22 new two member boroughs and 20 new single member boroughs were created.
- 62 seats went to the counties (Yorkshire to have six, 26 counties to be divided and to have four, seven to have three, and the Isle of Wight to have one).

Voting qualifications
- Counties: adult males who were
— 40 shilling freeholders
— £10 copyholders
— £10 and £50 long leaseholders
— £50 annual leaseholders (the Chandos Clause).
- Boroughs: adult males owning or occupying property rated at £10.

Voting procedures
- A register of voters was to be kept for county and borough seats.
- Counties were to be divided into polling districts.
- Polling was to be limited to two days in all constituencies.

Wales
- Three counties now returned 2 members.
- There was an increase of one in borough members.
- Total increase of 4 seats.

Scotland
- County representation unchanged.
- Edinburgh and Glasgow to have 2 members.
- Aberdeen, Dundee, Greenock, Paisley and Perth one member each.
- Total increase of 8 seats.
- Voting qualifications in Scotland followed the English ones except that in counties all owners of property with a yearly value of at least £10 voted. This had been the original county qualification.

Ireland
- Four boroughs upgraded to two members.
- One extra to Trinity College, Dublin.
- Total increase of 5 seats.
- County franchise remained at £10 freeholder (1829 legislation), £10 householder in boroughs.

The reformed House of Commons

The diarist Greville was surprised that the first House elected under the Reform Act turned out 'to be very much like every other Parliament.' The landed interest continued to dominate the Commons and the aristocracy continued to dominate Cabinets through the nineteenth century. Few commercial men and industrialists could afford the time to become MPs until they had secured their future and had joined the gentry by purchasing a country estate. As the historian M. Brock has observed, 'Most of the new voters wanted, not to challenge the aristocracy, but to win recognition from it: once they had their rightful position they did not favour further adventures' (*The Great Reform Act*, 1973).

FOCUS

4.1 The Impact of the Reform Act – Hopes, Fears and Realities

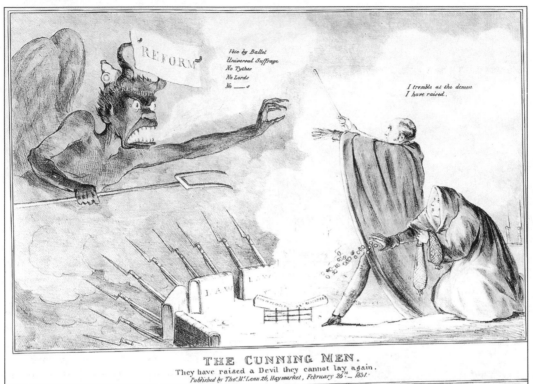

THE CUNNING MEN.
They have raised a Devil they cannot lay again.
Published by Tho. McLean 26, Haymarket, February 26th— 1831.

LORD GREY HAS SUMMONED A DEMON WHILE HIS CHANCELLOR OF THE EXCHEQUER, VISCOUNT ALTHORP, THROWS IT MONEY.

What is Grey's reaction? What is the cartoonist implying about the government's reform proposals?

Whatever the intentions of the framers, or the supporters of this measure may be, I am quite sure, that, if carried, it will sweep clean the House of Peers in ten years.

Sir Robert Inglis opposing the Bill, 1 March 1831.

The field of coal would beat the field of barley; the population of the manufacturing districts was more condensed, and would act with more energy, backed by clubs and large assemblages of people, than the population of the agricultural districts. They would act with such force in the House that the more divided agriculturalists would be unable to withstand it, and the latter would be overwhelmed.

Alexander Baring opposing the Bill, July 1831.

J. W. Croker writing to the Duke of Wellington, 11 August 1832 explaining his decision not to seek election to the reformed Parliament.

I believe, in my conscience, that Parliament will substantially be as complete a usurpation, leading to as complete a subversion of our ancient Constitution, as the Long Parliament ... I will not spontaneously take an active share in a system which must ... subvert the Church, the Peerage, and the Throne – in one word, the Constitution of England.

THE STEPING STONE or John Bull peeping into Futurity !!!
Pub.d by J.L.Marks 91 Long Lane Smithfield.

THE MAN Wot pays the TAXES !!
London J.L.Marks Long Lane

Before and after – compare these comments on the Reform Bill and the Reform Act.

The true mode of relieving the working class is to repeal the Corn Laws and the taxes on the necessities of life, and this gives them cheap food; to open the ... [commerce] of this country to the East Indies and China, and thus to extend the demand for our manufactures; and to reduce the expenditure of the state, which can only be done by a Reformed Parliament.

Leeds Mercury, 7 January 1832.

But I say, the Reform Bill is a trick – it's nothing but swearing-in special constables to keep the aristocrats safe in their monopoly; it's bribing some of the people with votes to make them hold their tongues about giving votes to the rest.

A radical orator in George Eliot's novel **Felix Holt, the Radical (1866).**

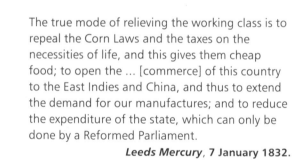

TALKING POINT

Why did the Reform Crisis provoke so many contrasting reactions?

Focus

4.2 The Impact of the Reform Act – What Changed?

TALKING POINT

Compare the pre-reform (see page 6) and post-reform electoral systems. To what extent, and in what ways, had the 1832 Reform Act changed and improved the electoral system?

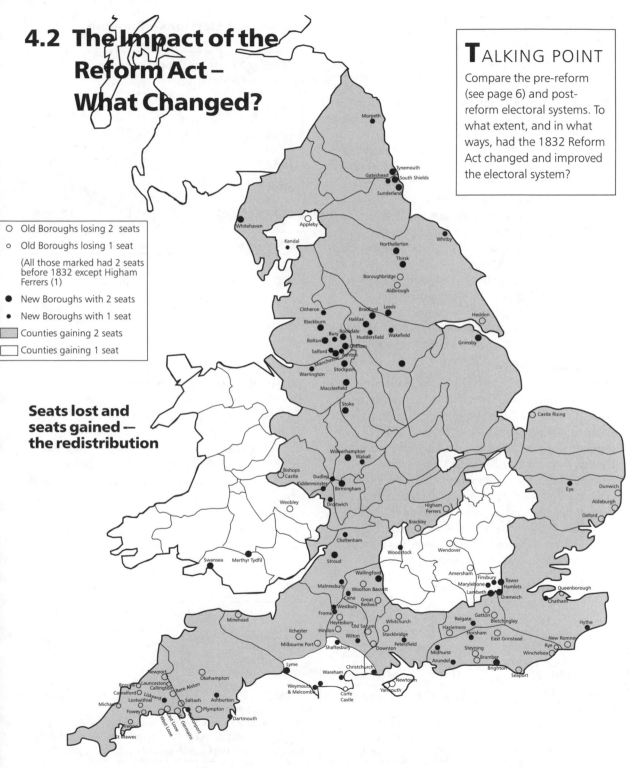

Old Boroughs losing 2 seats

Old Boroughs losing 1 seat

(All those marked had 2 seats before 1832 except Higham Ferrers (1)

New Boroughs with 2 seats

New Boroughs with 1 seat

Counties gaining 2 seats

Counties gaining 1 seat

Seats lost and seats gained – the redistribution

From the evidence of the map comment on the location of the disfranchised and newly enfranchised boroughs.

The English counties were still under-represented. Although they contained 56 per cent of the electors they only made up 31 per cent of the seats. In practice, however, this was counter balanced by the large number of small borough seats in rural areas.

The ten southern counties, with a quarter of England's population, had one third of the MPs (representing county seats and boroughs); Middlesex, Lancashire and the West Riding of Yorkshire, with over a quarter of the population, only had an eighth of the MPs.

The London area was still badly under-represented. Middlesex (London north of the Thames) had roughly the same population as Lancashire and Yorkshire put together, but Yorkshire had 37 MPs, Lancashire 26, and Middlesex only 14.

£10 Householders

The new franchise was designed to exclude non-property-holders, who were deemed unsuitable, and to create a standard qualification for all voters. The nature of the new voters varied from borough to borough since rental values differed. High rents in London meant that skilled working men were enfranchised but in most industrial towns where rents were lower this was not the case. In Leeds only 5,000 were entitled to vote out of a population of 125,000. In Preston, Westminster and Coventry, where the old franchises had been exceptionally wide, the number of voters decreased under the new regulations.

Contested Elections – England

Year	No. of contests	Constituencies	%
1832	188	254	74.02
1835	153	254	60.24
1837	176	254	69.29
1841	138	254	54.33
1847	120	254	47.24

Compare this with the similar table in the Focus on the unreformed electoral system in Chapter 1. What has changed, and why?

Size of Borough Electorates

The Whigs had no intention of equalising electorates. New boroughs were created not because of size, but to represent a trade or interest. Doncaster, Loughborough and Croydon, each with more than 10,000 population, did not have their own MPs, but in 1832 eight English boroughs polled under 200 voters, and five of these returned 2 Members. Totnes, with 179 votes cast in 1832, had two MPs, the same as Liverpool where over 8,500 voted. In 1832 31 boroughs had fewer than 300 registered electors; 29 had over 2,000.

The size of the electorate

	1831	1833		1831	1833
England & Wales			**Scotland**		
Counties	201,859	370,379	**Counties**	c.3,000	33,000
Boroughs	164,391	282,398	**Boroughs**	c.1,500	31,000
Totals	366,250	652,777	**Totals**	4,500	64,000

This gives an increase of about 80 per cent. Approximately 11 per cent of adult males had the vote in 1831; in 1833 it was about 18 per cent.

The most significant increase was in Scotland, where the Reform Act completely changed the electoral fortunes of the groupings in favour of the Whigs/Liberals.

Electoral Behaviour

Influence

The influence of social superiors – landlords, clergy and employers – remained undiminished. In the counties the exercise of landlord influence over tenants was natural and expected. Only in exceptional circumstances would tenants rebel. Old practices like 'exclusive dealing' with tradesmen of the right political opinion continued.

Bribery and corruption

This continued unabated. As late as 1844 the borough of Sudbury was disfranchised for corruption. At the 1841 election the Liberal candidates spent about £3,000 and the Conservatives £2,000. Liberal voters were paid £7 as well as receiving the usual treating. When Lord Aberdeen wanted a seat for his son he told F. R. Bonham, the Conservative Party organiser, that he was prepared to spend £2,500 if that guaranteed a seat without the uncertainty of a contest.

Electoral violence

Abducting opposition voters, getting them drunk, and locking them up was common; the reverse was 'cooping' the candidate's own voters to keep them safe. In Nottingham the 'lambs' were employed to bully opponents and break windows, in Lewes the 'bullies'. At Hertford in 1832 the Tory candidate hired a gang of gypsies and the radical a gang of bargees to intimidate each other's supporters. A Southampton man spoke of 'the inconvenience to the innocent electors of an election ... the electors would be glad if the town were disfranchised.'

Proprietary and controlled boroughs

Professor Gash has estimated that possibly 73 MPs continued to be returned by patrons after 1832. These included Gladstone, who entered Parliament in 1832 for the Duke of Newcastle's borough of Newark, following in the footsteps of young aspiring politicians of the previous hundred years.

Managing the new voters

With the introduction of annual registration of voters, the way was opened for a new approach to party organisation and management. Sympathetic voters could be registered and opponents' right to vote challenged in the Revising Courts. For the Tories, F. R. Bonham operated from the Carlton Club from 1835 encouraging and advising on registration procedures, finding candidates for constituencies, and constituencies for prospective MPs. From 1836 the Whigs/Liberals had the Reform Club, which under Joseph Parkes and James Coppock became the centre of their national organisation.

TALKING POINT

Lord John Russell stated that the Reform Act was a final measure. Suggest reasons, from this focus, why that was unlikely.

REVIEW

What was the reform crisis about?

Writing an essay

The ability to write a good essay is necessary for success at A level.

Most essays fall into two categories. They either ask for explanations, the 'why' question, or for evaluation and analysis. Essays of the latter type might have phrases like 'account for', 'comment on', 'discuss', 'to what extent' somewhere in the question. At any level History is an inquiry into the past, and the examiner wants you to investigate the topic and issue selected for you.

There are three initial stages for essay writing:

1 Unpacking the question – this can be straightforward. Ask the following questions:

● Is this a 'why', or an evaluative question?

● What is the topic?

● What aspect or issue around the topic is to be investigated?

2 Be relevant by focusing on the question set. Don't be tempted to write everything you know about a topic. Much of it will not be needed and will detract from your answer.

3 Select appropriate material to support the argument, and stick to this content.

Here are some essay questions about the reform crisis:

1 'More concerned to stave off democracy than to bring it nearer.' Comment on this view of the Parliamentary Reform Act of 1832.

2 'An essentially conservative measure, which nevertheless alarmed the ruling classes, but naturally angered radicals.' Examine the validity of this view of the Great Reform Act of 1832.

3 How far did the Reform Act of 1832 warrant the excitement aroused in its passing?

Quotations often seem to make a question more obscure. After reading it through carefully try re-writing the question in your own words. This can often clarify your ideas about the task.

Using the material in this chapter, and your wider knowledge, plan your approach to each of these essays. Discuss with others in your group: the interpretation of the question, the relevant content to include, and the argument to be developed. Then choose one title and write the essay.

5 Years of Whig Achievement and Conservative Renewal, 1833–41

The political parties

Tory and Conservative: Peel's ministry, 1834–35, was the first government to be called Conservative, though Tory remained an alternative name.

Whig, Liberal and Radical: The Whigs were never a Party in the formal sense. Whig governments included Whigs, liberals and radicals. Liberalism and radicalism were associated with the middle class. Radicals wanted major changes in the institutions of church and state. The name Liberal Party came into use around 1859.

Party numbers in the Commons can only be approximate since there was still some cross-voting, but whips and party managers were reasonably accurate in their estimates. The figures for the Whigs include the Radicals and the Irish group led by O'Connell.

1 Compare these opinions with the parliamentary situation before 1832. What appears to have changed?

2 Given the nature of the Reform Crisis what do you find surprising about the political developments shown here? Can you offer any explanations for them?

PREVIEW

A two party system?

Prime Minister	Party	General election	Whigs and supporters	Conservatives
(Nov.1830) Lord Grey	Whig	Dec.1832	483	175
July 1834 Lord Melbourne	Whig			
Dec.1834 Sir Robert Peel	Cons.	Jan.1835	385	273
Apr.1835 Lord Melbourne	Whig	Aug.1837	345	313
		July 1841	291	367
Aug.1841 Sir Robert Peel	Cons.			

In 1836 E.L. Bulwer wrote of 'times like the present, when two parties, professing two perfectly distinct creeds, are struggling for power'. Gladstone, in 1841, noted that 'the principle of party has long predominated in this country', adding 'it now has a sway almost unlimited.'

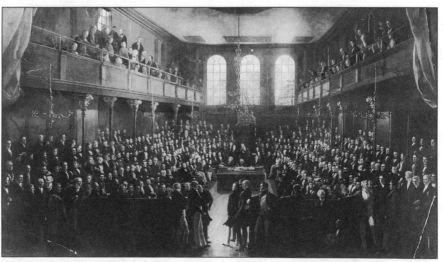

WHIG MINISTERS FOUND IT VERY DIFFICULT TO MANAGE THE REFORMED HOUSE OF COMMONS.

5.1 Whig leadership, 1833–41: A problem of credibility?

> What particularly discredited the Whigs was the visible lack of firm and incisive leadership ... This defect of leadership ran back to the immediate post-Reform years. Neither Grey nor Melbourne was fitted to be leader of a Liberal party, and Russell suffered from both temperamental flaws and lack of sufficient authority.
>
> N. Gash, *Reaction and Reconstruction in English Politics 1832–1852*, 1965.

Lord Grey, the hero of the reform crisis, was unchallengeable as Whig leader. His successful management of a difficult Cabinet through those years had left him exhausted. Now he wanted to slow down the pace of change. Constant bickering in the Cabinet stretched his nerves to breaking point and he increasingly looked forward to retirement to his estates. Attempts to resign in 1833 and in the spring of 1834 were frustrated by appeals from the King and his colleagues. He was, explained Cabinet minister Lord Holland, 'the keystone that holds the whole edifice together'. His eventual resignation in July 1834 was soon followed by William's dismissal of the Melbourne Cabinet. Out of office Grey continued to meddle in government through his son, Lord Howick, a critical member of the Melbourne Cabinet.

William Lamb, 2nd Lord Melbourne, was not a member of the aristocratic Whig circle. His marriage to

Caroline Ponsonby became one of the causes célèbres of the period. Her wild affair with the poet Byron and eventual collapse into mental instability led to a formal separation. His unhappy family life – his only son was a permanent invalid – contributed to a detached and cynical view of life, but Melbourne's easy manners and wit made him a congenial companion.

He had served under Canning and Wellington as Chief Secretary for Ireland, resigning with Huskisson in 1828. He joined the Grey government as Home Secretary, succeeding Grey as premier in July 1834. Dismissed by William IV in November 1834, he returned in April 1835, his standing with the King immeasurably strengthened by William's failure to impose a Conservative Peel government on the country. Following the accession of the 18-year-old Queen Victoria in 1837, Melbourne enjoyed the respect of the monarch, supervising her political education until his electoral defeat in 1841.

Melbourne was a reluctant reformer. As Home Secretary, he dealt severely with the Swing rioters and the Tolpuddle Martyrs (see page 00). The Reform Act was, for Melbourne, an unfortunate necessity. Consider his view of the role of government: 'the principal duty of Parliament is to consider the estimates for the public service, to retrench what is superfluous, to correct what is amiss, and to assist the Crown with those supplies and subsidies which it thinks right and necessary to afford.' His government was not one of great reforms.

Melbourne's reputation as an indolent man about town concealed the ruthlessness of an accomplished politician. In 1831 Grey had been contemplating removing him from the Home Office; Lord Holland recorded his comments when the proposal was discussed:

> His motive ... was alleged indolence in Melbourne. I combated the grounds and told him a dislike to meddling legislation and his careless nonchalant Manner might give him the character of an indolent man with the unobservant, but those who had business with the office did not find him so.

In contrast, Lord Campbell later commented that 'Lord Melbourne as Minister had not displayed proper activity and energy', neglecting to keep himself informed of his colleagues purposes thereby creating '"a government of departments" without unity or pervading plan.'

Melbourne's successor as Whig leader, Lord John Russell, came from the greatest of the grand Whig families. Having been the leading advocate of parliamentary reform during the twenties, Grey entrusted him with the task of guiding the Reform Bill through the Commons. Entering the Cabinet in 1831 as Paymaster General, his outspokenness helped to drive Lord Stanley to resign in 1834. This, and Althorp's succession to the peerage in the autumn of 1834, left Russell as the leading Whig in the House of Commons. He masterminded the alliance of Whigs, Radicals and Irish, the Lichfield House Compact, which defeated Peel in 1835. Melbourne rewarded him with the position of Home Secretary and the Leadership of the House of Commons. In 1839 he became Secretary for War and the Colonies to tackle the complicated affairs of Canada.

Russell was never really popular and could be insensitive. His ill-considered outbursts under stress in the Commons were potentially disastrous. Nevertheless he proved a more than competent departmental minister and was responsible for the reform successes of the second Melbourne administration. Unlike Melbourne, he recognised the need for new policy departures if the Whigs were to stem the tide of opinion flowing in Peel's favour. He eventually persuaded the Prime Minister to make the secret ballot and the Corn Laws open questions for ministers in 1839, and initiated the 1841 free trade budget proposals in a vain attempt to win back moderate voters.

TALKING POINT

E.P. Thompson warns against the 'enormous condescension of posterity' – judging the past by what we think ought to have happened rather than by what actually happened. Consider the difficulties of interpreting the 1830s, and the role of the Whigs, bearing that danger in mind.

5.2 Reform: The Whig dilemma, 1833–41

Unless Ministers produced 'Popular measures', Althorp warned Grey after the 1832 General Election, 'the Reform will lead to Revolution.' Expectations had been raised, candidates had made pledges; the Whigs now had to balance conflicting hopes and aspirations.

Pressures for reform

1 The Irish dimension – In the short term the tithe question had to be settled and the anomalous status of the Church of Ireland resolved. In the longer term the Irish might be reconciled to the Union by a period of fair government. The presence of O'Connell in the reformed Commons with about forty supporters made this a pressing issue.

2 The Nonconformists expected the Whigs, their allies in the campaign for civil and religious equality, to remove their remaining grievances.

• To be legally recognised, marriages had to take place in the parish church (Hardwicke's Marriage Act, 1753).

The parish baptismal register was the only legally accepted birth document.

• Anglican clergy often prevented Nonconformist ministers from holding funeral services in parish burial grounds.

• Religious tests excluded Nonconformists from the universities.

• All parishioners were required to pay church rates for the maintenance of the parish church.

• For militants the very existence of an established church was anathema.

3 Political radicals wanted to continue the reform process by reducing the powers of the House of Lords, further extending the franchise, establishing a secret ballot, and beginning to reform the Church of England.

4 The short-time movement was a heterogeneous alliance of millworkers, Tory radicals like Richard Oastler, evangelical clergymen from the West Riding of Yorkshire and humanitarians pressing for a ten hour working day for children. Their propaganda and evidence had shocked public opinion.

5 Humanitarian and religious demands for the abolition of slavery.

6 A new breed of reformer, the Philosophic Radicals or Utilitarians, who sought efficient and effective administrative action by the state. Edwin Chadwick was the most active of this group outside Parliament.

The Whig dilemma

In 1841 Edward Ellice reminded Russell that since 1832 a negative response to pressure for reform had been out of the question: 'Our Whig party can only do good when leading and moderating the actions of the popular party below and beyond them.' The Whigs, however, were natural conservatives. The Reform Act had not been devised as the starting point of an era of reform. Russell impatiently told the Commons in 1837 that it had been intended as a 'final' measure, whilst Melbourne believed that government's job was to 'rule', not to legislate. Neither Grey's nor Melbourne's Cabinets had clear priorities and they often seemed to be reacting to pressures rather than framing their own solutions. They did, however, believe in careful and measured legislation and began to use expert opinion through Royal Commissions to collect information and clarify policy. There were Royal Commissions on the Poor Law, Factory Conditions, Local Government, Rural Policing and Children's Employment. Russell pinpointed the Whig dilemma in 1837: 'if they attempt little, their friends grow slack; and if they attempt much, their enemies grow strong.'

Resistance to reform

1 The Tory Ultras – uncompromising opponents of any change in the institutions of church and state.

2 Peel's new conservatism, with its promise of stability, but enough reform to remove the worst abuses from the threatened institutions, was increasingly attractive to voters.

3 Interest groups which felt threatened: the Church of England, West Indian plantation owners and merchants (slave owners), factory owners.

4 The overwhelming desire for 'cheap government'.

5 Reluctance of voters to contemplate further political change, coupled with alarm at the increasingly close Whig alliance with O'Connell after 1835.

6 Orthodox political economy, which emphasised individualism and freedom from restriction, was an effective brake on any inclination to widen the scope of government action into social reform. This was reinforced by the widespread belief that central government was corrupt and inefficient, and that local initiatives and control were to be preferred.

Stanley was moved from the Irish Chief Secretaryship in 1833 because of his opposition to the conciliatory policies preferred by the Cabinet. He became Secretary for War and the Colonies, hence his responsibility for slavery. A brilliant debater, Stanley (later Lord Derby) was to be a Conservative premier 1852, 1858–59, 1866–68. At this stage in his career he was marked as a future Whig leader and premier.

Lord Ashley was a leading Evangelical social reformer. Entering Parliament as a Tory in 1826, he campaigned for improved conditions for the mentally ill and working children. He was a member of the first Public Health Board (1848–54) and supported the Ragged School Union. He became Lord Shaftesbury in 1851.

TALKING POINT

Gladstone faced a similar dilemma during his second ministry, 1880–85 (see chapter 15).

Why did nineteenth century Conservative administrations (Peel, 1841–46, Salisbury 1886–92) find it easier to control Irish agitation than the Liberals and Whigs?

The end of Lord Grey's coalition

Abolition of slavery and factory reform

Apparent Whig strength in the Commons soon proved illusory. Ministers were faced by a divided and leaderless Tory opposition that was outnumbered by a phalanx of about 190 Radicals and O'Connellites. Ministers could expect greater challenges from these nominal supporters. Their first stumble, therefore, was the failure to promise the abolition of slavery in the King's Speech, although it had been a significant issue for many voters. When Lord Stanley eventually responded to the outcry and introduced an abolition Bill its offer of compensation to the slave owners and a seven year apprenticeship scheme for the slaves, rather than immediate abolition, failed to satisfy his critics.

Ministers were also caught unawares by the tactics of the factory reformers. Their parliamentary spokesman, Lord Ashley, introduced a Ten Hours Bill which the government, accepting the critical arguments of its supporters amongst the mill owners, had to resist. They successfully blocked Ashley by appointing a Royal Commission. Its Report provided the basis for the government's own Factory Act which angered the reformers, because there was no provision for a ten hour day, and annoyed the mill owners because of the restrictions it placed on them.

The Factory Act of 1833 restricted working hours for children to a maximum of eight hours per day for children under 13 and twelve hours for 13–18 year-olds. Children under 9 were excluded from factories. Adult working hours were unaffected.

The heavy fines which factory reformers had demanded were not introduced but inspectors were appointed to help enforce the law.

The Irish problem

It was Ireland that provided the real test of ministerial resolve and unity. Since emancipation the 'tithe war' had disrupted the countryside. The catholic peasantry, encouraged by their priests, refused to pay for an alien church. Troops were used to enforce payment but with little success, the violence merging into a general attack on landlords. Ministers faced the dilemma of all liberal governments when faced by disorder – what balance to strike between coercion and conciliation.

Grey distrusted O'Connell and was unsympathetic to Irish grievances. He much preferred the coercive policies favoured by Stanley, the Irish Chief Secretary, to the remedial legislation proposed by Lord Anglesey, the Lord Lieutenant of Ireland. The Tithe Act (1832) attempted to defuse the situation by making tithe a rent charge paid by the landlord rather than a direct payment by the peasantry. However, this failed to satisfy the Irish and did nothing to lessen tension in the countryside.

O'Connell's ultimate aim remained repeal of the Act of Union, but when the new Parliament met he concentrated his attack on the anomalous position of the Church of Ireland. This attracted the support of large numbers of Radical MPs, some of whom viewed reform of the Irish Church as a first step to reform of the Church of England. This alliance of the O'Connellites and the Radicals offered a formidable challenge to the authority of Ministers in the House of Commons.

Stanley's initial reaction was to maintain law and order with a harsh coercion measure. Contrary pressures within the Cabinet ensured that this was accompanied by a reform of the Church of Ireland. The impact of the Church Reform Bill was blunted by the Coercion Bill that preceded it, and its terms failed to satisfy radical expectations. However, the indirect threat it posed to the Church of England alarmed both the Conservative opposition and more moderate Whig reformers.

The proposed diocesan and parish rationalisation created a financial surplus, so debate centred on the purposes to which this revenue could be applied. The Bill was ambiguous, but the O'Connellites, the Radicals and some members of the government felt that the money should be appropriated for secular purposes to benefit the whole population of Ireland. Education and poor relief were obvious candidates for support. A Cabinet in disarray abandoned this proposal to get the rest of the measure through. A disappointed O'Connell rejected the final measure as one whose 'pith, substance … had been plucked out.'

The end of Lord Grey

The appropriation issue remained a source of discord within the Cabinet and between the parties for the rest of the decade. An uneasy agreement amongst Cabinet ministers to leave it as an open question was shattered by Lord John Russell on 6 May 1834. During the Commons debate on a new Tithe Bill, Stanley re-stated his opposition. Russell, believing that Ireland could only be quietened by concessions, rose to state his own opinion that 'the revenues of the Church of Ireland were larger than necessary for the religious and moral instruction of the persons belonging to the Church and for the stability of the Church itself.' Stanley passed a hastily scribbled note to Sir James Graham – 'John Russell has upset the coach.' Grey tried in vain to prevent their resignations. Eventually they were joined by Lord Ripon (formerly Goderich) and the Duke of Richmond.

In April 1833 Lord Durham, always a difficult minister to manage, had resigned. The resignation of three more ministers in May–June 1834 intensified Grey's personal despondency. It was well known that he was looking for a suitable opportunity to retire. He found his moment in July 1834 when the Coercion Act was being renewed. O'Connell revealed to the Commons that there had been secret negotiations between himself and Littleton, Stanley's successor as Irish Chief Secretary. Grey had not sanctioned the talks and knew nothing about them. Scenting a conspiracy, he submitted his resignation to the King.

Grey's successor, Lord Melbourne, only survived as premier until the autumn. Althorp was persuaded to remain in the Cabinet under Melbourne, but his elevation to the House of Lords on the death of his father left the leadership of the House of Commons vacant. Russell was the obvious successor to this post. Unfortunately the King disliked him, and held him responsible for the government's Irish policies. Melbourne was summoned to Brighton for a long discussion of the alternatives and a close questioning on Cabinet disunity on Irish and other matters. William wanted the assurance of a Conservative administration, and sent Melbourne back to London on 14 November with a letter of dismissal.

The Act reduced the four Irish Anglican archbishoprics to two, abolished ten episcopal sees and any parish in which no service had been held for three years. Church cess, a tax levied on all parishioners for the upkeep of church buildings, was also abolished.

Appropriation – the use of surplus church revenue for secular purposes. This became a key political issue in Irish politics.

None of these men were impeccable Whigs. Graham had not been firmly committed during the previous decade, Stanley came from a great Whig family but had held office under both Canning and Wellington, Ripon was a Canningite, and Richmond was a Tory Ultra.

The Leader of the House, when the Prime Minister was a peer, had the duty of reporting daily to the monarch on Commons business. Hence William's insistence that he dealt with a minister he personally respected and trusted.

Peel – building an opposition

Melbourne's difficulties were Peel's opportunities. He had soon established his authority on the opposition benches but he remained estranged from the Ultras of the Tory party who still distrusted him for his role in Catholic emancipation and scorned his refusal to join Wellington in 1832.

Outnumbered by Radicals and Irish MPs, there was perhaps little that a Conservative opposition could do in 1833. Peel used his influence to help as well as criticise ministers. He voted against the government on three occasions during that session, but supported the Irish Church Reform Bill once appropriation had been abandoned, persuaded Wellington to allow it through the Lords, defended Stanley from the attacks of O'Connell and annoyed the Ultras by his refusal to launch all-out opposition to every government measure.

Peel's vision of a future Conservative revival ignored the posturings of the Ultras. A new Conservative Party had to attract those on the government side who were becoming increasingly disenchanted at the lengths to which ministers seemed prepared to go to retain the support of Radical and Irish allies. It had to be a party, therefore, of moderate and considered reform. Such an approach would appeal to those amongst the new voters who were satisfied by the Reform Act and alarmed at the prospect of further debate and instability. What Peel envisaged was a return to something like the pragmatic Liberal Toryism he had shared in under Liverpool's leadership. In these circumstances Peel was not going to turn to the Ultras; he could afford to wait until they realised that they needed the prestige and authority of his leadership.

The departure of Stanley, Graham and the others from the Whig benches gave hope of an exodus of moderates, frightened away by the excesses of the Radicals and the Irish group. During the decade about forty MPs crossed the floor of the House, but the real catches remained Stanley and Graham. Both had had Cabinet experience, the former would grace any front bench with his oratorial skills, whilst Graham's command of detail and administrative expertise rivalled that of Peel himself. However, both declined places in Peel's first Cabinet; Stanley aspired to be the leader of a moderate third force attracting support from both sides, and both distrusted the link between Peel and Wellington, and were concerned to preserve some element of political consistency. Opposition tactics – Peel's reluctance to join all-out assaults on Melbourne's ministry, and his less than aggressive criticism of government measures – were partially dictated by the need to win Stanley over. The Lichfield House Compact, which drew the Whigs even closer to the Radicals and Irish MPs, gave an added impetus, and by the end of 1835 Graham was in correspondence with the opposition leader. Stanley did not make the formal move until 1837, but by 1838 the two men were Peel's closest collaborators in the Commons.

EXAMINING THE EVIDENCE

The principles of a Conservative opposition

Source A

I presume that the chief object of that party which is called Conservative, whatever its number may be, will be to resist Radicalism, to prevent those further encroachments of democratic influence which will be attempted (probably successfully attempted) as the natural consequence of the triumph already achieved. I certainly think that – as that party will be comparatively weak in numbers; as victories gained by mere union with the radicals will promote mainly the views of the Radicals; as there is no use in defeating, no use in excluding a Government, unless you can replace it by one framed on principles more consonant to your own – our policy ought to be rather to conciliate the good will of the sober-minded and well-disposed portion of the community, and thus lay the foundations of future strength, than to urge an opposition on mere party grounds, and for the purpose of mere temporary triumph.

Sir Robert Peel to Henry Goulburn, 3 January 1833.

Source B

Peel spoke. He spoke last, & for nearly two hours – never with more effect. All parties admit that he astonished the new members, Irishmen & lawyers. It is evident to me that from the state of the House & the impotence of Ministers to manage it, he will, before two months are gone by, practically be at its head. He will by that time have often saved the Government, and their own friends will tell them he alone can lead the House.

Lord Ellenborough on a Commons debate, February 1833.

Source C

respecting the measure of reform. He would … consider that question as finally and irrevocably disposed of. He was now determined to look forward to the future alone, and considering the constitution as it existed, to take his stand on main and essential matters – to join in resisting every attempt at new measures, which could not be stirred without unsettling the public mind, and endangering public prosperity.

Report of Sir Robert Peel, House of Commons, 7 February 1833.

Source D

my opinion is decidedly against all manoeuvring, all coquetting with Radicals, for the mere purpose of a temporary triumph over the Government … How can the Conservative party, if again called to the Government, hope to maintain itself, except by conciliating the goodwill, at least by mitigating the hostility, of many of the more moderate and respectable supporters of the present Government? The surest way to prevent this is by finesse and party tactics.

Sir Robert Peel to Henry Goulburn, 25 May 1834.

1 With reference to sources A and F and your own knowledge explain what is meant by the following phrases.
a 'the natural consequence of the triumph already achieved' (source A)
b 'avail myself … of this legitimate opportunity' (source F)
c 'that great and intelligent class of society of which you are a portion' (source F).

2 Discuss Peel's understanding of the role of a 'Conservative Opposition' (source G), referring to sources A, D and E.

3 Show how the Tamworth Manifesto (source F) is consistent with the tactics and statements of Peel in 1833 (sources A and C).

4 What evidence is there in source F that Peel was also making an indirect approach to the Ultras? How successful, given the other sources here, was that likely to be?

5 Comment on the language and tone of the Tamworth Manifesto, indicating its suitability for Peel's purpose.

6 Refer to the section on the 1841 election at the end of this chapter. To what extent had the message of the Tamworth Manifesto contributed to a change in Tory attitudes, and helped to win support for the Party?

Source E

I believe ... that the present strength of the Conservative party and the present condition of the Government have mainly resulted ... from our having kept aloof from Radical union, and from our having honestly supported the Government whenever we thought the Government right.

Sir Robert Peel to Charles Arbuthnot, 27 May 1834.

Source F

The 'Tamworth Manifesto'
To the Electors of the Borough of Tamworth ...

I gladly avail myself ... of this legitimate opportunity, of making a more public appeal – of addressing, through you, to that great and intelligent class of society of which you are a portion ... to that class which is much less interested in the contentions of party, than in the maintenance of order and the cause of good government, that frank exposition of general principles and views which appears to be anxiously expected ... and cannot be the interest, of a Minister of this country to withhold ...

I never will admit that I have been, either before or after the Reform Bill, the defender of abuses, or the enemy of judicious reforms ...

With respect to the Reform Bill itself, I will repeat now the declaration ... that I consider the Reform Bill a final and irrevocable settlement of a great Constitutional question – a settlement which no friend to the peace and welfare of this country would attempt to disturb ...

Then, as to the spirit of the Reform Bill, and the willingness to adopt and enforce it as a rule of government: if ... it be meant that we are to live in a perpetual vortex of agitation; that public men can only support themselves in public estimation by adopting every popular impression of the day, – by promising instant redress of anything which anybody may call an abuse, – by abandoning altogether that great aid of government ... the respect for ancient rights, and the deference to prescriptive authority; if this be the spirit of the Reform Bill, I will not undertake to adopt it. But if the spirit of the Reform Bill implies merely a careful review of institutions, civil and ecclesiastical, undertaken in a friendly temper, combining, with the firm maintenance of established rights, the correction of proved abuses and the redress of real grievances, – in that case, I can for myself and colleagues undertake to act in such a spirit and with such intentions.

The 'Tamworth Manifesto' was Peel's address to the Tamworth electors when he sought re-election in December 1834 following his appointment as Prime Minister. It was novel because of the wide publicity it received. It was significant because its writer was Prime Minister and because it was intended by the Cabinet to be an agreed statement of the new government's position. It was not, however, designed to be the foundation document of a new conservatism.

Source G

The recourse to faction, or temporary alliances with extreme opinions for the purposes of faction, is not reconcilable with Conservative Opposition.

Sir Robert Peel in a memorandum written in 1837.

The significance of Peel's first ministry

Source H

In his first short premiership, Peel emerged from the shadows of the reform crisis as a major national figure, standing at the head of a revived party which, after the 1835 election, was, if the Whigs and Radicals are considered separately, the largest single party in the House of Commons.

R. Stewart, *The Foundations of the Conservative Party, 1830–67*, 1978.

SIR ROBERT PEEL

7 Using your knowledge of the period 1833–35 discuss the validity of these views.

Source I

To a large number of his fellow countrymen he had presented a fresh and welcome political leadership, dissociated from the anti-reform image of old Toryism and yet different from the radical propensities of the new Whiggery ... One thing at least was clear. Peel had emerged as a national leader.

N. Gash, *Sir Robert Peel*, 1972.

The 'Hundred Days' – Peel's ministry 1834–35

When William IV dismissed Melbourne and invited Wellington to form a government the Duke advised the King to send for Peel, then holidaying in Italy. This decision made Peel leader of the Party, forcing him on the Ultras. By the time his government fell in April 1835 Peel had the status of the premiership behind him, had presided over a General Election which pulled the Party together and increased its parliamentary membership by some 90 MPs.

James Grant, a journalist, observed in 1836: 'Never had the leader of a party a more complete ascendancy over that party than has this Tory Coryphaeus over the Conservatives in the House of Commons.'

Through the medium of the Tamworth Manifesto, Peel was able to present his case to a wider public. This document can only be understood in the political context that existed in December 1834. Peel returned to England to find that Wellington had single-handedly been managing the affairs of state. Wellington's name was tainted by his reactionary reputation. Peel was urged by his friends to make some public statement to rid his government of the stain of Wellingtonism with its Ultra connections, and to win over moderate opinion before Parliament was formally dissolved to give the new premier the General Election he had requested from the King.

Peel's Tamworth Manifesto was strong on generalities, but it did make a commitment to moderate reform, and it formalised Peel's acceptance of the Reform Act. It also indicated that the Royal Commission on Municipal

Peel's 'Hundred Days'
demonstrated that the
Reform Act had eroded the
prerogatives of the
monarch. George III had
been able to appoint
William Pitt as Prime
Minister in 1783, who like
Peel had a minority in the
House of Commons, and see
him secure a victory in the
subsequent general election.
Peel knew that things had
changed, even if William IV
did not, and the election of
1835, without the old
sources of influence, still left
him in a minority.

TALKING POINT

Compare this definition of
Conservatism with the
Tamworth Manifesto
(Source F, page 113). What
do they agree on? In what
ways do they differ? What
dangers might there be in
the differences for Peel?

Corporations would be allowed to continue its work, and that Nonconformist grievances would be sympathetically handled, whilst the promise of necessary reforms to 'remove every abuse that can impair the efficiency of the Establishment' offered reassurance to the Ultras. Although the appeal was mainly to the new middle class voters, Peel did not want to abandon the Tory extremists; rather, he wanted them to join him on his own terms.

By setting up the Ecclesiastical Commission to enable the Church of England to reform itself, Peel removed the Church from the arena of political debate and danger. It was the one great success of his short ministry. Although he asked the House for a fair trial, defeat for his minority government was only a matter of time. The Lichfield House Compact, negotiated by Russell, brought Whigs, Radicals and O'Connellites together on the one issue that could unite them – appropriation of Irish Church revenues. Peel could offer no compromise and on 8 April it was all over.

It was a defeat, but the Party had gained a new identity – the term Conservative Party began to be used. In 1836 Sir John Walsh could reply to the question 'What is a Conservative?':

A Conservative is a man attached upon principle to the English Constitution, to the Established Church, to our mixed institutions ... a Conservative is one who, having this loyalty to the Constitution, believes it is threatened with subversion by the encroachments of democracy, and is prepared to defend it against that danger. The Conservative party, therefore, includes all those shades and degrees of political opinion, from the disciple of moderate Whig principles to the most devoted champion of ancient usages, who agree in these two points – attachment to King, Lords, Commons, Church, and State, and a belief that there is a pressing danger of these institutions being overborne by the weight of the Democracy.

Sir J. B. Walsh, *Chapters of Contemporary History*, 1836.

Organisation was the other gain from 1834–35. An ad hoc committee, the 'Charles Street Gang', had been set up in 1831, independent of Peel, to co-ordinate electoral arrangements. The Carlton Club was established as the Party's London headquarters in 1832 and became the centre of activity in preparation for the 1835 election. F. R. Bonham proved indispensable in his co-ordinating and managerial role, and he proposed to Peel that a permanent electoral committee should be established. Bonham became the first full-time electoral agent, although he was unpaid and did not use that title. The complexities of the new registration processes required both central and local management. Bonham's committee found seats for candidates, candidates for constituencies, controlled an electoral fund, and proffered advise and encouragement. The party fielded 390 candidates in 1835, and more than 450 in 1837. In 1841 Graham was able to write to Bonham, 'Thanks to you and your indefatigable industry, no party out of office ever possessed such sources of intelligence and such means for active war.'

Decline and fall – the Whigs 1835–41

Melbourne was able to return on his own terms. The King had to accept Russell as Leader of the House of Commons, and a government now committed to appropriation, however unrealistic that policy might be. Melbourne picked a new Cabinet with only two ministers inherited from Grey. In particular, Brougham, Grey's uncooperative Lord Chancellor was dropped from the government.

The agreement with O'Connell made the Commons easier to manage. To their credit, ministers made every effort to pay O'Connell's price, a more even handed administration in Dublin and a willingness to give Irish legislation a high priority. Even the radicals were quieter, the more moderate being prepared to give ministers a chance whilst the ranks of the more extreme were reduced by the elections of 1835 and 1837. Their greatest difficulties now were with Peel and the reviving Conservatives in the Commons, and with the obstructionist tactics adopted by the Ultras in the House of Lords. The Municipal Corporations Act (1835) only passed because they were able to negotiate a compromise through Peel, and successive Irish measures were lost in the Lords. When the Irish reforms were allowed through in 1838 and 1840 they reflected less what the Whigs wanted than what the Conservatives would allow them to have. Appropriation was quietly forgotten.

Henry Brougham, as an MP, had always been a thorn in the side of the Whig leadership. Too awkward to leave out of the government, but too unpredictable to leave in the Commons, Grey had moved him to the Lords as Lord Chancellor. He had masterminded a considerable reform of the legal system, but remained an unstable element in the Cabinet. Melbourne was glad to be rid of him.

THE ALLIANCE WITH O'CONNELL WAS TURNED AGAINST THE GOVERNMENT BY ITS OPPONENTS, AS IN THIS CARTOON, 'THE GALLEY SLAVES'. O'CONNELL LEADS MELBOURNE, RUSSELL AND OTHER MINISTERS IN CHAINS BEHIND HIM.

Alliance with O'Connell held political dangers. Opponents accused ministers of dancing to the tune of a dangerous Irish radical. Anti-Irish racial antagonisms mixed with religious antipathy into a heady mixture. Who, asked *The Times* in 1837, wrote Victoria's first speech from the throne?

No other than Lord MELBOURNE, the Whig slave of the Radical Joseph Hume, and of the anti-Saxon Papist, O'CONNELL – the same Lord MELBOURNE, who has for these last two years and more been levying open war against, or trickily undermining, the ancient laws, the fundamental institutions, and the Protestant monarchy of Great Britain

Sir Harry Verney, Whig MP for Buckingham, reported in 1836 that 'at the present moment the fault found with government is that they are too much influenced by O'Connell.' After further election losses in 1837, however, ministers were almost totally dependent on O'Connell's continued support for survival.

Russell's skilful management held the government alliance together. Up to 1837 its reform record was impressive, but after the electoral losses of that year ministers lost their way. The Whig governments never had clear policy aims, reacting to needs rather than trying to impose their own views on legislation. This expedient approach became more marked.

Appreciating that survival after the 1837 election demanded some concession to the Radicals, Russell unsuccessfully tried to persuade Melbourne to make concessions on constitutional reform.

Hounded by the Radicals through 1838 and into 1839 because of their Canadian policies (both provinces had been in revolt), ministers, divided on so many issues, were weary and dispirited. When a Radical motion condemning their Jamaican policy won opposition support, and pushed the majority down to five, they took the opportunity and resigned. Within a week they were back. Victoria had resented Peel's reasonable request that some of the Whig ladies in the royal household should be replaced by Conservatives to show her confidence in the incoming ministry. Melbourne knew that Peel was right, if tactless, but he allowed his colleagues to display their gallantry and come to the rescue of their young monarch. Peel gratefully abandoned his attempt to form a government, and the Radicals, frightened by the possible consequences of their opposition, sought a reconciliation with Whig ministers. Melbourne reluctantly gave way to Russell's arguments and the secret ballot was made an open question for ministers. In 1838 about 200 government supporters had voted with George Grote for his secret ballot motion. In 1839 they were joined by 17 members of the government. It was hard to escape the conclusion that ministers were more interested in hanging on to office than in political principles.

Despite a reshuffle to remove some less effective ministers and to enable Russell to tackle the colonial problems, ministers appeared increasingly inept. They had no solution for the economic crisis facing the country and Chartism was sweeping the industrial districts. Melbourne, at best a languid leader, became more distant and remote, and more reluctant to authorise change. The diarist Greville recorded that the government was 'in a wretched state of weakness, utterly ignorant whether it can scramble through the session.' Cabinet ministers despaired. A dissatisfied Lord Howick (he resigned in 1839) wrote that it

MELBOURNE IS AT THE HELM OF 'THE WHIG RADICAL' AS 'THE TIMES' BLOWS IT ONTO THE CLIFFS (STANLEY, PEEL AND WELLINGTON). WHAT POINT IS BEING MADE?

was 'a government of departments some very ill, some moderately administered but of which the various measures have never been animated by one spirit or directed with energy to one common object.'

The free trade budget proposals of 1841 were a last gamble to gain some electoral popularity, and to force Peel onto the defensive by placing the Corn Laws at the centre of political debate. The Whig government was heading for a financial crisis as the economic depression lead to a fall in consumption and a corresponding fall in tax revenue. During Melbourne's term of office no new sources of revenue had been explored and from 1837 each year saw a budget deficit. In 1840 both direct and indirect taxes had been increased. The 1841 budget aimed to boost consumption by reducing import duties, including those on timber and sugar. However, by adding a modification of the Corn Laws, Russell turned a budgetary expedient into an electioneering move.

The 1841 election results would suggest that commitment to a more enlightened commercial policy came too late, and that the electorate remained suspicious of Whig intentions. The aura of ineptitude, failure and compromise which surrounded ministers could not be shaken off by the jaded men in office. The jibe that O'Connell ruled Ireland, Peel ruled England, and that the Whigs were content with office and patronage without power, whilst the opposition had power without office and patronage, rang true.

5.3 The legislative achievement

I feel great satisfaction and pride in the thought that I was so long connected in office with men who,
I sincerely believe, did more to improve our institutions and to promote our prosperity than any who have ever governed this country.

     Memoirs of Lord Campbell, who held junior office during the 1830s.

Study the summary below, and follow up the references. Does the record justify Campbell's claim?

Dealing with Social Issues

1833
Factory Act
• Applied to all cotton, woollen and linen mills
• No child under age of 9 to work in a mill
• Children aged 9 – 13 to work a maximum eight hour day
• Young people, aged 13 – 18 to work a twelve hour day with no night work
• Children under 13 to receive two hours schooling per day
• Factory inspectors to be appointed
First government grant for education – £20,000 to be shared between the education societies.

1834
Poor Law Amendment Act (see Focus on p232)

Local Government Reforms

1835
The Municipal Corporations Act
This Act was a logical consequence of the Reform Act, defining the functions of local authorities and reforming the 178 existing corporations.
• All ratepayers with three years residence could vote in municipal elections.
• Councillors were to serve for three years with one third being re-elected annually.
• Aldermen were to be elected by the councillors, and were to be one third of the council. This was a Conservative amendment.
• New towns could become incorporated - Manchester and Birmingham were among those which took early advantage of this provision.

1839
The Rural Police Act
This act enabled county magistrates to set up local police forces with Home Office approval. The 1835 Municipal Corporations Act had given town councils these powers. Nevertheless, the cost of a police force meant that many rural areas remained unpoliced.

Education

The government was forced to modify its education proposals because of opposition from the Church of England. The annual grant was increased, a Privy Council Committee for Education was to administer it, and inspectors were to supervise inspect grant-aided schools. (Refer to Chapter 10 for the education controversies.)

Church Reform
(see Chapter 10 for the religious context)

1835
Peel's Ecclesiastical Commission of churchmen and ministers began to plan and supervise the process of reform. Whig legislation adopted the recommendations of the Commission.

1836
Tithe Act commuted tithe into a money payment.
The Established Church Act rationalised the size of the dioceses, and created two new ones – Manchester and Ripon. Episcopal incomes were equalised, and the Ecclesiastical Commission made permanent.

1838
The Pluralities Act limited the benefices (parishes) held by a person to two, no more than ten miles apart.

1840
Surplus cathedral posts were abolished. The revenues were to be used to finance new parishes and increase the lowest clergy incomes.

Religious and Civil Equality

1834
Government Bills to remedy the Nonconformists' marriage grievance and to reform church rates were unacceptable to them. A Bill to end religious tests for university entrance was defeated in the Lords.

1836
Charter granted to London University. University College had no religious entrance tests.
Marriage Act – Dissenters could be married in their own chapels.
Registration Act set up a central registry of births, deaths and marriages. This had other purposes – e.g. enforcement of Factory Acts.

1837
Government abandons its attempts to deal with church rates when its majority falls to 5 in the vote on an abolition scheme.

Ireland

1834
Irish Church Reform Act

1835
Ministry begins policy of making the administration of Ireland fairer to all its people. Catholics were made magistrates and appointed to important legal and administrative posts; the Orange Order was suppressed.

1838
After persistent Conservative opposition in the Lords, an acceptable Tithe Act is passed.
New Poor Law extended to Ireland.

1840
Irish Municipal Reform Act extends the reforms of 1835 to Ireland. The Act is less liberal than the English reform – the price paid to get it through the Lords.

Other measures

1833
Abolition of slavery within the British Empire.
Bank Charter Act to regulate the Bank of England.
East India Company Act ends the Company's monopoly of trade with the Far East.
Major legal reforms and a re-organisation of the legal system managed by Brougham, the Lord Chancellor.

1838
Process of emancipation for slaves begun in 1833 speeded up. The previous seven year apprenticeship scheme abandoned in favour of immediate abolition.

1839
Legislation passed to enable the penny post to be launched in 1840.

> We are endeavouring to improve our institutions. We think they have been lax, careless, wasteful, injudicious to an extreme; but the country governed itself, and was blind to its own faults. We are busy in introducing system, method, science, economy, regularity, and discipline.
> Sir John Russell to Edwin Chadwick, August 1836.

The Whigs introduced the system of expert advisers. All the major domestic legislation of the decade was preceded by a Royal Commission – Factory Reform, Poor Law Reform, the Municipal Corporations Act, the Rural Police Act – and the Royal Commission on Children's Employment, whose Report led to the passing of the Mines Act of 1842, began its work under the Whigs. Legislation was now based on carefully collected evidence, however dubious the conclusions drawn from it sometimes were. Meanwhile, the Poor Law, and the Registration and Factory Acts led to the appointment of the first of an army of bureaucrats.

The Whigs and the Nonconformists

UNION CHAPEL HARPURHEY.

R. MOFFAT SMITH ARCH

THE INCREASING CONFIDENCE OF NONCONFORMISTS WAS REFLECTED IN THE ARCHITECTURE OF THEIR CHAPELS.

Some of the religious issues and debates are covered in Chapter 10.

Dissenters were members of the Protestant denominations outside the Church of England – Congregationalists, Baptists, Quakers, Presbyterians, Unitarians, etc. From the mid-nineteenth century, 'Dissenters' became known as 'Nonconformists'.

Nonconformists were one of the groups who expected to gain from the Reform Act and a Whig Government. The Marriage and Registration Acts (1836) removed two of their grievances, but the slowness with which any reform, however moderate, emerged embittered the more militant Nonconformists and turned them against the Whigs.

Source A

A circular from the United Committee to co-ordinate the campaign for the redress of Dissenters' grievances.

That this Committee, although deeply sensible of the importance of other just and reasonable claims upon the Legislature, decidedly recommend, that in all petitions to Parliament prominence should be given, and the chief exertions of the body be directed, to the removal of specific and practical grievances peculiar to Dissenters, and directly affecting religious liberty.

Congregational Magazine, July 1833.

Draw up a list of the 'practical grievances' affecting the Nonconformists.

Source B

A letter written by George Hadfield which appeared in several denominational magazines and newspapers.

It is a matter of deepest regret and surprise, that no steps are taking by the Dissenters in England, at this critical juncture, to assert their principles and claim their just rights, when it is generally understood that his Majesty's ministers, or at least the majority of them, will concede nothing to us which they can possibly avoid, and that they intend to bring forward next session, their plan of Church Reform, the tendency of which will be decidedly unfavourable to our interests, and will consolidate the political power and influence of one dominant sect.

If ... we owed Earl Grey and his colleagues any debt of gratitude, for doing us an act of justice before they took office, in getting the Test Laws repealed, we have now paid it; and it is time to look to our own interests ...

We are required to submit to the domination of a corrupt state church; to be governed by bishops; to see £3,500,000 at the least ... annually expended in the maintenance of a clergy, of whom a vast majority do not preach the gospel; to see the cure of souls bought and sold in open market; to have the Universities closed against us, and all the iniquities of those degraded places continued; to be taxed, tithed, and rated to the support of a system which we abjure; to be compelled to submit to objectionable rites and ceremonies at marriage, baptism, and burial;– in one word, to be left out of the social compact, and degraded ... We have hitherto demanded too little; and, consequently, we have been refused everything worth caring about ... The real points at issue between the Government and us are very few ...

1st. A total disconnection between church and state ...

2nd. The repeal of the Act of Charles II, which enables bishops to sit in the House of Lords.

3rd. The repeal of all laws which grant compulsory powers to raise money for the support of any church whatever.

4th. The reformation of the Universities, the repeal of all religious tests ...

5th. A reformation of all the laws relating to marriage and registration with equal rights in places of public burial.

No Government whatever could long resist any of these just and reasonable requirements, if perseveringly demanded; and it is well known that several members of the present administration would gladly and promptly grant them all.

The Patriot newspaper, 13 November 1833.

Hadfield was a Manchester Congregationalist and solicitor; he led the campaign which ended the collection of church rates in Manchester in 1835; unsuccessfully contested Bradford as a Liberal in 1835 and was MP for Sheffield, 1852–74. During 1833 and 1834 he wrote several letters to Joshua Wilson, a leading London Nonconformist, urging alliance with the Radicals and O'Connell.

Source C

Edward Baines, editor of the *Leeds Mercury* and MP for Leeds, 1834–41, was a Congregationalist. The more militant Nonconformists accused him of damaging their cause by his support of the Whigs throughout the 1830s.

There has never been a Ministry disposed to do a tenth part so much as the present on behalf of the Dissenters; but we certainly expect nothing from Ministers beyond what liberal Churchmen would grant. They are connected to the Church by too many ties, and they will naturally be averse to take anything from the Church, without a strong motive. They will introduce a measure of Church Reform, but it will doubtless be intended to strengthen the Establishment, not to weaken it. Nor are we disposed to call Ministers dishonest, because they differ in opinion from ourselves as to the expediency of Church Establishments.

Leeds Mercury, 16 November 1833.

Source D

George Hadfield to Joshua Wilson, 13 January 1834, to express his 'grief & disappointment' at the recommendation of the United Committee that Dissenters should only petition for the redress of their 'practical grievances'.

[They advise us] to petition for the redress of comparatively trifling grievances, and even to venture so far as to suggest to us to talk about great principles ... yet they enjoin us to take no step whatever to promote them, but to exclude them altogether from the prayer of our petitions! This is to me unaccountable, but Earl Grey was, no doubt very civil to the deputation for 20 minutes together! He was even kind! It is true he would promise us nothing; but he must not be embarrassed until he is strong enough to unite with the lovers of a corrupt Church & set the Dissenters at defiance.

Source E

Nonconformists were divided on the tactics to follow. Government proposals on marriage and church rates were rejected as unsatisfactory. In May 1834 a conference met in London, organised by the United Committee. The Rev. John Angell James attended as the delegate from his congregation in Birmingham. He was approached by one of the United Committee members:

we want a MODERATE MAN from the country to move the resolution we have prepared, and knowing you to be such, it is our wish that you should be entrusted with that business. We go only for a redress of specific grievances, but do not touch the question of separation of Church and State. There are some delegates from Manchester and Nottingham who wish to go further, but we cannot consent to it.

R.W. Dale, *Life and Letters of John Angell James*, 1861.

Source F

The Whig Ministry cannot stand without the Dissenters: the Dissenters have no hopes but from the Whig Ministry.

But, say some . . . warm Dissenters, we have nothing to hope from the Whig Ministry. We ask in reply – what is there to hope from the Tories? If the Whigs are cold and timid, the Tories are hotly and boldly hostile. If the Whigs bring forward half-measures of relief, the Tories will be more likely to propose new measures of restriction ...

We hold, therefore, that the Dissenters have far more to hope from the Whigs than from the Tories. Nay, we maintain that the Dissenters will in time gain everything from the Whigs, except the separation of Church and State. The Whig Ministers have in fact admitted all the principles for which the Dissenters contend; and they have attempted – clumsily and timidly we admit – to give them practical redress. Looking to the past and to the present, we entertain a perfect confidence that the Dissenters will in a short time have all their practical grievances removed, if the present Ministers keep office.

Leeds Mercury, 17 May 1834.

---

1   With reference to source B, and your wider knowledge of the period, explain:
a   'influence of one dominant sect'
b   'Test Laws'
c   'Debt of gratitude' owed to 'Earl Grey and his colleagues'
d   'Church Establishments' (source C).
2   How, according to Hadfield, are the Nonconformists 'degraded' by the existence of an Established Church?
3   Outline the main differences between the proposals of the United Committee (source A) and those recommended by Hadfield (source B).
4   Compare and contrast the arguments, tone and language used by Hadfield in sources B and D with that of Baines in sources C and F.
5   Use all these sources, and your wider knowledge of the period, to comment on the dilemma faced by all the pressure groups after 1832 in their relationship with the Whigs. What alternatives did they have, and which, if any, was the more realistic approach?
6   The 'Church in danger' became a potent Tory election cry. How might these sources contribute to that fear? How was Peel able to remove the Church of England from the realm of political debate?

Peel's problem – leading an opposition

The parliamentary opposition was united by the perceived threat to the Union and protestantism from O'Connell, to the Church of England from Nonconformism, and to the constitution from radicalism. These anxieties were increasingly shared by the electorate. The Whig MP Francis Baring explained his Party's losses in the 1837 election: 'squires and clergy are dead against us, and the county voters are under the sway of the "Church in danger" cry ... the real truth is that the great body of the English people have been, and are, against anything like liberal government in Ireland ... O'Connell and the "Church in danger" have been the cause of our being beaten in England.'

In his public speeches of the late 1830s Peel reminded his audiences that 'With me you ought now to combine for the defence of the existing institutions of the country', and that 'By Conservative principles we mean the rescuing from threatened danger our Protestant establishments.'

The 'Church in danger' remained a potent cry, but after 1837 the danger was receding. The influence of radicalism was rapidly becoming a myth - frightening for the imagination, but with no real power. Peel's conservatism was not, however, about negatives. He talked of 'governing in opposition', and Whig measures often got through only 'by his leave' after suitable amendment.

The House of Lords was frequently as much a problem for Peel and Wellington in opposition as it was for Melbourne. It nearly threw out the Municipal Corporations Act in 1835, and under Lyndhurst's leadership the Ultras mangled Irish legislation which had been carefully framed by Peel to pass through the Commons.

Peel wanted to display moderation, an image of cautious progressivism, and a respect for stability and order which would attract the newly enfranchised voters. His control over the backbenches was not always absolute. Following the 1837 election, with ministers reeling on the ropes and an increased Tory presence in the Commons, there was increasing discontent with Peel's policy of propping up the Whig Government. In 1838 over Canada, and in 1839 over Jamaica, he found himself fending off backbench pressure to support the Radicals' attacks on government policy, and in 1840 he was forced into an unsuccessful 'no confidence' motion. Generally, however, opposition unity held. For the division on the decisive 'no confidence' motion in 1841, carried by a majority of one, no Conservative MP was absent.

Examining the Evidence

The 1841 election

The 1841 election had a constitutional significance as the first time that a government with a majority in the House of Commons was defeated in a General Election and replaced by the winning Party. Queen Victoria had to accept Peel as Prime Minister despite her preference for Melbourne.

Contemporary opinions

Source A

The elections are wonderful, and the curiosity is that all turns on the name of Sir Robert Peel. 'Tis the first time that I remember in our history that the people have chosen the first Minister for the Sovereign ... here every Conservative candidate professed himself in plain words to be Sir Robert Peel's man, and on that ground was elected.

J. W. Croker to Sir Robert Peel, 20 July 1841.

Source B

Until now the world has never known an instance of a party being installed in power expressly by the voice of a great people – not for any pledges or promises which they have given, not for the sake of any particular measure or series of measures which they have advocated, but solely because the nation places confidence in their capacity and disinterestedness, and recognises in them a tone of principle which it feels to be necessary for wise and good government.

The Times, 27 July 1841.

The issues

Source C

If his votes respecting the Church injured him with Churchmen – his votes with an Anti-Corn Law Government must affect him with Electors, whose trade and prosperity depend solely on the Farmers of the neighbourhood or on persons deriving their entire existence from the soil.

The *Bucks Herald* commenting on the withdrawal of Sir Harry Verney, Whig MP for Buckingham, before the nomination.

Source D

Our great force has been Protestantism. We began the reaction with it; every step of success has been founded on it.

Lord Ashley in his diary, 16 March 1841.

Source E

I was elected by an agricultural body, who expected, undoubtedly, that what they called 'Protection', should be maintained.

Lord Ashley in his diary, 23 December 1845.

Source F

The Whigs complain bitterly of the apathy and indifference that have prevailed, and cannot recover from their surprise that their promises of cheap bread and cheap sugar have not proved more attractive. But they do not comprehend the real cause of this apathy. It is true that there has not been any violent Tory reaction, because there have been no great topics on which enthusiasm could fasten, but there has been a revival of Conservative influence, which has been gradually increasing for some time, and together with it a continually decreasing confidence in the Government. They have been getting more unpopular every day with almost all classes, and when they brought forward their Budget the majority of the country, even those who approved of its principles, gave them little or no credit for the measure, and besides doubting whether the advantages it held out were very great or important, believed that their real motives and object were to recover the popularity they had lost, and to make a desperate plunge to maintain themselves in office.

Greville reviewing the election results in his diary, 11 July 1841.

Source G

In many a constituency the gist of the Conservative appeal was simply that Sir Robert could provide more efficient management of the national affairs than Lord Melbourne. The achievement of almost exact parity with the Reformers in the returns from the English boroughs was a remarkable tribute to Peel's moderation and empiricism, as well as to his reputation as an administrator and his supremacy as a parliamentarian.

D. Southgate, *The Passing of the Whigs* (1962).

For details of the elections during this period, please consult the chart on p. 105.

Source H

There was ... little difference between Whigs and Conservatives on a number of issues; but the Whigs always gave the impression of being susceptible to radical pressure ... on the positive side, the Conservative revival was due to efficient party organisation ... and, of course, to the leadership and policy of Peel, with its assurance of government which would be strong, orderly and anti-radical, but not reactionary. It was an assurance which contrasted very favourably with the impression given by the Whigs of drift and indecision, and one which seemed to have peculiar merits at a time when the economic crisis of the late thirties was engendering social discontent and the threat of disorder.

G. Finlayson, *England in the Eighteen Thirties* (1969).

Source I

He [Peel] addressed himself repeatedly to the professional, mercantile and industrial middle classes. He sought to convince them that, supporters of the Reform Act though they might have been, their duty was now to combine with the Conservative party in maintaining peace, order and the prosperous evolution of society; and that in turn the Conservative party stood for the defence not merely of the landed aristocracy but of the interests of the solid middle classes of early-Victorian Britain ... The electoral successes in the urban constituencies which, added to the more predictable victories in the counties, provided the majority of 1841, were a practical reward for all that he had worked for in the previous decade.

N. Gash, 'Wellington and Peel, 1832–1846' in *The Conservative Leadership, 1832–1932*, edited by D. Southgate (1974).

Source J

The electoral power of his name and reputation ... has been exaggerated. It is almost beyond question that the two great issues which swayed Conservative voters in 1841 were the defence of agricultural protection against the Whigs' readiness to tamper with the corn laws and the defence of the Church against the designs of the Dissenters and the Irish Roman Catholics.

R. Stewart, *Party and Politics, 1830–1852* (1989).

TALKING POINT

General elections are lost more often than they are won. Discuss the 1841 election with this comment in mind.

1 What, according to sources A and B, was the significance of the 1841 election?

2 Comment on the reasons for Conservative success and Whig defeat suggested in sources C, D, E, and F.

3 After a visit to Blackburn in 1834 Peel remarked that 'The professional men and chief shopkeepers were Conservative.' Use the electoral statistics provided to analyse the results. Is there any evidence that Peel's Conservative Party was making substantial gains in urban areas, or in the industrial towns?

4 Referring to all the sources, discuss the view that the 1841 election was a victory for old-fashioned protectionist Toryism rather than for Peelite Conservatism.

5 'The election of 1841 was a striking vindication of Peel's policy.' (R. Blake, The Conservative Party from Peel to Churchill (1970).)

'Sir Robert Peel and the Conservative party, 1832–1841: A Study in Failure?' (Title of an article by I. Newbould in English Historical Review, 1983).

Referring to the sources, and to your wider knowledge of the decade and Peel's purposes, how can each of these contrasting opinions be justified, and challenged?

REVIEW

A minister's explanation

Lord Campbell's assessment of the Whigs in government, 1833–41, and their defeat in 1841, emphasised their weaknesses and difficulties, rather than Peel's achievements.

I begin with the extravagant expectations which the masses fostered of the benefits to be derived from the Reform Bill ... Deep disappointment was felt, much discontent was created ... The Reform Bill was blamed, and its framers fell in public estimation more serious mischief arose from the absurd conduct of the ultra-Radicals in the House of Commons ... still aiming at what was impracticable or mischievous – they would not give the Reform Bill any fair chance of retaining popularity ...The people ... were thus taught to believe that very little had been done for them, and ... Ministers in the House of Commons had the invidious task cast upon them of resisting popular measures ... one section of their former supporters deserted them from fear of further innovation, and another because the Whigs were charged with having ceased to be reformers. A serious detriment to them likewise arose from Sir Robert Peel's moderation, and his giving a new name to his party ... they had not any grand principle of action, they wavered between the two extremes of their supporters, by turns disgusting both ...

[Lord Melbourne] displayed too great a disposition to cultivate the Duke of Wellington. His own inclinations were in favour of Conservative principles ... A more fatal fault was our Premier's listlessness ...

I will only add to the causes of our downfall the delay and reluctance with which popular measures were brought forward – such as the uniform Penny Post and Free Trade in Corn – which caused serious doubts as to the sincerity of Ministers, and gave rise to the noted saying that they were of 'squeezable materials.'

Life of John, Lord Campbell, edited by Mrs Hardcastle (1881).

1 Explain Campbell's references to the Radicals, with examples, and his description of ministers as being made of 'squeezable materials'.

2 Show how Campbell's language reflects his prejudices, and reinforces his argument.

3 Campbell believed that the Whigs ran a constructive reforming ministry with many achievements to its credit. To what extent did these 'achievements' (Poor Law reform, Church reform, Irish policies etc.) in fact contribute to their decline in popularity?

4 **Essay** Why did the Whigs fail to retain, in the period 1833–1841, the dominant political position with which they had emerged from the Reform Act crisis?

6 Peel's Prime – Ireland, Corn and the Collapse of the Conservative Party, 1841–50

Preview

Peel's reputation

Source A

THE MAN WOT PLAYS SEVERAL INSTRUMENTS
AT ONCE.

PUNCH'S VIEW OF PEEL IN 1845; RUSSELL GAWPS IN AMAZEMENT AT HIS VIRTUOSITY.

Source B

I will not speak of the populace, which to a man is with you; but of the active and intelligent middle classes, with whom you have engrossed a sympathy and interest greater than ever before possessed by a minister ... the whole interest centres in yourself. You represent the IDEA of the age, and it has no other representative amongst statesmen.

Richard Cobden to Sir Robert Peel, 23 June 1846.

Discuss the impressions these sources give of Peel, the Prime Minister. To what extent do they confirm opinions expressed in the 1830s; to what extent do you find them surprising?

6.1 'A real working government' – Peel's second ministry (1841–45)

The best man of business who was ever Prime Minister

Gladstone on Peel.

I defy the Minister of this country to perform properly the duties of his office – to read all that he ought to read, including the whole foreign correspondence; to keep up the constant communication with the Queen, and the Prince; to see all whom he ought to see; to superintend the grant of honours and the disposal of civil and ecclesiastical patronage; to write with his own hand to every person of note who chooses to write to him; to be prepared for every debate, including the most trumpery concerns; and to do all these indispensable things, and also to sit in the House of Commons eight hours a day for 118 days.

Sir Robert Peel to Charles Arbuthnot, 14 August 1845.

Compare Peel's assessment of the Prime Minister's role with that of Melbourne (see page 106).

Problems to be solved, not evaded

1 Financial
The Whigs had failed to balance the budget, having 'burned the candle at both ends, increasing expenditure and diminishing revenue.' (Peel to J.W. Croker, 21 February 1842).

2 The 'condition of England' question
This was highlighted by Chartist agitation (see chapter 7) and Anti-Corn Law League propaganda (see chapter 8).
Something effectual must be done to revive, and revive permanently, the languishing commerce and ... manufacturing industry of this country.
Sir Robert Peel to J.W. Croker, 27 July 1842.

Without improvement we are on the brink of a convulsion ... We must make this country a cheap country for living.
Sir Robert Peel to J.W. Croker, 3 August 1842.

3 Ireland
O'Connell's repeal campaign peaked in 1843.
What we must aim at ... is to reconcile ... the Roman Catholics ... to two great principles, the maintenance of the Union, and the maintenance of the Church Establishment. Every concession we can make consistent with these principles must be made, sooner or later.
Sir Robert Peel, memorandum to the Cabinet, 17 February 1844.

The Cabinet

It was a talented team containing three future Prime Ministers (Lord Stanley (who became Lord Derby), Lord Aberdeen and Gladstone). Peel tried to ensure that all elements in the Party were represented at the highest level – the old Tories (Lord Lyndhurst, Lord Wharncliffe, the Duke of Wellington), Peel's contemporaries (Henry Goulburn, Lord Aberdeen), the Stanleyites (Sir James Graham, Lord Stanley, Lord Ripon) and the agriculturalists (Duke of Buckingham , Sir Edward Knatchbull). Goulburn, as Chancellor of the Exchequer, was a self effacing figure who allowed Peel to dominate. The Prime Minister himself presented the innovatory budgets of 1842 and 1845. Graham, as Home Secretary, was the ideal number two for Peel – they were described in Punch as 'two persons with only one intellect '. Buckingham resigned in 1842 and Knatchbull in 1845, but Stanley, who let the Cabinet in 1845, was the only significant figure to desert Peel.

Gladstone entered the Cabinet as President of the Board of Trade in 1843, where he had been Vice-President since 1841.

Budgetary policy

Aims

- To stabilise government finances.
- To reduce cost of living, increase employment and remove discontent by stimulating trade and prosperity.

Means

- End government dependence on indirect taxation by re-introducing the income tax, a policy discussed by the Liverpool Cabinet in the 1820s.
- Reduce import duties to encourage industry and consumption.

The Budgets

1842

- Modification of the Corn Laws and the sliding scale to secure more stable prices.
- Income tax introduced as a temporary measure for three years; 7d in the £ on income above £150 a year.
- Income tax was linked to a drastic policy of tariff reductions on imported raw materials, semi-manufactured articles and foreign manufactured goods. Duties on 750 other commodities (including timber, cattle and coffee) were also cut.

1844

- Duties abolished on raw wool and reduced on coffee and sugar.

1845

- The budget 'was a series of exceptionally well-matured measures' (N. Gash, *Sir Robert Peel* (1972)) founded on the success of the 1842 measures.
- Income tax renewed for a further three years despite a £5 million surplus.
- All export duties, and over 400 import duties, were abolished. The duty on raw cotton was among those to go. Excise duties were modified and the sugar duties re-organised.

Social policy

Social concerns could not be neglected. Chartism focused attention on them, and the Poor Law had been an election issue in the North.

- Poor Law renewed, 1842.
- Ashley felt betrayed by a government which accepted colliery owners' amendments to his Mines Bill. The Act outlawed underground work for women, girls, and boys under 10 (rather than Ashley's original proposal of 13).
- Graham's Factory Bill (1843) attempted to regulate hours of work for children, and to provide them with schooling. The Bill was dropped following Nonconformist opposition to the leading role given to Anglican clergy in the proposed schools.
- The 1844 Factory Act gave young children a 6½ hour working day. Women and 13–18 year-olds were restricted to 12 hours.
- Both Peel and Graham accepted orthodox political economy and sympathised with the mill owners' case. Peel believed that prosperity was the best way to remove social problems, not legislation.

Business confidence and regulation

- The Bank Charter Act (1844) aimed to increase confidence in the banking system by giving the Bank of England greater control over bank note issue. The Bank was split into two departments, one for note issue the other for normal banking functions. Note issue was limited to a total of £14 million in circulation, unless backed by gold bullion.

- The Companies Act (1844) set out to regulate and control 'reckless speculation'. Companies had to be registered, publish prospectuses and issue regular balance sheets.

- The Railways Act (1844) increased government powers of regulation and inspection and protected the interests of poorer travellers

Ireland (See pages 138–147)

For Peel there could be no concession to O'Connell's National Repeal Association, but he also felt that 'mere force ... will do nothing as a permanent remedy for the social evils of that country.' (Peel to Graham, 1843).

> Perhaps Peel's greatest claim to fame is that, alone of the Conservative leaders ... he made a serious effort to deal with the Irish question.
>
> R. Blake, *The Conservative Party from Peel to Churchill* (1970).

- Positive discrimination in making appointments in the Irish administration to benefit Catholics.

- Devon Commission, 1843, set up to examine the land question.

- Charitable Bequests Act, 1844.

- Increase in the grant to Maynooth College, 1845.

- Irish Colleges Act, 1845.

TALKING POINT

Discuss the appropriateness of Greville's description of the ministry as 'a real working government'. It was written in 1841.

EXAMINING THE EVIDENCE
Sir Robert Peel – A Flawed Personality?

Source A

The Cabinet dined with me at Roehampton. I asked Peel to drink a glass of wine with me, and showed him two or three pictures. I really believe he is only rather a proud, touchy man, and that the least attempt at management would make him very cordial.

Lord Ellenborough, *A Political Diary 1828–1830*, 1881.

Source B

15 March 1830

He asks immense parties of the H. of Commons to dinner every week & treats them so *de haut en bas* & is so haughty & silent that they come away swearing they will never go to his house again, so that his civilities do him more harm rather than otherwise.

The Journal of Mrs Arbuthnot.

Source C

Lady de Grey's advice to Peel on the eve of his audience with Victoria, 7 May 1839.

I wish you success from my friendship for you, from my high esteem and admiration of your noble character, and from the belief that you alone can avert the evils which threaten my country; and I fear that even with such qualities you may not succeed in gaining the Queen's confidence, as I think your bearing too reserved and too cautious.

Source D

Sir Robert Peel had a bad manner of which he was sensible; he was by nature very shy, but forced early in life into eminent positions, he had formed an artificial manner, haughtily stiff or exuberantly bland, of which, generally speaking, he could not divest himself. There were, however, occasions when he did succeed in this, and on these, usually when he was alone with an individual whom he wished to please, his manner was not only unaffectedly cordial, but he could even charm

Benjamin Disraeli, *Lord George Bentinck*, 1852.

Source E

His great merit consists in his judgement, tact, and discretion, his facility, promptitude, thorough knowledge of the assembly he addresses, familiarity with the details of every sort of Parliamentary business, and the great command he has over himself. He never was a great favourite of mine, but I am satisfied that he is the fittest man to be Minister, and I therefore wish to see him return to power.

The Greville Memoirs, 22 February 1834.

Peel on premiership and party leadership

Source F

I feel a want of many essential qualifications which are requisite in party leaders; among the rest, personal gratification in the game of politics and patience to listen to the sentiments of individuals whom it is equally imprudent to neglect and an intolerable bore to consult.

Sir Robert Peel from his *Private Papers*, edited by C.S. Parker, 1899.

1 How far do these witnesses agree about Peel's defects, and their probable origin?
2 Using the evidence of these sources suggest why Peel would have found party leadership difficult.
3 In what ways does Greville help us to understand Peel's rise to pre-eminence despite his aloof and distant manner?

Source G

If I exercise power, it shall be upon my conception – perhaps imperfect – perhaps mistaken – but my sincere conception of public duty. That power I will not hold, unless I can hold it consistently with the maintenance of my own opinions – and that power I will relinquish the moment I am satisfied I am not supported in the maintenance of them by the confidence of this House and the people of this country.

Sir Robert Peel, House of Commons, August 1841.

Source H

Is it likely that I would go through the labour which is daily imposed upon me, if I could not claim for myself the liberty of proposing to Parliament those measures which I believe conducive to the public weal? ... no consideration of mere political support shall induce me to hold such an office ... by a servile tenure, which would compel me to be the instrument of carrying other men's opinions into effect.

Sir Robert Peel, House of Commons, September 1841.

Source I

Peel writing after his fall from power.

To incur the deepest responsibility, to bear the heaviest toil, to reconcile colleagues with conflicting opinions to a common course of action, to keep together in harmony the Sovereign, the Lords and the Commons; to have to do these things, and to be at the same time the tool of a party – that is to say to adopt the opinions of men who have not access to your knowledge, and would not profit by it if they had, who spend their time in eating and drinking, and hunting, shooting, gambling, horse-racing, and so forth – would be an odious servitude, to which I never will submit. I will take care ... not again to burn my fingers by organising a party. There is too much truth in the saying, 'The head of a party must be directed by the tail.'

Sir Robert Peel to Lord Hardinge, 24 September 1846.

A model for the future

Source J

He is my leader still, though invisible. I never take a step in public life without reflecting, how would he have thought it.

The Duke of Newcastle to Lady Peel, 29 December 1851.

Source K

... as I was inspired with the thought of treading, however unequally, in the ways of my great teacher and master in public affairs, so it was one of my keenest anxieties not to do dishonour to his memory, or injustice to the patriotic policy with which his name is for ever associated.

W.E. Gladstone to Lady Peel, 20 April 1853, after introducing his first budget.

4 In what ways do these sources reinforce the impressions given by Peel's contemporaries?

5 What can be learnt from these sources of Peel's understanding of the Prime Minister's role?

6 How could these sources be used to support the view that Peel was a good Prime Minister but a bad party leader?

7 Comment on the opinions expressed here, and the implied contradictions with sources A, B, C and D.

8 Referring to all the sources, comment on their value as explanations for the problems that beset Peel in the 1840s as leader of the Conservative Party.

The strains of office – Peel and the Conservative Party, 1841–44

Praising Peel's 1842 Budget, Greville observed:

> ... it is really remarkable to see the attitude Peel has taken in this Parliament, his complete mastery over both his friends and foes. His own party . . . have surrendered at discretion, and he has got them as well disciplined and as obedient as the crew of a man-of-war.
>
> *The Greville Memoirs*, 13 March 1842.

The premiership offered Peel the opportunity to safeguard both the Church of England and the influence of the landed gentry and aristocracy in government from the threats of Chartism and the Anti-Corn Law League. He aimed to remove the strains within society that created the discontent on which protest thrived. His budget measures in 1842 were a direct response to the 'condition of England' question. The bold innovation of income tax solved pressing financial difficulties inherited from the Whigs, whilst reducing the burden of indirect taxation which fell most heavily on the poor. Changes in tariffs were designed to stimulate economic growth, prosperity and employment. Modification of the Corn Laws was to stabilise both supply and prices. When Peel extended his policies in the 1845 budget, a substantial surplus, an improving economic climate and calm in the industrial districts proved their success.

There were, however, underlying tensions within the Conservative Party which had never been resolved. Many of Peel's backbenchers held a very different view of the role of government, and did not feel that his policies were 'Conservative' at all. Thus Disraeli's ringing charge in 1845 that 'a Conservative government is an organised hypocrisy' was greeted with thunderous applause from both sides of the House.

Victory in 1841 was, for many ordinary Conservative MPs, a guarantee that the Church and agriculture were safe from any challenge, and that the radical threat had been averted. They viewed their leader's apparent departure from their negative and defensive understanding of Conservative principles with some disquiet.

Although the Duke of Buckingham resigned from the Cabinet in protest at Peel's modification of the Corn Laws, the vast majority of Conservative backbenchers accepted the change. Responding to constituency pressure, more voted against the removal of restrictions on the import of cattle, part of the tariff reform proposals. The following year there were mutterings against Stanley's plan to lower the duty on imported Canadian corn, but reviving prosperity stilled the doubts the agriculturalists might have felt.

Buckingham was not a significant political figure, but Peel had included him in the Cabinet as a representative of the agricultural interest.

As the 1843 session came to an end, Ashley recorded that Peel had 'committed great and grievous mistakes in omitting to call his friends together to state his desires & rouse their zeal.' Bankbenchers resented the expectation that they would be 'followers in drill'. These feelings were exacerbated during the 1844 session with its controversies over factory reform and alteration of the sugar duties.

Sugar from the British West Indies, grown by free labourers, paid a lower duty than slave-grown sugar. An equalisation of duties would, it was argued, put British producers, with higher costs, at a disadvantage.

Ashley's Ten Hour amendment to Graham's Factory Bill won the support of enough Conservative MPs, hostile to the Anti-Corn Law League and manufacturers, for it to be carried against ministers by 179 – 170. However, confronted with Peel's threat of resignation, Conservative backbenchers dutifully trooped through the division lobby to reverse their vote. This pattern was repeated over proposals to reduce sugar duties. This roused the latent fears of agriculturalists, the ire of the West Indian sugar interest, and the arguments over slavery. A hostile amendment wrecked the government Bill. Once more Peel cracked the whip, warned of the consequences at a party meeting, and saw the vote rescinded.

Peel's government was never in any serious danger. The Whig alternative was totally unacceptable to Peel's critics, who in any case lacked an effective and commanding leader. At issue were conflicting views of the role of the Party. Whilst Ashley and Disraeli argued that Ministers should recognise and not betray the opinions of their supporters, Peel was adamant that the 'tail' should not direct the 'head'. MPs might assert their right to independence of judgement, but 'a Conservative Government should be supported by a Conservative party' (Peel to Wellington, 21 June 1846). Independent voting was incompatible with this. Both Peel and Graham saw party discipline as the means of getting government measures through parliament, and they expected MPs to defer to the greater knowledge and appreciation of national needs which office, and its access to information, gave.

Peel could welcome resignation in December 1845 (during the Corn Law crisis) because it allowed him to escape from these quarrels:

> For myself ... I heartily rejoice at being released from the thankless and dangerous post of having the responsibility of conducting public affairs, and being expected to conform not to my own sense of the public necessities, but to party doctrines, to be blindly followed, whatever new circumstances may arise, or whatever the information which a government may receive.
>
> Sir Robert Peel to Sir Thomas Fremantle, 19 December 1845.

TALKING POINT

Comment on the apparent inconsistency in Peel's view, that sets him above party constraints, but imposes party discipline on everybody else.

TALKING POINT

'It was the fate of the great Conservative party of 1841 ... that the problems it had to face when it came to power, were not the problems it had been created to solve.' (Norman Gash)
Discuss the validity of this statement, comparing the pre-1841 Party and its objectives with the changed situation after 1841.

Peel and Ireland – the challenge of O'Connell

See chapter 3 for O'Connell and Catholic emancipation, and chapter 5 for his relationship with the Whigs.

When the first reformed parliament assembled it was estimated that O'Connell's Party numbered 39 MPs, and that he could expect support from half of the 36 Whig / Liberal Irish members and co-operation from the Radicals. Tories viewed O'Connell as a formidable opponent likely to attack both the Union and, through the Church of Ireland, the Protestant ascendancy. Whig attitudes were more ambivalent. Whilst recognising a debt owed to him for his support during the reform crisis, Grey and Lord Stanley, the Irish Chief Secretary, were reluctant to make reforms that would undermine the Church of Ireland or appear to be concessions to violence. Grey's distrust of the Irish leader made co-operation unlikely.

Grey's resignation and the dismissal of the Melbourne government by William IV changed the situation. O'Connell expected nothing for Ireland from a Peel ministry and welcomed the opportunity to work with the Whigs and Radicals in the Lichfield House Compact to overthrow the Conservative administration. O'Connell had made this alliance possible in 1834 when he was able to persuade his Party that immediate repeal of the Act of Union was an unrealistic aim, and should be dropped. The Whigs would not have worked with a party that retained repeal as its main aim.

Neither side had made any specific commitments but O'Connell viewed it as 'an alliance on honourable terms for mutual co-operation.' Irish votes were helpful to the government after 1835, and enabled it to survive the difficult parliamentary situation after 1837. To maintain this support, the Whigs were expected to deliver a programme of Irish reform acceptable to O'Connell. As an alternative to repeal, he sought equality in legislation. He had sacrificed some freedom of manoeuvre, but if the Union failed to deliver justice and fairness for Ireland the repeal campaign could be re-activated.

The results of this strategy were not totally satisfactory to O'Connell. Both the Tithe and the Municipal Corporations Bills were passed after long struggles with the House of Lords, and neither met O'Connell's requirements. The Irish wanted total abolition of tithe payments, but the 1838 Act converted it instead into a rent charge paid by the landlord. Appropriation had to be abandoned. O'Connell expected a local government measure modelled on the 1835 Municipal Corporations Act to place the boroughs 'under popular control', but the 1840 Act was a victory for the right wing of the Conservative Party in the Lords. The extension of the Poor Law to Ireland (1838) was opposed by O'Connell against all-party support in the Commons. 'Ireland', he told the House, 'is too poor for a Poor Law.'

Alliance with the Whigs had 'required great sacrifices of opinion and consistency ... Political compromise was the inevitable consequence of alliance with an English Government' (A. MacIntyre, *The Liberator – Daniel O'Connell and the Irish Party 1830–1847* (1965)). Legislation was disappointing because the Whigs were unwilling to take up the challenge from the Lords. O'Connell had not acquired any real influence on policy, but he had gained access to patronage and appointments in Ireland. Whig Lord Lieutenants and Chief Secretaries removed the worst Orangemen from the magistracy and took positive steps to promote Catholics. Thus the administration became fairer and more even-handed.

The renewal of the repeal agitation

The success of Peel in the 1841 General Election, the decimation of O'Connell's own following, and Whig ineffectiveness in opposition persuaded O'Connell that it was time to launch once again the mass agitation for repeal of the Act of Union. His personal antipathy towards Peel convinced him that a Conservative government would do nothing willingly for Ireland. The Repeal Association revived the organisational methods of the Catholic Association but it was 1843 before the agitation became formidable. During 1842 Parliament and the government were preoccupied with the 'condition of England' question; and Peel dismissed repeal as a 'failing concern'. O'Connell, however, dubbed 1843 'Repeal Year'. The Association won the support of the Catholic clergy, the Catholic middle class and the peasantry. As huge repeal meetings followed one another in all parts of Ireland support grew. The government had to act.

If O'Connell believed that he could repeat his triumph of 1829 he was badly mistaken. Speaking in the Commons in May 1843, Peel made it clear that the Union was not negotiable: 'Deprecating as I do all war, but, above all, civil war, yet there is no alternative which I do not think preferable to the dismemberment of this empire.' English opinion, both in the country and in the Commons, divided in 1829, was now united on this issue.

The government did not suppress the Repeal Association, although a coercion measure was passed in 1843. Ministers played for time. A meeting at Clontarf, site of a great Irish victory over the Danes, was planned for October to be the climax of O'Connell's campaign. When the authorities finally acted and banned it, the 'Liberator' accepted the decision and advised his followers to stay away. His power began to ebb away despite his arrest, conviction on a conspiracy change and subsequent release on appeal to the Law Lords in 1844.

PUNCH'S PENCILLINGS.___Nº· LXI.

THE "REPEAL FARCE;"
OR, MOTHER GOOSE AND THE GOLDEN EGGS.

Perhaps the banning of Clontarf had saved him from the embarrassment of failure when Repeal Year did not succeed, but he was now an old man and imprisonment hastened his physical decline. Instead of repeal he now talked of federalism. The new men of Irish nationalism, Young Ireland, finally split from the repeal movement in 1846, rejecting O'Connell's constitutional approach, arguing that armed force would have to be used as a last resort.

WHAT IS THE ENGLISH OPINION ON REPEAL?

FOCUS

6.2 The achievement of Daniel O'Connell

O'Connell was a dominant figure in the politics of Britain and Ireland for twenty years. Catholic emancipation was unquestionably his triumph, but there is more room for debate about his achievements after 1830. He was never a revolutionary, and believed in maintaining the status quo. O'Connell did not favour Chartism in England, and did much to prevent Irish participation in that movement, but he could offer no solutions for Ireland's pressing social and economic problems. Instead he unrealistically held up repeal of the Union as a panacea. He did, however, point Irish nationalism down the path of constitutional action and, by his actions in and out of Parliament, made it impossible for English politicians to ignore the Irish question.

> **TALKING POINT**
>
> Review O'Connell's career and consider the view that 'O'Connell's best work for Ireland was done before 1830' (Sir Llewellyn Woodward). Refer to the evidence in the Focus and your wider knowledge of his activities.

HOSTILE CONTEMPORARY WITNESSES

Source A

John Mitchel, a member of Young Ireland, acknowledged O'Connell as a great popular leader but saw that he was not a republican.

He led them, as I believe, all wrong for forty years. He was a lawyer; and never could come to the point of denying and defying British law. He was a Catholic, sincere and devout; and would not see that the Church had ever been the enemy of Irish Freedom. He was an aristocrat, by position and by taste; and the name of a Republic was odious to him.

John Mitchel, Jail Journal.

Source B

Up to the conquest of Catholic Emancipation his was certainly a great and glorious career. What he might have done and what he ought to have done after that, it is not easy to say, but undoubtedly he did far more mischief than good, and exhibited anything but a wise, generous, and patriotic spirit. In Peel's Administration he did nothing but mischief, and it is difficult to comprehend with what object and what hope he threw Ireland into confusion, and got up that Repeal agitation, the folly and impracticability of which nobody must have known so well as himself.

Charles Greville, The Greville Memoirs, 7 June 1847.

Source C

The untruthfulness of O'Connell must be regarded as a constitutional attribute in O'Connell two sets of characteristics were united ... He was genuinely impetuous, ardent, open-hearted, patriotic, and devoted; and then again, he was genuinely cautious and astute; calculating, sly, untruthful; grasping, selfish, and hypocritical. He was profuse, and he was sordid; he was rash, and he was unfathomably politic; now he was flowing out, and now he was circumventing. Among all his charges, however, he never was brave, he never was reliable or accurate; and he never kept his eye off the money-boxes which supplied his annual income from the scrapings of the earnings of the poor.

Harriet Martineau, History of the Thirty Years Peace 1816–1846, 1848.

> **TALKING POINT**
>
> An Irish revolutionary and two English observers with liberal views – how reliable and useful are these opinions of O'Connell and his achievements?

The Historians

Source D

The age of O'Connell witnessed a series of important reforms in Ireland, undertaken by Government partly in obedience to current ideas about economics and society but also, in a more tangible and immediate fashion, in response to the presence and activity of the O'Connellite party in Parliament.

Whatever the final judgement on O'Connell's party, there can be no doubt of its success as a political pressure group. From the conclusion in 1832 of the struggle for Parliamentary Reform until the effective rise of Chartism and the Anti-Corn Law League in the early 1840s, the Irish question formed a central theme of British politics.

A. MacIntyre, *The Liberator – Daniel O'Connell and the Irish Party 1830–1847*, 1965.

Source F

It was his earlier pressure which had forced Peel and his Cabinet, at last, onto the path of concession in Ireland; and, once committed to that path, they saw the breaking of O'Connell's power as the necessary preliminary to a course of Irish reform. The fact that it was a Tory and not a Whig administration which intended to yield ground should not blind us ... to the essential fact that it was a British government which would yield, in the face of Irish agitation. O'Connell himself had repeatedly, if partly rhetorically, begged to be put out of business – the business of Repeal – by being outbid by 'Justice for Ireland'. Up to a point, this was precisely Peel's intention – to undercut O'Connell's movement by concessions.

O. MacDonagh, *The Emancipist – Daniel O'Connell 1830–1847*, 1989.

Source E

O'Connell, with remarkable political genius, contrived a marriage of convenience between religion and national politics ... He welded an effective and enduring alliance between nationalism and Catholicism in Ireland ... O'Connell enlisted the power of Irish Catholicism to reformist political objectives.

P. O'Farrell, *Ireland's English Question*, 1971.

Source G

His part in the later campaigns for Catholic emancipation had both promoted him to a sort of a national leadership and cleared away what was, in many ways, a great cross-issue obstructing the path of reform. His entry into parliament in 1830 transformed his situation and both enabled and induced him to develop an entirely new grammar of pressure politics ... Well before he shifted his focus from Westminster again, he had established his domination in Catholic Ireland by persuading or compelling his political rivals, the trade unions, the priests, the Catholic bourgeoisie, and the rural masses to support him ... throughout his parliamentary manoeuvres. In short, he had turned Catholic Ireland into something like a gigantic political party, which, of course, the leader had to tend and listen to, but which in the last resort he could count on to back him, even blindly.

O. MacDonagh in *A New History of Ireland*, volume 5, edited by W. E. Vaughan, 1989.

Examining the Evidence

Peel's response to the Irish challenge

Peel's experience of Irish affairs exceeded that of any other nineteenth century politician. As Chief Secretary for Ireland (1812–18) his defence of the rights of the Church of Ireland and the vigour with which he dealt with the perennial problem of lawlessness earned him the nickname 'Orange Peel'. As the Home Secretary (1821–27, 1828–30) who had to deal with the crisis created by O'Connell and the Catholic Association he had not shirked his responsibilities. In 1843 O'Connell's forceful revival of the repeal movement once again focused attention on Ireland. The collapse of that campaign gave Peel the opportunity to persuade Parliament and the public of the need for more radical measures.

Source A

REPEAL MEETING AT TARA.

THE MASS REPEAL MEETING AT TARA, BELIEVED TO BE THE SEAT OF THE ANCIENT HIGH KINGS OF ALL IRELAND. MYTHOLOGY, LEGEND AND THE CREATION OF AN IRISH HISTORY ALL PLAYED A PART IN THE REPEAL MOVEMENT.

Source B

Matters are looking so serious, that delay or temporising will be ruin ... Many motives are at work to swell the Repeal party. Many are beginning to say 'We feel assured it will be granted, like the Catholic claim, and we may as well go with the stream, and profit by it.'

The Roman Catholic hierarchy support Repeal. Dr. McHale remits subscriptions from nearly every priest in his diocese. America gives increased support to it. This can only be with *separation* in view. The corporations, following the example of Dublin, have nearly all declared

Dr McHale was the Catholic Archbishop of Tuam.

Earl de Grey was the Lord Lieutenant. He took the Protestant side, and was at odds with his Chief Secretary, the more liberal Lord Eliot.

for it ... All Ireland is organised by 'Repeal Wardens', sent down, appointed, and paid, by the head Association.

Till within these few weeks only one or two magistrates, exclusive of O'Connell and his family, had joined the ranks. The numbers are daily on the increase.

The money now raised is very considerable. From weekly sums under £60 it has risen to near £700.

The meetings are enormous, and most formidable. Their numbers are grossly exaggerated but when O'Connell states that he has been addressing 70,000; 80,000; 120,000; more; the world believes him.

Earl de Grey to Sir Robert Peel, 6 May 1843.

---

1 Explain the following phrases from de Grey's letter: 'we feel assured it will be granted, like the Catholic claim', and 'with separation in view'.
2 How does de Grey convey his alarm and anxiety to Peel?

Source C

We must look out for respectable Roman Catholics for office. There are many grounds for not rigidly acting in Ireland on that specious principle that, if Protestants are better qualified for appointments that fall vacant, Protestants ought to be preferred to Catholics.

Sir Robert Peel to Sir James Graham, Home Secretary, 16 June 1843.

Source D

We cannot abandon the Protestant Church in Ireland ... We cannot give to the Roman Catholics an Establishment, and we must not yield to their threats or open violence. But no opportunity should be omitted of winning them to the State, of softening their resentment, of improving their education, of reconciling their clergy, of admitting them to a share of patronage, and of giving them full scope to the Act of Emancipation, of which we have incurred the dangers and have failed to reap the promised fruit.

Sir James Graham to Sir Robert Peel, 18 June 1843.

Source E

Without an adequate provision for the clergy of the national church, a conciliatory policy would be incomplete and ineffectual. In my own conscience I feel no objection, while the Protestant Church is maintained in Ireland, to a grant, even on a liberal scale, to the Roman Catholic hierarchy and to the parochial priesthood. But I foresee that on the part of the British public in their present temper invincible repugnance will be felt to any such proposal.

Sir James Graham to Sir Robert Peel, 20 October 1843.

Source F

MAYNOOTH COLLEGE FOR THE TRAINING OF CATHOLIC PRIESTS IN IRELAND, FOUNDED IN 1795, RECEIVED AN ANNUAL GRANT OF £8,000 FROM THE STATE, BUT THERE WAS NO INSPECTION OR CONTROL. PRIESTS TRAINED AT MAYNOOTH WERE ALLEGED TO BE POORLY EDUCATED MEN WHO USED THEIR INFLUENCE OVER THE PEASANTRY TO ENCOURAGE SUPPORT FOR O'CONNELL AND THE REPEAL MOVEMENT.

Source G

11 February 1844

Each year we grant a sum of money for the education of the priesthood. It is insufficient for its purpose, and the practical result seems anything but favourable ... The style of living, the habits engendered at the College ... all combine to send forth a priesthood embittered rather than conciliated by the aid granted by the State for their education ... It is said '... you refuse endowment from the public funds for the clergy of the Roman Catholic Church; you make that clergy depend altogether upon the contributions of their flock – that flock mostly composed of the poorest and most prejudiced classes – and hold out a premium to the clergy to agitate, and encourage agitation, in order that they may maintain their influence over those on whose goodwill they are dependent for their existence.'

17 February 1844

I know not what remedy there can be for such an evil as this [total collapse of the government's authority] but the detaching ... from the ranks of Repeal, agitation, and disaffection a considerable portion of the respectable and influential classes of the Roman Catholic population. It may be said that this is impossible, the attempt will fail. But if we act on this assumption, what is the result? You have the whole Roman Catholic population banded against you.

The immediate domestic evil will be impunity for conspiracy and sedition. The danger in the event of foreign war will be extreme ...

What we must aim at ... is to reconcile ... the Roman Catholics ... to two great principles, the maintenance of the Union, and the maintenance of the Church Establishment. Every concession we can make consistent with those principles must be made, sooner or later.

Sir Robert Peel, memoranda to the Cabinet.

Source H

Peel in the House of Commons, 18 April 1845, closing the Maynooth debate, recalled the situation at the height of the repeal campaign:

There was a universal feeling at that time that you ought not merely to rely on applications of force ... that it was the duty of the Government to take into consideration the condition of Ireland ... you must break up ... that formidable confederacy which exists in that country against ... the British connection. I do not believe you can break it up by force ... You can do much to break it up by acting in a spirit of kindness, forbearance and generosity.

Source I

The Measures

Measure	Purpose	Impact
1843 The Devon Commission	To investigate the problems of land tenure.	Its report was authoritative, but legislation had to be abandoned. **FAILURE**
1844 The Charitable Bequests Act	To encourage private bequests and endowments to the Catholic Church. Parish priests would be less dependent on their parishioners for financial support.	After much opposition it did win the support of the Catholic bishops. They agreed to serve on the administrative Board despite O'Connell's continued resistance. **SUCCESS**
1845 Maynooth Grant increase	Grant increased to £26,000 a year; building grant of £30,000. Aim was to improve the quality of the clergy, and to make them more loyal to the Union.	The Bishops welcomed the concession. They were consulted in advance. O'Connell gave his support. The political reaction was in England. **SUCCESS**
1845 The Academic Colleges Act – this was the concession to the Catholic laity to match Maynooth, and to split them from the repeal movement.	Three university colleges were to be set up with building grants and an annual subsidy. Colleges were to be open to all denominations. There was to be no religious teaching or tests.	The Bishops were hostile fearing that 'godless' colleges would undermine the faith. Government motives were distrusted. The colleges seemed part of an anti-Catholic plot. The benefits from Maynooth were lost. **FAILURE**

Source J

By this time, the 'Year of Repeal', as O'Connell had confidently called 1843, had come and gone. If he had failed to achieve Repeal ... he had brought the Irish question to the centre of English politics; and his efforts to win over the Irish clergy had been ... successful ... The secret investigation into the Repeal movement ... showed the government that the clergy was at the heart of the movement, findings which were confirmed by the reports of the sermons and speeches and by the signing by the Dublin priests of the requisition for the Clontarf meeting. Peel, fearing that this union between O'Connell and the clergy might eventually result in the dismemberment of the Empire, made the breaking up of this 'powerful combination' the cornerstone of his Irish policy...

Peel's chief concern was not to reform or control Maynooth but to break up 'that formidable conspiracy' against the government – a task that he saw as necessary both for domestic and foreign reasons. In short, his policy was to kill Repeal by kindness ...

Justice was not done then (nor has it been since) to Peel's Irish reforms which, considered in the context of the time and the prejudices of his own party, were remarkable ... By May 1845 the distinct possibility emerged that his government might succeed in their policy of reconciliation.

To Peel belongs the credit of being the first Tory premier to make a serious effort to solve the Irish problem by conciliation ... Apart from the calamitous effects of the Famine in deepening mutual suspicions, the success of the premier ... was limited by ... failure to take sufficient account of the views and feelings of the majority of Irish Catholics – including the clergy. The loyalty of most Irishmen to O'Connell was too strong and their political and religious distrust of the Tory party too deep, to be overcome by the measure of reform which Peel could offer.

D. A. Kerr, Peel, Priests and Politics, 1982.

---

3 Referring to sources C, D, E, G and H:

a Outline what Graham and Peel feel should be done to pacify Ireland.

b What constraints did they recognise which could limit the scope of any ameliorative measures?

4 Using the evidence of sources G and H explain the purpose of Peel's policy, and his justification for it.

5 Using your wider knowledge, why was any alteration of the State's relationship with the Catholic Church in Ireland likely to be hazardous for the government; how justified, in the event, was Graham's caution?

6 To what extent might source I lead you to qualify your assessment of O'Connell's achievement during the 1840s?

7 Explain how the measures summarised in the chart aimed to conciliate different groups, showing how they fit in with the purposes outlined by Peel in sources D, G and H.

8

> How wonderful is Peel
> He changes with the time...
> He gives whate'er they want
> To those who ask with zeal
> He yields the Maynooth grant
> To the clamour for Repeal

Punch, 1846.

O'Connell had forced Peel's hand in 1828 over emancipation. How far did he repeat this feat in 1843, and was Peel's response that of a pragmatic politician reacting to a temporary difficulty, or that of a truly conservative statesman? Refer to the sources and your wider knowledge.

The political impact of the Maynooth Act

The proposals to increase the Maynooth grant stirred up the Protestantism and anti-Catholicism of both the Conservative Party and the country at large. Nonconformist ministers and evangelical Anglican clergy shared the same platforms and urged on the opposition to the proposals in the Commons. Graham was right to be cautious.

A majority of Conservative MPs voted against the Bill on its third reading, but the government won through with Whig and Radical support. Members who remembered 1829 accused Peel of betraying the principles of his Party, and Protestantism, once more. Many felt they had been elected in 1841 to protect the Church of England from further assault. Now their government was preparing to endow Roman Catholicism in Ireland. Rebel backbenchers rejected the sophisticated conservative arguments that justified the policy. Peel could not tamper with religion with impunity.

What does this statement tell us about Peel's attitude to party leadership?

Peel remained unrepentant: 'All this raises a storm at which I look with much indifference, being resolved on carrying the Bill, and being very careless as to the consequences which may follow it' (Peel to J.W. Croker, 22 April 1845).

Graham was more pessimistic:

How had the government 'laboured hard … to restore … prosperity' and to improve the condition and lessen 'the discontent of the great masses of the people', and why were they 'scouted as traitors'?

> I am aware … that our country gentlemen are out of humour, and that the existence of the Government is endangered by their present temper and recent proceedings. We have laboured hard, and not in vain, to restore the prosperity of the country … by improving the condition and diminishing the discontent of the great masses of the people. We have effected this object without inflicting any injury on the landed proprietors; yet we are scouted as traitors, and are denounced as if we were time-serving traders in politics, seeking to retain place by the sacrifice of the interests of our friends.
>
> The country gentlemen cannot be more ready to give us the death-blow than we are prepared to receive it.
>
> Sir James Graham to J.W. Croker, 22 March 1845.

> … a large Body of our supporters is mortally offended, and in their anger are ready to do anything either to defeat the bill or to revenge themselves upon us.
>
> Sir James Graham to Lord Heytesbury, 18 April 1845.

The opportunity for that revenge soon came. It is significant that of 147 Conservative MPs who voted against Maynooth only nineteen supported the repeal of the Corn Laws twelve months later.

6.3 Repeal of the Corn Laws: a crisis within the Conservative Party

Lord George Bentinck (1802–48), fourth son of the Duke of Portland, had been an MP since 1826 but had rarely spoken in the House. His reputation rested on his success in ridding horse racing of its criminal element. In January 1846 he emerged as the leader the Conservative backbenchers lacked. They would cheer Disraeli's attacks on Peel, but his flamboyant appearance and unorthodox background made him an unacceptable leader. Bentinck possessed all the right credentials. He did not aspire to lead a party but viewed Peel as 'no better than Common Cheats', a man who had indulged in 'wholesale examples of political lying and pledge-breaking'. It was necessary, he wrote, 'for the sake of Political Morals and the Character of Public Men … a salutary lesson should in all cases be taught to the delinquent Politicians.' It was his determination to destroy Peel politically, to drive him out of office and Party leadership, that ensured the defeat of the government's Irish Coercion Bill which forced Peel's resignation. 'It was his energy and persistence which raised the protectionist opposition to the government from a protest into a rebellion.' R. Stewart, *The Foundation of the Conservative Party, 1830–1867*, 1978.

NOVEMBER

The extent and seriousness of the Irish potato crop failure was rapidly becoming more apparent. This was compounded by a poor grain harvest across Europe. The Cabinet was reluctant to take the decisive step of suspending the Corn Laws and opening the ports to the free import of grain. Peel wanted to prepare repeal legislation since it would be impossible to close the ports again once the Corn Laws were suspended. On 22 November Russell announced the Whig conversion to immediate repeal in his 'Edinburgh letter' to his London constituents.

DECEMBER

At a final Cabinet meeting on the 5th, two ministers still stood out against Peel; and many of the rest were reluctant converts. Uncertain of being able to carry a repeal measure without the full support of his Cabinet, Peel offered his resignation to the Queen, who invited Russell to form a Whig administration. By the 20th Russell had to admit failure. Peel and all his ministers, except for Lord Stanley, agreed to continue in office, several out of loyalty rather than conviction.

JANUARY

There was evidence of growing opposition in the counties as rumours of the government's new policy spread. The Central Agricultural Protection Society formed an election committee and recommended the lobbying of MPs. Peel introduced a comprehensive programme of tariff reform, with gradual abolition of the Corn Laws over a three year period as one element of a much broader scheme which included some compensation for farmers and grants for improvements.

FEBRUARY TO MAY

Peel was shocked by the strength of the opposition to repeal, and its virulence. Gladstone, freshly recruited to the Cabinet as Stanley's replacement, decided not to contest Newark against the wishes of the seat's patron, the Duke of Newcastle. Lord Lincoln was defeated in South Nottinghamshire after his appointment as Irish Chief Secretary. His opponent was supported by his father, the Duke of Newcastle, and the Central Agricultural Protection Society. Backbenchers who resigned and sought re-election on their new free trade opinions universally met with disaster. Nevertheless, Peel steered the legislation through the Commons, making five major speeches, but he suffered the constant abuse of his former supporters and vituperative attacks from Disraeli. On the third reading (15 May) the government had a majority of 98 but 241 conservatives voted against and only 112 for.

JUNE

Repeal passed in the Lords with Wellington keeping the Conservative peers in order and Russell threatening resignation from the Whig leadership if his supporters voted to defeat the measure. In fact, the great landowners in the Lords did not feel threatened by repeal, as the tenant farmers did. On 25 June, 74 Conservative backbenchers followed Bentinck into the division lobby to 'kick out' both Peel and the government's Irish Coercion Bill. Fifty-one abstained. This was what Wellington described as a 'blackguard combination', voting against a measure they would normally have supported, to get revenge on Peel. Tenant farmers were unimpressed by Peel's confidence in the future of British agriculture. Like Conservative backbenchers they felt betrayed by the man in whom they had placed their trust and whom they believed had gained office in 1841 on the basis of continued protection for agriculture.

TALKING POINT

Croker, Peel's old friend, wrote bitterly of his fears for the future: 'is the great Conservative Party dissolved? and are the Landed Interests, and ultimately the aristocracy, and the monarchy, to be handed over to the fierce democracy of the League?' (to Peel, 16 December 1845) 'your repeal of the Corn Laws will feed nothing but agitation. You have rendered it quite impossible to constitute a strong Government. You have divided the only party on which any Government could rely for stemming agitation' (to Graham, 3 April 1846).

Contrast Croker's view of the likely effect of repeal with that of Peel himself.

MANAGER PEEL TAKING HIS FAREWELL BENEFIT.

WHO IS BEING EVICTED FROM THE THEATRE, AND WHY?

Peel and the Corn Laws

Norman Gash has described Peel's change of mind on the Corn Laws as 'a process of continuous erosion' in which 1842 was probably the critical year. Boyd Hilton, however, has suggested that Peel's intellectual conversion to free trade came in the 1820s when it was being put forward by Huskisson in Cabinet meetings. For the Liberal Tories and their successors, the Corn Laws were increasingly anomalous. They did not fit in with a tradition of liberal economic policy that went back to Pitt, and Peel's own budgets of 1842 and 1845 merely served to highlight the problem. It was difficult to justify a special case for agriculture while other tariff barriers were being removed.

A growing population also required increased food supplies. If British agriculture could not meet that need, then the Corn Laws would have to go, otherwise they really would become 'starvation laws'. In the immediate post-war years when there had been grain surpluses on the Continent, the Corn Laws had kept up the home price and successfully defended the interests of British agriculture. By the 1840s, however, these surpluses no longer existed and Peel believed that efficient British farmers could compete with foreign importers. Repeal might mean bankruptcy for those farming marginal land, but Peel's concerns were wider than that, and he accepted the consequences of economic laws and free competition.

Peel may have been converted to repeal before 1841, and the evidence would certainly suggest that his mind was made up by 1842. Why, then, did he wait until the Irish famine crisis of 1845 before making the policy decision? Firstly, Peel was the leader of an essentially protectionist party which would have to be led gently to the new policy. An immediate change would be politically disastrous for Peel. Secondly, repeal was the purpose of the Anti-Corn Law League, and Peel did not want to appear as the League's agent acting under duress. Thirdly, the League and Chartism had dressed their attacks on the Corn Laws in class terms. Peel did not want to encourage the anti-aristocratic spirit that had been engendered.

Examining the Evidence

Peel and the case for repeal

Source A

It is a question of time. The next change in the Corn Laws must be to an open trade; and if our population increases for two or three years at the rate of 300,000 per annum, you may throw open the ports, and British agriculture will not suffer. But the next change must be the last; it is not prudent to hurry it; next Session is too soon; and as you cannot make a decisive alteration, it is far wiser to make none.

Sir James Graham to Sir Robert Peel, 30 December 1842.

Source B

The next change in the Corn Laws would be total repeal.

Sir Robert Peel in a conversation with W.E. Gladstone, 1843.

Source C

Does not the state of the revenue, buoyant under all our reductions, the state of commerce and manufactures, above all, the spirit of contentment and loyalty for the last three years, speak volumes in favour of the continued application – to articles of manufacture as well as to the produce of the land – of those principles the cautious and deliberate adoption of which has mainly led to our present prosperity?

Sir Robert Peel to E. B. Denison, 1845.

Source D

Sir Robert has an *immense scheme in view*; he thinks he shall be able to remove the contest entirely from the dangerous ground upon which it has got – that of a war between the manufacturers, the hungry and the poor against the landed proprietors, the aristocracy, which can only end in the ruin of the latter; he will not bring forward a measure upon the Corn Laws, but a much more comprehensive one. He will deal with the whole commercial system of the country. He will adopt the principle of the League, *that of removing all protection and abolishing all monopoly*, but not in favour of one class as a triumph over another, but to the benefit of the nation, farmers as well as manufacturers

Memorandum by Prince Albert, Windsor Castle, 25 December 1845.

Source E

I think you could have continued this law [the Corn Law] ... for a shorter time longer; but I believe that the interval of its maintenance would have been but short, and that there would have been, during its period of continuance, a desperate conflict between different classes of society ... [and] that you might at an early period have had no alternative but to concede an alteration of this law under circumstances infinitely less favourable than the present to a final settlement of the question ... It was the foresight of these consequences – it was the belief that you were about to enter into a bitter and, ultimately, an unsuccessful struggle, that has induced me to think that for the benefit of all classes, for the benefit of the agricultural class itself, it was desirable to come to a permanent and equitable solution of this question. These are the motives on which I acted ... The mere interests of the landlords – the mere interests of the occupying tenants, important as they are, are subordinate to the great question – what is calculated to increase the comforts, to improve the condition, and elevate the social character of the millions who subsist by manual labour ... My earnest wish has been, during my tenure of power, to impress the people of this country with a belief that the legislature was animated by a sincere desire to frame its legislation upon the principles of equity and justice.

Sir Robert Peel in the House of Commons, 15 May 1846.

1 Explain
a 'The next change ... must be to an open trade' (source A).
b 'these principles the cautious and deliberate adoption of which has mainly led to our present prosperity' (source C).
2 Is there anything in sources A, B and C which would justify the charge that Peel had deliberately deceived his Party?
3 Study sources C, D, and E. To what extent were Peel's motives economic, and to what extent were they political?
4 'The Irish famine provided the occasion for repeal, it was not the cause.' Comment on this view in the light of the evidence of these sources.
5 **Essay**
'A politician who thought more about the national need than the interests of a party.'
Discuss this view using the evidence of these sources and your wider knowledge.

How accurate is *Punch's* comment on the repeal of the Corn Laws in these two cartoons?

PEEL'S CHEAP BREAD SHOP,
OPENED JANUARY 22, 1846.

PUNCH'S MONUMENT TO PEEL.

WHAT IS THE SIGNIFICANCE OF THE DATE? WHAT IS THE SIGNIFICANCE OF THE DUKE OF WELLINGTON CARRYING THE PLACARD?

Peel – the twilight years

3   An Interesting Group by 'HB' 1847. 1. Lord Lincoln; 2. Sir Robert Peel; .
3. Mr Goulbourne; 4. Mr D'Israeli; 5. Lord George Bentinck; 6. Mr
Stafford O'Brien ('*HB*', *Political Sketches, vol. IX (1843), No. 876*)

THIS SKETCH OF THE OPPOSITION FRONT BENCH IN 1847 INDICATES THE DIFFICULTIES FACED BY THE CONSERVATIVE PARTY, AND THE AMBIGUITY OF PEEL'S PERSONAL POSITION. HE SITS (SECOND FROM LEFT) FLANKED BY LORD LINCOLN AND GOULBURN, ON THE RIGHT, INSULATED FROM CONTACT WITH HIS OPPONENTS DISRAELI, BENTINCK AND STAFFORD O'BRIEN.

Corn Law repeal split the Conservative Party. Peel's position was ambiguous. Although he sat on the opposition front bench he was determined not to subject himself again to the humiliations of party leadership. He made clear his intention of keeping the Whig government in office to prevent the protectionists, pledged to reversing his economic policies, from replacing them. Hence, he only once voted against the government. Following the banking crisis of 1847, Sir Charles Wood, Chancellor of the Exchequer, was in regular contact with Peel on budgetary matters, whilst Lord Clarendon, Irish Lord Lieutenant, began consulting the ex-premier on Irish policy in 1849. It is no surprise that when Peel died in 1850, Lord Campbell noted, 'His death is a very heavy blow to the Whigs'.

See chapter 11.

REVIEW

Peel – statesman or party leader?

Source A

Peel could hardly have created anything. His intellect, admirable in administrative routine, endlessly fertile in suggestions of detail, was not of a class which creates ... a new idea.   Walter Bagehot.

Source B

He [Peel] never originated a single great measure; but no man equalled him in accomplishing them; and he was signally skilled as an administrator.

J.C. Symons, *Sir Robert Peel as a Type of Statesmanship*, 1856.

Source C

[Peel] had always been an opportunist who took his ... decisions with an eye to the wishes of the country and the needs of the moment.

E. Halevy, *History of the English People in the Nineteenth Century*, 1961.

Source D

... he was a most able administrator. He possessed a remarkable capacity for hard work. He was humane. He cared intensely about the distress and poverty of the society in which he lived ... pursuing his cautious middle course ... [towards] consensus politics.

Lord Blake, *The Conservative Party from Peel to Churchill*, 1970.

Source E

The combination of practical experience and a pragmatic temperament ... gained Peel his reputation as a model administrator.

R. Stewart, *The Politics of Protection*, 1971.

Source F

What was important was his assertion that the aristocratic system could only survive if it showed a readiness to promote the welfare of all other classes in the community ... He based his power on party but his policy was neither sectional nor partisan ... By 1850 ... the age of revolt was giving way to the age of stability; and of that age Peel had been the chief architect ... His allegiance was to an older concept than party loyalty; it was to the service of the state.

N. Gash, *Sir Robert Peel*, 1972.

Source G

In essence, Peel was an expert who devoted his political career to developing professional expertise in government and administration. The benefits of this are clear. He got things done. His legislative record is second to none in nineteenth century politics. He dominated the House of Commons ... [because] He just knew more about the subject under discussion than almost anyone else in the House ... The negative aspects of 'expertism' ... include intolerance, aloofness and arrogance. Peel was persistently criticised for all three vices.

E. Evans, *Sir Robert Peel: Statesmanship, Power and Party*, 1991.

---

1 An 'opportunist', a 'pragmatist', a 'model administrator', an 'expert'. Illustrate these judgements from your knowledge of Peel's career. How apt are they?
2 Comment on Peel's strengths and weaknesses, and on the view that he implemented other men's ideas rather than originating new policies and ideas.

Source H

A view of the repeal of the Corn Laws.

In my judgement no charge of treachery can be maintained, and the change of opinion was honest. But we may regret that Sir Robert had not taken his supporters sooner into his confidence and 'educated' his party.

Quoted in Gash 'From the Origins to Sir Robert Peel' in Lord Butler (ed.) *The Conservatives*, 1977.

Source I

Peel drove his party in the 1840s too fast and too far.

N. Gash, *Pillars of Government*, 1986.

Source J

Peel's conception of party may be criticised as both narrow and selfish. In the 1830s, he had seen more clearly than most the implications of 1832 for political reorganisation in the constituencies. What he had not seen, or more likely had chosen to ignore, was that party was becoming a dynamic factor whose importance in government would inevitably grow. The backbench case that Peel deserved his fate in 1846 is ... a reasonable one. Between 1841 and 1845 Peel either ignored his followers' sensibilities or bludgeoned them into submission. He proved himself untrue to their Tory principles on Ireland, on religion, on commerce and, finally and fatally, on the English landed interest itself

E. Evans, *Sir Robert Peel: Statesmanship, Power and Party*, 1991.

The charge against Peel is that he misled his party, and deceived his backbenchers. For sympathisers, Peel is a great statesman who sacrificed his party and his own political future for what he perceived to be the real interests of the nation as a whole.

Prepare two statements:

● A defence of Peel the administrator and statesman from the accusation of betraying his party and its principles.

● The case against Peel from his opponents' point of view.

Make use of the sources in this Review, but also range widely through chapters 5 and 6 to research points to support your arguments. You may need to gather evidence from Peel's earlier career to substantiate or illustrate your arguments.

---

7 Pressure for Change: Chartism – Success or Failure?

PREVIEW

Source A

'CAPITAL AND LABOUR',
PUNCH (1843).

TALKING POINT

Can the historian learn anything worthwhile from nineteenth century novels?

CAPITAL AND LABOUR.

Source B

At all times it is a bewildering thing to the poor weaver to see his employer removing from house to house, each one grander than the last ... while all the time the weaver, who thinks he and his fellows are the real makers of this wealth, is struggling on for bread for his children, through the vicissitudes of lowered wages, short hours, fewer hands employed, etc. And when he knows trade is bad ... he would bear and endure much without complaining, could he also see his employers were bearing their share; he is ... bewildered and (to use his own word) 'aggravated' to see that all goes on just as usual with the mill-owners. Large houses are still occupied, while spinners' and weavers' cottages stand empty because the families that once filled them are obliged to live in rooms or cellars. Carriages still roll along the streets, concerts are still crowded by subscribers, the shops for expensive luxuries still find daily customers, while the workman loiters away his unemployed time in watching these things, and thinking of the pale, uncomplaining wife at home, and the wailing children asking in vain for enough of food, – of the sinking health, of the dying life of those near and dear to him. The contrast is too great. Why should he alone suffer from bad times?

Elizabeth Gaskell, *Mary Barton*, 1848.

> Describe, and discuss, the view of mid-nineteenth century society suggested by these sources.

FOCUS

7.1 Chartism: the origins

The radical tradition
There was nothing new about the Six Points. The London Corresponding Society had called for universal suffrage, the secret ballot and equal constituencies in 1792, the post-war Radicals had the same programme, and Henry Hunt had opposed the Reform Bill as MP for Preston because it did not concede universal suffrage.

Attacks on trade unions by the authorities
1834   The Tolpuddle Martyrs were convicted on dubious grounds for administering illegal oaths. This was part of the campaign against the Grand National Consolidated Trades Union.
1837   During the Glasgow Spinners' Strike a blackleg was killed. The Union's leaders were charged with murder, acquitted, but transported for a lesser offence.

The London Working Men's Association published the 'People's Charter' in May 18[?]. The 'six points' set out in the Charter were be the focus of the Chartist campaigns of t next 20 years:
1 Universal manhood suffrage over age of
2 Secret ballot
3 Equal electoral districts
4 No property qualification for MPs
5 Payment of MPs
6 Annual parliaments
By summer 1838 the Charter had been adopted by the revived Birmingham Politic[al] Union and the radical societies in the Nort[h]

From 1831 the government conducted a vigorous campaign against the unstamped press.
Editors, newsagents and street sellers were prosecuted and imprisoned. A campaign by Radical MPs secured the Newspaper Act in 1836. The stamp duty was reduced to 1d which persuaded unstamped papers, including Feargus O'Connor's *Northern Star*, to go legal. O'Connor observed that the Act made newspapers cheaper for the rich, and more expensive for the poor.

The economic boom of the mid 1830s broke in 1836. To unemployment, wage reductions and short-time working was added high food prices as a cycle of poor harvests began.
The state of the unhappy hand-loom weavers is distressing in the greatest degree; an industrious man in full work and on the highest wages starves.
General Sir Charles Napier, 1839. These conditions continued into the 'Hungry Forties'.

lusionment with the results of
Reform Act
reformed House of Commons ignored
ands for further reform, and its
ation seemed designed to oppress
working class.
nce their accession to the franchise
. the middle classes thought only of
hemselves ... the experience of the
st three months convinces us that
he spirit in which they desire to
xercise the franchise is as exclusively
lfish as the aristocratic spirit which
ave them a monopoly of it was
bitrary and unjust.
Poor Man's Guardian, 6 April 1833.

The Ten Hours Movement, led by
Richard Oastler, had raised the
expectations of textile workers in
Lancashire and the West Riding of
Yorkshire. Matthew Sadler's parliamentary select committee (1832) had
collected appalling evidence about
children working in the mills, but in
1833 the government defeated Lord
Ashley's Ten Hours Bill. The 1833
Factory Act, based on the evidence
collected by the Royal Commission,
offered nothing to adult workers.
Ministers seemed to have capitulated
to the millowners.

The extension of the New Poor Law to the
North in 1837 coincided with the onset of
economic depression. Richard Oastler became
a leading campaigner in the Anti-Poor Law
movement as it merged with the short-time
movement.

> The passage of the New Poor Law
> Amendment Act did more to sour the
> hearts of the labouring population than
> did the privations consequent on all the
> actual poverty of the land ... the labourers
> of England believed that the new poor law
> was a law to punish poverty; and the
> effects of that belief were to sap the loyalty
> of the working men, to make them dislike
> the country of their birth ... to hate the rich
> of the land.
>
> Samuel Kydd, *History of the Factory
> Movement*, 1857.

The Irish 'Coercion Act' of 1833 was
claimed to be a model for the legislation
the government wanted to enact to keep
order in the rest of Britain.
The Municipal Corporations Act
(1835) seemed to extend middle class
power over the lives of working people.
In Manchester working class leaders
opposed incorporation as it meant rule
by the mill owners.
**The extension of policing arrange-
ments** through the Municipal
Corporations Act and the Rural Police Act
(1839) was alleged to be a threat to
liberty and freedom.

TALKING
POINT
Why did the Charter
become the focus for
this mass of grievance
and discontent?

Examining the Evidence

The roots of Chartism

Source A

Chartism means the bitter discontent grown fierce and mad, the wrong condition therefore, or the wrong disposition, of the Working Classes of England.

Thomas Carlyle, Chartism, 1840.

Source B

The cry of millions suffering under a diseased condition of society.

Comment in the Morning Chronicle.

Source C

The Rev James Rayner Stephens at the great Manchester demonstration on Kersal Moor, 1838.

This question of Universal Suffrage was a knife and fork question after all; this question was a bread and cheese question ... and if any man should ask him what he meant by Universal Suffrage, he would answer that every working man in the land had the right to have a good coat to his back, a comfortable abode in which to shelter himself and his family, a good dinner upon his table, and no more work than was necessary for keeping him in health, and as much wages for that work as would keep him in plenty, and afford him the enjoyment of all the blessings of life which a respectable man could desire.

Northern Star, 29 September 1838.

Source D

Our conviction is that the real cause of the present Insurrection is long-continued, wide-spread, gnawing Distress

Leeds Mercury, 20 August 1842.

Source E

Whatever it may have been with others it has been a wages question with me. And I do say that if Mr. O'Connor has made it a Chartist question, he has done wonders to make it extend through England, Ireland and Scotland. But it was always a wages question, and ten hours bill with me.

Richard Pilling, strike leader in 1842 and local Chartist leader in Ashton and Stockport, at his trial in 1843.

---

1 Chartism has been dismissed as 'hunger politics'.
a To what extent could these sources be used to sustain that view?
b Study the chart on page 43. What background factor links the three main periods of Chartist activity?
c Consider the likely weaknesses of a movement rooted in these motives.

Source F

The landlords and capitalists make the law, – the law makes the institutions, – the institutions place the producers in such a position that they must either starve or sell their produce for a fraction of its value, that is to say, give up a major portion of it to the landlords and capitalists. Thus are the producers robbed, and thus do the rich acquire their riches.

Poor Man's Guardian, 21 June 1834.

'The great strength of Chartism 1838–9 lay in its identification of political power as the source of social oppression, and thus in its ability to concentrate the discontent of the unrepresented upon one common aim.' (G. Stedman Jones)

Discuss this comment on the nature and strength of Chartism. Would you agree that this awareness was a source of strength?

Source G

... the end I have in view is social equality for all and each, to obtain this we must first have political equality for each and all. To obtain political equality, we must have a more extensive and effective organization of the working classes, and of that portion of the middle class which is immediately dependent on their custom, than has hitherto been even thought of, much less accomplished.

Bronterre O'Brien in *Bronterre's National Reformer*, 7 January 1837.

Source H

The Chartists were called ugly names, the swinish multitude, unwashed and levellers. I never knew levelling advocated amongst Chartists, neither in public nor in private, for they did not believe in it, nor have I known a case of plunder in the town, though thousands have marched through its streets to meetings in various places. What they wanted was a voice in making the laws they were called upon to obey; they believed that taxation without representation was a tyranny, and ought to be resisted; they took a leading part in agitating in favour of the ten hours question, the repeal of the taxes on knowledge, education, co-operation, civil and religious liberties and the land question, for they were the true pioneers in all the great movements of their time.

Benjamin Wilson, *The Struggles of an Old Chartist*, 1887.

Source I

Chartism was a political movement and political movements cannot satisfactorily be defined in terms of anger and disgruntlement of disaffected social groups, or even the consciousness of a particular class. A political movement is not simply a manifestation of distress and pain, its existence is distinguished by a shared conviction articulating a political solution to distress and a political diagnosis of its cause.

G. Stedman Jones, *Languages of Class: Studies in English Working Class History*, 1983.

Source J

Chartism was a political movement, demanding political rights and political participation.

Dorothy Thompson, *Chartist Studies*, 1984.

2 Chartism has been described as 'the creed of the excluded'. Use the evidence of sources F, G and H, and the information in Focus 7.1 to comment on the aptness of this view.

3 Comment on Wilson's remark in source H that the Chartists were not 'levellers'. From the evidence here, and in Focus 7.1, was there a class element in Chartism?

4 Sources I and J emphasise the political nature of the movement. Was Chartism a political movement first, and a social movement second? Use the evidence of these sources and your wider knowledge to explain your answer.

1838–40 – Chartism's initial surge

In 1838 several radical strands came together. These provided Chartism with its initial surge in the period 1838–40.

The Charter

The London Working Men's Association (LWMA) had been formed in 1836. A year later, after a meeting with a group of Radical MPs, it set up a committee of six MPs and six London radicals to devise a new reform plan. This became The People's Charter. There was nothing new about its six points, but they were soon to become the objectives of a new working class movement – Chartism.

THIS IMAGE OF THE CHARTIST MEETING, WITH ITS FLAMING TORCHES AND THE DISPLAY OF WEAPONS, ALARMED THE AUTHORITIES. DURING THE AUTUMN OF 1838 THEY WERE HELD THROUGHOUT THE INDUSTRIAL DISTRICTS AS PREPARATIONS WERE MADE TO PETITION PARLIAMENT TO ENACT THE PEOPLE'S CHARTER AND TO ELECT DELEGATES TO ATTEND THE NATIONAL CONVENTION.

The Petition

Thomas Attwood, elected MP for Birmingham in 1832, was disillusioned by the refusal of the reformed House of Commons to consider his currency reform proposals. In 1837 he revived the BPU with a programme of household suffrage, triennial parliaments and the secret ballot; by the end of the year the Union's council had decided to campaign for universal suffrage. In August 1838 the BPU's public demonstration in Birmingham endorsed the People's Charter, and launched the petitioning strategy which was to form a major part of Chartist campaigning.

The newspaper

Disappointed by the ineffectiveness of London radicalism, O'Connor turned to the North. He unsuccessfully contested the Oldham seat vacated by the death of Cobbett, but speaking tours in 1835 and 1836, when he consciously imitated Henry Hunt as the radical gentleman on the platform, made him more widely known. At the height of the Anti-Poor Law agitation he shared platforms with Oastler and the Rev J.R. Stephens, but added the radical programme of political reform and universal suffrage. Aware of the need for organisation and publicity, if reform was to become a national issue, O'Connor launched the *Northern Star* in November 1837.

FEARGUS O'CONNOR, AN IRISHMAN, HAD BEEN ELECTED MP FOR COUNTY CORK IN 1832 AS A SUPPORTER OF O'CONNELL. A LAWYER AND A PROTESTANT LANDOWNER, HE CAME FROM A FAMILY WELL KNOWN FOR ITS NATIONALIST SYMPATHIES. HE QUARRELLED WITH O'CONNELL WHEN THE IRISH LEADER SHOWED HIS WILLINGNESS TO POSTPONE REPEAL OF THE ACT OF UNION TO REACH AN ACCOMMODATION WITH THE WHIGS. WHEN HE LOST HIS SEAT IN 1835 HE DISCOVERED THAT HIS VOTES FOR ASHLEY'S TEN HOURS BILL AND AGAINST THE NEW POOR LAW, AND HIS SUPPORT FOR THE TOLPUDDLE MARTYRS AND A

FREE PRESS, HAD WON HIM ALLIES AMONGST THE LONDON RADICALS.

Its success was crucial for the emergence of Chartism as a national movement. The *Star* came to provide a sense of identity and held the movement together during its most difficult years. Selling at 4½d, the *Northern Star* was not cheap, but because it was a stamped newspaper it was able to benefit from the advantage of free postage. It assumed a literate audience, and was a serious political paper written by highly skilled professional journalists. O'Connor used the profits to finance the Chartist movement, to build up defence funds for the inevitable trials, and to support the families of imprisoned Chartists. The *Northern Star*'s paid agents became Chartism's local organisers.

Weekly sales of the *Northern Star*

Year	Sales		Year	Sales
1838	11,000		1845	6,500
1839	36,000		1846	6,000
1840	18,700		1848	12,000
1843	8,700		1850	5,000

At Chartism's peak in 1839 weekly sales exceeded 50,000, an unprecedented circulation figure for the mid-nineteenth century, and the readership was much greater. In the Pennine town of Todmorden the streets were crammed with people when the *Star* was due. Ben Brierley remembered reading the paper aloud to his father and five other people who shared the subscription cost, and Benjamin Wilson recorded that 'it was a common practice, particularly in villages, to meet at friends' houses to read the paper and talk over political matters.'

O'Connor's enemies accused him of misappropriating the profits and of using the *Star* to stamp his own personality on the movement by ensuring that his critics were not heard. In fact, apart from his weekly letter and full reports of his many speeches, he left control to his editors. G.J. Harney, editor in the late 1840s, assured Engels in 1846 that the proprietor 'never interferes with what I write in the paper nor does he know what I write until he sees the paper.' As the historian Dorothy Thompson points out, 'The paper succeeded because it was considered by its readers to be the paper of the Chartist movement, not simply the voice of Feargus O'Connor' (*The Chartists*, 1984).

WILLIAM LOVETT, CABINET MAKER AND SECRETARY OF THE LWMA, DRAFTED THE PEOPLE'S CHARTER. WITHIN THE CHARTIST MOVEMENT, DESPITE HIS IMPRISONMENT FOR INCITING THE BIRMINGHAM RIOTS IN 1839, HE REMAINED A MODERATE FIGURE INCREASINGLY RESENTFUL OF THE INFLUENCE AND DOMINANCE OF FEARGUS O'CONNOR. AFTER 1840 HE WAS MARGINALISED BY O'CONNOR'S HOSTILITY TO THE VIEW THAT WORKING MEN WOULD ONLY GET THE VOTE IF THEY COULD DEMONSTRATE, BY RESPONSIBLE BEHAVIOUR, THAT THEY WERE WORTHY OF IT.

The National Convention

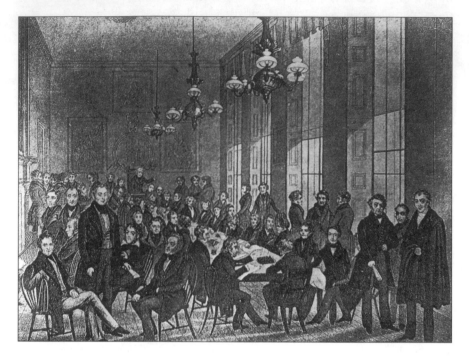

The purpose of the National Convention had never been made clear. Was it there solely to manage the presentation of the petition, or was it meant to debate and decide the strategy to be adopted if the Commons rejected it? The arguments, and the violent opinions, of some delegates persuaded the more moderate, mainly from the middle class, to withdraw.

Adjourning to Birmingham in May, the remaining delegates recommended vague 'Ulterior measures' if the petition failed. More threatening was the extremist rhetoric of some delegates coupled with their advice that Chartists should arm themselves for the struggle. Many Chartists reasoned that if the establishment had succumbed to threat and pressure in 1832 it would do the same in 1839. The circumstances, however, were very different. Neither ministers nor the propertied and newly enfranchised classes were prepared to submit to these tactics.

Not unexpectedly, the Commons refused to consider the National Petition by a vote of 235 to 46. Despite all their talk the Convention delegates had no agreed strategy. Hastily they devised the ambitious concept of a general strike which they described as a 'sacred month'. Scattering to their districts to sound out opinion they discovered that no plans were being made and that the people were not prepared to come out on strike in this way. Reluctant to force a confrontation with the authorities, and compelled to face reality, O'Connor proposed abandonment of the 'sacred month' and its replacement by a 'holiday' – a three day general strike at the beginning of August. O'Connor was always realistic about the chances of workers against armed and disciplined troops.

Some delegates hoped to provoke the authorities into making mass arrests. The government never gave them this justification for a violent reaction, delaying arrests until after the Newport Rising of November 1839 had discredited the movement.

On each occasion that the Chartist petitions were considered, in 1839, 1842 and 1848, fewer than half of the MPs actually voted. Parliament had no intention of even discussing the Chartist demands.

The reaction

O'Connor's innate caution – his enemies called it cowardice – ensured that the aftermath of the strike was relatively peaceful. Focus 7.2 indicates that there were some preparations for an insurrection in the summer of 1839, but the only violent outbreak was in Newport. O'Connor's opponents alleged that he knew what was intended, and that his intervention could have stopped the South Wales Chartist leader, John Frost. O'Connor discretely left for Ireland at the end of October. In Bradford Peter Bussey, believed to have been involved in the conspiracy with Frost, was strangely taken ill and could not be contacted.

. Newport gave the authorities the excuse they needed. Frost and his lieutenants, Zephaniah Williams and William Jones, were convicted of treason, despite the judge's strong hints to the jurymen that *not guilty* verdicts should be returned. Melbourne and the Cabinet initially agreed to uphold the death sentences, but then decided that transportation for life would avoid creating martyrs. William Lovett had been arrested in July 1839 after the Birmingham riots; now prominent Chartists, including O'Connor, were rounded up. By the following spring most were serving terms of imprisonment.

Newport was a lesson to the Chartists. It destroyed the myth that soldiers would never fire on fellow working men, and it emphasised the dangers of insurrection and violent talk. Working class agitation was directed more than ever down the constitutional path.

FOCUS

7.2 Chartism and the Revolutionary Tradition

Source A
Extracts from the diary and letters of General Sir Charles Napier.

Napier was appointed as commander of the northern military district by Russell in March 1839.

Diary entry, March

The northern district embraces eleven counties, and it is said arms are being provided for insurrection: this is the result of bad government, which has produced want, and the people are rather to be pitied than blamed. They are indeed putting themselves in the wrong, but that does not make those right whose misgovernment has produced this terrible feeling.

Diary entry, April

These poor people are inclined to rise, and if they do what horrid bloodshed!
Letter to the Home Office, 25 April
... we know that printed extracts from Maceroni's book on pike exercises are ... in circulation; and we have information, though vague, that drilling without arms goes on nightly. We are also informed ... that the purchase of fire-arms and the manufacture of pikes goes on.
We have also the fragment of a letter showing that barricades are contemplated and understood ... Finally, the conversation among the poorest classes who meet in public houses is, that one hundred Chartists may destroy fifty soldiers in billets and small detachments; and that the first thing is to cut the railroad and all communications between towns ... of its being speedily put down there can be no doubt, because funds, leaders, and that discipline which is required to move large bodies, are all wanting.

Diary entry, 25 July

... the people should have universal suffrage – it is their right. The ballot – it is their security ... and therefore their right also; and the new poor law should be reformed.

Diary entry, 6 August

The Duke of Portland tells me there is no doubt of an intended general rising. Poor people! ... We have physical force not they. They talk of their hundred thousands of men. Who is to move them when I am dancing round them with cavalry and pelting them with cannon-shot?

> Lieutenant General Sir W. Napier, *Life and Opinions of General Sir Charles James Napier, G.C.B.* (1857).

1 Summarise Napier's attitude towards the Chartists. What do you find surprising? Why might he have been a good appointment?
2 What Chartist weaknesses do these sources highlight?
3 Is there any evidence in these sources that an insurrection was planned, or expected? Explain your answer.

The Newport Rising, 3–4 November 1839

The Newport Rising can only be properly understood within the context of the South Wales valleys communities. Rapid expansion of the iron and coal industries meant relatively high wages, but appalling living and working conditions. Most employers had little interest in the welfare of their employees who responded with a fierce class hatred and a violent union tradition enforced through intimidation.

Source B

AN ARTIST'S IMPRESSION OF THE 'ATTACK' ON THE WESTGATE HOTEL, 4 NOVEMBER 1839. WHO APPEAR TO BE THE AGGRESSORS? WHO ARE BEING SHOT AT? COMPARE THIS WITH THE EYE-WITNESS ACCOUNT.

The leader

Source C

JOHN FROST, FORMER MAYOR OF NEWPORT, RECENTLY DISMISSED J.P, AND CHAIRMAN OF THE NATIONAL CONVENTION, LED THE MINERS, QUARRYMEN AND IRONWORKERS WHO GATHERED IN THE HILLS ABOVE THE TOWN ON THE NIGHT OF 3 NOVEMBER. SENTENCED TO DEATH ON A TREASON CHARGE THIS WAS LATER COMMUTED TO TRANSPORTATION FOR LIFE.

The participant

Source D

I saw Jenkin Morgan at Newport ... I ... know him to be a Chartist ... On ... the 3rd of November ... he came to my house and said he was a captain of men, and that I was appointed his man; he said that Frost was on the hills, and was coming down with thousands of men to attack the soldiers. He said ... that the Charter would be the law of the town of Newport on Monday night, and that it would be the law of the land before daylight.... He told me there was powder at Crossfield's warehouse ... but we found no powder. He also told me that there was to be a rising through the whole kingdom on the same night, and the same hour'

The Charter, 17 November 1839.

The eye-witness

Source E

The parcel of people I saw ... were armed; they had guns, sticks, etc; the sticks had iron points, I did not see many with guns. I saw of this body two hundred or three hundred.... They were not very tumultuous. They drew up in front of the Westgate ... and asked for the prisoners who were taken before daylight ... then a rush was made. Then I heard firing, and took to my heels. I cannot say whether the mob had guns, pikes or clubs. I cannot tell whether they were armed for the biggest part ... I could not say where the firing began .... It is likely enough the firing began from the Westgate inn.

Edward Patton giving evidence at the trial of John Frost.

Source F

Letter found in the pocket of one of the Chartists killed at Newport.

Dear Parents, – I hope this will find you well, as I am myself at present. I shall this night be engaged in a struggle for freedom, and should it please God to spare my life, I shall see you soon; but if not, grieve not for me. I shall fall in a noble cause.

The newspaper report

Source G

At least eight thousand men ... were engaged in the attack ... many of them were armed. Their design seems to have been to wreak vengeance upon the Newport magistrates, for the prosecution of Vincent ... and ... to advance to

> Henry Vincent was a Chartist organiser in South Wales. Reports of his ill-treatment after his arrest appalled Frost and angered the miners.

Monmouth, to liberate these prisoners. The ultimate design of the leaders ... probably was to rear the standard of rebellion throughout Wales ... until the people of England ... should rise ... for the same objects ... On entering Newport, the people marched straight to the Westgate Hotel, where the magistrates and about forty soldiers were assembled ... The Riot Act was read, and the soldiers fired down, with ease and security, upon the people who had first broken and fired into the windows ... About thirty of the people are known to have been killed, and several to have been wounded.'

The Charter, 17 November 1839.

The historians

Source H

It is safest to assume that the only common purpose ... was a great demonstration of strength in Newport.

D. Williams in *Chartist Studies*, edited by Asa Briggs, 1959.

Source I

... some form of local rising is the most satisfying explanation of what was intended ... [that] local rising was originally conceived as part of a general insurrection.

D. Jones, *The Last Rising: The Newport Insurrection of 1839,* 1985.

Source J

If 4 November was simply intended as a 'monster demonstration' ... it was unlike any other Chartist demonstration. It had been preceded by secret discussions through the country. It was itself mounted with the utmost secrecy. The participants were exclusively men, and they carried arms – clubs, muskets and pikes – rather than banners.

Dorothy Thompson, *The Chartists*, 1984.

TALKING POINT

Discuss the evidence of these sources. How far do they support the view that there was an organised conspiracy with revolutionary aims behind the Newport Rising of 1839?

Chartism 1840–42: consolidation, revival, and failure

The National Charter Association

With its leaders imprisoned the movement seemed finished but O'Connor continued to exercise his authority from York jail. With his approval the National Charter Association was formed at a Chartist Convention in July 1840. The Association provided the central organisation that Chartism had lacked.

Managed by working men, the NCA has been described as the first working class political party. A weekly subscription of 1d per week ensured a wide membership; in 1842, at the Association's highpoint, there were over 400 affiliated branches. Together with the *Star*, the NCA created the sense of unity and brotherhood which kept Chartism alive, although the link with O'Connor caused disquiet in some quarters.

Chartism – a way of life

In towns and villages where Chartism was strong it came to be more than just a political movement; a 'Chartist culture' emerged. From November 1839 Nottingham, for example, had a Democratic Chapel. A religious service was held on Sunday, the Charter Association met on Monday, the Chartist Total Abstinence Society (teetotallers) gathered on Tuesday, and on Wednesday there was Chartist singing practice. On Saturdays members assembled to read and discuss Chartist newspapers. During the day the premises housed the Nottingham Democratic Day School and on Sunday the Chartist Sunday School; there were also evening classes for adults. Elsewhere in the town 'Operative Libraries' were open to working men for a small subscription and Chartist discussion groups met in public houses and coffee houses. Special entertainments such as teas and balls were organised, and in the summer there were open air sermons every Sunday and regular demonstrations. Being a Chartist meant more than just agreeing with the six points of the People's Charter.

The 'New Move'

Some Chartists emerged from prison with a new vision for the movement. In his pamphlet *Chartism, a new organisation for the People*, Lovett argued that working men would have to win acceptance of the Charter by displaying their moral worth through a programme of education, Henry Vincent turned to teetotalism, and in Birmingham there was a move to Christian Chartism. O'Connor decried all diversion from the Charter, denouncing 'Knowledge Chartism, Christian Chartism and Temperance Chartism' in the *Star*. He made enemies, but the mass of Chartists stayed with him.

The Complete Suffrage Movement

This was an attempt to unite middle class radical reformers with the Chartists. Its leading advocates were Joseph Sturge of Birmingham and Edward Miall, editor of the *Nonconformist*. They were willing to work with leaders like Lovett, but were unsure of O'Connor. A first conference at the beginning of 1842 went well, and the six points were accepted by the middle class representatives. However, O'Connor was opposed to this new development, and, in December 1842, a second conference broke up on his insistence that the Charter itself should become the objective of a new movement. Lovett and O'Connor agreed on this if on nothing else. By 1842 no working class leader who wanted to retain his credibility could abandon the Charter, and for many, its acceptance was an essential guarantee of middle class good faith.

The Second Petition

ON HIS RELEASE FROM PRISON O'CONNOR IMMEDIATELY BEGAN THE CAMPAIGN TO COLLECT SIGNATURES FOR A SECOND NATIONAL PETITION. IN MAY 1842 A MOTION TO CONSIDER IT WAS OVERWHELMINGLY REJECTED BY THE HOUSE OF COMMONS, BY 287 VOTES TO 46. COMMENT ON THE IMPRESSION CREATED BY THIS ILLUSTRATION OF THE PROCESSION TAKING THE PETITION TO PARLIAMENT.

The 'Plug' Strikes

Once more the ineffectiveness of peaceful petitioning had been demonstrated, and once again the National Convention had no agreed alternative strategy. Meanwhile, discontent continued to grow. By July 1842 the economic depression was at its worst, and the prevailing mood of political bitterness was intensified by the death in prison of Samuel Holberry, the leader of Sheffield's 1840 riot. Over the following months the Chartist leaders saw the mainstream of working class activism drift out of their control.

The strikes of that summer affected 23 counties across Wales, England and Scotland, but they were most severe and most political in the Black Country, the Potteries, Lancashire and the West Riding. In the Potteries

The 'Plug' Strikes were so called because the strikers closed down working mills by removing the plugs from the steam engine boilers.

miners first went on strike against wage reductions. They spread their action by marching on working pits and forcing them to close by putting out the engine fires. On 14 August the Leicester Chartist leader, Thomas Cooper, addressed a meeting in Hanley, when, he later wrote, 'I caught the spirit of the oppressed and discontented thousands, and ... struck the spark which kindled all into combustion.' An industrial dispute became a political strike and the town became the scene of 24 hours of destruction and looting.

In Manchester the trade societies had been active in the Chartist movement in 1838–39 and several became NCA branches. The first strikes were in the Ashton-under-Lyne, Hyde and Staleybridge areas. From here bands of strikers spread the action to the other cotton towns, to Manchester, and across into Yorkshire. Several strike leaders were active Chartists, and on 7 August it was decided 'to remain out until the Charter, which is the only guarantee you have for your wages, becomes the law of the land.' A week later a meeting of representatives from all trades agreed to make it a general strike for the Charter.

The general council of the NCA, meeting in Manchester, found itself with a strike it had not organised or planned. Some members, like Thomas Cooper, believed that the time had come to force the authorities to give way, or to fight. Eventually a half-hearted endorsement was given, with O'Connor adding many qualifications. Like the government, he suspected that the mills had closed too easily and that millowner members of the Anti-Corn Law League were plotting behind the scenes. This belated involvement lead to the Chartist leadership being punished for a national strike which they had not instituted, although O'Connor and 58 others were acquitted on a technicality at the Lancaster Assizes in the spring of 1843. Peel's government did not want to seem too repressive or to create unnecessary martyrs.

See chapter 8 for the involvement of the Anti-Corn Law League in the strikes.

Chartism 1843–48: survival

In this year [1847] flour was very dear ... whilst trade was also very bad. This was the time to make politicians, as the easiest way to get to an Englishman's brains is through his stomach. It was said by its enemies that Chartism was dead and buried and would never rise again, but they were doomed to disappointment. It is true there had been no meetings or processions ... but it was going on. Amongst [wool] combers, handloom weavers, and others politics was the chief topic. The *Northern Star* was their principal paper ... We were only waiting for the time to come again.

Benjamin Wilson, *The Struggles of an Old Chartist*, 1887.

TALKING POINT

Comment on the kind of workers who remained Chartists, and on the light this throws on the movement as 'hunger politics'.

The Chartist Land Plan

The renewed prosperity of the mid-1840s, fuelled by 'railway mania', diverted working men away from Chartism. Miners in the North East, who had been disillusioned by the fiasco of 1839, were not the only workers to turn to trade union activity. O'Connor's language became more moderate and he devoted himself to the Land Plan, a scheme to settle Chartists in the countryside as smallholders.

The Chartist Land Company was launched in 1845. As a practical venture the plan was not a success. Its failure, through financial mismanagement, discredited both O'Connor and the movement as a whole, and his critics later accused O'Connor of diverting attention from the Charter. It did, however, hold the Chartists together in the second half of the decade. Men who had been prominent in the earlier local agitations appear amongst its list of shareholders and local agents. Chartism was encouraging that sense of self-help amongst its followers that would eventually give them 'respectability'.

'Railway mania' – a period of intense speculation in railway construction.

SNIG'S END IN GLOUCESTERSHIRE WAS ONE OF THE LAND COMPANY'S VILLAGES. SETTLERS WERE CHOSEN BY LOT FROM AMONGST THE SHAREHOLDERS. FEW BECAME SUCCESSFUL SMALLHOLDERS AND MANY RETURNED DISILLUSIONED TO THE TOWNS.

The Third Petition

In 1847 O'Connor was elected MP for Nottingham. A new Chartist Convention and a national petition, to be presented by a Chartist MP, was planned. The campaign coincided with a downturn in trade and a run of bad harvests, and in February 1848 Chartists were filled with excitement by news of revolution in France.

During 1848, for the first time, London played a leading part in the agitation, and the Irish, long excluded from Chartism on O'Connell's insistence, became involved in large numbers. There had always been some Irishmen in Chartist ranks, but after O'Connell's death in 1847, his successors were prepared to consider alliance with O'Connor. The Irish element added to the sense of alarm felt by the government and the propertied classes as the April deadline for the petition approached.

O'Connor was elected as the first Chartist MP via an anti-Liberal alliance with local Tories.

Equally the Chartists had been reluctant to work with O'Connell, who had compromised with the Whigs and supported legislation like the New Poor Law.

THE GREAT CHARTIST MEETING AT KENNINGTON COMMON, 10 APRIL 1848; O'CONNOR ACCEPTED THE ADVICE OF THE POLICE AND THE PETITION WAS TAKEN TO THE COMMONS IN THREE CABS ACCOMPANIED BY THE MOVEMENT'S LEADERS. WELLINGTON HAD ORGANISED THE DEFENCE OF LONDON, AND THOUSANDS OF SPECIAL CONSTABLES HAD BEEN ENROLLED. O'CONNOR WAS WARNED THAT THE PLANNED PROCESSION WOULD NOT BE ALLOWED TO CROSS THE RIVER THAMES.

TALKING POINT

Consider the effect on Chartism, Chartists, and their opponents, of O'Connor's decision and of the revelations of the Commons committee.

One recent historian of working class movements has argued that O'Connor's 'surrender' at Kennington Common marked the end of the 'mass platform' agitation begun by Hunt – the huge demonstration, the leader on the platform, the rhetoric of violence, the attempt to intimidate through sheer force of numbers. In fact, the threat of violence remained through the summer. There were disturbances in London, and possibly conspiracy in the North. Benjamin Wilson recalled having a pistol ready in 1848, and a friend who had a bullet mould in his house. The inevitable arrests, trials, and imprisonments followed.

THE CHARTIST PROCESSION ACCORDING TO THE SIGNATURES OF THE PETITION.

It is a very remarkable fact connected with the late Chartist Petition, that the parties who appear to have contributed the largest amount of signatures were not forthcoming to back the document on the day of its presentation. Our artist, in his beautiful simplicity following the pictorial practice of the present day, has drawn from his own imagination the exact representation of the passing of the procession; and, in order to place our periodical quite on a par with our illustrated contemporaries, he has introduced almost as many characters that never were engaged in the ceremony, as are usually to be found in the views of passing events that are drawn expressly by "artists on the spot" —which spot, by the way, is always that convenient spot, their own lodgings—for the illuminated journals.

The Chartist Procession, with which we this day present our readers, is in accordance with the view we should be justified in taking of it, if the signatures to the Petition were *bonâ fide*, and comprised of the actual autographs of the illustrious personages whose names were found appended to the document in conjunction with those of the heroic PUGNOSES, FLATNOSES, and other great nasal organs of Chartist opinion that seemed desirous of being heard in favour of the six pints, or three quarts, as our friend CUFFEY has ingeniously designated his favourite measures. Had the petition been anything but a hoax, HER MAJESTY would have been at an early hour wending her way towards Kennington Common with seventeen DUKES OF WELLINGTON at her side, and SIR R. PEEL would have been conspicuous in the van that was bearing the monster document.

Perhaps, after all, the two Premiers—ex and present—have as much interest as the CUFFEYS the REYNOLDSES, and the M'GRATHS in one

CHEEKS THE MARINE

LONGNOSE AND EXTENSION OF THE SUFFRAGE

SIBTHORPE AND DOWN WITH OUR OLD INSTITUTIONS

PUGNOSES FOR EVER!

PUNCH RIDICULES THE PETITION. ON EXAMINATION OF THE SIGNATURES BY A COMMONS COMMITTEE IT APPEARED THAT QUEEN VICTORIA AND SEVENTEEN DUKES OF WELLINGTON HAD SIGNED.

The epilogue: 1848–58

Despite humiliation and ridicule, Chartism survived in a few places, like Halifax, where deep roots had been put down. O'Connor's powers failed, in 1852 he was confined in a lunatic asylum, and the *Northern Star* collapsed into insolvency, but Ernest Jones, who became a Chartist in 1846, continued to lecture and to edit new Chartist journals. During the rising prosperity of the mid-Victorian years it was a hopeless cause. The last Chartist Convention met in Manchester in 1858, and the following year

TALKING POINT

Review your thoughts on Chartism as 'hunger politics', or Chartism as primarily a political movement.

one old Halifax Chartist responded to a renewed appeal from Jones with the dismal news:

> I am sorry to inform you that there is no Chartist organisation in Halifax, nor in any of the numerous villages surrounding it ... Many of those that were once Chartists have emigrated. And others, though residing here as usual, have become so thoroughly disgusted at the indifference and utter inattention of the multitude to their best wishes that they too are resolved to make no more sacrifice in a public cause.

EXAMINING THE EVIDENCE

Feargus O'Connor: creative or destructive force?

The man and his contemporaries

Source A

Verses from a Chartist hymn composed by Thomas Cooper to celebrate O'Connor's release from prison in 1841.

> The lion of freedom comes from his den,
> We'll rally around him again and again,
> We'll crown him with laurels our champion to be,
> O'Connor, the patriot of sweet liberty.
>
> The pride of the nation, he's noble and brave,
> He's the terror of tyrants, the friend of the slave,
> The bright star of freedom, the noblest of men,
> We'll rally around him again and again.

Source B

O'Connor's impact from the platform:

> His figure was tall and well-proportioned, and his bearing decidedly aristocratic. He wore a blue frock-coat and buff waistcoat, and had rings on the fingers of each hand. In a graceful manner and in emphatic language, he told the Radicals of Barnsley that he had sold off his horses and dogs, greatly reduced his establishment, and come weal, come woe he would henceforth devote his whole life to promote the well-being of the working-classes ... The language of O'Connor, to ears accustomed to little else than the Barnsley dialect spoken by pale-faced weavers and swart cobblers, sounded like rich music.
>
> John Hugh Burland's recollections in the *Barnsley Times,* May 1882.

Source C

Julian Harney, editor of the *Northern Star*, replies to Engels who wanted Harney to replace O'Connor as leader (1846).

> A popular chief should be possessed of a magnificent bodily appearance, an iron frame, eloquence or at least a ready fluency of tongue. I have none of these. O'C has them all – at least in degree. A popular leader should possess great animal courage, contempt of pain and death, and not be altogether ignorant of military arms and science

... From a knowledge of myself and all the men who have, and do figure in the Chartist movement, I am convinced that even in this respect, was O'C thrown overboard, we might go further and fare worse.

Source D

... the immense majority of Chartists in Leicester, as well as in many other towns, regarded him as the only really disinterested and incorruptible leader. I adopted this belief because it was the belief of the people.

Thomas Cooper, *The Life of Thomas Cooper. Written by Himself*, 1872.

Source E

William Lovett on O'Connor. Remember that Lovett had always been suspicious of O'Connor's motives, and that the *Northern Star* had condemned and ridiculed Lovett's 'new move'.

i)   ... your own vain self must be supreme – you must be 'the leader of the people' ... You carry your fame about with you on all occasions to sink all other topics in the shade – you are the great 'I AM' of politics, the great personification of Radicalism ...

ii)   I regard Feargus O'Connor as the chief marplot of our movement ... a man who, by his personal conduct joined to his malignant influence in the Northern Star, has been the blight of democracy from the first moment he opened his mouth as its professed advocate ... By his great professions, by trickery and deceit, he got the aid of the working classes to establish an organ to promulgate their principles, which he soon converted into an instrument for destroying everything intellectual and moral in our movement ... the *Star*, a mere reflex of the nature of its master ... By his constant appeals to the selfishness, vanity, and mere animal propensities of man, he succeeded in calling up a spirit of hate, intolerance and brute feeling, previously unknown among Reformers.

William Lovett, *The Life and Struggles of William Lovett*, 1876.

---

1   What reasons do sources B, C, and D offer to explain O'Connor's enormous popularity and success?
2   Compare and contrast the impressions of O'Connor in sources A and E, commenting on their tone and the language used.
3   How reliable and useful are these sources as evaluations of O'Connor and his contribution to the movement?

The man and the historians

Source F

O'Connor ... was unworthy of the trust ... so strangely reposed in him. He was an egoist who spent much of his time consolidating his own position and eliminating other leaders of whom he very early became jealous, and he was a braggart, a man who used rhetoric about force without clearly understanding what the words meant, and as a result under his inspiration the movement came to be conspicuously ill led.

G. Kitson Clark, The Making of Victorian England, 1962.

Source G

... among O'Connor's most important contributions as a national leader was his ability to turn his appeal as a charismatic demagogue towards the creation of more permanent forms of working class organisation and leadership.

As Chartism's most prominent national leader, O'Connor played a central role in maintaining the movement's national challenge. At least until 1848, he was able to unite the forces of Chartism behind his leadership .... O'Connor's popularity was based upon his unrivalled talents as an agitator, his brilliance as an orator, his indefatigable energy in the radical cause; but his standing within the ranks of Chartism was also founded upon the consistent and intelligent leadership which he had provided since the mid-1830s, his insistent class perspective and class tone, his emphasis upon the need to establish permanent organisations of independent working class political struggle. He came to symbolise the independence of working class radicalism. Certain aspects of his style of leadership, particularly its highly personalised character, may appear unattractive, and may have proved detrimental to the cause ... O'Connor clearly understood the attraction of a leadership style that looked back to Hunt ... the movement's great charismatic leader attempted to channel the spontaneous energy of Chartist protest into support for national institutions capable of sustaining agitation over the long-term.

J. Epstein, The Lion of Freedom, 1982.

Source H

In fact, so far from being the exploiter and distorter of the Chartist movement, O'Connor was so much the centre of it, that had the name Chartist not been coined, the radical movement between 1838 and 1848 must surely have been called O'Connorite Radicalism. Remove him and his newspaper from the picture and the movement fragments, localises and loses its continuity.

Dorothy Thompson, The Chartists, 1984.

---

4 Discuss the interpretation of O'Connor's role in source F, relating it to sources A, B, C, D and E.

5 'O'Connor did more harm than good to the Chartist movement.' Comment on this view, referring to all the sources and your wider knowledge of the movement's history.

Who were the Chartists?

> The Charter was a symbol of unity, but it concealed as much as it proclaimed – the diversity of local social pressures, the variety of local leaderships, and the relative sense of urgency among different people and different groups.
>
> Asa Briggs, *Chartist Studies*, 1959.

Chartism was stronger in some parts of the country than others. London was not a major centre of Chartist activity until 1848 – it lacked the sense of community shared in the single-industry towns of the industrial districts. The London radicals were divided amongst themselves and resented outside leadership, whilst the very size of the city meant that local loyalties were difficult to overcome. One reason for the move of the National Convention to Birmingham in 1839 was the lack of enthusiasm in London.

The movement was at its most militant in the single-industry outworking villages and small towns of the Midlands, and in the expanding textile towns of Lancashire and the West Riding. In 1842 it was strikers from the outlying cotton towns like Ashton-under-Lyne, Hyde, and Staleybridge, who took the general strike into Manchester and closed its mills. Leeds, Manchester and Sheffield had their Chartists, but there were too many trades affected by change and depression in different ways and times. Leeds and Sheffield, however, saw 'municipal Chartism', with Chartists being elected to the local councils.

On the other hand in small single-industry towns dominated by a paternalistic employer, like Glossop, there was little agitation. The Wesleyan Methodist network kept Chartist lecturers and missionaries away from the Cornish tin miners. Despite the events at Newport, the miners of South Wales played little further part in the movement, while in the North East the miners turned to trade union activity after 1839. Agricultural labourers were hardly touched by the movement.

Chartists in Scotland tended to be more moderate than the 'physical force' English leaders. Glasgow was the centre of Scottish Chartism but that city did not experience the full severity of the economic depression. The Scottish shipbuilding and heavy engineering industries were just beginning to grow at the end of the 1830s, and there was no Poor Law Amendment Act in Scotland to excite discontent. Trade societies were more closely integrated into a movement which had its roots in the prosecution of the leaders of the spinner's strike of 1837.

Outworkers faced particular problems which made the political demands of Chartism attractive. Handloom weavers, superseded by technological innovation, were trying to survive in a dying trade. Leicestershire framework knitters were increasingly exploited by manufacturers and middlemen who hired out the knitting frames as well as providing the raw materials, and were trying to force down wages by ignoring apprenticeship regulations. Handloom weavers and stockingers had seen their appeals to Parliament for protection rejected. The Charter seemed to offer a ray of hope.

Factory workers were active in the movement. Cotton spinners and power-loom weavers appear on lists of Chartists. Skilled male cotton spinners felt threatened by the introduction of the new self-acting mules which could be managed by women and children. In some mills double banked mules were being installed – the spinner had more to supervise and production increased, but wages did not. These grievances contributed to the outbreak of the 'Plug' Strikes in August and September 1842. Chartists wanted the regulation of machinery and of factories. Factory workers in the woollen industry also became Chartists, for similar reasons.

Craft workers are well represented on lists of active Chartists – shoemakers, tailors, and building workers. These trades were being transformed by employers seeking to increase production by methods including the ending of apprenticeships and moving workers into supervised workshops. Craft skills were being devalued. Men became Chartists to defend their skill, status and labour against the pressures imposed by the employers' desire to meet the needs of the new mass markets.

Chartism was not, however, solely the province of workers threatened by change. Trade societies were probably more closely linked to Chartism than earlier historians supposed, and in August 1842 it was a conference of the five metal trades – mechanics, engineers, millwrights, smiths and moulders – a major area of growth in the industrial economy, which transformed an industrial dispute into a strike for the Charter. The Charter seemed to promise protection to all those whose earnings, status or employment seemed insecure.

TALKING POINT

Chartism meant different things to different groups of workers at different times. It can only be fully understood if the local dimension is taken into account. Why, then, and in what ways, was Chartism so successful as a working class movement? To what extent does that success surprise you?

Examining the Evidence

Women in Chartism

The Belle alliance, or the Female Reformers of Blackburn!!!

THERE HAD BEEN FEMALE REFORM SOCIETIES DURING EARLIER AGITATIONS, AND
THERE WERE REPRESENTATIVES FROM THEM ON THE PLATFORM AT PETERLOO. WHAT
DOES THE CARTOON FROM 1819 SUGGEST ABOUT ATTITUDES TOWARDS FEMALE
INVOLVEMENT IN POLITICS, AND THE PREJUDICES WOMEN WOULD FACE?

Source A

Let every man, woman and child sign the petition ... Go on, good men!
Go on, virtuous women! ... we are engaged in the cause of justice
which is the cause of God. Sign the petition!

Feargus O'Connor writing from the National Convention, 1839.

Source B

The formation of political societies amongst the women may be justly
ranked as one of the most important features in the present political
movement; for on no other occasion have women been aroused to a
just sense of their social and political importance.

Henry Vincent, *Western Vindicator*, 28 September 1839.

Source C

A description of the banner of the Female Political Union of Newcastle-on-Tyne.

... on one side the keeper of the Bastille about to part the mother and her children, with the motto 'Tyrants beware – think ye a mother's love is not stronger than your laws?' on the other the inhuman monster parting man and wife with 'whome God has joined together let no man put asunder.'

Northern Star, 2 February 1839.

Source D

We have been told that the province of woman is her home, and that the field of politics should be left to men, this we deny; the nature of things renders it impossible ... Is it not true that the interests of our fathers, husbands, and brothers, ought to be ours? If they are oppressed and impoverished, do we not share those evils with them? ...

We have seen that because the husband's earnings could not support his family, the wife has been compelled to leave her home neglected and, with her infant children, work at soul and body degrading toil. We have seen the father dragged from his home by a ruffian press-gang ... We have seen the poor robbed of their inheritance and a law enacted to treat poverty as a crime, to deny misery consolation, to take from the unfortunate their freedom, to drive the poor from their homes and their fatherland, to separate those whom God has joined together, and tear the children from their parents' care ...

We have struggled to maintain our homes in comfort, such as our hearts told us should greet our husbands after their fatiguing labours. Year after year has passed away, and even now our wishes have no prospect of being realised, our husbands are overwrought, our homes half-furnished, our families ill-fed, and our children uneducated ...

We have searched and found that the cause of these evils is the government of the country being in the hands of a few of the upper and middle classes, while the working men who form the millions, the strength and wealth of the country, are left without the pale of the Constitution ... for these evils there is no remedy but the just measure of allowing every citizen of the United Kingdom the right of voting in the election of the members of Parliament, who have to make the laws that he has to be governed by, and grant the taxes he has to pay for ... in other words, to pass the people's Charter into a law ... This is what the working men ... are struggling for, and we have banded ourselves together in union to assist them.

'Address of the Female Political Union of Newcastle-upon-Tyne to their Fellow-Countrywomen', *Northern Star*, 2 February 1839.

Source E

Extract from the Address of the female Chartists of Ashton-under-Lyne.

... we are determined that no man shall ever enjoy our hands, our hearts, or share our beds, that will not stand forward as the advocate of the rights of man, and as the determined enemy of the damnable New Poor Law ... we do not despair of yet seeing intelligence the necessary qualification for voting, and then sisters, we shall be placed in our proper position in society, and enjoy the elective franchise as well as our kinsmen.

Northern Star, 2 February 1839.

1. How do the women justify their political involvement?
2. Female Anti-Poor Law Societies were active in many northern mill towns. Why were women prominent in that movement and what evidence of their concern is there here?
3. Is there any evidence in either address (source D or E) that votes for women as part of universal suffrage were required or deemed attainable?

Source F

... every inducement or threat that could be held out to goad forward the men was fully applied by these harpies, whose expressions on every occasion, whose oaths and blasphemy, groans and yells, really made us blush for the feminine sex of England ... In Lees close, when the Mayor read the riot act, the scene was truly horrifying: a decided majority in number of women, many with children, were assembled, and attempting by all the means in their power, to raise a disturbance or promote a riot against the authorities. 'I wish I were a man', said one, 'I'd soon put the ******* police to rout.' Another exclaimed, 'What are they running at! why don't they cut them to pieces now they have them here ...' – while shouts of 'At 'em lads,' and 'Down with them,' burst from the mouths of the mothers of families and wives of hardworking men ... We do not hesitate to say, that the men would never have met in the Market Place or on the Forest on Monday were it not for the women; the taunts and revilings at their conduct in not turning on the soldiers, and sticking up for their rights cannot be described.

Nottingham Mercury, 16 August 1839.

Source G

London is threatened with an irruption of female Chartists, and every man of experience is naturally alarmed, for he knows that the VOX FOEMINAE is the VOX DIABOLI when it is set going ... we have, however, something to propose that will easily meet the emergency. A heroine who could never run from a man, would fly in dismay before an industrious flea or a burly black beetle. We have only to collect together a good supply of cockroaches, with a fair sprinkling of rats, and a muster of mice, in order to disperse the largest and most ferocious crowd of females that was ever collected.

Punch, 1848.

Women in Chartism – a changing role

In 1839 O'Connor and Vincent appeared to be encouraging female involvement. The evidence suggests that women were active in the Chartist movement, though generally acting in support of their menfolk rather than with a separate feminist agenda. Early chroniclers of Chartism, like R. C. Gammage, ignored their role. Dorothy Thompson, in her study of Chartism, has concluded that women largely disappeared from working class politics by the middle of the century.

Here are some issues to consider:

● Opponents of Chartism used the female presence to ridicule the movement as a whole.

● Early historians of Chartism were men who wanted to portray a mature working class movement. Female involvement did not fit into their picture.

4 In what ways do both the reporter on the *Nottingham Mercury* and the writer in *Punch* display their prejudices against female Chartists?

5 How could both articles be used to discredit the whole movement?

TALKING POINT

Discuss these points. How far do they explain the neglect of female Chartists by historians, and do they provide a reasonable explanation for the withdrawal of working class women from political activity?

- The formalisation of Chartism in the National Charter Association and the Chartist Land Company meant that women and unskilled low-paid male workers were excluded.
- As society became more prosperous, a domestic female stereotype permeated down from the middle class for working class women to aspire to.

Why did Chartism fail?

1858 Abolition of property qualifications for MPs
1872 Secret ballot
1884 Third Reform Act created equal sized one-member constituencies
1911 Payment of MPs
1918 Universal manhood suffrage over age 21 (votes for women over 30 were also granted)

In 1848 ten years of agitation seemed to have achieved very little. The six points were still unattainable. Chartist activity played no part in the removal of property qualifications for MPs in 1858. The gains were less tangible. Attention had been drawn to the discontent of the industrial areas, and reforms had been instituted to 'kill Chartism with kindness'. Working people had also shown that they could organise a movement for themselves, and this experience of self-help, working class culture and fellowship provided a foundation for the building of the Labour movement in the second half of the century. These were small rewards for the optimism and commitment of those who had marched for the Charter in the autumn of 1838. What had gone wrong?

TALKING POINT

Why was the call for annual parliaments the only one of the six points that was not eventually adopted? Do the Chartists deserve any credit for these developments?

'Doomed to failure'?

In the circumstances of post-1832 politics there was no chance that the House of Commons would legislate for the Charter, and no reason at all why the propertied middle class should support the working class protest.

The Chartist class analysis of events since 1832 alienated potential sympathisers amongst middle class radicals. There could be no alliance with employers and manufacturers who exploited working people, or with Radicals who advocated the new economic thinking, who had voted for the Poor Laws and who wanted repeal of the Corn Laws, even if they had wished to join forces with the Chartists.

The Anti-Corn Law League was suspect because the Chartists feared the motives of its mill-owner members – repeal of the Corn Laws might make bread cheaper, but that would merely enable the mill owners to cut wages. O'Connor proposed the retention of protection and payment of higher wages to give manufacturers a larger home market, not the export market the League hoped for.

At no time did the authorities, whether under Whig or Tory government, weaken in their handling of the crisis. Whig restraint during the meetings of the Chartist Convention in 1839 prevented a confrontation. Only after the Chartists had discredited themselves at Newport were there large numbers of arrests. A confident Conservative government struck decisively in 1842. Convicted Chartists were severely dealt with but, although prison conditions were harsh and unhealthy, the sentences were, in most cases, relatively short, to avoid creating martyrs.

AS THIS ILLUSTRATION OF TROOPS MARCHING INTO EUSTON STATION IN AUGUST 1842 SUGGESTS, THE EXPANDING RAILWAY NETWORK, AND THE TELEGRAPH SYSTEM THAT ACCOMPANIED IT, ENABLED THE AUTHORITIES TO RESPOND QUICKLY TO DISTURBANCES. THE METROPOLITAN POLICE, TRAINED IN CROWD CONTROL, HAD BEEN DISPATCHED TO BIRMINGHAM AND OTHER TOWNS DURING 1839. IN 1848 THE METROPOLITAN POLICE WERE ABLE TO DISPERSE RIOTS AND THREATENING CROWDS IN LONDON WITHOUT MILITARY ASSISTANCE. SOME IMPROVEMENT IN POLICING IN THE INDUSTRIAL AREAS, AS A RESULT OF THE MUNICIPAL CORPORATIONS ACT AND THE RURAL POLICE ACT, MEANT GREATER SOCIAL CONTROL AND FEWER OPPORTUNITIES FOR MEETINGS AND DEMONSTRATIONS TO ERUPT INTO SERIOUS TROUBLE.

'Extraordinary feebleness'

PART OF THE PROCESSION.—SKETCHED AT BLACKFRIARS-BRIDGE.

IMPRESSIVE MARCHES AND DEMONSTRATIONS, LIKE THIS PROCESSION IN SUPPORT OF THE CHARTER THROUGH LONDON IN 1848, IMPLIED GREATER STRENGTH THAN THE MOVEMENT ACTUALLY POSSESSED.

That the Chartists expected to batter down prejudice and authority with petitions says more about their naivety than their understanding of the reality of the situation. By adopting the constitutional route through the national petition the Chartist leadership condemned the movement to the humiliation of repeated failure. The failure of the petition in 1838, and the subsequent lack of direction of the Chartist leadership, brought about immense disillusionment, and this was repeated in 1842 and 1848. No popular agitation could afford these rebuffs, but no credible alternative strategy was offered.

Serious differences over strategy were reflected by the division of the leaders into 'moral force' and 'physical force' factions. Lovett, Vincent and others looked to the 'New Move' and alliance with sympathetic middle class radicals. O'Connor is often seen as the leader of the 'physical force' group, but his was the rhetoric of the platform, and he always hedged his exhortations with qualifications and conditions. His purpose was intimidation – what C.P. Villiers, the Anti-Corn Law MP, called the 'brickbat argument'.

TALKING POINT

'Chartism is dead in these parts. The Ten Hours Act and cheap provisions have slain it outright.' (Lord Ashley writing to Lord John Russell from Manchester in 1851) To what extent does this comment help us to understand the 'feebleness' of Chartism? Comment on and explain Ashley's failure to understand Chartism.

The changing political climate

Chartist decline was not initially the result of prosperity and economic stabilization, for it effectively preceded them. Attention to the language of Chartism suggests that its rise and fall is to be related in the first instance not to movements in the economy, divisions in the movement or an immature class consciousness, but to the changing character and policies of the state – the principal enemy upon whose actions radicals had always found credibility depended.

G. Stedman Jones, *Rethinking Chartism.*

Whether influenced by the need to remove Chartist discontent or not, the governments of Peel and Russell reduced the cost of living, repealed the Corn Laws, passed the Mines Act and the Ten Hours Act, and began to think seriously about public health. Repeal of the Corn Laws was not the calamity Chartist leaders had forecast, and the economic prosperity and falling prices of the next decade merely reinforced the bankruptcy of their case.

A changing working class?

By the 1850s those workers who had been threatened by changes at work, new technology, falling piece rates, and attacks on the restriction and protection of their craft, had lost the battle. It is perhaps significant that Chartism retained its vitality longest in towns like Bradford and Halifax where handworkers survived against mechanisation the longest. Elsewhere the battle between employer and employee still continued, but on different terms. For the skilled 'aristocracy of labour', there were new trade unions and leaders who believed that the direct challenge to society was not the best means of protecting the interests of the working man. Amongst this group there was an increasing approximation to middle class values and standards of respectability as co-operatives, friendly societies and savings banks developed in the calmer economic climate of the mid-Victorian years.

TALKING POINT

'The Chartists were doomed to failure even before the final form of their Charter was drafted.' (Asa Briggs)
'The historian of Chartism ... can hardly fail to be saddened by the extraordinary feebleness of this greatest of all the mass movements of British labour.' (E.J. Hobsbawm) Discuss these views, explaining 'doomed to failure' and 'the extraordinary feebleness'.

REVIEW

'The Chartist movement was born of genuine distress but ruined by inept leadership.' Discuss this statement.
This essay encompasses all the issues you will be expected to cover in any question on Chartism. Examiners are likely to ask you about the reasons for the emergence of a militant working class movement in the late 1830s, or for some explanation for its decline and eventual collapse. As part of your review of this chapter make a diagram, chart or pattern notes to bring both these aspects of Chartism together on one sheet of paper, as they are closely linked. You may have to refer to other chapters. Now use this as your plan, and write the essay.

8 The Anti-Corn Law League – Successful Politics of Pressure?

PREVIEW

The League's case

Source A

THIS WAS THE LABEL INSIDE A HAT – SOLD AS THE 'CORN LAW REPEAL HAT' – IT PROVIDES A SUMMARY OF THE CORE ARGUMENTS FOR FREE TRADE

Source B
Extract from the petition of the Nonconformists attending the Old Gravel Pit Chapel in Hackney to the House of Commons in favour of repeal of the Corn Laws, 1841.

That the results of those unhappy Laws are now made manifest in the extreme sufferings of those classes of our fellow subjects which constitute the basis of our national strength, in the depression of manufactures, and their exportation to rival countries, in the miserable inadequate wages of both agricultural and manufacturing industry, in the entire want of work to an alarming extent, in the hazardous and pernicious direction given to mercantile pursuits, and in a fearful tendency to the impoverishment and ruin of the nation. That your Petitioners are especially affected by a rational and Christian conviction of the impiety involved in those Laws, as being in their nature a crime against God, and as in their practical operation productive of discontent, disloyalty, infidelity, profligacy of conduct, a rejection of the authority of religion, and by necessary consequence the most appalling dangers to the peace and security of all classes as to both property and person.

1 Using both sources, make a list of the points in favour of free trade, and against the Corn Laws.
2 Comment on the religious and Biblical references in the sources. Suggest why the Anti-Corn Law League might want to highlight them.

The Anti-Corn Law League: the contexts

The economic context
The League, like Chartism, was a product of the economic depression of the late 1830s. Like Chartism, it offered a solution to the 'condition of England question'.

The Corn Laws were attacked as the symbol of a protective economic policy that had failed to bring to British industry the prosperity the efforts of the manufacturers deserved. Repeal seemed to offer a simple and immediate solution to the difficulties that industry, and particularly the textile industry, was facing. For most cotton manufacturers it was, commented Henry Ashworth, 'a pocket question'. The League's greatest support, both financial and moral, came from Lancashire and the exporting cotton industry. Cobden recognised these realities as early as 1839 after experiencing the apathy of London – 'My hopes of agitation are anchored in Manchester' (Letter to J.B. Smith, 3 February 1839).

The political context
If the immediate context was the economic depression, the roots of the League must be viewed in the wider context of the collapse of political radicalism. By the late 1830s the heady optimism of 1833, when the presence of 60 to 70 Radical MPs in the reformed House of Commons promised a period of further reform, had gone sour. The parliamentary Radicals differed in background, temperament and political aims. Thomas

Attwood had his currency theories, George Grote seemed obsessed with the ballot, Joseph Hume with government expenditure, and John Roebuck with indiscriminately attacking the government. Co-operation was impossible, and no leader emerged to mould them into an effective parliamentary force. Some lost their seats in the 1835 General Election, and many more followed in 1837. 'Amateurs in politics', they were unwilling to give a lead to extra-parliamentary movements and reluctant to compromise with the Whigs in an alliance that could keep Peel out.

The League's clear, single purpose – total and immediate repeal of the Corn Laws – seemed to provide a focus on which Radicals of all persuasions might unite. Cobden certainly viewed the agitation with that wider perspective. In his speeches the Corn Laws became a symbol of the aristocracy's privileged position in society and government.

Both he and John Bright exploited the resentments of the rising commercial middle class, conscious of their role as wealth creators and makers of the nation's current and future greatness, but jealous of the political status and influence of aristocracy.

> I believe this to be a movement of the commercial and industrial classes against the lords and great proprietors of the soil.
>
> John Bright speaking at the League's Covent Garden meeting, 19 December 1845.

TALKING POINT

If these resentments existed, why did so many successful manufacturers aspire to purchase landed estates, send their sons to public schools and become members of the landed gentry?

The humanitarian and religious context

> I think the scattered elements may yet be rallied round the question of the corn laws. It appears to me that a moral and even a religious spirit may be infused into that topic, and if agitated in the same manner that the question of slavery has been, it will be irresistible.
>
> Richard Cobden to his brother Frederick, 5 October 1838.

Repeal had an immense humanitarian appeal – here was the means by which the starving could be fed, a process blocked by the selfish interests of the few. The Bible provided propagandists with many appropriate texts. In August 1841 the League arranged a four day conference for ministers of religion on the Corn Laws. Its proceedings were carefully orchestrated by Manchester ministers, the League provided the secretarial assistance and the resolutions were all carefully prepared beforehand. Some 700 attended, the vast majority Nonconformists, some sent by their congregations and some by local Leaguers in their home towns. The dividends for the League were incalculable. Many of the ministers were convinced that the Corn Laws were a social evil and contrary to the word of God. They took these views back to their congregations, and their petitions increased the flood the League could direct at the Commons at the beginning of the parliamentary session.

The assault on the Corn Laws also led to attacks on the Church of England for taking tithes and revenues which depended on a system that robbed the poor of food: 'The Church clergy are almost to a man guilty of causing the present distress by upholding the Corn Law – they having themselves an interest in the high price of bread' (Cobden to Bright, 12 May 1842).

TALKING POINT

A rallying point for the Radicals, an attack on inherited privilege, a promise of cheap food and economic stability, a solution for the problems of poverty and hunger, and a stick to beat the Church of England? How could the League offer all these things, and what would the advantages be if it succeeded?

Focus

8.1 The Anti-Corn Law League – prototype pressure group

THE TIMES

18 November 1843

THE ANTI-CORN LAW LEAGUE

A single issue pressure group with one clearly understood aim – total and immediate repeal of the Corn Laws.

THE LEAGUE IS A GREAT FACT ... It is a great fact that there should have been created in the homesteads of our manufacturers a confederacy devoted to the agitation of one political question, persevering in it year after year, shrinking from no trouble, dismayed by no danger, making light of every obstacle ... These are facts important and worthy of consideration. No moralist can disregard them; no politician can sneer at them; no statesman can undervalue them .... A NEW POWER HAS ARISEN IN THE STATE.

Talking point

Pressure groups

Many of the techniques used by modern pressure groups were developed by similar organisations in the eighteenth and nineteenth centuries. The anti-slavery campaigns have been regarded as the first successful attempts to organise mass public opinion to persuade parliament to abolish first the slave trade (1807), and then slavery itself (1833) within the British Empire. The Anti-Corn Law League gave pressure group politics a totally new dimension, and a new range of methods to apply.

The League took pressure group politics to a new level of sophistication and professionalism.

Wilson chaired the League Council which exercised a firm central control. All subscribers of £50 were entitled to attend – in practice that meant a nucleus of Manchester men. Even after the League's HQ was moved to London in 1843 Newell's Buildings in Manchester remained the powerhouse from which all documents were issued and where all decisions were made.

The League organised petitions in 1840, 1841 and 1842. This was a traditional pressure group tactic which Cobden abandoned as ineffective and demoralising until there was some chance of parliamentary success. Regular large majorities in the Commons against repeal did not encourage supporters.

Propaganda and popular education was essential. The League appointed its first lecturers in 1839, had its own journal (*The Anti-Corn Law Circular,* renamed *The Anti-Bread Tax Circular*, and in 1843 *The League*) and employed an army of pamphlet writers. In 1843 300 people were employed in the League's publications department, and 500 in distribution. Apparently independent writers were secretly subsidised, payments were made to newspapers to publish favourable articles, and the League gave financial support at the launch of the Economist in 1843. In 1843 Cobden and Bright began their joint speaking tours drawing huge audiences and keeping the League in touch with its supporters.

Modern communications were exploited by the League:

● The League pioneered the political mailshot in selected constituencies from 1843 by making use of the penny post. Cobden perceived clearly the power of this new medium:

> ... we shall radicalise the country in the process of carrying repeal of the Corn Laws; and we are effecting such an organisation by means of the penny postage (that destined scourge of the aristocracy) that we shall, by and by, be able to carry any measure by a coup de billet.
>
> Richard Cobden to C.P. Villiers, 1840.

● The expanding railway network was also vital for the League's activities, enabling Cobden and Bright to undertake their extensive tours.

As MPs, Cobden and Bright gave the League spokesmen whose parliamentary speeches would gain coverage for their ideas in a generally unsympathetic press. 'You speak with a loud voice when talking on the floor of the House.' (Cobden, June 1845) The League became a wealthy organisation. The £50,000 fund of 1842 was followed by an appeal for £100,000 in 1844 and £250,000 in 1845. In the depression years funds were difficult to raise, but in the good years after 1842 support from manufacturers was readily available.

> ... the return of better times may have diminished the ardour of many repealers, but it filled the League's coffers to overflowing, and that was the main point.
>
> N.C. Edsall, *Richard Cobden: Independent Radical*, 1986.

Continuous agitation and propaganda could be financed.

THE LEADING PERSONALITIES

'Of the free traders Mr. Cobden is, unquestionably, the natural leader. His talents are considerable and always available. He is quick, fluent, unscrupulous.' (Morning Chronicle, hostile Tory newspaper, July 1842) He was the League's tactician and spokesman possessing 'the great quality in a leader of a public question, of sticking exclusively to your object.' (Joseph Parkes to Cobden, 1843). MP in 1841.

RICHARD COBDEN

The manipulator and 'wheeler dealer' who kept the organisation oiled. Cobden wrote to him in 1846: 'You and I made the League, and the League made others.'

GEORGE WILSON

Quaker and Rochdale mill owner who began actively working for the League in 1841 after the death of his wife. He soon became Cobden's number two. On their dual speaking tours his biblical and emotional oratory neatly complemented the quiet rational approach adopted by Cobden. MP in 1843.

JOHN BRIGHT

THE ELECTORAL STRATEGY

The House must be changed before we can go further.

Richard Cobden to J. B. Smith, February 1839.

Stage 1 – 1840:

Leaguers were recommended to demand repeal pledges from election candidates.

Stage 2 – 1841:

League contested Walsall by-election when the Whig candidate refused to make a repeal pledge. J.B. Smith was only 27 votes behind the winning Tory – gaining a moral victory for the League. At the General Election Walsall was won, Cobden was returned for Stockport, and free traders were successful in other Lancashire towns.

Stage 3 – 1842–44:

The decision to contest borough seats was preceded by a general survey of constituencies and their accessibility to a repeal candidate. Electors in targeted boroughs received mailshots, and there was work on electoral registration to increase the number of favourable voters. After 1844 efforts were concentrated on winnable seats following a series of damaging failures in small boroughs where local influences were too strong.

Stage 4 – 1844–46:

Winnable county seats were targeted. Urban freeholders in the industrial towns were encouraged to register their county votes; supporters were urged to create new votes by buying rural properties and splitting them up into 40 shilling freeholds. In this way an investment of £50 could buy a vote. Special attention was paid to South and North Lancashire, North Cheshire, South Staffordshire, Middlesex and the West Riding. The annual registration process was used to challenge protectionist voters and remove them from the roll. In 1845 a South Lancashire by-election was won easily. In 1846 the protectionists did not bother to contest the West Riding.

1 What factors and techniques do you think are needed to make a successful pressure group?
2 Both Chartism and the League were pressure groups. One saw its objective achieved, albeit not directly as a result of its campaign, the other is dubbed a failure. Compare and examine the differing approaches of these movements. To what extent did they contribute to success or failure?

FOCUS

8.2 Chartists and the League

Source A

> Who are that blustering, canting crew,
> Who keep the cheap loaf in our view,
> And would from us more profit screw?
>
> The League.
>
> Who cry 'Repeal the curs'd Corn law',
> And would their workmen feed with straw,
> That they may filthy lucre paw?
>
> The League.
>
> Who wish to gull the working man,
> And burk the Charter, if they can,
> With their self-aggrandising plan?
>
> The League.

Northern Star

Source B

Not that Corn Law Repeal is wrong; when we get the Charter we will repeal the Corn Laws and all the other bad laws. But if you give up your agitation for the Charter to help the Free Traders, they will not help you to get the Charter. Don't be deceived by the middle classes again. You helped them get their votes – you swelled their cry of 'The Bill, the whole Bill, and nothing but the Bill!' But where are the fine promises they made you? Gone to the winds! They said when they had gotten their votes, they would help you to get yours. But they and the rotten Whigs have never remembered you ... And now they want to get the Corn Laws repealed – not for your benefit – but for their own. 'Cheap Bread!' they cry. But they mean 'Low Wages'. Do not listen to their cant and humbug. Stick to your Charter. You are veritable slaves without your votes.

Speech made by the Leicester Chartist John Mason.

> What do these sources suggest about the relationship between the League and the Chartists? List the accusations made against the League and its middle class supporters, commenting on their validity and on Chartist priorities.

Some Chartist leaders looked forward to repeal, but only after the Charter had been achieved and parliament had legislated to safeguard wages and to protect workers. O'Connor took a protectionist stance, both in print and on the platform, emphasising the divergent interests of mill owners and their employees.

Violence

In Manchester the local Chartists disrupted League meetings. The Leaguers retaliated by allying with the local Irish who were incensed by O'Connor's attacks on O'Connell.

> The Chartist leaders attacked us on the platform at the head of their deluded followers. We were nearly the victims of physical force; I lost my hat, and all but had my head split open with the leg of a stool.
>
> Richard Cobden describing an early League meeting.

In October 1841 the Chartists moved their own amendment to the main resolution at a League public meeting in Manchester. The following extract is an eye-witness account:

> ... one speech in support of it was listened to, the second speaker was refused a hearing. Mr Acland then spoke in support of the original motion, but was interrupted by a Chartist in the centre of the room. Upon this, a body of Irish [Corn Law repealers] rose. A cry of 'Put him out' was raised, and presently a forest of shillelahs was seen flourishing in the air. The forms were upset, and the sides of several of them torn off, and converted into short staves ... In a short time the Irish became almost exclusive possessors of the room.

In March 1842 the Manchester free traders successfully broke up a Chartist rally attended by O'Connor himself.

3 Why was Manchester likely to be at the centre of disputes between Chartists and the League, and why was the League prepared to use dubious methods to assert their control?

The League – 'a middle-class agitation'

> I have no objection in admitting here ... that these artifices and manoeuvres [Chartist inspired disruptions of League meetings] have ... compelled us to make our agitation a middle-class agitation. I do not deny that the working classes generally have attended our lectures and signed our petitions; but I will admit, that so far as the fervour and efficiency of our agitation has gone, it has eminently been a middle-class agitation. We have carried it on by those means by which the middle class usually carries on its movements. We have had our meetings of dissenting ministers; we have obtained the co-operation of the ladies; we have resorted to tea-parties, and taken those pacific means for carrying out our views, which mark us rather as a middle-class set of agitators ... We are no political body; we have refused to be bought by the Tories; we have kept aloof from the Whigs; and we will not join partnership with either Radicals or Chartists, but we hold out our hand ready to give it to all who are willing to advocate the total and immediate repeal of the corn and provision laws.
>
> Richard Cobden speaking to the League Council, September 1842.

4 Comment on Cobden's attitude towards the middle and working classes in this source, showing how it is reflected in the tone and language used.

TALKING POINT

Using the evidence from this Focus, and your wider knowledge, explain why Leaguers and Chartists found it impossible to work together, commenting on the class emphasis underlying both movements.

Richard Cobden – agitator and strategist

Although Cobden is inextricably connected with Manchester, the cotton industry and free trade he did not settle in that city until he was 28. Born in Sussex, his roots were rural and agricultural. When he first rose to prominence, in the campaign to gain incorporation for Manchester in 1838 he was looked upon as an upstart by the middle class élite who managed the affairs of the town.

Cobden and repeal

For Cobden the League was about more than repeal of the Corn Laws. It was an organisation which could unite reformers of all classes, place the Tories on the defensive – opposing what was morally and socially, as well as economically, right – and regain for the Radicals their ascendancy over the Whigs. The free trade argument was respectable with a pedigree stretching back to Adam Smith. It had convinced supporters in the Board of Trade. There was nothing revolutionary about it to frighten off the moderates.

Repeal was one more step to the overthrow of aristocratic power, the realisation of the promise of 1832, and the establishment of government by the enlightened middle class.

> The sooner the power in this country is transferred from the landed oligarchy, which has so misused it, and is placed absolutely ... in the hands of the intelligent middle and industrious classes, the better for the conditions and destinies of this country.
>
> Richard Cobden in a speech, 15 January 1845.

This vision of what the anti-Corn Law agitation should be was Cobden's special contribution to the movement, and largely because of it he was able to assume a central role in the campaign from its inception.

N.C. Edsall, *Richard Cobden – Independent Radical*,1986.

Cobden's case for repeal

Cobden recognised the negative impact of the argument that cheap food would lead to lower wages, and so did not use the simplistic call for 'cheap bread'. His case for repeal was that:
- Manufacturers would benefit from repeal, which would open export markets by giving food producers money to spend.
- Workers would benefit from the increasing demand for labour and, therefore, from higher and more regular wages at a time when food prices were falling.
- Increasing international trade would bring peoples and governments into closer relationships and interdependence. International relations would improve, and a new era of peace be ushered in. Economic self interest would make war unthinkable.

Cobden and strategy

Cobden's case for repeal did not convince the Chartists, but as early as 1839 Cobden was pointing the League at the electors, rather than the masses.

> I formed my conviction [that C.P. Villiers' repeal motion would be defeated] upon the present constitution of the House of Commons, which forbids us hoping for success. *That House must be changed*

With part of the £75,000 gift he received from League supporters after repeal Cobden purchased his birthplace in Sussex and made it the core of a new residence. Although he continued to represent industrial constituencies in Parliament – the West Riding and later Rochdale – he never lived in the North again.

Discuss the reasons why
Cobden rejected a
parliamentary reform
campaign as the means of
changing the Commons, and
consider the likely impact of
the electoral strategy at a
General Election.

before we can get justice. All our efforts must therefore be directed upon the constituencies, and, to strike a blow that will be responded to by every large town, let us begin in Manchester. I propose ... our association call a meeting of the electoral body ... by which a pledge shall be entered into ... not to return any man to represent them in the future who will not vote for ... total and immediate repeal.

Richard Cobden to J.B. Smith, 3 February 1839.

The electoral strategy developed from seeking pledges to targeting winnable constituencies (see Focus 8.1). Cobden encouraged the exploitation of the registration procedures, and the use of the postal service to inform electors. He discovered the loopholes which enabled borough electors to purchase rural freeholds and thus an additional vote for a county seat, and this, together with careful scrutiny of the registers, became the main focus of League activity for the last two years of its existence.

Cobden and pressure group politics

Cobden's other contribution to the League was the insistence that it stick to the one clear objective of total and immediate repeal. He did not object to other reform movements but he was not prepared to associate the League with them. Joseph Sturge's Complete Suffrage Association (1842) was given his blessing, but even in this his aim was to further the cause of repeal: 'Nothing will frighten the aristocracy into free trade measures as soon as a threatened union of the classes upon the suffrage.'

THE ANTI-CORN LAW LEAGUE MEETS IN DRURY LANE THEATRE.

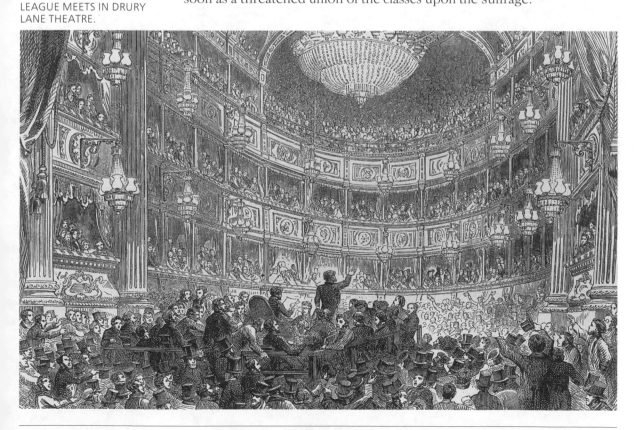

Cobden the campaigner

The commitment of both Cobden and John Bright to the League was total and punishing. Membership of the House of Commons, where Cobden was increasingly liked and respected, made its own demands. Cobden was more the member for the League, than for Stockport. Outside their presence was constantly required. A meeting was a guaranteed success if one or both men attended. The railways made their travels possible. In January 1844 Cobden began a Scottish tour in Glasgow and Edinburgh, proceeding to Perth, Aberdeen, Montrose and Dundee, then back to Manchester via Sunderland, Sheffield, York and Hull; after two days rest he was off to Blackburn and Stockport, to Wakefield on the 31st before catching the night train to London for the opening of Parliament the next day. His calico printing business, under the less than competent management of his brother, Frederick, was on the verge of bankruptcy by 1845.

THE ANTI-CORN LAW LEAGUE BAZAAR.

THE conversion of Covent Garden Theatre into a Gothic Hall is a transformation so complete, as to be worthy the best days of Pantomime and the high reputation of our old friend GRIEVE. The massy beams of ⅜ canvas, emblazoned with the Anti-corn Law cognizance—the roof of stained calico admitting "a dim rushlightish light," the Chinese lanterns trying to look Gothic, all tend to aid the delusion without entirely dispelling it. The aspect of the place is not, however, more marvellous than the regularity of the proceedings, when it is remembered that a committee of *one thousand ladies* has had the management of the arrangements. Scarcely a town has been without a female secretary and a committee of local ladies, all of whom have had a voice in the matter ; so that the unanimity with which the plan has been carried out is indeed wonderful.

The contributions to the bazaar comprise every conceivable commodity. We were particularly struck with three or four free millstones, which would form an elegant addition to the *bijouterie* of a lady of fashion. Some highly-polished circular saws seemed to be objects of great attraction, and we can fancy a gentleman presenting to his lady-love one of them, labelled, " A trifle from the League Bazaar."

There is a post-office, too, where you may buy one of our old jokes and a smile—such a smile !—for sixpence. The pretty politicians who preside at the various counters fulfil their task with admirable tact, and we repeatedly found our hands diving into our pockets, in obedience to the mute solicitations of the bright eyes of the fair Leaguers.

Contributions to the Bazaar.

THE GREAT LEAGUE BAZAAR AT THE COVENT GARDEN THEATRE IN 1845 WAS IMPORTANT AS BOTH A FUND RAISING AND A PUBLICITY EVENT. HOW WOULD YOU CONTRAST THE ROLE PLAYED BY WOMEN IN THE LEAGUE, AS SUGGESTED IN THIS ARTICLE, WITH THE ROLE OF WOMEN IN THE CHARTIST MOVEMENT DESCRIBED IN CHAPTER 7?

Examining the Evidence

The League and the 'Plug' Plot

Both the Government and the Chartists suspected that League manipulation lay behind the strikes in the cotton districts in the August of 1842.

Source A

Let a circular signed so as to give it some weight, be issued to every firm ... in the Cotton district, calling a special meeting ... A deputation to be sent off to Peel to lay before him the facts, and to have authority from the meeting to declare that the property of all these parties is rapidly wasting away, that the state of Trade renders it impossible to keep up wages – that they feel themselves merely the tool in the hands of the landowners to extract the greatest possible amount of labour for the smallest possible amount of food – that this course they will no longer pursue, seeing that it will bring ruin to themselves and suffering to their work-people, and that unless the Govt. consent to open their trade by repealing the Corn Law they will at a given time close their works ... At the same time a meeting of the Yorkshire Woollen district should be held to do the same. This would shake Peel either from office or into a new Bill or the Total Repeal, and it would show the country to what a crisis we are arrived. But is it practicable? To a great extent I think it is.

John Bright to Richard Cobden, 9 March 1842.

Source B

Depend on it the plan of a simultaneous stopping of the factories would not succeed. In the first place you can't get people to unite. In the next any attempt on the part of the Members of the League would draw upon us the odium from the working class of throwing them overboard.

Richard Cobden to John Bright, March 1842.

---

1 What precisely is Bright proposing in source A, and for what reasons does Cobden discourage him?

Source C

Bright describes the arrival of striking workers in Rochdale.

This morning about 10 o'clock, they entered Rochdale from Oldham, turning out the hands at all the mills and workshops in their progress – no opposition being made, no violence was necessary. At 11 they had passed through the town and were approaching our premises – some turned down to the Engine house and boilers and let the water out of the boilers to prevent their being started after their departure. They called to the people at work 'Come out,' 'Come out.' I was not inclined to resist, especially when the chances were all against us, and ordered the mills to be stopped.

John Bright to Richard Cobden, 11 August 1842.

Source D
Bright reports to George Wilson the outcome of a meeting in Rochdale of local mill owners and magistrates.

Boyds is very anxious some mill should start, & he will engage to defend it ... I strongly rebuked his disposition, told them we had predicted this – we knew the cause – they ought to know it, & recommended a resolution agreeing to do what we could to keep the peace, but imploring the Govt. to repeal the Corn law & do justice to the people.

John Bright to George Wilson, 12 August 1842.

Source E

I think some great meetings of the middle classes to declare that the tyranny of the aristocracy has brought this on would do good – & force at least the repeal of the Corn Laws ...

John Bright to George Wilson, 14 August 1842.

Source F

I have written to Wilson who tells me the League meets tomorrow morning & have advised very strongly that they should be cautious & quiet just now – the League is at this moment under trial by the public for charges laid on by the Tories, Standard & other papers – All that is necessary to rise higher than ever is for us to keep aloof in Manchester from all connection with the present commotions. The result of the present disturbances will be to weaken the government by the unpopularity which it will acquire in putting down the rioters. – The trades & Chartists will be weakened by their reverses.

Richard Cobden to his brother Frederick, 15 August 1842.

Source G
Bright reports to Cobden on the League Council meetings.

We have had two meetings ... A majority were for the resolutions I proposed ... but ... a lot were against them – Greg, Wilson, Evans – Wilson sent for Brooks and Callender who spoke strongly against them. I keep my opinion but rather than sacrifice our union I consented to withdraw them .... There is little pluck or firmness in this room.

John Bright to Richard Cobden, 16 August 1842.

Source H

I will venture to say, in the name of the Council of the Anti-Corn-Law League, that not only did not the members of that body know or dream of anything of the kind such as has now taken place,– I mean the turnout for wages – not only did they not know, concoct, wish for, or contemplate such things, but I believe the very last thing which the body of our subscribers would have wished for or desired, is the suspension of their business, and the confusion which has taken place in this district ....

Speech by Cobden at a League meeting, 25 August 1842.

2 Using sources C, D, E, F and G write accounts of the events of August 1842 from the points of view of Bright and Cobden.

3 From your wider knowledge of events explain why the League faced policy and tactical problems in 1842 which led Cobden and Bright to consider the methods outlined in these sources.

4 In source I, N. McCord writes that 'this denial was partly false.' To what extent was Cobden (source H) misleading his audience?

5 The government suspected the League of active involvement in the strikes and, for a week in August, all Cobden's letters were intercepted and read. From the evidence here, what, if anything, were the League and Cobden guilty of?

6 Sources I and J make a similar assessment of Cobden's motives. Can they be supported from the evidence you have seen, and can Edsall's apportioning of blame be justified?

Source I

It is clear ... that the reluctance of the Leaguers to have anything to do with extreme measures was due, not to any scrupulous regard for law and order, but solely to reasons of expediency.

N. McCord, *The Anti-Corn Law League*, 1958.

Source J

That 1842 was not the 1832 of Corn Law repeal was not due to want of hoping and trying on his [Cobden's] part. The League, under his direction, had done much to create the atmosphere of crisis, and it was considerations of tactics not of principle that led him to step back from the brink in August.

N. Edsall, *Richard Cobden – Independent Radical*, 1986.

EXAMINING THE EVIDENCE

The myth of the Anti-Corn Law League

After the repeal of the Corn Laws in 1846 the League quickly claimed the credit, and its responsibility for the free trade policies of Peel and later of Gladstone was widely accepted. Peel, it was asserted, had been converted by Cobden's arguments in the House of Commons. The other factors present during the crisis of 1845–46 were conveniently forgotten. How was this myth created, and how true was it?

Source A

PAPA COBDEN TAKING MASTER ROBERT A FREE TRADE WALK.

PAPA COBDEN.—"Come along, MASTER ROBERT, do step out."
MASTER ROBERT.—"That's all very well, but you know I cannot go so fast as you do."

Source B

THE ANTI-CORN LAW ORGAN.

Source C

Peel speaking in the House of Commons on his resignation, 29 June 1846.

The name which ought to be, and will be, associated with these measures is the name of one who, acting ... from pure and disinterested motives, has, with untiring energy, made appeals to our reason ... is the name of Richard Cobden.

Source D

The League would not have carried the repeal of the Corn Laws when they did, had it not been for the Irish famine and the circumstance that we had a Minister who thought more of the lives of the people than his own continuance in power ...

Richard Cobden.

---

1 Consult sources A and B. Explain how both cartoons could help in the creation of the League myth and, using your wider knowledge, comment on the accuracy of their comment.

2 Source D mixes myth and reality. Show how this is, and comment on Peel's remarks in source C.

Source E

The repeal of the Corn Laws in 1846 had not been the direct result of the League's agitation; certainly the League had made a great deal of noise during its life, had kept the question of the Corn Laws in the forefront of public attention, and had produced a considerable effect by its propaganda, but the final repeal was implemented by other hands and in the last crisis the whole settlement of the question was taken out of the League's hands. The League had certainly not yet succeeded in its aim of building up its own independent strength to a point at which repeal could have been carried in the face of the influence of the united landed interest. It is very unlikely that the free traders would have emerged victorious from a general election in 1846 if such a trial of strength proved necessary.

N. McCord, *The Anti-Corn Law League*, 1958.

Source F

The task he had set for the League in its early days, that of 'preparing the public mind,' had been accomplished. By keeping the issue alive for seven years and gradually undermining the theoretical foundations of protection, the League had altered the balance of opinion. The League had not converted Peel or Russell or the nation at large, but it had shifted the weight of doubt from repeal to protectionism and the heavy burden of being considered a narrow special interest from the League to the landed interest. For political reasons, the claims of that interest could not be ignored and were generally tolerated, at least in good times. The League did not, even in 1846, yet have the power to do very much about that. But once the claims of the landed interest were seen as coming into conflict with those of the mass of the population, as happened late in 1845, the Corn Laws were finished; the public would not quietly have accepted their continuance. That Cobden believed, with good reason, was the work of the League.

N.C. Edsall, Richard Cobden – Independent Radical, 1986.

Source G

Though he [Peel] certainly believed that free-trade in corn would alleviate the lot of the working classes in time of scarcity, he did not attach to the abolition of the corn laws the magical effects which the League orators sometimes predicted. More important in his view was the knowledge that their repeal would remove a feeling of class injustice and demonstrate to the voteless and unpropertied masses that a legislature of landowners was not indifferent to their wants. Only so could the aristocratic system in which Peel believed hope to survive in mid-Victorian society.

For him the repeal of the corn laws, as the Reform Act had been for Grey, was essentially a preserving measure.

N. Gash, Aristocracy and People, 1979.

Source H

Yet it is difficult to contend that the Corn Laws were repealed because of League pressure. That pressure had certainly kept the question closely in the public eye, but interest was not so strong in 1845-46 as it had been in 1843–44 ... The Corn Laws were repealed because Peel no longer believed in them ... Peel knew that a substantial proportion of the landed interest no longer set great store by protection. The Irish famine brought the ... question ... to a head in both parties ... He believed also that repeal in 1846 would spike radical guns ... Peel's actions in 1846 ... completed the process whereby the forces of property were strengthened , not weakened, during a period of monumental change.

E. Evans, The Forging of the Modern State, 1983.

---

3 How far do sources E and F qualify the myth of the League, and what do they see as its achievement?

Review

Essay

Sources G and H place the greatest emphasis on the role of Peel in the final repeal of the Corn Laws. Using your wider knowledge, and referring to the sources in this section, discuss the view that: 'It is difficult to contend that the Corn Laws were repealed because of League pressure.'

9 Britain, Europe and the World 1815–65

PREVIEW

Conflicting traditions in foreign policy

THE GREAT POWERS MET IN VIENNA 1814–15 TO SETTLE THE AFFAIRS OF EUROPE
FOLLOWING THE DEFEAT OF FRANCE IN 1814. WHAT DOES THIS SUGGEST ABOUT
BRITAIN'S ROLE AS A EUROPEAN POWER AT THAT TIME?

There were two broad approaches to Europe in British foreign policy in the nineteenth century. Lord Castlereagh (Foreign Secretary 1812–22), Lord Aberdeen (Foreign Secretary 1828–30, 1841–46, Prime Minister 1852–55) and the Duke of Wellington (Prime Minister 1828–30, Foreign Secretary 1834–35) saw Britain as part of Europe. All three had experienced the continental diplomacy of the final years of the Napoleonic Wars and of the peacemaking. Gladstone, who regarded Aberdeen as his mentor in foreign affairs, took this cosmopolitan European outlook into the last part of the century. The alternative tradition was represented by George Canning (Foreign Secretary 1822–27, Prime Minister 1827) and Lord Palmerston (Foreign Secretary 1830–34, 1835–41, 1846–51, Prime Minister 1855–58, 1859–65). They aggressively promoted British interests and took a more insular stance, preferring to stand aloof from European affairs unless British interests were directly threatened. Disraeli was their heir in this and in their flair for managing public opinion.

TALKING POINT

It could be argued that any study of the nineteenth century needs to begin with Pitt; why then is 1815 so often taken as the start date? What are the dangers to students from the period structure into which historians divide the past?

FOCUS

9.1 British Interests – a European and a World Power

On 1 March 1848, Palmerston explained the principles on which foreign policy was based to the House of Commons:

... I say that it is narrow policy to suppose that this country or that is marked out as the eternal ally or the perpetual enemy of England. We have no eternal allies, and we have no perpetual enemies. Our interests are eternal and perpetual, and those interests it is our duty to follow. ... And if I might be allowed to express in one sentence the principle which I think ought to guide an English Minister, I would adopt the expression of Canning, and say that with every British minister, the interests of England ought to be the shibboleth of his policy.

Castlereagh, Canning, Palmerston and Aberdeen differed in personality and style, but their common pursuit of unchanging British interests gave a continuity to foreign policy.

Britain depended on trade and had become an importer of foodstuffs and raw materials. Trade was her life-blood. By 1860 only about 40 per cent of British trade was with the continent. Europe was important but not exclusively so. Foreign secretaries had to be concerned with protecting and expanding opportunities for trade.

The traditional concern for the security of the Netherlands against a powerful France was reiterated by Pitt in his war aims of 1805. French incursions into northern Europe had been through the Low Countries, whilst Antwerp and the Scheldt estuary could provide the bases and harbours for an invasion of Britain. The Union of Belgium and Holland in 1815 was a response to this vital British interest.

Naval supremacy had to be maintained but there was no serious challenge until the last quarter of the century. In 1848 129 British warships were scattered across the world, but the Navy did not have a universal application. It could not deter the great European land powers and Britain did not possess the resources to fight a land war. The French military took the lead in the Crimean War. Nevertheless the worldwide naval presence and its selective exploitation by Canning and Palmerston helped to create the myth of "Pax Britannica".

Distrust of French intentions and ambitions influenced policy throughout the period. In 1815 Castlereagh sought security through the reconstruction of Europe and the Quadruple Alliance. Confrontations and differences of view marked every decade. Palmerston's last premiership saw increased military expenditure to counter a perceived threat from Imperial France.

TALKING POINT

Explain the term 'Pax Britannica' and why it was thought appropriate.

At the Vienna Congress Castlereagh sought to establish an equilibrium, a balance between the great powers. The maintenance of the balance of power was regarded as a sure guarantee of European peace and stability, Palmerston defined it in 1864:

'It means that it is to the interest of the community of nations that no nation should acquire such a preponderance as to endanger the security of the rest; and it is for the advantage of all that the smaller Powers should be respected in their independence and not swallowed up by their more powerful neighbours.

Russia was the restless power in eastern Europe. Its capacity to destabilise central Europe had to be countered by Castlereagh in the Treaty of Vienna whilst its intentions towards its Ottoman neighbour were always suspect. Russian expansion into central Asia was viewed with considerable misgivings as a potential threat to British rule in India.

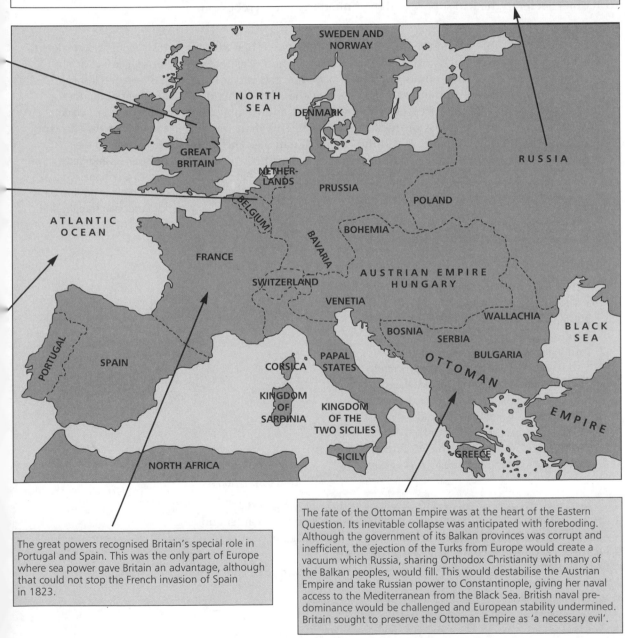

The great powers recognised Britain's special role in Portugal and Spain. This was the only part of Europe where sea power gave Britain an advantage, although that could not stop the French invasion of Spain in 1823.

The fate of the Ottoman Empire was at the heart of the Eastern Question. Its inevitable collapse was anticipated with foreboding. Although the government of its Balkan provinces was corrupt and inefficient, the ejection of the Turks from Europe would create a vacuum which Russia, sharing Orthodox Christianity with many of the Balkan peoples, would fill. This would destabilise the Austrian Empire and take Russian power to Constantinople, giving her naval access to the Mediterranean from the Black Sea. British naval predominance would be challenged and European stability undermined. Britain sought to preserve the Ottoman Empire as 'a necessary evil'.

Examining the Evidence

Castlereagh the Villain?

Contemporary radical opinion alleged that Castlereagh, deluded by his contacts with emperors and princes at Vienna, had become the tool of Metternich in forcing despotic states on the peoples of Europe. As Leader of the House of Commons, he was held responsible for the repressive legislation of 1817 and 1819. His critics went back to 1798, when, as Pitt's Irish Chief Secretary, he had suppressed the United Irishman's rebellion.

Source A

There are some now who, in mature years, cannot remember without emotion, what they saw and heard that day [when Castlereagh committed suicide]. They could not know how the calamity of one man, – a man amiable, winning and generous in the walk of his daily life, – could penetrate the recesses of the world, not as a calamity, but as a ray of hope in the midst of thickest darkness. This man was the screw by which England had revetted the chains of nations. The screw was drawn, and the immovable despotism might be overthrown.

Harriet Martineau, *A History of the Thirty Years' Peace,* 1848.

His opponents were right to see significance in Castlereagh's Irish experiences, but for the wrong reason. Ireland showed him the effects of revolution and the divisiveness and destructiveness of a nationalism that could provide no firm basis for European stability and security.

Source B

Cold-blooded, smooth-faced, placid miscreant!
Dabbling its sleep young hands in Erin's gore,
And thus for wider carnage taught to pant,
Transferred to gorge upon sister shore,
The vulgarest tool that Tyranny could want,
With just enough talent, and no more,
To lengthen fetters by another fixed,
And offer poison long already mixed.
A bungler even in its disgusting trade,
And botching, patching, leaving still behind
Something of which its masters are afraid –
States to be curbed, and thought to be confined,
Conspiracy or Congress to be made –
Cobbling at manacles for all mankind –
A tinkering slave-maker who mends old chains,
With God and Man's abhorrence for its gains.

Lord Byron, *Don Juan*.

---

1 How do Martineau and Byron sum up Castlereagh's political career and his foreign policy in sources A and B?
2 Is this kind of evidence of any value to the historian?

Castlereagh's achievements: Making War and Making Peace

● He held the anti-Napoleonic coalition (Britain, Austria, Prussia, Russia) together during the early months of 1814, when his allies were considering a separate peace with France that would have met their needs in central Europe but ignored Britain's vital interests in the Netherlands. The Treaty of Chaumont (March 1814) was one of 'the highest points' of his influence in Europe. His refusal to compromise, the power of his personal diplomacy and the promise of British subsidies secured an agreement that no separate peace would be made.

● In the peace negotiations in Paris (1814, 1815) and at Vienna all Britain's vital interests were met and no great power was left with sufficient sense of grievance to resort to war. Castlereagh helped devise a practical and realistic settlement to give Europe peace and stability.

> Peace founded upon a satisfactory and equitable balance of power was his aim; if, in the process, he appeared to favour despotic states and conservative principles, this tendency arose out of more than his own admittedly strong political prejudices; it arose out of a belief that these would best subserve his basic policy.

C.J. Bartlett, *Castlereagh*, 1966.

Source A

British interests and the peace treaties:

1st Treaty of Paris, May 1814
● Bourbon monarchy restored in France, with Louis XVIII as king.
● France to retain its 1792 frontiers.

Treaty of Vienna, June 1815
● Holland and Belgium united to form the Kingdom of the Netherlands under the Prince of Orange.
● Prussian territory extended westward to the Rhine.
● Germany consolidated into a Confederation of States under the leadership of Prussia and Austria.
● The Republic of Venetia given to Austria.
● The Republic of Genoa given to the King of Sardinia.
● Britain returned most of her colonial conquests except those required for strategic reasons. The Dutch East Indies were handed back but the Cape of Good Hope was retained. The Dutch were given £2,000,000 in compensation to be spent on fortifying the frontier with France. Malta and Heligoland became naval bases.
● There was agreement in principle to the abolition of the slave trade.

2nd Treaty of Paris, November 1815
● France to pay an indemnity to the allies.
● There was to be an army of occupation for five years.
● France was to be restricted to its frontiers of 1789.

Source B

The Quadruple Alliance committed the powers to oppose any future French aggression. Clause VI, Castlereagh's insertion, seemed to imply something more.

To facilitate and to secure the execution of the present Treaty, and to consolidate the connections which at the present moment so closely unite the four Sovereigns for the happiness of the World, the High Contracting Parties have agreed to renew their meetings at fixed periods ... for the purpose of consulting upon their common interests, and for the consideration of the measures which at each of these periods shall be considered the most salutary for the repose and prosperity of Nations, and for the maintenance of the Peace of Europe.

Castlereagh wished to implement a Concert of Europe – an informal arrangement between the great powers to maintain peace and settle disputes by negotiation.

CASTLEREAGH DEVELOPED A CLOSE PERSONAL RELATIONSHIP WITH BOTH METTERNICH (LEFT) AND ALEXANDER I (BELOW) WHICH ENABLED HIM TO INTERVENE DECISIVELY AT KEY POINTS IN THE NEGOTIATIONS. HE MADE BRITAIN INTO THE MEDIATOR POWER WITH NO DEMANDS IN EUROPE, BUT HE COULD NOT STOP ALEXANDER ACQUIRING POLAND. HE DID, HOWEVER, OBTAIN A CENTRAL EUROPEAN SETTLEMENT WITH WHICH BOTH PRUSSIA AND AUSTRIA COULD FEEL SATISFIED AND WHICH OFFERED A BARRIER TO RUSSIAN AMBITIONS.

As the victor of Waterloo, Wellington used his immense prestige to support Castlereagh. The first allied commander to enter Paris in 1815, he immediately commenced negotiating the lenient peace that both he and the Foreign Secretary believed essential to restore a stable Bourbon monarchy and to secure French acceptance of the settlement.

Source C

A CRITICAL COMMENT ON THE VIENNA CONGRESS. WELLINGTON TRIES TO BALANCE THE SCALES WITH THE KING OF PRUSSIA AND METTERNICH. ON THE RIGHT THE TSAR IS IN CONFERENCE WITH TALLEYRAND, THE FRENCH MINISTER.

1 Referring to the map in Focus 9.1 and to source A, indicate how the Vienna Treaty provided Europe with security against France and satisfied Britain's vital interests.
2 What criticism is source C making about the Congress of Vienna? Castlereagh was accused of betraying the Poles and the republics of Venetia and Genoa. In the context of Europe in 1815, and his main aim, is this accusation fair?
3 What appears to be the implications of Clause VI of the Quadruple Alliance (source B)?

TALKING POINT

Debate this assessment of Castlereagh's achievement 1814–15:
'It was the measure of Castlereagh's personal triumph that, with hardly a diplomatic or military card in his hand, he negotiated a peace settlement with the other allies … which would protect all Britain's vital interests.' (M. Chamberlain, 'New Light on British Foreign Policy' in *History Today*, July 1985)

Castlereagh and the Congress System, 1815–22

Purposes and Objectives

No British interest had been neglected at the peace conferences. France was surrounded by newly strengthened states, the Netherlands was secure, central European questions had been settled to the satisfaction of Russia, Austria and Prussia. Britain's claim to maritime rights had not been challenged, her generosity in handing back most of her colonial conquests marvelled at, her commercial interests safeguarded, whilst her humanitarian conscience had been salved by Castlereagh's earnest endeavours to obtain agreement to suppress the slave trade.

For Castlereagh the Quadruple Alliance had two purposes. Firstly it was an alliance against France. Secondly, through the periodic meetings proposed in Clause VI, it could provide a mechanism for the orderly management of change in the European balance. Castlereagh knew that change was inevitable; occasional meetings of the great powers would ensure that peace and stability were not undermined. Unfortunately differences soon emerged over what constituted a threat to European stability and the extent to which change was permissible.

Castlereagh's policy was 'one of the most personal ever pursued by a British Foreign Secretary.' He did not explain himself in the House of Commons and his authority in Cabinet effectively silenced criticism. By 1818, however, some aspects of his European policy were being queried by Cabinet colleagues and questioned by the opposition in the Commons. C.J. Bartlett argues that Castlereagh's 'New Diplomacy' was an attempt to break away from the traditions of the eighteenth century. Influenced by the success of his personal diplomacy, 1814–15, he wished to continue and extend the contacts that had been made. Castlereagh's skills as a negotiator and a mediator were considerable and the power of his personality was unquestionable.

> Maritime rights: Britain's claim, as the leading sea power, to be able to stop and search neutral as well as belligerent ships attempting to trade with blockaded ports. The War of 1812–14 with the United States was partly about Britain's exercise of maritime rights.

The Congress System under Pressure

His authoritarian European allies never understood Castlereagh's flexibility of purpose in 1815 and the tensions within the Alliance that emerged in 1820 should not have been unexpected. At Aix-la-Chapelle the Tsar revived vague ideas for a guarantee of all monarchs and thrones. Castlereagh and Metternich diverted him from this but the seeds that so seriously damaged the Alliance two years later had been sown. Castlereagh made it very clear that the internal affairs of states were of no concern to the Alliance unless they offered a threat to wider European stability. Alexander was thinking much more about preserving the 'status quo' and responding to the ideological challenges posed by the forces unleashed by the French Revolution.

Revolutions in Spain and Naples, and unrest in Germany changed the situation by 1820. The first outbreak was in Spain where Ferdinand VII was forced to accept the extreme Spanish constitution of 1812; this was followed by a successful rising in Naples. Castlereagh deplored the extremism of the 1812 constitution but argued that the Spanish revolution was an internal matter and that intervention was unnecessary. Events in Italy were less clearcut. Italy had been placed in Austria's sphere of

The Congresses	
1818	Aix-la-Chapelle
1820	Troppau
1821	Laibuch
1822	Verona

influence at Vienna and her presence in the North was a barrier to French aggression. Anything that might weaken the Austrian position was, therefore, to be resisted. Castlereagh could have supported independent action by Austria to deal with the Neapolitan crisis. He could not accept any form of joint action by the powers which would have given that intervention a wider significance. Hence he only sent observers to the Congresses at Troppau and Laibuch. The Troppau Protocol seemed to distance Russia, Austria and Prussia from Britain and to suggest that the close post-war co-operation was coming to an end.

Yet Castlereagh was planning to attend the Verona Congress, 1822, himself. The Greek War of Independence had given Britain and Austria a new common interest – to control the activities of the Tsar strongly attracted by the cause of fellow Orthodox Christians against a Muslim overlord. The interests of both powers would be damaged by a Russo-Turkish conflict over Greece. Co-operation between the powers seemed to offer the best means of resolving that crisis, preventing French intervention in Spain and protecting the new South American states. Castlereagh's death disrupted improving relations with Metternich. His policy was European, but British interests were at its heart. Canning endorsed the instructions Castlereagh had prepared for the Congress and published his State Paper of May 1820.

Castlereagh's State Paper of 5 May 1820

Following revolution in Spain, the following paper was sent to all British ambassadors. Its primary purpose was to explain British policy towards the Spanish insurrection, but Castlereagh also took the opportunity to clarify the British position on intervention in general and the purpose of the Quadruple Alliance.

There can be no doubt of the general Danger which menaces more or less the stability of all existing Governments from the Principles which are afloat, and from the circumstances that so many States of Europe are now employed in the difficult task of casting anew their Governments upon the Representative Principle; but the notion of revising, limiting or regulating the course of such Experiments, either by foreign Council or by foreign force, would be as dangerous to avow as it would be impossible to execute ...

...It [the Quadruple Alliance] was an union for the Reconquest and liberation of a great proportion of the Continent of Europe from the Military Dominion of France ... It never was ... intended as an Union for the Government of the World, or for the Superintendence of the Internal Affairs of other States ...

... it was the Revolutionary Power more particularly in its Military Character actual and existent within France against which it intended to take Precautions, rather than against the Democratic Principles, then as now, but too generally spread throughout Europe ...

... We shall be found in our place when actual danger threatens the System of Europe, but this Country cannot, and will not, act upon abstract and speculative Principles of Precaution ...

1 What, according to Castlereagh, was the purpose of the Alliance?

2 How, according to Castlereagh, was it being perverted?

3 Comment on Castlereagh's attitude to 'the Principles which are afloat'.

4 Referring to this source, and to your wider knowledge, explain why Canning published this State Paper in 1823?

George Canning: Showmanship in Foreign Policy

Despite his conservatism and his membership of the reviled post-war cabinet Canning, the Foreign Secretary, became the hero of the liberals. He was naturally more isolationist than Castlereagh, lacking his predecessor's continental contacts, but the main difference between the two was a matter of style and rhetoric rather than policy. Canning possessed the flair to turn routine operations into personal triumphs and to popularise his policies with dramatic gestures and flourishes.

The Failure – Spain

Canning sent Wellington to Verona. The powers rejected Alexander's offer of a Russian army to suppress the Spanish revolution, but Wellington was not consulted when French intervention to restore the autocratic regime of Ferdinand VII was authorised. In April 1823 French troops crossed the Pyrennees. Britain was left isolated and humiliated, powerless to stop a reassertion of French influence in a country from which Wellington had driven their armies in 1813.

The Successes – Portugal and South America

On the other hand, Canning successfully defended British interests in Portugal and kept the French out. In 1826 5000 British troops were sent to Lisbon to defend the young Queen Maria and the liberal constitution her father had given to the Portuguese people. It was a dramatic gesture but Canning knew that the risk of war was negligible.

More important was the fate of the former Spanish colonies in South and Central America.

The French, firmly established in Spain after 1823, possessed the only fleet capable of transporting an invasion force. An attempt at Anglo-American co-operation floundered because of United States suspicion of Canning's motives. In December 1823 the American President Monroe declared the American continent closed to further European colonisation. This was directed against Britain and her Canadian claims as much as in defence of the South American states.

Canning had already obtained assurances from Polignac (the French ambassador) that France had no intention of assisting a Spanish assault on South America. The record of these conversations was made public as the Polignac Memorandum. Since the meeting preceded the Monroe Doctrine by two months, the Latin Americans were reminded that they owed their security to Canning and the Royal Navy, not the United States.

A last attempt to persuade the Spanish to accept mediation was abandoned and recognition became government policy. With French armies still in Spain, a dramatic gesture was needed to restore British pride and prestige whilst commercial pressures demanded full attention. In February 1825 Britain took the final steps to recognise the republics of Mexico, Colombia and Buenos Aires. The outcry from Europe turned a routine act into a triumphant one which Canning was able to exploit to the full. He had done nothing that Castlereagh had not intended, but he did it with a flair the other man would have deplored.

Canning had been Foreign Secretary 1807–09. In 1812 he turned down the Foreign Office since Castlereagh was to take the lead in the Commons. In Cabinet 1816–20 he had supported Castlereagh although he expressed some concerns at open-ended commitments to Europe. The continuity between their policies is reflected in Canning's publication of the 1820 State Paper.

The Spanish South American colonies had broken away from the Spanish Empire after 1808. They had rapidly become significant new markets for British goods and investment. These were good commercial reasons why they should not be restored to Spain. Castlereagh had tried to mediate a settlement that would give the new states some independence whilst retaining the Spanish link. By 1817 he was acknowledging that this was unattainable and that Britain would eventually have to recognise their independence.

The Holy Alliance had been Alexander I's creation in 1815. It seemed innocuous at the time but became the mechanism through which Austria, Prussia and Russia imposed their interpretation of the Vienna Settlement on Europe

TALKING POINT

Canning has been accused of opportunism in foreign policy. Suggest a definition for opportunism. Why is this a criticism?

THE BRITISH ADMIRAL CODRINGTON LED THE ALLIED FLEET IN ITS ATTACK ON THE COMBINED EGYPTIAN AND TURKISH FLEETS AT NAVERINO. THE TREATY OF LONDON GUARANTEED THE GREEKS THEIR INDEPENDENCE. CANNING GOT THE CREDIT FOR THAT. HIS SUCCESSORS LOST CONTROL. RUSSIA DECLARED WAR AND ALMOST ADVANCED AS FAR AS CONSTANTINOPLE BEFORE IMPOSING TERMS ON THE TURKS BY THE TREATY OF ADRIANOPLE IN 1829. CANNING WOULD NOT HAVE STOOD ON THE SIDELINES WRINGING HIS HANDS, BUT HIS POLICY HAD RAISED THE SPECTRE OF WAR AND HAD GIVEN THE RUSSIANS THE EXCUSE TO ACT.

Russia and Greek Independence

Canning had no sympathy with the Greeks although he did nothing to restrain the swelling support for them in Britain. Recognition of the Greeks as belligerents in March 1823 was to protect British trade in the Eastern Mediterranean not to offer encouragement. Like Castlereagh he wanted to prevent Russian intervention and a war between Russia and the Ottoman Empire. Unlike Castlereagh he was not prepared to work through the old alliance and consistently dismayed Metternich by rejecting requests for a Congress to resolve the crisis. He maintained a strict neutrality ready for the time when Britain could adopt a mediatory role between the Turks and their rebellious subjects.

By 1825 the war was going badly for the Greeks. Mehemet Ali, the Pasha of Egypt, had lent the sultan his army and fleet. Alexander I was restless under Metternich's control. Canning opened talks with the Russians. In 1826 Wellington was sent to St Petersburg to greet the new Tsar, Nicholas I, and to negotiate a direct agreement between Russia and Britain to force mediation on the Turks. Canning hoped to prevent a war by working with Russia to persuade the Turks to reasonableness. The Protocol of St Petersburg was extended into the Treaty of London (1827) which brought France into the alliance. The threat of force if the Turks refused to accept terms was now overt. British mediation was rejected in July 1827. The powers prepared their fleets for action but Canning, now Prime Minister, died in August.

Canning had effected a diplomatic revolution. Metternich was marginalised. Canning was at the head of a new European concert to deal with the Eastern Question, had a good working relationship with Russia and had effected a rapprochement with France. It fitted with his belief that only the powers directly interested in a question needed to be involved in its solution but Canning turned it into a defeat for the Holy Alliance and a triumph for Britain's prestige and status in Europe. Despite his criticisms of Castlereagh he was not an isolationist and was prepared to co-operate with the great powers and to intervene when British interests demanded it.

EXAMINING THE EVIDENCE

Canning and Castlereagh – Reputations

Castlereagh – For Radicals, the personification of repression and reaction at home and abroad, he became, for historians working after 1918, the international statesman whose Congress System attempted to give Europe a forum to settle disputes without war. Both views distort the truth.

Canning – The 'hero' who defended the Portuguese constitution, recognised the independence of Latin America, created an independent Greece, undermined Metternich's European system and raised British prestige throughout the world.

Source A

I consider it to be the duty of a British statesman ... to hold a middle course between extremes; avoiding alike extravagancies of despotism, or the licentiousness of unbridled freedom – reconciling power with liberty; not adopting hasty or ill-advised experiments, or pursuing any airy and unsubstantial theories; but not rejecting ... the application of sound and wholesome knowledge to practical affairs, and pressing with sobriety and caution, into the service of his country, any generous and liberal principles whose excess, indeed, may be dangerous, but whose foundation is truth ...

Who do you think made this statement – Castlereagh or Canning? Refer to its sentiments in your answer. Could the statement have been made by either of them?
See bottom of page for the answer.

The historians' view

Source B

...Although practice showed that they were in rough agreement as to British interests ... a considerable gulf existed between them as to the means by which these objectives could best be pursued. Where Castlereagh rested his hopes on the Alliance, Canning believed that Britain could disengage herself from continental affairs and become 'a spectatress' ...

... whatever the continuity in aim, Canning's style of diplomatic conduct was bound to be different. Not for him the pressing desire to preserve the unity of the great powers if at all practicable and consistent with British interests; not for him the reluctance to publicise one's diplomatic quarrels or triumphs. Above all, Canning gave British foreign policy a positive, exciting, patriotic, even liberal appearance, which would have been anathema to Castlereagh. And differing methods led, to a certain extent, to different results, for Britain's relations with all the leading powers could hardly be so generally cordial when the tone of British diplomacy was so strident and positive.

C.J. Bartlett, *Castlereagh*, 1966.

Source C

Castlereagh strove to avoid having to make a choice between the defence of British interests (which he was bound to regard as his primary

ANSWER
Speech by Canning in the House of Commons, 24 February 1826.

responsibility) and the preservation of equilibrium in Europe. He believed that it was impossible adequately to achieve the first object without attaining the second. He never allowed Britain to lose her freedom of action, but he never gave up his conviction that Britain had a role to play in Europe, and he believed that British interests could not be divorced from the balance of power in Europe. British interests could not and would not be preserved merely by pretending that Europe did not exist or that European problems and conflicts could be ignored in a mood of complacent isolationism ... Events would change the balance of interests ... but if Britain withdrew from Europe she should eventually find that her interests were being threatened by forces which were outside her control, but which she could ignore at her peril.

J.W. Derry, Castlereagh, 1976.

Source D

He [Canning] claimed credit for destroying the congress System; this self-imposed task proved popular; its necessity ... is more open to question ... Canning allowed great importance to the affairs of the Iberian Peninsula; defeats and triumphs ... proved almost equally ephemeral; while British naval superiority was so pronounced, and provided Gibraltar remained in British hands, the politics of Spain and of Portugal were not perhaps as relevant to national interests as even Canning ... believed. Where Latin America was concerned, recognition ... was an obvious commercial interest ... Castlereagh had made it clear as early as 1817 that British recognition was only a matter of time ... had Castlereagh lived the result might have been achieved more quickly but surely in less dramatic circumstances; Canning converted a routine operation into a splendid publicity campaign ... Danger could ... only threaten in the Eastern Mediterranean from Russia. Perhaps, like many British statesmen ... Canning was too sensitive about his threat. But his method of meeting it was imaginative and sound. Direct co-operation with Russia was probably the best means of exercising a restraining influence on Russian ambitions which, after a successful clash with Turkey, might threaten to run riot.

P.J.V. Rolo, Canning, 1965.

1 'Both men shared the same aims, their methods were very different.' Referring to sources B, C and D, and to your broader knowledge, consider and discuss the validity of this statement.

2 Now write this essay:
'They differed in style and personality rather than in substance and objectives.' How far do you agree with this assessment of the foreign policies of Castlereagh and Canning in the years 1815–27?

TALKING POINT

Both Castlereagh and Canning have been nominated as candidates for the title 'Greatest British Foreign Secretary of the nineteenth century'. Prepare and argue the case for one of them.

9.2 The Eastern Question and the Crimean War, 1830–56

Source A

Letter from Palmerston to Lord Granville, British ambassador in Paris, 8 June 1838.

The Cabinet yesterday agreed that it would not do to let Mehemet Ali declare himself independent, and separate Egypt and Syria from the Turkish Empire. They see that the consequences of such a declaration on his part must be either immediately or at no distant time conflict between him and the Sultan. That in such a conflict the Turkish troops would probably be defeated; that then the Russians would fly to the aid of the Sultan, and a Russian garrison would occupy Constantinople and the Dardanelles; and once in possession of those points, the Russians would never quit them. We are, therefore, prepared to give naval aid to the Sultan against Mehemet, if necessary and demanded; and we intend to order our Mediterranean fleet immediately to Alexandria to give Mehemet an outward and visible sign of our inward resolve.

Source B

Letter from Palmerston to Henry Lytton Bulwer an official at the Constantinople embassy, 22 September 1838.

There can be no doubt that it is for the interest of England that the Sultan should be strong; and it is evident that he would be stronger with Syria and Egypt than without them. I am, therefore, the continuing to aim at a maintenance of the integrity of the empire …

People go on talking of the inevitable and progressive decay of the Turkish empire …

But I should be disposed to think that, for some years past, the foundations at least of improvement have been laid; and it is certain that the daily increasing intercourse between Turkey and the other countries of Europe must in a few years, if peace can be preserved, throw much light on the defects and weaknesses of the Turkish system, and lead to various improvements therein.

TALKING POINT

Sources A and B establish two important principles of British foreign policy until the 1870s. How does A justify intervention to protect the Sultan and what hopes does B express about the Ottoman Empire?

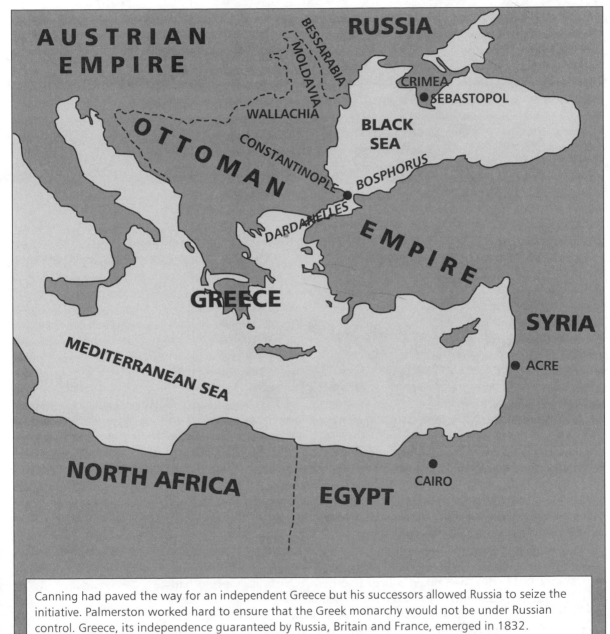

AUSTRIAN EMPIRE

RUSSIA

BESSARABIA

MOLDAVIA

WALLACHIA

CRIMEA

SEBASTOPOL

BLACK SEA

O T T O M A N

CONSTANTINOPLE

BOSPHORUS

E M P I R E

DARDANELLES

GREECE

SYRIA

ACRE

MEDITERRANEAN SEA

NORTH AFRICA

EGYPT

CAIRO

Canning had paved the way for an independent Greece but his successors allowed Russia to seize the initiative. Palmerston worked hard to ensure that the Greek monarchy would not be under Russian control. Greece, its independence guaranteed by Russia, Britain and France, emerged in 1832.

Britain and the Crimean War

THE "MONTAGNE RUSSE."—A VERY DANGEROUS GAME.

RUSSIAN INTRANSIGENCE, AS DEPICTED IN *PUNCH*. CARTOONS LIKE THIS BOTH REFLECTED AND FUELLED PUBLIC OPINION.

In 1853 there was a coalition cabinet. One former Foreign Secretary was Prime Minister (Aberdeen), another was Home Secretary (Palmerston) whilst Russell occupied the Foreign Office.

The principal cause of the Crimean War was undoubtedly Nicholas's clumsy truculence. But he could have been stopped ... if only the Cabinet in London had taken a firm line before Nicholas's pride had become too committed to a collision course. But it was the fatal weakness of the Coalition Cabinet that its counsels were divided and that it was never strong enough, not so much to resist public opinion in England, but to make Nicholas stop.

K. Bourne, *The Foreign Policy of Victorian England 1830–1902*, 1970.

Tsar Nicholas I, emperor 1825 – 55

Palmerston would probably have prevented a war by taking firm action to warn Russia early in the crisis. On the other hand Aberdeen's preference for negotiation would have been successful given time and goodwill. Unfortunately the Cabinet's decisions lacked consistency and Britain failed to impose its control on events or on the Turks.

Britain had no interest in the original dispute about the Holy Places but became involved when Nicholas opened talks with the British ambassador at the beginning of 1853. The Tsar suggested that since the collapse of the Ottoman Empire was imminent the two powers should work together. He assumed that informal discussions on the future of the Ottoman Empire between Aberdeen and Nesselrode, the Russian Chancellor, in 1844 implied that general agreement had been reached. Russell's reply to Nicholas's proposals failed to emphasise sufficiently the British view that the Turks were not on the verge of collapse. Its very vagueness left Nicholas believing he could rely on British co-operation and support.

At Constantinople the British ambassador, Stratford Canning, encouraged Turkish resistance to Prince Menschikov's demands. If the Russian claims were accepted they would have constant excuses for meddling in the affairs of the Ottoman Empire. The invasion of the Danubian Principalities (July 1853) finally shattered any possible Anglo-Russian agreement. In the summer of 1853 Britain took the lead in the diplomatic moves against Russia at Constantinople.

Russia was accused of secretly planning the partition to the Ottoman Empire. Her 'crimes' in Poland were condemned. Strident 'Russophobia' was fuelled by a press which seemed to drive government policy before it. Britain, like France and Russia, blundered into war in 1854 with no clear purpose or reason except to maintain the integrity of the Ottoman Empire.

Examining the evidence

Palmerston and Foreign Policy

See chapter 11 for details of Palmerston's career.

Palmerston's appointment to the Foreign Office in 1830 was totally unexpected. There was nothing about his previous political career which had suggested an interest in foreign affairs, but he was to dominate British foreign policy for the next 35 years.

Source A

Palmerston on the principles of foreign policy, 1838:

> ... my doctrine is that we should reckon upon ourselves; and act upon principles of our own; use other governments as we can, when we want them and find them willing to serve us; but never place ourselves in the wake of any of them; lead when and where we can, but follow, never. The system of England ought to be to maintain the liberties and independence of all other nations; out of the conflicting interest for other countries to secure her own independence; to throw her moral weight into the scale of any people who are spontaneously striving for freedom, by which I mean rational government, and to extend as far and as fast as possible civilisation all over the world.

Letter to Frederick Lamb, 21 March 1838.

Source B
Palmerston on foreign policy, House of Commons 1 March 1848:

I hold that the real policy of England – apart from questions which involve her own particular interests, political or commercial – is to be the champion of justice and right, pursuing that course with moderation and prudence, not becoming the Quixote of the world, but giving the weight of her moral sanction and support wherever she thinks that justice is, and wherever she thinks that wrong has been done.

Source C
Canning and Palmerston:

Canning is most remarkable for a profound intellectual conception of foreign policy ... Here we have the essential difference between Canning and Palmerston. The one took no step without weighing its consequences in relation to the whole ... the other was a man of expedients and of the moment. Both believed in public opinion, but Canning usually controlled what Palmerston sometimes had to follow. He [Palmerston] was a man of great courage and of boundless energy and vivacity ... He was indeed not a man of principle or system, yet he was a superb opportunist. He excelled in calling 'bluffs' and in making them. It was not the highest statesmanship but it often served.

H.M.V. Temperley, *England and the Near East: The Crimes*, 1964.

---

1 'A pragmatic statesman who put British interests first.'
   Referring to sources A and B, comment on this view of Palmerston.
2 To what extent would sources A, B and C sustain Palmerston's claim to be the heir of Canning?
3 Return to these sources when you have read to the end of the chapter. To what extent did Palmerston follow the guidelines of sources A and B, and, by 1865, was he guilty of creating 'a myth of British foreign policy'?

Palmerston at the Foreign Office 1830–41

... Palmerston proved himself a masterly Foreign Secretary. His pragmatic grasp of Britain's material interests and his realistic and flexible approach to the balance of power set him above Castlereagh; his manipulation of conference diplomacy and his tactical skill in ensuring that Britain was never isolated were superior even to Canning's. His successes were substantial and undoubted. Nor was he lacking in vision.

K. Bourne, *Palmerston: The Early Years 1784–1841*, 1982.

He was out of office during Peel's first ministry, November 1834 to April 1835.

The Affair of Belgium
On entering office, Palmerston inherited the Belgian crisis and the London Conference from the outgoing Tory administration. Wellington had recognised the revolutionary regime of Louis Philippe in France but revolution in that country had sparked off revolution in Poland, Italy and

the Low Countries. Austrian concern for Italy and Russian involvement in Poland left Britain and France free to resolve the issues raised by the Belgian demand for independence from Holland. Palmerston viewed a liberal constitutional France as Britain's natural ally in Europe and there was little difference on the basic question of independence. Disputes arose over the details – the fate of Luxembourg, the status of the barrier fortresses and the identity of the future King of the Belgians.

Palmerston could not afford to give the French any concessions in Belgium or to allow French influence to be paramount in Brussels. He had made his position clear to the French during 1831 when the two powers combined to impose the settlement on William of Holland. The French army showed a marked reluctance to withdraw from Belgium once the Dutch king had removed his forces.

> One thing is certain – the French must get out of Belgium or we have a general war, and war in a given number of days.
>
> Palmerston to Lord Granville, British ambassador in Paris, 16 August 1831.

The French took the hint. Palmerston knew that Louis Philippe could not afford to fight a European war for Belgium. When the British and the French combined to coerce the Dutch king again in 1832 Palmerston laid down clear objectives. William gave up Antwerp and the French had no excuse to stay. Dutch hostility delayed full international recognition of Belgian independence until the 1839 Treaty of London which, by guaranteeing Belgium's neutrality, effectively settled long-standing British concerns. Palmerston did not lead a crusade for Belgian independence. His main purpose was to protect vital British interests in the Low Countries and to ensure that French influence was kept to a minimum. In those aims he was supremely successful.

Palmerston was able to prevent the imposition of a French king on Belgium, the candidate was one of Louis Philippe's sons. The final choice, Leopold of Saxe-Coburg, was much more suitable.

The Liberal Alliance of the West

Palmerston was criticised for his low key reaction to events in Poland where the Russians clinically repressed the revolution. In fact, he was realistic. Britain could do nothing to help the Poles beyond routine protests. Italy presented a greater dilemma. Austria's presence was essential to maintain the balance of power and Palmerston did not want to encourage French meddling.

Rivalries in the Low Countries had kept Britain and France together. They seemed to have common interests in the Iberian Peninsula, where constitutionalist regimes in both Spain and Portugal were engaged in civil wars. Palmerston actively intervened in Portugal with both troops and naval support although French activities in Spain cause him much concern.

He responded to the renewal of the Holy Alliance at Munchengratz (1833) by proposing an alliance of Britain, France and the constitutional governments in Spain and Portugal. Palmerston hoped that the alliance would settle affairs in both Spain and Portugal but he gave it a much broader significance as 'a quadruple alliance among the constitutional states of the west, which will serve as a powerful counterpoise to the Holy Alliance of the east' (Letter to Williams Temple, 21 April 1834).

This grossly overstated the case. The Portuguese and Spanish governments were ineffective whilst relations between France and Britain were already strained. As the renewal of the Eastern Question revealed in 1840 Palmerston was willing to work with both Russia and Austria against France when British interests demanded. Dealing with the Russian threat might sometimes require a flexibility in defining British interests.

Concern with Russia was wider than Constantinople and the Near East. Russian inroads into Persia and her territorial expansion into central Asia offered a worrying threat to the British position in India. Afghanistan became a key border state. To establish British predominance in the region Palmerston ordered garrisons into the main Afghan towns (1838). The Russians backed down partly because Nicholas wanted to work with Britain to maintain the integrity of the Ottoman Empire against Mehemet Ali. The wisdom of Palmerston's troop movements was questioned in 1841 when the garrisons were attacked and Kabul had to be abandoned. Peel's government launched a punitive war against the Afghans but the garrisons were not replaced.

Palmerston got his way 1839–41 in the Near East. The Treaty of Unkiar Skelessi was abandoned by the Tsar, Mehemet Ali was driven back to Egypt, the Ottoman Empire was preserved, the Porte looked to Britain as its saviour and the Straits Convention gave Palmerston an international agreement. The price was French animosity and opposition from Cabinet colleagues alarmed by his bellicose attitude and the willingness of Thiers, the French Prime Minister, to respond. Mehemet Ali's defeat would not only strengthen the Ottoman Empire but weaken French influence throughout the Levant. Palmerston's lack of magnanimity in victory – the French were allowed back into the Concert for the Straits Convention but with an ill-grace – left Whig ministers and others with a feeling that Palmerston was too dangerous for the post he held. On the other hand he dismissed Nicholas' offer of an anti-French alliance with an impeccable summary of the principles upon which British policy was based.

The background to Palmerston's handling of the Eastern Question is covered in Focus 9.2

The Treaty of Unkiar Skelessi (1833) had made Russia the sultan's protector against Mehemet Ali. Palmerston's aim was to overturn this special relationship.

THE FIRST CHINESE WAR (1840–42) WAS OSTENSIBLY ABOUT THE RIGHT OF BRITISH MERCHANTS TO SELL OPIUM TO THE CHINESE. IN REALITY EQUAL AND CIVILISED TREATMENT FOR BRITISH TRADERS AND REPRESENTATIVES BY THE CHINESE AUTHORITIES WAS AT STAKE. IT WAS NOT A WAR FOR EXCLUSIVE TRADE. BOTH PALMERSTON AND ABERDEEN WANTED TO OPEN CHINA UP TO BRITISH MERCHANTS BUT THE PRIVILEGES OF THE TREATY PORTS (TREATY OF NANKING 1842) WERE OPEN TO ALL NATIONALITIES.

Lord Aberdeen 1841–46: the Trials of a Conciliator

When he became Foreign Secretary in 1841, Lord Aberdeen inherited a very difficult situation – war with China; war in Afghanistan; difficult relations with France; and the risk of war with the United States. His declared aims in foreign policy were to improve relations with France, and to remove the outstanding obstacles to better relations with the United States.

France

QUEEN VICTORIA RECEIVING LOUIS PHILIPPE, THE KING OF THE FRENCH, AT WINDSOR IN OCTOBER 1844.

Aberdeen hoped that his friendship with Guizot, the French Prime Minister, would lead to better relations. The 'entente' seemed to be consolidated by an exchange of royal visits. Unfortunately the old suspicions and latent animosities could not be removed as easily and by 1845 Wellington was sounding the alarm as the French began to construct a steamship navy. French ambitions in North Africa and in the Pacific helped to heat up public opinion. In 1845 the French made Tahiti a protectorate, imprisoning a British Protestant missionary. A heady mixture of 'Francophobia' and anti-Catholicism undermined Aberdeen's work.

The United States

Castlereagh was 'the first British Foreign Secretary to accept the reality of American independence'. Although he did not concede Britain's claim to maritime rights and impressment he helped to make a conciliatory peace at Ghent in 1814. Economic considerations (need for raw cotton), and finance (cost of defending Canada) were powerful arguments for a settlement of outstanding disputes. The Rush–Bagot Agreement of 1817 reduced forces on the Great Lakes and the 49th Parallel border was extended to the Rockies.

Canning and Palmerston both contributed to a worsening of relations. Aberdeen was determined to settle the remaining border problems. In his opinion, acres of forest did not seem worth fighting about.

The Webster–Ashburton Treaty (1842) dealt with the Maine boundary in the north east but quarrels over the future of Texas (newly independent), American ambitions in California (part of Mexico) and slavery made progress difficult. When the anti-British Polk was elected President in 1844, no progress had been made in defining the Oregon frontier in the far north west. There was talk of a Franco-American alliance against Britain. Polk, however, finally agreed to the extension of the 49th Parallel line to the Pacific coast in 1846.

Source A

Letter from Lord Aberdeen to Lord Ashburton, 28 September 1842.

The treaty was at first either well, or silently received; but under the inspiration of Palmerston, the *Chronicle* has opened a series of attacks, and the *Globe* has quite changed the language it had first employed. Other papers have joined in taking up the same views, and we must expect a fierce hostility. But I am well satisfied, and am not at all afraid. The more the whole subject shall be discussed, the more favourable I think the result will be ...

The good temper in which you have left them all, and the prospect of a continued peace, with I trust improved friendly relations, far outweigh in my mind the value of any additional extent of Pine Swamp.

Source B

Aberdeen's statement to the House of Lords on the Oregon Question, 4 April, 1845.

...I am accustomed almost daily to see myself characterised as pusillanimous, cowardly, mean, dastardly, truckling and base. I hope I need not say that I view these appellations with indifference ... I feel perfectly satisfied that these vituperative terms are to be translated as applicable to conduct consistent with justice, reason, moderation, and with common sense ... I believe I may conscientiously say that no man ever filled the high situation which I have the honour unworthily to hold, who felt more ardently desirous than I do to preserve to the country the blessing of peace, or who would be disposed to make greater sacrifices, consistent with propriety, to maintain it.

A favourable assessment

Historians have tended to accept Palmerston's judgement of Aberdeen and accuse him of failing to stand up for national interests, allowing his dislike of war to be too well known, and relying too much on personal contact. But it is as well to remember that this was not the judgement of contemporaries. In 1846 Aberdeen was regarded as a sound statesman, who had extricated Britain from potentially dangerous quarrels with France and the United States, kept the Eastern Question quiet, safeguarded Britain's trading interests from China to South America ... It was Palmerston who failed to inspire confidence.

M.E. Chamberlain, *'Pax Britannica': British Foreign Policy 1789–1914*, 1988

TALKING POINT

Aberdeen was accused of appeasing Britain's enemies and sacrificing her vital interests. Compare and contrast his handling of foreign affairs with that of Palmerston.

Palmerston: Revolution and Popularity, 1846–51

During these years Palmerston convinced the court and most of his colleagues that he was too dangerous and unpredictable to be Foreign Secretary, but he became popular. His reputation as a defender of liberal movements abroad, as the champion of British citizens in trouble, as 'the most English Minister that ever presided over the foreign affairs of this country', date from this period.

He began in 1846 by destroying Aberdeen's careful attempt to rebuild Anglo-French relations through an informal agreement over the marriage of the Spanish Queen and her sister. Palmerston's clumsy intervention (although it has been suggested that he was deliberately provoking the French) persuaded the French government to arrange a series of marriages that could result in an Orleanist prince becoming King of Spain – the very thing that both Aberdeen and Palmerston had wanted to prevent.

The Queen was married to a cousin who was believed to be impotent. Her sister married a son of Louis Philippe.

In 1847 he angered Metternich by the support he gave to the liberal cantons in Switzerland and by the dispatch of Lord Minto to Italy. Minto took Palmerston's message to the Italian rulers that reform would stave off revolution. Palmerston held Austria responsible for the chronic misgovernment throughout Italy and when revolution did break out in the spring of 1848 forcing the Austrians to retreat from Lombardy he advised them to evacuate Italy totally. An enlarged Piedmontese kingdom in northern Italy would become the new barrier to French ambitions. The remarkable Austrian recovery and the defeat of Charles Albert of Piedmont in 1848 and 1849 took Palmerston by surprise. However the balance of power dictated that Austria should remain in Italy to deter French intervention – Louis Philippe had been ejected in 1848 and France was now a republic.

1848 was the Year of Revolutions. France, Italy, Germany, Austria (Metternich was forced out of office) and Hungary were all affected.

Palmerston was not a nationalist in Italy and he was not a nationalist in Germany. By threatening Austria's status as a European power, revolution could undermine the balance of power in favour of Russia. It is significant that he only began to condemn Austrian and Russian behaviour in Hungary after the revolution had been suppressed. In 1849 he backed the Porte's refusal to hand over Hungarian refugees to Austria and Russia – although this was another twist in the Eastern Question rather than sympathy for the rebels. The Ottoman Empire could not be allowed to succumb to any pressure from Russia.

Throughout the Year of Revolutions Palmerston's concern was the preservation of the balance of power. Austria would be stronger if she abandoned Italy. The Austrian Empire had to survive as a counterpoise to Russia in Central Europe. Palmerston freely advised continental rulers and their ministers of the value of constitutions, but that was because he believed they would create stable regimes and prevent more violent change. He began to cultivate a popular reputation as the defender of liberalism.

Victoria and Albert resented the cavalier fashion with which Palmerston admonished the rulers of Europe. They deplored his Austrian policy. Victoria believed that she had real grounds for complaint because copies of official dispatches either never reached her, or did so after the originals had left the country. Palmerston offered contrite apology but there was little that Russell or the Queen could do to control the Foreign Secretary. In the Don Pacifico debate (June 1850) his popularity and indispensability to the survival of the Ministry were underlined.

For the background to the Don Pacifico debate, see chapter 11.

The Palmerstonian Legacy

In his later years Palmerston created a myth which did not always reflect his cautious and careful protection of British interests. Becoming Prime Minister in 1855 as the strong man who would win the Crimean War he quietly forgot the wider aims of an independent Poland or of restoring the Crimea to Turkey and accepted a peace in 1856 which was hissed when the heralds proclaimed it in the City of London.

In 1856 his bold championing of the rights of British Hong Kong citizens, albeit accused of piracy by the Chinese authorities, led to war with China to wrest more trading concessions out of the imperial government. Defeated in the Commons on Cobden's censure motion, February 1857, he swept his critics aside in the ensuring general election. His defeat and resignation the following year over the Conspiracy to Murder Bill was a surprising lapse for a minister who knew how to lead public opinion.

THE DIRTY DOORSTEP.

P—lm—rst—n (an active lad). "WELL! THIS IS THE GREATEST MESS I EVER SAW AT ANYBODY'S DOOR."
Little Jack R—ss—ll. "AH! I LIVED THERE ONCE—BUT I WAS OBLIGED TO LEAVE—IT WAS SUCH A VERY IRREGULAR FAMILY."

In 1858 an Italian, Orsini, had attempted to assassinate the Emperor Napoleon. Evidence that the bombs were of English manufacture persuaded Palmerston of the need to legislate to control the activities of political refugees. His succumbing to French pressure turned an unexpected coalition of Radicals and Conservatives against him.

'THE DIRTY DOORSTEP', PUNCH, 3 FEBRUARY 1855.

THE ABERDEEN ADMINISTRATION ENDED ON 29 JANUARY. THIS CARTOON PRESENTS PALMERSTON AS THE MAN OF DECISIVE ACTION

Italian Unification

Prime Minister again in 1859, with Lord John Russell as Foreign Secretary, Palmerston contrived to turn inactivity during the crisis of Italian unification into a political triumph. Indeed, with Garibaldi in Sicily threatening to invade the Kingdom of Naples in May 1860 the fleet was ordered to the Straits of Messina to prevent a crossing. Both Russell and Palmerston feared a secret deal between Napoleon, the Kingdom of Piedmont and Garibaldi. An approach from the French, proposing joint Anglo-French action against Garibaldi, showed that there was no conspiracy, and British policy changed to neutrality. Palmerston was credited with making a significant contribution to unification and nationalism in Italy. He had done nothing.

Bullying had worked against the Chinese, masterly inactivity in Italy. Bluff and bluster – Palmerston believed that the threat of war was a viable diplomatic tool – secured concessions from the North during the early stages of the American Civil War, but failed to move Bismarck over the Danish Duchies, 1863–64.

The American Civil War

From a British point of view, there was much to be said for a break-up of the United States. The cotton industry's dependence on the South and an initial sympathy with the Confederate States predisposed the Cabinet to favour the seceders. Gladstone's impolitic statement in his Newcastle speech, October 1862, that Jefferson Davis and the other southern leaders 'have made an army ... are making, it appears, a navy; and they have made ... a nation', brought him a hail of criticism but it did reflect ministerial thinking. The previous year Britain had declared its neutrality, recognising the South as belligerents not as rebels. Palmerston gained some popularity by the firmness with which his government responded to the seizure of two southern politicians, on mission to London, from a British ship by Union warships. A strong letter was sent to Washington, toned down by Prince Albert, and troops were moved to the Canadian border. The Confederate representatives were released. Confederate commerce raiders were built on Merseyside, although the government eventually intervened once it became clear that the North would win. Palmerston had had a life-long hatred of slavery, but the Emancipation Declaration, which so strongly influenced public opinion, did not have the same impact on official policy.

Poland and the Danish Duchies

Policy was driven by suspicion of France and Napoleon III. Continental interventions were hamstrung by an unwillingness to co-operate with the French if that might mean French armies streaming across the Rhine. In 1863 Russell snubbed a French proposal for a joint protest to the Tsar about Russian suppression of rebellion in Poland. When Palmerston needed French support against Bismarck during the Danish Duchies crisis it was not forth-coming.

The Schleswig-Holstein question, whether the Duchies remained possessions of the Danish crown or became German, was complex and difficult to resolve. In 1863 Bismarck sought to force the pace by demanding their incorporation into the German Confederation. Bouyed up by Palmerston's Commons statement that if anyone interfered with Danish independence 'it would not be Denmark alone with which they would have to contend', and by the marriage of the Danish Princess Alexandra to the Prince of Wales, the Danes refused all concessions. When the German Confederation sent troops into the Duchies, the Danes turned to Britain for help. Russell suggested joint intervention with France; Palmerston was opposed to this, but, in any case Napoleon preferred to deal with Bismarck. When the Cabinet eventually discussed the sending of the fleet to Copenhagen it split evenly with Palmerston's casting vote in favour. He conceded that on such a majority action was impossible. The Danes were left to face the invader alone. A Conservative censure motion was carried in the Lords. In the Commons the censure debate covered all aspects of Palmerstonian policy. It was his last great Commons triumph. By astute manoeuvres he split the radicals from the opposition and won by 18 votes. His reputation was unharmed, and he swept to a convincing victory in the 1865 General Election.

Palmerston had become the typical 'John Bull' figure, the 'English' minister, but bluff and bluster did not work when Britain was isolated and when his opponent was determined and skilful. His populist approach and manipulation of the press created the myth on which his political success had been based. His immediate successors made it very clear that they would not continue his interference in continental affairs, but Palmerston had tapped a rich nationalist vein which had sustained him in power for ten years. A reaction was to be expected after the humiliation of 1864, but English nationalism remained a potent political force.

Review

European or World Power?

1 Refer back to the Preview. In what ways had Britain's European role been diminished by 1865?
2 Now consider this extract from B. Porter, *Britain, Europe and the World, 1850–1986*, 2nd edn, 1986.

   ... disengagement from Europe ... was the central fact of British foreign policy from the 1830s onwards, though before the 1860s it tended to be obscured by Napoleonic memories, and Balance of Power myths, and Palmerstonian bluster, and a haze of rhetoric from every quarter. In the middle of the nineteenth century Britain was scarcely in any sense at all a 'European' power. It would have been impossible for her to be so: impossible, that is, without changing her social and economic structure and her political nature fundamentally. It would have been impossible for Britain as she was then to become part of the continent as it was then: a different world, with different interests and values and priorities; full of tadpoles still, with not a frog in sight.

   Using your wider knowledge, consider Porter's view that Britain had 'disengaged' from Europe. How far can it be sustained for the period 1815–65?

Talking Point

How far did Britain's worldwide interests make it difficult for her to assume a European role?

10 A Changing Society?

The Great Exhibition, 1851

Source A

THE POUND AND THE SHILLING.

"Whoever Thought of Meeting You Here?"

OVER 4,500,000 VISITED THE GREAT EXHIBITION ON THE CHEAP 'SHILLING DAYS'. THE ORGANISERS ASSUMED THAT THE RICH AND THE POOR WOULD NOT MEET, BUT THE CARTOON MAKES A SIGNIFICANT COMMENT ON CHANGES THAT SEEMED TO BE OCCURRING BY 1851.

TALKING POINT

Explain the anxiety many people felt before the first 'shilling day' and suggest ways in which society seemed to be changing by 1851.

Discuss why it would have been impossible to anticipate an event like the Great Exhibition ten years before.

10.1 The Problem of Poverty: Problems and Solutions

The Working of the Old Poor Law

The relief of poverty was laid down in a number of acts which had been passed down over the centuries.

> ### 1597, 1601 Poor Law Act:
> – made parishes responsible for maintaining their own poor
> – all property-holders were to pay the poor rate
> – in each parish the overseer of the poor administered the fund and the poor rate.

1662 Law of Settlement
Paupers were only entitled to relief in the parish of their birth. This restriction n the mobility of labour was condemned by the nineteenth century political economists..

A workhouse was where the poor were lodged and worked to help pay for their own relief.

The allowance system is often referred to as the Speenhamland System since one of the earliest allowance scales was devised at Speen in Berkshire in 1797.

Gilbert's Act, 1782
Allowed parishes to unite to construct workhouses.
The allowance system developed at the end of the eighteenth century in the rural South of England. Wage supplements were paid to the low paid working poor (agricultural labourers), linked to the size of the man's family and the price of bread.

Poor Laws in Crisis – the Contemporary Perspective

Source A

A critical view of the working of the Poor Laws.

The first obvious tendency is to increase population, without increasing food for its support ... They are taught that there is no occasion whatever for them to put any sort of restraint upon their inclination or exercise any degree of prudence in the affair of marriage because the parish is bound to provide for all that are borne.

The poor-laws tend in the most marked manner to make the supply of labour exceed the demand for it.

... the labouring poor ... seem always to live from hand to mouth. Their present wants employ their whole attention, and they seldom think of the future. Even when they have an opportunity of saving they seldom exercise it, but all that is beyond their present necessities goes, generally speaking, to the alehouse. The poor-laws ... may ... be said to diminish both the power and the will to save among the common people.

Thomas Malthus, *An Essay on the Principles of Population*, 1798.

Source B

A ratepayers' protest at the allowance system.

... a practice like this must necessarily raise the rate far beyond its usual amount ... it is thus made subsidiary to wages ... it becomes an assessment, not so much for the relief of the poor as of their employers; a great proportion of whose agricultural labour is paid for by the public.

Memorial of the Magistrates of the Country of Suffolk, respecting poor rates, 1817.

The Problem Solved – Recommendations of the Royal Commission on the Poor Laws, 1834

... the great source of abuse is the outdoor relief afforded to the able-bodied on their own account or on that of their families.

... ALL RELIEF WHATEVER TO ABLE-BODIED PERSONS OR TO THEIR FAMILIES, OTHERWISE THAN IN WELL-REGULATED WORKHOUSES ... SHALL BE DECLARED UNLAWFUL, AND SHALL CEASE ...

Historians on the Poor Laws

Most recent historical analysis disagrees with the analysis of contemporaries and the Royal Commission Report.

- The allowance system was needed because of over-population in rural areas which created a pool of surplus labour and under-employment.
- Systematic allowance payments were a response to the low wages and rural unemployment of the agricultural depression after 1814.
- The allowance system was a reaction to population increase and low wages rather than their cause.
- 'The evidence they collected ... should have taught the commissioners that they had misinterpreted the consequences of the old poor law. But their minds were made up, and where they did not ignore the findings, they twisted them to suit their pre-conceived opinions.' (M. Blaugh, 'The Myth of the Old Poor Law and the Making of the New' in *Journal of Economic History*, 1963)
- 'Recent investigations on the Old Poor Law by historians, economists, and demographers have therefore produced convergent conclusions. They emphasis that relief under the Old Poor Law was essentially a response to population growth, under-employment, and low wages, rather than their cause as the Royal Commission's 'Report' alleged.' (A. Digby, *The Poor Law in Nineteenth-century England and Wales*, 1982)

Using the evidence of these sources, outline the contemporary case against the old Poor Laws.

In what ways do modern historians disagree with the contemporary view of the old Poor Laws?

Focus

10.2 The Working of the New Poor Law

The New Poor Law Act, 1834

The key provisions of the 1834 Act were:
- A deterrent system with local management and central control.
- No outdoor relief for the able-bodied poor.
- The 'workhouse test' operated – relief was only available in the workhouse.
- Conditions in the workhouse were to be 'less eligible' than those of the lowest paid labourer. Inmates were to be disciplined to deter the able-bodied from seeking relief.
- There was to be local management of the workhouse by a Board of Guardians elected by the ratepayers.
- Parishes were to be grouped into new administrative units – Poor Law Unions.
- The Board of Central Commissioners was to ensure uniformity in poor law administration and workhouse conditions.

By 1839 about 350 workhouses had been built, mainly in the South. Outdoor Relief Prohibition Orders were being issued to southern Unions.

In what ways did the New Poor Law apparently solve the perceived problems of the old Poor Law?

The New Poor Law – a Success?

Source A

Of the first eighty-seven labourers with families to whom outdoor relief was refused … and to all of whom an order for the workhouse was given for themselves and their families, not one half availed themselves of that offer, but immediately found means of providing for themselves.

Of the rest … some stayed one day, some two, some three, and excepting two, none remained more than four days …

Thus were 85 men with their families at one removed from the degradation of pauperism … taught that they could honestly and independently support themselves and their families by their industry.

> Report from the Faringdon Union in the '1st Report of the Poor Law Commissioners', 1835.

Source B

… the average annual expenditure of this Union for three years ending 1835 was £11.387, or £2,846.15s. a quarter. in the quarter from Christmas to Lady-day our expenditure, … is only £1,545 1s. 11d.

> Report from the Swindon Union in the '2nd Report of the Poor Law Commissioners', 1836.

Source C

Norfolk property-owners collaborated with central administration in introducing the New Poor Law … because they found the punitive, class element in this legislation congenial, and welcomed the more rigorous relief system as a means of disciplining the labouring poor.

> A. Digby, *Pauper Palaces*, 1978.

The New Poor Law – the Reality?

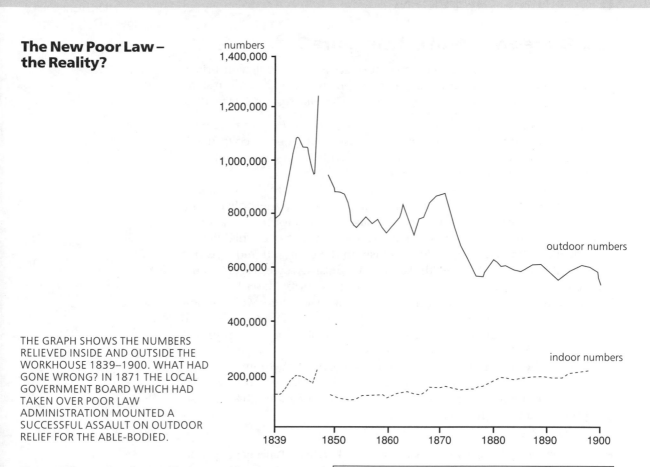

numbers

THE GRAPH SHOWS THE NUMBERS RELIEVED INSIDE AND OUTSIDE THE WORKHOUSE 1839–1900. WHAT HAD GONE WRONG? IN 1871 THE LOCAL GOVERNMENT BOARD WHICH HAD TAKEN OVER POOR LAW ADMINISTRATION MOUNTED A SUCCESSFUL ASSAULT ON OUTDOOR RELIEF FOR THE ABLE-BODIED.

There was some local opposition to workhouses in the South but in the North it was vigorous and fierce. The 'Whig Bastilles' were denounced by the poor and centralisation by the middle class ratepayers. No workhouses were built in the West Riding during the 1840s; several were closed.

Outdoor relief never stopped in the industrial areas. In 1847–48 over 17,000 were receiving outdoor relief in Leicester, in Bradford 13,000 were on relief in July 1848 when the workhouse only held 260.

Outdoor relief for the able-bodied continued in rural areas. It was cheaper than putting whole families into the workhouse and kept a pool of cheap labour available for the local farmers.

Rural guardians used relief ostensibly in aid of sickness as a means of relieving low-paid, irregularly employed agricultural labourers.

A. Digby, *Pauper Palaces*, 1978.

TALKING POINT

The great weakness of the New Poor Law Act was that it expected a system designed to solve difficulties in the agricultural South to cope with the problems of an industrialising society. Is this all that was wrong with the New Poor Law?

Examining the Evidence

You will find references to all the legislation mentioned on pages 302–3.

Was there an 'Age of Laissez-faire'?

By the middle of the nineteenth century government policy in Britain came as near laissez-faire as has ever been practicable in a modern state.

E.J. Hobsbawm, *Industry and Empire*, 1968.

Writing in 1905, A.V. Dicey *(Law and Public Opinion in England)* labelled the years 1865–1900 the 'Period of Collectivism'. He defined collectivism as action by the State, even at some loss of individual freedom, to improve conditions for the people as a whole.

There were two aspects to 'laissez faire': the State's role in economic affairs and its role in social policy. By following free trade policies, the State withdrew from economic regulation. Social reform was another matter. Dicey and Hobsbawm both ignore the fact that there had been a great deal of administrative interventionism in the early and mid-Victorian periods (Poor Law, public health, factories), whilst Dicey exaggerates the extent to which the State had extended its powers by 1905. The 1870 Education Act encouraged local and voluntary activity. There were no new principles underpinning the social legislation of Disraeli's second government, although the Public Health Act compelled local authorities to take a central role in public health regulation.

On the other hand, there was a fourfold increase in the number of civil servants, 1870–1914 and government expenditure increased ten times during a period of falling prices and then of gentle inflation. This suggests a significant increase in government activity.

Source A

Extracts from the evidence of Joseph Hebergam, aged 17, to the Parliamentary Select Committee on the Employment of Children in Factories, 1832.

At what age did you commence? – Seven years of age.

What were your hours of labour ...? – From 5 in the morning till 8 at night.

What intervals had you for refreshment and rest? – Thirty minutes at noon.

You had fourteen and a half hours of actual labour at 7 years of age? – Yes.

What wages had you at that time? – Two shillings and sixpence a week.

State to the Committee how this excessive labour agreed with the health of the children so employed? – They were often sick and poorly...

Did you not become very drowsy and sleepy towards the end of the day ...? Yes; that began about 3 o'clock, and grew worse and worse ...

What means were taken to keep you at your work so long? – There were three overlookers ... they was kept on purpose to strap.

[Hebergam's brother had died three years before.]

To what was his death attributed by your mother and the medical attendants? – It was attributed to this, that he died from working such long hours, and that it had been brought on by the factory. They have to stop the flies with their knees, because they go so swift they cannot stop them with their hands; he got a bruise on the shin by a spindle-board, and ... it burst; the surgeon cured that ... then he went to work again; but when he had worked about two months more his spine became affected, and he died.

[Hebergam became crippled and could hardly walk.]

Was it very painful for you to move? – Yes, in the morning I could scarcely walk, and my brother and sister used out of kindness to take me under each arm, and run with me to the mill, and my legs dragged on the ground in consequence of the pain ...

Were you sometimes late? – Yes; and if we were five minutes too late, the overlooker would take a strap, and beat us till we were black and blue.

Source B

Opposition to the Ten Hours Movement:

There are the strongest possible objections to any legislative interference between the master and the workman – to any law that would constrain the free course of industry, or pretend to adjust either wages or the time of labour. The true policy is to leave the workman to get as much as he can for his labour, and the master to purchase labour as cheaply as he can. But the case of children under fourteen years of age is an exception to the general rule: they are not free agents, but are subject to their parents or to their employers, and their tender age requires that they should be protected from a combination of parents and employers to extract from them an undue amount of labour.

Leeds Mercury, 16 October 1830.

Source C

The *Leeds Mercury* comments on the Whig Factory Bill of 1833:

This measure seems to us to be dictated by the best intentions, but to be a crude piece of legislation, calculated greatly to harass the manufacturers by the strict surveillance and minute interference which it establishes, whilst it secures for the children more leisure and less wages than their parents will approve.

Leeds Mercury, 10 August 1833.

1 Refer to source A.
  It was alleged that the evidence taken by the Committee was rehearsed and exaggerated. Why do you think that the reformers thought it necessary to collect evidence of this kind?
  It has been suggested that the regulation of child labour in the mills had to come because 'the intolerability barrier' had been breached. What do you think this means?
2 Read sources B and C. Outline the *Leeds Mercury*'s objections to factory legislation in general and the 1833 Bill in particular. (Check the terms of the Bill on p. 109.)

The Ten Hours Movement sought a ten-hour working day for children in textile mills.

Source D

What are the duties of Government? Generally speaking, to maintain the frame of society; and for this end to restrain violence and crime, – to protect person and property, – to enact and administer the laws needful for the maintenance of peace, order, and justice, – to sanction public works called for by the general convenience ... to conduct the relations of society with other communities, – to appoint officers, raise the taxes, pass the laws, construct the buildings, &c., requisite for these purposes.

On the other hand, it is *not* the duty of Government to interfere with the free action of the subject beyond what is necessary for these protective and defensive objects. It is *not* the duty of Government to feed the people, to clothe them, to build houses for them, to direct their industry or their commerce, to superintend their families, to cultivate their minds, to shape their opinions, or to supply them with religious teachers, physicians, schoolmasters, books, or newspapers.

These are things that the people can and ought to do for themselves, and which it is not the province of Government to do for them.

Edward Baines jun. 'Letters to the Right Hon. Lord John Russell, First Lord of the Treasury, on State Education', 1846.

Edward Baines Jnr. was the leading Nonconformist campaigner against the extension of state grants for education. Nonconformists feared that the bulk of the money would go to the Church of England schools thus giving that Church money from taxes. Baines argued that elementary education should be provided through voluntary agencies – the churches and the education societies – without any state support.

EDWIN CHADWICK'S 'REPORT ON THE SANITARY CONDITION OF THE LABOURING POPULATION', 1842, PROVIDED DETAILED FACTUAL AND STATISTICAL EVIDENCE TO SHOW THE EFFECTS AND COSTS OF INADEQUATE PUBLIC HEALTH. HIS RECOMMENDATIONS FOR CENTRAL AND LOCAL GOVERNMENT ACTION WERE CLEARLY BASED ON THE EVIDENCE. THE 'REPORT' SHOCKED, BUT OPPOSITION FROM VESTED INTERESTS, ARGUMENTS OVER THE FEASIBILITY OF THE WATER AND SEWAGE SYSTEMS HE PROPOSED, AND FEAR OF CENTRALISATION DELAYED LEGISLATION UNTIL 1848. THE 1848 PUBLIC HEALTH ACT ESTABLISHED A PUBLIC HEALTH BOARD BUT IT HAD NO COMPULSORY POWERS, COULD ONLY ADVISE LOCAL HEALTH BOARDS AND COULD ONLY SET THEM UP IF THE RATEPAYERS REQUESTED IT UNLESS THE DEATH-RATE WAS EXCESSIVELY HIGH. ITS POWERS WERE REDUCED IN 1854 WHEN CHADWICK, LORD SHAFTESBURY AND DR SOUTHWOOD SMITH, ITS MOST ACTIVE MEMBERS, WERE FORCED TO RESIGN. IT WAS ABOLISHED IN 1858.

Source E

'An 'obituary' for the Public Health Board:

... a few doctrinaires, nursed in the narrow conceits of bureaucracy, scornful alike of popular knowledge and of popular government, seized upon the sanitary theory as a means of exercising a central power of domiciliary inspection and irresponsible interference with the conduct and property of Englishmen. The ready plea was the inherent right of every man to the enjoyment of the means necessary to health; and hence the duty incumbent upon the Government of making every man healthy. Well, if it could be shown that half a dozen men, constituting a board and sitting in a Government office, could so regulate the social and domestic conduct of the inhabitants of this country as to ensure to them the safe removal of all those causes which unnaturally impair their health, and shorten their lives, it might admit of an argument, whether, for the sake of the inestimable boon of health, it would not be desirable to surrender to such a board our most cherished political institutions. But this has not been proved. ... The truth is we do not like paternal governments.

The Lancet, 13 February 1858.

Source F

The 1866 Sanitary Act compelled local authorities to act for the first time. This was a significant step forward.

Sir John Simon, a far more tactful and discreet public health reformer than Chadwick, could claim in 1865 that 'the time has arrived when it ought not to be discretional in a place whether that place should be kept filthy or not. The language of the law besides making it a power, should name it also a duty to proceed for the removal of nuisances to which attention is drawn.'

Source G

Birmingham and Leeds local authorities launched into the era of 'gas and water socialism'. They took over the supply of basic necessities, often from private companies. Joseph Chamberlain's theory was simple enough:

Here was a new radical ideal – that the state should be the agent for the physical improvement of the people.

All regulated monopolies, sustained by the State, in the interests of the inhabitants generally, should be controlled by the representatives of the people, and not left in the hands of private speculators. The Water Works should never be a source of profit, as all profit should go in the reduction of the price of water.

Source H

Joseph Chamberlain campaigning on his Unauthorised Programme, 5 August 1885:

See page 373 for the background to the Unauthorised Programme and its proposals.

I have always had a deep conviction that when the people came to govern themselves, and when the clamour of vested interests and class privileges was overborne by the powerful voice of the whole nation, that then the social evils which disgrace our civilisation, and the wrongs which have cried vainly for redress, would at last find a hearing and a remedy ... I do not want you to think that I suggest to you that legislation can accomplish all that we desire. But ... I want you not to accept as final or as perfect, arrangements under which millions of your fellow-countrymen are subject to untold privations and misery, with the evidence all around them of accumulated wealth and unbounded luxury. I believe that the great evil with which we have to deal is excessive inequality in the distribution of riches ... It is not our duty, it is not our wish, to pull down and abase the rich. But our object is to elevate the poor, to raise the general condition of the people.

Source I

The last twenty years of the century saw the publication of several reports on poverty. They revealed an appalling picture of human misery and deprivation.

1883 Andrew Mearns, *Bitter Cry of Outcast London*
1890 William Booth, *In Darkest England and the Way Out*
1889–1903 Charles Booth, *Life and Labour of the People in London*

That in this land of abounding wealth, during a time of perhaps unexampled prosperity, probably more than one-fourth of the population are living in poverty, is a fact which may well cause great searchings of heart. There is surely need for a greater concentration of through by the nation upon the well-being of its own people, for no civilisation can be sound or stable which has at its base this mass of stunted human life.

Seebohm Rowntree, *Poverty: A Study of Town Life*, 1902.

Source J

However it is looked at economically, State interference in the dominion of civil life and with the machinery of production is an evil.

The Economist, 1895.

Source K

Even in those areas of social policy where state intervention was least inhibited by considerations of economic individualism, the limitations of governmental action are readily discernible. Intervention was prompted not by any conviction of its innate desirability but by the inescapable need to meet pressing problems, created largely by the twin forces of industrialisation and urbanisation, which were incapable of individualist solutions. The government of early and mid-Victorian England did not so much seek to provide new remedies for old problems as to come to terms with the new crises which accompanied a rapidly changing social order. Although parliament legislated widely and purposefully and the bureaucracy worked powerfully and at time heroically within the limits which successive governments set for it, Victorian social policy was basically negative and unconstructive.

A.J.P. Taylor, *Laissez-faire and State Intervention in Nineteenth Century Britain*, 1972.

TALKING POINT

Debate Taylor's view in source K that 'Victorian social policy was basically negative and unconstructive.'

---

3 Now refer to sources B, D and E. How do they define and restrict the role of government and sustain the view that the first half of the nineteenth century was an age of individualism?

4 To what extent do sources F, G and H suggest that there was a move to 'collectivism' in the last part of the century?

5 Read source K, refer back to the Hobsbawm quotation which opened this section, and using your wider knowledge of legislation and change and the evidence of these sources, discuss the view that there never was an era of 'laissez-faire'.

Women in Victorian England – Myths and Realities

'The Angel in the House'

Coventry Patmore's poem encapsulated the middle class ideal of separate spheres – the public sphere of business and politics for men, the private sphere of home and family for women.

The writings of Hannah More (1745–1833) were instrumental in developing the concept. She believed that men and women occupied separate spheres by nature as well as custom. Men were formed for 'the more public exhibitions on the great theatre of human life,' whilst women were best suited to the smaller scale of the domestic. Men, she argued, preferred their wives to be meek and virtuous. Wives should find their fulfilment through service to others and through the exercise of moral influence. Through their example they could make all those around them in the family circle better people and provide the truly religious home that

TALKING POINT

Should the history of women be written by women? What is omitted when it is written by men?

was the foundation of all morality.

Evangelical religion reinforced the message. John Angell James, the influential Congregationalist minister of Carr's Lane Chapel in Birmingham, stated that:

> To be a good wife is a high attainment in female excellence: *it is woman's brightest glory since the fall.*

Following the teaching of St Paul, Evangelicals offered spiritual equality but social subordination; in the home women's natural gentleness and passivity would create the space for true family religion.

Outside the home the proper activity for women was in philanthropic work. This enabled them to apply their natural aptitudes effectually in aspects of life that were part of the domestic sphere – visiting the sick or poor, education, moral and religious work.

The Reality

That was the ideal. Many middle class women happily accepted it and opposed the challenges to the concept that emerged in the second half of the century. Working class women had different priorities and problems, but they were also not unaffected by the ideal. The Factory and Mines legislation of the 1840s which restricted female employment was motivated less by concern about working conditions than for the moral environment in which women and girls were working, particularly in the mines. If female hours of work were limited (1844, 1847, 1850 Factory Acts) then married women would have more time to spend in domestic tasks and family management, their proper sphere.

TALKING POINT

'The Angel in the House' is the title of a poem by Coventry Patmore, published in 1854: what image does it suggest about the wife's role?

TALKING POINT

What point is the artist making? Does the concept of separate spheres have any relevance here?

PIN MONEY.

NEEDLE MONEY.

Marriage became both symbol and institution of women's containment, it was marriage which would safely domesticate the burgeoning garden flower into an indoor pot plant; the beautiful object potentially open to all men's gaze became the possession of one man when kept within the house like a picture fixed to the wall.

L. Davidoff and C. Hall, *Family Fortunes*, 1987.

Marriage protected and constrained. The legal system enforced subordination – a wife gave up all her property to her husband, her husband legally acquired all her earnings, her children were his and in the event of a separation the law gave him custody. Most women still actively sought marriage. In many cases the legal restrictions were an irrelevance. In many middle class marriages there was a greater equality than the ideal suggests whilst working class women were often the dominant partners skilfully managing the family budget.

The Challenge to Separate Spheres

From the 1850s pressure groups began to challenge the prevailing ideology. Led by Barbara Leigh Smith, 'the Ladies of Langham Place' campaigned for changes in the law. John Stuart Mill published *The Subjection of Women* in 1869. Two years before, he had launched the movement for women's suffrage with an unsuccessful amendment to Disraeli's Reform Bill. In 1872 the Central Committee of the National Society for Women's Suffrage was formed to co-ordinate the campaign. In 1897 it was transformed into the National Union of Women's Suffrage Societies, led by Millicent Fawcett. The NUWSS stressed its non-party and non-militant character. It was a typical nineteenth-century single issue pressure group, and in 1897 a private member's Bill won a majority of the votes cast by both Conservative and Liberal MPs. The Pankhursts were to allege, when founding the Women's Social and Political Union in 1905, that the non-militants had achieved nothing but considerable progress had been made.

Female property-owners and ratepayers were given the local government vote in 1869. They could stand for election for School Boards, Poor Law Guardians and for the new parish, rural district and urban district councils. Although they could vote for the new county councils (1888 Local Government Act) they could not become county councillors until 1907. Increasingly the political parties required female support. Through the Primrose League and the Women's Liberal Federation they secured the party workers they needed once the Corrupt Practices Act (1883) had set limits on election expenditure. As local and national elections became more orderly, female participation and local government work helped to undermine the anti-suffragist case.

Not all feminists were suffragist. Many argued that it was more important to secure real practical advances, not to wait for the vote. Emily Davies withdrew from the agitation in case association with it damaged the reputation of her college for women at Cambridge (Girton College). She wanted to open education to middle class women to provide them with opportunities and careers that would otherwise remain closed to them.

128 women had been elected to School Boards by 1895 and 893 to Poor Law Boards – although education and caring for the poor were regarded as part of the female sphere.

The Contagious Diseases Acts authorised military doctors to give prostitutes medical examinations in garrison towns and naval ports. The campaign focused attention on society's double standards about sexual behaviour by men and women in and out of marriage.

The Victoria University – a federation of colleges in Manchester, Liverpool and Leeds.

Despite the social pressure for marriage there were large numbers of single women for whom the only opening was as governesses. Octavia Hill and Beatrice Webb were two other active women who remained aloof from the suffrage movement. Josephine Butler concentrated on the campaign for the repeal of the Contagious Diseases Acts.

There was little agreement between feminist groups. Some wanted more legislative protection for women, others wanted to remove the protection that existed to enable men and women to compete equally.

In 1857 the Divorce Law was reformed, but it still favoured the husband. The Married Women's Property Acts (1870, 1882) allowed a wife to retain ownership of her property and to keep her earnings. Legislation in 1873 and 1886 made it easier for mothers to get custody of their children and to appoint guardians. In 1895 violence became grounds for a judicial separation with the payment of maintenance by the husband. The barriers of training and education set up as occupations were professionalised were gradually breached – there were only 8 female doctors in 1871, by 1901 there were 212, women could graduate from London University in 1878, the Victoria University in 1880, the Scottish universities in 1892, the University of Wales in 1893 and Durham in 1895.

FOOD VALUES IN OUR RESTAURANTS.

Customer. "What do you suggest for to-day, Miss?"
Waitress (late of Girton). "Well, Sir, roast mutton, two vegetables and sweets will give you the necessary protein, calories and carbo-hydrates."

THIS CARTOON FROM *PUNCH* SUGGESTS THAT ATTITUDES TO WOMEN'S EDUCATION WERE STILL UNCHANGED IN MANY QUARTERS.

By 1906 substantial progress had been made in freeing women from the restrictions of mid-century but they only directly affected a minority of women among the more privileged, affluent and sophisticated social groups.

Throughout society both 'individualist' and 'collectivist' attitudes to economics and public policy coexisted with large residues of pre-industrial paternalism and patriarchalism in the sphere of private relationships. A growing emphasis upon individual rights that undoubtedly embraced women as well as men was nevertheless tempered by the view that social cohesion, personal morality, reproduction and family life all required the relative confinement of women to the home – a view shared not just by men but by large numbers of women, who maintained that the sexes occupied generically 'separate spheres'.

J. Harris, *Private Lives, Public Spirit: Britain 1870–1914*, 1993.

Women and Work

Main occupations of females (all ages) in Britain, 1881 and 1911 (thousands)				
	1881	%	1911	%
Domestic service	1,756	45.2	2,127	39.3
Textiles	745	19.2	870	16.1
Clothing	667	17.2	825	15.2
Professional occupations	203	5.2	383	7.1
Food, drink, tobacco	98	2.5	308	5.7
Commercial occupations	11	0.3	157	2.9
Papers, printing, books and stationery	53	1.4	144	2.7
Metal-working and manufacture	49	1.3	128	2.4
Agriculture	116	3.0	117	2.1
Public administration	9	0.2	50	0.9

WHAT TRENDS IN FEMALE EMPLOYMENT CAN BE DEDUCED FROM THESE STATISTICS? IT IS WORTH NOTING THAT 39% OF THE WORKFORCE WAS FEMALE IN 1881 BUT ONLY 35% IN 1911.

Widening work opportunities were available to the higher social groups by the end of the century. The revolution in the office with the advent of the typewriter and the telephone were the most obvious examples of the changes that were taking place. Women operated them more readily than men, and did not appear to be challenging traditional male occupations when they did so. The proportion of clerks who were female increased from 3 per cent in 1881 to 25 per cent twenty years later. The Post Office rapidly became a major employer of women.

Working class women did not necessarily work from choice and many looked forward to marriage as a release. In 1911 90 per cent of married women did not work. this figure varied in different parts of the country. In the cotton districts, the Potteries and Dundee (jute industry) 30 per cent of married women were in employment. The censuses underestimate the total number of women who contributed to the family budget because it did not allow for part-time work, seasonal work, or domestic outworking. The cheap sewing machine provided a new source of employment at home or in small sweated workshops where women were exploited on low piece rates and long hours. With very few exceptions men earned more than women for the same work. Unions were slow to organise female

THE EXPANSION OF
ELEMENTARY EDUCATION
AFTER 1870 AND THE
INTRODUCTION OF NEW
TECHNOLOGY INTO THE
OFFICE CREATED
ACCEPTABLE EMPLOYMENT
OPENINGS FOR MIDDLE
CLASS WOMEN.

workers fearing that they would undermine male wage rates and de-skill the trades they entered. The Unions wanted a 'family wage' to enable a man to support his family without the need for extra sources of income. Attitudes were ambivalent. Men wanted to relieve their wives of the double burden of work and family but were concerned about the wages of their daughters.

By the early years of the twentieth century there were new and 'respectable' occupations for those middle class women who wanted to work, or who had to work before marriage. Strangely, at a time when middle class women were challenging the family ideal and seeking to break out from it, working class men were demanding the family wage that would put their wives firmly into the home.

MOTHERHOOD
TOOK ON A NEW
SIGNIFICANCE AT
THE TURN OF THE
CENTURY. THE
GROWING
CHALLENGE FROM
OTHER EUROPEAN
POWERS,
IMPERIALLY AND
INDUSTRIALLY,
CREATED AN
AWARENESS OF THE
NEED FOR A
HEALTHY AND
GROWING
POPULATION. THE
CRUCIAL ROLE OF
STABLE FAMILY LIFE
IN THIS TENDED TO
REINFORCE THE
OLD IDEAL.

TALKING POINT

What progress had women really made by the early years of the twentieth century?

10.3 Improving Living Standards for the Working Class?

Wages and Prices

The slow increase in money wages that seems to have begun after 1850 was halted in the late 1870s by the Great Depression. After 1875, there was a dramatic drop in prices, the consequence of the import of cheap North American grain, falling sugar and tea prices, the importation of refrigerated and canned meat. One estimate suggests an increase in real wages of about 80 per cent by 1900 when prices were beginning to rise.

There were variations within this

It is easy to generalise about living standards and conditions. Experiences differed from community to community, from area to area, from industry to industry and from family to family but most working class memoirs from the end of the century agree that standards were improving. This Focus can only point to some aspect of working class life that were changing whilst raising the questions – how far had things improved, and for whom?

overall pattern. Carpenters' rates were 4 7/8d per hour in Falmouth and 10 1/2d per hour in London. Agricultural labourers in Dorset still got half the rate paid in Lancashire. Many workers were casual labourers and there was no job security. Highly skilled workers could expect from 30 to 40 shillings a week or more.

Diet

Legislation to stop food adulteration (1860, 1872, 1875) improved the working class diet, but the rapid fall in bread prices after 1875 meant that there was more to spend on other foodstuffs. Three quarters of a wage was spent on food before 1850, the bulk of it on bread. Consumption of tea, sugar, cocoa and meat increased as their prices fell. The first fish and chip shops provided cheap nourishing meals at a time when many working class homes had inadequate cooking facilities. Cheap flour and sugar enabled biscuit manufacturers like Huntley and

AS WAGES ROSE, THE BETTER OFF SECTIONS OF THE WORKING CLASS COULD PATRONISE THE NEW MULTIPLE GROCER CHAINS WHERE THE RANGE OF PRODUCE WAS MUCH WIDER THAN COULD BE PURCHASED IN THE OLDER CORNER SHOPS.

Palmer to cater for a new mass market, Chivers and Robertsons produced jams and the first convenience foods appeared. The vogue for white bread, the growing use of margarine and condensed milk counter-balanced other nutritional changes.

Housing

Dreadful slum housing still existed at the end of the century. Although the working class elite aspired to move into superior housing, there was not much alternative for the majority. Conditions were worsened in many towns by railway construction and urban improvements which often replaced demolished slums by civic buildings or housing with rents beyond most working people. The Census revealed less overcrowding (more than two people to a room). In 1891 11.2 per cent of the population were overcrowded, in 1901 8.2 per cent and in 1911 7.8 per cent. After 1875 each new house was required to have its own lavatory and a tap. In 1911 about half of all the towns in England and Wales could boast that 96 per cent of their lavatories were water closets.

The public health movement improved living conditions, but many old style houses survived in town and country and the provision of low rent council housing was still in the future.

THE OLD ROOM IN SLUMLAND.

TALKING POINT

What were the obstacles to the provision of cheap affordable good quality housing for the working class?

Leisure and recreation

By 1880 the great majority of industrial workers had gained the six and a half day week. The Bank Holiday Act (1871) provided statutory holidays. Increased leisure time led to the commercial provision of entertainment. Day excursions by rail were increasingly taken at holiday time, and in Lancashire towns where the 'Wakes week' was taken the better off could afford a few days at the seaside.

10.4   Religion in the Nineteenth Century

It is difficult for us to understand the centrality of religion in the lives of many nineteenth century men and women. Religious issues had a political significance throughout the century. Catholic Emancipation in 1829, reform of the Church of England in the 1830s, Papal Aggression in 1851 and issues around education which continued into the twentieth century. In one form or another religious questions seemed to have impinged on virtually every Victorian general election.

The Church of England

A Report on clerical incomes (1833) showed that 47 per cent of parish clergy had incomes of less that £200 but that 14 per cent received more than £500. In 1831, 52 per cent of incumbents were non-resident in their parishes. Many, however, lived just outside the parish in more suitable accommodation and still performed their duties. Pluralism was the holding of more than one benefice. The general situation was undoubtedly better than the Church's critics portrayed.

At the beginning of our period, the Church of England was perceived as being Tory and reactionary. Radicals expected to reform its corruptions and abuses after 1832. There were three main complaints – the great diversity of clerical incomes, absenteeism and pluralism. In addition the continued payment of tithe caused friction in the countryside whilst militant Nonconformists and radicals demanded disestablishment. Peel's first administration (1834–35) lessened the pressure on the Church by establishing the Ecclesiastical Commission to enable the Church to reform itself. The Whigs (1833–41) implemented the reforms the Commission recommended.

For details of Church reform, see page 119.

THE PARISH STRUCTURE MADE IT DIFFICULT FOR THE CHURCH OF ENGLAND TO RESPOND TO THE RELIGIOUS NEEDS OF THE GROWING URBAN AND INDUSTRIAL DISTRICTS. BETWEEN 1811 AND 1831, WHEN THE POPULATION ALMOST DOUBLED, ONLY 439 NEW CHURCHES WERE BUILT. THE CHANGES INSTITUTED BY THE ECCLESIASTICAL COMMISSION ENSURED A RAPID EXPANSION OF CHURCH BUILDING AFTER 1840, MAINLY FINANCED OUT OF VOLUNTARY CONTRIBUTIONS. THE VAST MAJORITY WERE BUILT IN THE GOTHIC REVIVAL STYLE.

Evangelicals were the most prominent group within the Church at the beginning of the period. They achieved their greatest influence when Palmerston was Prime Minister, advised by his son-in-law, the leading Evangelical layman Lord Shaftesbury. With their roots in the Evangelical Revival of the eighteenth century, they believed in the necessity of the conversion experience for salvation, that the Bible was the foundation of faith, and lived strict and ordered lives.

The Tractarian Movement began in Oxford in 1833. It was a reaction to state interference and enforced reform, an attempt to defend the Church from Radical attack and to restate the traditions of the Church. At first the movement had considerable support within the Church. The 'Tracts for the Times' were widely read. 'Tract XC''s claim that the Thirty Nine Articles were not at variance with Roman Catholic teaching confirmed the suspicion that the Oxford Movement was inclining the Church of England toward Rome. The Movement's continued influence was reflected in the emergence of a High Church party within the Church. The second half of the century was marked by disputes over ritual and the internal arrangement of churches as High Churchmen sought to revive traditional practices abandoned since the seventeenth century.

> The Thirty Nine Articles: the Church of England's statement of belief.

The Nonconformist Denominations

The Methodists, as befitted the church that had been formed in the Evangelical Revival by John Wesley, expanded most rapidly in the new social and industrial conditions. The first major secession from the Wesleyan connection was that of the Primitive Methodists after 1807. Later splits did not weaken Methodism. It was able to react quickly to urban and industrial growth and its chapels sprang up in slums, in industrial villages and rural areas. Both the Congregationalists and the Baptists benefitted from the Evangelical Revival, with numbers of members and chapels increasing.

> JOHN HENRY NEWMAN'S SECESSION TO THE ROMAN CATHOLIC CHURCH IN 1845 SEEMED TO JUSTIFY ALL THE DOUBTS ABOUT THE OXFORD MOVEMENT. HE HAD BEEN ONE OF ITS FOUNDERS AND LEADERS IN THE 1830S.

> The Wesleyan Methodists did not regard themselves as Nonconformists since John Wesley had never seceded from the Church of England.
> The Roman Catholic Church was the denomination that grew most rapidly. Irish immigration following the Famine gave it 28 per cent of all church members in 1860.
> The Congregationalists and the Baptists were the dissenting denominations that originated in the seventeenth century – 'Old Dissent'.

TALKING POINT

The Church of England was the established church – what does this mean, and why was that status challenged during the nineteenth century?

Estimated membership of the main Nonconformist denominations (in thousands)

Date	Methodists		Congregationalists		Baptists	
	A	B	A	B	A	B
1800	96	8	55	4	40	3
1820	208	12	117	7	79	4
1840	451	18	196	8	138	6
1860	525	13	291	7	203	5

A = Church Members (this is not the same as attenders)
B = % of all Church Members (including the Church of England)

The shattering of Victorian complacency

Source A
Proportion of the population in receipt of poor relief:

1834   8.8 per cent
1850   5.7 per cent
1880   3.2 per cent.

Source B
Titles of books about the London slums and the people who lived in them:

The Bitter Cry of Outcast London (1883)
In Darkest England and the Way Out (1890)
The People of the Abyss (1903)
From the Abyss (1902)
Glimpses into the Abyss (1906).

Source C
... the average wage for a labourer in York is from 18s. to 21s. whereas ... the minimum expenditure necessary to maintain in a state of physical efficiency a family of two adults and three children is 21s. 8d., or, if there are four children, the sum required would be 26s.

It is thus seen that the *wages paid for unskilled labour in York are insufficient to provide food, shelter, and clothing adequate to maintain a family in a state of bare physical efficiency.*

And let us clearly understand what merely physical efficiency means. A family ... must never spend a penny on a railway fare or omnibus ... They cannot save, nor can they join a sick club or Trade Union ... The children must have no pocket money... Should a child fall ill, it must be attended by the parish doctor, should it die, it must be buried by the parish. Finally the wage-earner must never be absent from his work for a single day.'

Seebohm Rowntree, *Poverty: a study of town life*, 1901.

1 How might source A contribute to the view that most working people were better off in late-Victorian England?

2 Comment on the titles chosen by the authors for the books listed in source B.

3 Why would the findings of social investigators like Rowntree and Charles Booth be so disturbing? How could they contribute to changes in attitude and policy?

TALKING POINT

Charles Booth (*Lives and Labours of the People of London*) concluded that about 30.7 per cent lived in poverty; Rowntree's figure for York was 27.84 per cent; Maud Pember Reeves (*Round about a pound a week*, 1913) suggested that life on a wage of 18 to 26 shillings a week was a struggle, but it was above a bare subsistence level. Do the findings of these investigators invalidate the claim that the standard of living of the working class had improved greatly by 1906?

EXAMINING THE EVIDENCE

The Churches and the People

Source A
Details from the 1851 Religious Census in which attendance at church or chapel was recorded separately for London parliamentary boroughs and 65 large towns. The table gives the findings for selected towns.

Town	% of population attending place of worship	Church of England		Methodists		Baptists		Congregation		Roman Catholics	
		A	B	A	B	A	B	A	B	A	B
Birmingham	36.1	17.0	47.1	5.2	14.5	4.2	11.6	3.3	9.1	2.2	6.1
Bristol	56.7	25.2	44.9	9.8	17.3	4.8	8.4	9.0	15.8	3.4	5.9
Leeds	47.4	16.4	34.5	19.8	41.9	2.7	5.6	3.5	7.4	2.9	6.1
Liverpool	45.2	18.4	40.7	6.0	13.2	1.1	2.4	1.9	4.3	14.7	32.5
Manchester	34.7	11.9	34.4	7.0	20.2	1.3	3.7	3.1	8.8	8.1	23.3
Preston	25.5	5.2	20.4	6.4	25.2	1.0	4.1	2.6	10.3	9.1	35.8
Stockport	42.8	15.4	36.0	14.2	33.2	1.5	3.6	6.2	14.4	3.7	8.7
Stoke	40.9	12.9	31.6	21.8	53.2	0.9	2.1	2.6	6.4	2.0	5.0

Key:
A: attendance as a percentage of total population
B: attendance as a percentage of total attendance at a place of worship in each town

Source B
Summary of total attendance at places of worship on Census Sunday.

Total population of England and Wales	**17,927,609**
Number of possible worshippers	12,549,326
(This estimate assumed that 30 per cent of the population would not be able to attend because of illness, old age, infants etc.)	
Number of actual worshippers	7,261,032
Which included: Church of England	3,773,474
Independents (Congregationalists)	793,142
Baptists	587,978
Wesleyan Methodists	1,385,382
Roman Catholics	303,393
Others	416,013

Source C

The conclusion to the 1851 Census Report:

The most important fact which this investigation ... brings before us is, unquestionably, the alarming number of non-attendants. Even in the least unfavourable aspect of the figures ... it must be apparent that a sadly formidable portion of the English people are habitual neglecters of the public ordinances of religion. Nor is it difficult to indicate to what particular class of the community this portion in the main belongs ... While the labouring myriads of our country have been multiplying with our multiplied material prosperity, it cannot, it is feared, be stated that a corresponding increase has occurred in the attendance of this class in our religious edifices.

Source D

The Rev Algernon Wells speaking to the Congregational Union, 1848:

... preaching, buildings, ministers, manners, notions, and practices – all have on them the air and impress of English middle class life. Are they not at this time far more exclusively of that class than was the case a century ago?

Source E

The Rev Dr W.F. Hook, Vicar of Leeds, to Archdeacon Samuel Wilberforce, 5 July 1843:

...in the manufacturing districts she [the Church of England] is the object of detestation to the working classes ... The working classes consider themselves to be an oppressed people ... they consider the church to belong to the Party of their oppressors; hence they hate it, and consider a man of the working classes who is a Churchman to be a traitor to his Party or Order – he is outlawed in the society in which he moves.

A. R. Ashwell, *Life of the Right Reverend Samuel Wilberforce, Vol. 1*, 1880.

Source F

In the school and the church, the people are taught that passive obedience is a virtue ... They are taught to believe that they are mercifully created to endure poverty, and that the rich are very unfortunate in being born to the care and trouble of ruling over the poor. They are also taught, that God has created them poor, for the salvation of their immortal souls; and that through tribulation they must enter heaven. They are taught that to fret at their earthly privations, is to rebel against the goodness of God ...

Chartist Circular, 30 November 1839.

Source G

Some of the pews for the rich were padded, lined, cushioned, and supplied with every comfort ... The poor ... were seated on stools in the aisles; many of the seats were without backs, to prevent the occupants from falling asleep during the sermon, and the cold, damp stone beneath their feet was the only place to kneel during prayer ... Some of our Church ministers ... appeared to have fellowship only with the wealthy.

John Glyde, *Suffolk in the Nineteenth Century: Physical, Social, Moral, Religious and Industrial*, 1855.

1 Study sources A, B and C:
What shocking facts did the Census reveal about the new urban areas?
How did the census encourage the Nonconformists but alarm the Church of England?
How far does the wider evidence support the conclusion in source C?

2 Referring to sources E, F, G, H and I, and to your wider knowledge, comment on the reasons why the working class stayed away from the churches in the first half of the century.

3 'The churches largely remained middle class institutions.'
How far would sources D, H, I and J support this?

TALKING POINT

In 1851 the churches believed that they faced a crisis. By 1900 new scientific knowledge and the theory of evolution had challenged the veracity of the Old Testament. Starting from source K, the other evidence and your broader knowledge of the nineteenth century explore the view that Britain was a less religious society in 1900 than in 1815.

Source H

A barrow boy explains why working people did not go to church: 'They see people come out of church and chapel, and they're mostly well-dressed, and there's very few of their own sort among the church-goers, the costers somehow mix up being religious with being respectable, and so they have a queer sort of feeling about it.'

Henry Mayhew, *London Life and Labour*, 1851.

Source I

It is evident at once that Methodism has been much too exclusively the sect of the lower middle class

Methodist Times, 19 August 1886.

Source J

The great section of the population, which passes by the name of the working classes ... remains, as a whole, outside of all the religious bodies, whether organised as churches or as missions ...

Charles Booth, *Lives and Labours of the People of London*, Vol. VII.

Source K

Though many Nonconformist groups in the late 1900s were failing to keep pace with demographic growth, the Anglican Church in the Edwardian period was attracting a higher proportion of the population as Easter communicants than at any time in the previous century. Attendance at Sunday schools ... nearly trebled between the 1860s and 1906. Membership of Bands of Hope, Boys' Brigades, Mens Societies, the Girls Friendly Society and the Young Men's and Women's Christian Associations (all of them late Victorian foundations) ran into many millions.

... The churches maintained their hold upon the major rites of passage ... The 1870 Education Act entrenched ... Christian teaching within the popular culture, and made a generalised Christian morality more nearly universal than ever before ... The threat to organised religion from the new recreational culture of the 1880s and 1890s has probably been exaggerated ... the churches themselves were leading purveyors of this new culture ...

J. Harris, *Private Lives, Public Spirit: Britain 1870 – 1914*, 1993.

REVIEW

This chapter has examined some of the topics and issues that were controversial at the time and which have been debated by historians since:
● 'laissez faire' and 'Collectivism',
● the changing role of the State,
● the role of women and the challenge to convention,
● the quality of life for the working class,
● the significance of religion.

Review the topics covered in this chapter and consider:
● In what ways had conditions changed for the better?
● In what ways were attitudes and policies still very much the same at the century's end as they had been around 1850?

11 The Dominance of Lord Palmerston

PREVIEW

The disruption of party politics?

Source A

The Session of 1845 was the last of those that witnessed party connection in its normal state. Throughout the decade which preceded that year it was in full and brilliant blossom. Since then we have had properly speaking ... none in the best sense of the term: none compact and organised after the ancient manner.

W.E. Gladstone, writing in 1855.

Source B

Confusion was the legacy of repeal among politicians.

M. Bentley, *Politics without Democracy, 1815–1914*, 1984.

Source C

It was a period of easy-going rivalry between a number of aristocratic factions, to which the mass of the country was content to leave government, as long as prosperity rose, taxes fell, free trade remained sacrosanct, and British prestige was upheld against all comers.

R. Blake, *Disraeli*, 1966.

Source D

Parties and Elections

Election	Whigs/Libs	Conservatives	Peelites
July 1847	338	227	91
July 1852	310	299	45
April 1857	367	260	27
May 1859	325	306	23
July 1865	370	288	—
Nov. 1868	387	271	—

(Any figures of party strength can only be approximations)

TALKING POINT

Comment on Gladstone's view that the period from the Reform Act to the Corn Law crisis had 'witnessed the party connection in its normal state'.

Referring to sources D and E, comment on:

1 the accuracy of the judgements of Gladstone (source A) and the two historians (sources B and C);
2 the strengths and weaknesses of the parties and political groups.

Source E

Government and Leading Ministers					
Dates	Prime Minister	Foreign Secretary	Home Secretary	Chancellor of the Exchequer	Party
June 1846 – Feb. 1852	Lord John Russell	Lord Palmerston (until Dec. 1851)	Sir George Grey	Sir Charles Wood	Whig/ Liberal
Feb. 1852– Dec. 1852	Lord Derby	Lord Malmesbury	Spencer Walpole	B. Disraeli	Cons.
Dec. 1852– Feb. 1855	Lord Aberdeen	Lord John Russell (1852–3); Lord Clarendon	Lord Palmerston	W.E. Gladstone	Coalition Whig/Lib. Peelite
Feb. 1855– Feb. 1858	Lord Palmerston	Clarendon	Sir George Grey	Gladstone (3 weeks only); Sir G. Cornewall Lewis	Whig/Lib.
Feb. 1858– June 1859	Lord Derby	Malmesbury	Walpole	Disraeli	Cons.
June 1859– Oct. 1865	Lord Palmerston	Russell	Cornewall Lewis, then Sir George Grey	Gladstone	Liberal
Oct. 1865– June 1866	Russell	Clarendon	Sir George Grey	Gladstone	Liberal
June 1866– Feb. 1868	Lord Derby	Lord Stanley	Walpole, 1867-8; Gathorne-Hardy	Disraeli	Cons.
Feb. 1868– Dec. 1868	Disraeli	Lord Stanley	Gathorne-Hardy	G.Ward Hunt	Cons.
Dec. 1868 (formed)	Gladstone	Clarendon	H.A. Bruce	Robert Lowe	Lib.

The formation of the Liberal Party is traditionally dated from the meeting of opposition MPs at Willis's Rooms on 6 June 1859.

Mid-Victorian prosperity

The Great Exhibition of 1851 demonstrated how successfully Britain had come through the difficulties of the previous decade. It heralded a period of widespread prosperity that lasted until the late 1870s.

Contentment may not have been universal but economic calm, a gradual rise in living standards and the passivity of the working class appeared to vindicate Peel's policies.

A brief agricultural depression, 1848–52, was followed by 20 years of stable wheat prices. Farmers benefited from a steady rise in the prices of other grain crops, dairy produce and meat. The pessimistic forecasts of the Protectionists were forgotten, whilst Peel's optimism seemed fully justified as farmers adopted new scientific methods and invested in machinery and land improvements. An expanding home market meant that the landed interest was not immediately damaged by the repeal of the Corn Laws.

The Great Famine 1845–49

The potato blight, a fungal disease which rots the potato in the ground, struck Ireland in September 1845, spreading rapidly in an exceptionally wet autumn, and becoming more widespread in 1846. It declined in 1847, but returned with renewed vigour in 1848–49. The consequence, in districts where the labourers were dependent on a potato diet, was a severe subsistence crisis. Epidemics of typhus in 1847 and cholera in 1849 aggravated the situation, ravaging a population already weakened by hunger.

The impact of the Great Famine on British politics was first felt with the Corn Law crisis and the fall of Peel. But successive potato crop failures also had to be dealt with by the Whigs. Equally significant was the long- term impact on Anglo-Irish relations and attitudes.

Why did Ireland starve?

The Landowner's view
The Smiths resided on their estate in Co. Wicklow:

> The people are starving I believe... For years the failure of the potato crop has been expected, yet no preparations were made to meet this coming evil. They have no forethought. If they get a shilliing they must spend it .. . they have no store for the rainy day, then when it comes they rail at all the rest of the world for not stepping to their relief instantly...
>
> D. Thomson and M. McGinty (eds), *The Irish Journals of Elizabeth Smith 1840–1850*, 1980.

Government Policy
Peel's administration dealt 'effectively' with the initial stages of the crisis. Large quantities of corn were imported, accompanied by a programme of public works to provide employment. Unfortunately there was a general reluctance to interfere with market forces. There was no attempt at price control, and no ban on the export of food from Ireland. It was assumed that Irish ratepayers should pay for Irish poverty. The Poor Law became the only resort for the poor, and the workhouse system collapsed under the strain. By the Gregory clause of the 1847 Poor Law legislation relief was denied to smallholders occupying a quarter of an acre of land. Families starved rather than giving up their holdings.

The words of John Russell, the prime minister, stressed the vital part that Irish self-help and self-reliance was supposed to play in the alleviation of the Famine:

... there are some things which the Crown cannot grant, which Parliament cannot enact – these are the spirit of self-reliance and the spirit of co-operation ... happy will it be, indeed, if the Irish themselves take for their maxim, 'Help yourselves and Heaven will help you'; and then I trust they will find there have been some 'uses in adversity...

Lord John Russell in the House of Commons, 25 January 1847.

The Historical Perspective

Source A

... I see it ... as the tragic outcome of three factors: an ecological accident that could not have been predicted, an ideology ill-geared to saving lives and, of course, mass poverty. The role of sheer bad luck is important: Ireland's ability to cope with a potato failure would have been far greater a few decades later, and the political will – and the political pressure – to spend more money to save lives greater too ... Food availability *was* a problem; *nobody* wanted the extirpation of the Irish as a race.

C. O'Grada, *Ireland Before and After the Famine*, 1988.

Source B

... when the chips were down in the frightful summer of 1847, the British simply abandoned the Irish and let them perish. There is no doubt that Britain could have saved Ireland. The British Treasury spent a total of about £9.5 million on famine relief. While parts of the sum were considered a loan, most of it was never repaid. Financed largely by advances from London, the soup kitchen program ... saved many lives. When the last kitchens were closed in October 1847, Lord Clarendon wrote in despair to ... Russell: 'Ireland cannot be left to her own resources ... we are not to let the people die of starvation.' The reply was: 'The state of Ireland for the next few months must be one of great suffering. Unhappily the agitation for Repeal has contrived to destroy nearly all sympathy in this country.'

J. Mokyr, *Why Ireland Starved*, 1983.

TALKING POINT

What can the British government be accused of and criticised for during the Famine?

Source C

If the charge of genocide could be sustained simply by showing that blind adherence to the doctrines of *laissez-faire* led to countless thousands of deaths (though certainly not two million) in Ireland during the late 1840s, then it may be taken as proved. But if ... there must also be a demonstration that British statesmen and their agents in Ireland were knowing and willing collaborators in a deliberate campaign of extermination, then the allegation of genocide is not only unproven but not even worth making. Still, that the charge has been levelled at all is one measure of how radically mistaken were the actions and inactions of the politicians and administrators responsible for relief measures during the great famine. It is true that at times ... accepted econoimc principles were reluctantly abandoned. Yet what made by far the greater impression was not how many people were kept alive by soup in the late spring and summer of 1847, but rather how many people were allowed to die at other times because they were not fed when they might have been.

James S. Donnelly jr, in W.E. Vaughan (ed.), *A New History Of Ireland*, vol. V, 1989.

The Consequences of the Famine

Bitterness

That million and a half men, women and children were carefully, prudently, and peacefully *slain* by the English government.

John Mitchel, Young Ireland revolutionary, sentenced to 14 years transportation in 1848.

Disillusionment

Ireland had not been treated as an equal within the Union. The Poor rate burden had not been shared. The English government had worked for England's interests - Ireland's needs had been ignored.

Population decline

The continued emigration after 1850 contributed to a steady decline in Ireland's population. Demographers have traced the beginnings of this to the years before 1846, but the catastrophic losses of the famine years were not recovered in the nineteenth century.

Change on the land

In the countryside there was bitterness at the role played by landlords during the famine – their reluctance to help and their eagerness to clear their estates, taking advantage of the Gregory clause of the 1847 Poor Law Act. Landlords, however, suffered from falling rents and soaring rates. The Encumbered Estates Act (1849) freed property from the legal restrictions that prevented sale. Estates valued at £20 million changed hands. Landowners aimed to consolidate the farms on their estates. The number of small tenancies decreased and larger farms of over 30 acres increased. Apart from the far west of Ireland where subsistence agriculture survived, farmers turned increasingly to grazing and livestock production, benefiting from rising

prices in Britain and the expanding railway network. The Franchise Act (1850) gave these prosperous farmers the vote. With the cottiers eliminated by the Famine, this group was to take the lead in the next confrontation with the landlords.

cottiers – landless labourers

The fragmentation of the parties

The Whigs – the natural party of government?

After Peel's resignation in June 1846 Russell formed a Whig ministry. With few exceptions, Russell's Cabinet was selected from the same narrow circle of Whig families as those of Grey and Melbourne. The paucity of rising talent on the Whig side contrasted bleakly with the expertise ranged alongside Peel on the Opposition front bench. Some junior offices went to placate the Radicals, but the bold step of offering a Cabinet post to Cobden, all that he would have accepted, was avoided. Whig aristocrats and Queen alike demurred at such a rapid rise to high office for the leader of the Anti-Corn Law League and scourge of aristocratic privilege.

Russell was not a strong premier. Unlike Peel he was not interested in the details and processes of administration, and he lacked the self-assurance to impose his authority on either Cabinet or Commons. His colleagues resisted and frustrated his renewed interest in parliamentary reform, whilst his lack of tact and charm, and his pride and self-importance, sent potential government supporters into the Opposition lobbies. Lord Palmerston, his foreign secretary,

POLITICAL ECONOMY; OR, LORD JOHN IN PEEL'S CLOTHES.

THE QUEEN (log.)—"WELL! IT IS NOT THE BEST FIT IN THE WORLD, BUT WE'LL SEE HOW HE GOES ON!"

IT WAS RUSSELL'S MISFORTUNE TO BE OVERSHADOWED BY 'STRONGER AND BIGGER' MEN THROUGHOUT HIS POLITICAL CAREER. IN THE THIRTIES IT WAS MELBOURNE, THEN PEEL, UNTIL HIS DEATH IN 1850, AND FINALLY PALMERSTON. RUSSELL'S SIZE MADE HIM A READY TARGET FOR CARTOONISTS AND POLITICAL OPPONENTS.

defied his authority, and Russell was left intriguing with the Court to remove him from office. It was a ministry that lacked any constructive policy or purpose, a Cabinet, as Disraeli put it in 1848, 'who, in preparing their measures, have no conviction that those measures will be carried.'

Important measures were carried, but often in spite of, rather than because of, Russell's leadership. The Ten Hours Act of 1847 was the work of John Fielden the Tory factory owner from Todmorden, the 1848 Public

Repeal of the Navigation Laws removed the last remaining regulations that restricted cargo carrying to British ships.

In 1846 the government proposed the extension of the education grant to support the training of teachers. The Nonconformists opposed this, fearing that the bulk of the money would go to the National Schools supported by the Church of England.

Don Pacifico was a Portuguese Jew whose house had been looted and destroyed during anti-Semitic riots in Athens. Claiming birth in Gibraltar, he requested British government assistance in pursuing his demand for compensation. The case was unsavoury and his demands excessive, but Palmerston backed him by sending a naval force to blockade Piraeus. This flagrant defiance of Russia and France, the other powers which, with Britain, guaranteed Greek independence, caused the French to break off diplomatic relations. Conservative censure motions in both Lords and Commons became attacks on Palmerston's record since 1846.

Health Act was driven through the Commons by the fear of cholera, and the repeal of the Navigation Laws in 1849 was a logical extension of the free trade policies initiated by Peel. During 1848 about thirty government measures had to be abandoned. Russell got little credit for the successes, while the failures undermined his authority.

The General Election of 1847 had appeared to give ministers a Commons majority. Both Protectionists and Peelites lost ground, but the Whigs made few gains. Support for the increased Maynooth Grant in 1845 and association with the government's education proposals cost ministerial candidates the votes of Anglican evangelicals and Nonconfirmists. The Radicals made substantial gains, but Ministers could not rely on their unquestioning allegiance. Cobden remained their leading figure but no issue had been found that could replace repeal of the Corn Laws. They were a divided and dissatisfied group, some seeking parliamentary reform, some administrative reform, others focusing on financial matters or education. In 1848, however, some 50 to 60 Radical MPs ostentatiously formed themselves into a separate party with a programme of parliamentary reform and financial retrenchment – this left reliable government supporters in a minority and Russell dependent on Peel and his followers for political survival. Radical unity did not last, but it was embarrassing for the Whigs.

Lacking credibility and a secure majority in the Commons, the government possessed one asset – Lord Palmerston, the Foreign Secretary. His lecturing of foreign governments on liberalism, his sympathy for Hungarian nationalists, and his bold upholding of the rights of the British citizen abroad had endeared him to the public. His own astute handling of the press had also helped. He turned the Don Pacifico debate into a triumphant defence of his overall policy, whilst his justification of his vigorous support for Don Pacifico's claims gained him massive popularity. A government defeat in the Lords (169 votes to 132) was turned into victory by 46 votes in the Commons, but it was Palmerston's personal triumph, not a vindication of the Cabinet in which he sat.

Russell desperately sought an issue which would recapture some popularity. In the autumn of 1850 and the spring of 1851 he tried to capitalise on Protestant feelings by openly denouncing Papal plans to create English Catholic dioceses, condemning in his Durham Letter those Tractarian practices within the Church of England which seemed to be encouraging a drift to Rome. His Ecclesiastical Titles Act (1851) was unworkable and it cost Russell the support of the Peelite leadership in the Commons and of the Irish Catholic MPs. An attempted resignation in February 1851, following defeat on a reform motion, failed when Lord Stanley refused to form a Conservative administration. The Whigs limped on.

Both the Court and Russell seized on a premature note of congratulation which Palmerston sent to Louis Napoleon in December 1851 as an excuse for his dismissal. The dismissal of Palmerston was disastrous for the ministry. Two months later it was Palmerston who engineered the government's final defeat in the Commons over the Militia Bill. This time Stanley, now Lord Derby, agreed to form a Cabinet, and the Conservatives were once more in government even though they were a minority.

The Conservatives – a party in disarray

The rift caused by Corn Law repeal was not expected to be permanent. There could be no reconciliation between the Protectionists and Peel, but eventual reunion with the other Peelites was anticipated.

Lord Stanley was reluctantly persuaded to accept the leadership of the Protectionists. The split had left him as the only figure capable of leading the truncated Conservative Party, with experience and talent unequalled. In the House of Commons, Lord George Bentinck, the new leader, lacked tact, embarrassed by his clumsiness in debate and upset the Protestant prejudices of the backbenchers by his support for legislation to enable Jews to sit in the House of Commons. He gladly resigned from a position he had never sought.

Disraeli was the only man of ability on the Conservative side in the Commons, but his background and appearance made him an unlikely leader of the country gentlemen. Since he was held responsible for the vilification of their leader by the Peelites, his presence on the front bench made eventual reunion difficult. Nevertheless, during 1849 Disraeli emerged as Party leader in the Commons, the political beneficiary of the Corn Law crisis, although his leadership was tolerated more than welcomed. As the Duke of Newcastle observed to Stanley, 'we must of necessity choose the cleverest man that we possess'.

Disraeli, who never had been a Protectionist, realised that the Party would have to abandon that policy if it was to win an electoral majority. He began to press this change on Stanley in 1849 but a series of bad harvests, low prices and Stanley's own scruples about political consistency made progress slow, and protectionism was not abandoned until 1852.

Stanley succeeded to the Earldom of Derby in 1851. He was to be Conservative Party leader for 22 years and Prime Minister three times. His interests were wide-ranging, and often horse racing and estate management took priority over politics. His political caution frustrated Disraeli's ambitions on more than one occasion. It was Derby, however, who first raised the parliamentary reform issue in the autumn of 1866, and he fully backed Disraeli when he had to accept Radical amendments to the Conservative Reform Bill in the Commons.

Tractarians – High Church Anglicans whose observance was similar to Roman Catholicism. Leading members of the group later converted to the Catholic Church (see chapter 10).

Louis Napoleon, President of the French Second Republic, seized power in a *coup d'état* as his presidential term was coming to an end.

EDWARD STANLEY,
14TH EARL OF DERBY

Examining the evidence

The Peelite dilemma

Before the 1847 election there were about 120 MPs who could be labelled as Peelites. This number fell as seats were lost or backbench free traders drifted back to their Conservative roots. All but three members of Peel's government followed him in 1846. Graham, Aberdeen and Goulburn represented the older generation; Gladstone, Lord Lincoln, Lord Dalhousie, Sidney Herbert and Edward Cardwell were prominent amongst the younger men. It was the proven ability of these politicians which persuaded Russell to try to attract Graham into alliance with the government, and Derby to hope for the return of Gladstone to Conservative ranks to provide the weight his Party lacked in the Commons.

Source A

I intend to keep aloof from party combinations. So far as a man can be justified in forming such a resolution, I am determined not again to resume office.

I will take care to not again to burn my fingers by organising a party. There is too much truth in the saying, 'The head of a party must be directed by the tail'.

Sir Robert Peel to Lord Hardinge, 24 September 1846.

Source B

Peel explains his reasons for voting against Disraeli's motion for a Select Committee on Distress, 1849.

I wish it to be distinctly understood, that all I mean to imply by the vote I shall give tonight is this – that I cordially approve of the general principles of commercial policy by which Her Majesty's Government have been guided, and that I will not consent to a motion, the main object of which avowedly is, to censure them for their adherence to those principles, and to substitute in the place of that policy some other economic system.

Source C

Gladstone suggests why Peel voted with the Whig government on every critical division, 1846–50.

Certainly this was not due to any desire ... for, or contemplation of, coalition with the liberal party. It sprang entirely from a belief on his part that the chiefs of the protectionists would on their accession to power endeavour to establish a policy in accordance with the designation of their party, and would in so doing probably convulse the country ... We were flatly at issue with him on this opinion. We even considered that as long as the protectionists had no responsibilities but those of opposition ... there would be protectionists in plenty to fill the left hand benches.

Source D

The Peelites were not only small in numbers, but disunited among themselves. Peel and Graham stood on several occasions nearly alone – Gladstone, Lincoln and the minor Peelites going off in other directions. Peel appears to me to have abandoned definitively all idea of being a party leader or holding office.

Sir G. Cornewall Lewis to Sir Edmund Head, 4 September 1848.

TALKING POINT

Why, according to *The Times*, were the Peelites not a party?

Source E

Comment from *The Times* during the 1852 General Election campaign.

Sir ROBERT PEEL broke from party: he scattered his party to the four winds ... and substituted a policy in its place. His followers ceased to be partisans and at this moment it is only a convenient fiction to describe any number of men as 'Peelites', for, besides their original diversity of character, the men so described seemed to have received an additional impulse of separation and independence from the example of their late chief. Their present difficulty is that they are not a party, they have not its ties; they have not its facilities; they have not its obligations. They have not acted together, and no one can argue from the course taken by one what the other will do, or what opinions may be presumed from a mere historical connection with Sir ROBERT PEEL.

The Times, 10 July 1852.

TALKING POINT

Discuss the view that Peel's career ended in anti-climax and political inconsistency.

1 Referring to source B, explain and comment on Peel's reasons for opposing Disraeli and voting with the government.
2 Referring to sources A, B, C and D, and your wider knowledge, discuss the difficulties and frustrations revealed here in the relationship between the leading Peelites and Peel.
3 'They were trained for executive office and, deprived of it, they lacked purpose.' (E. Evans, *The Forging of the Modern State 1783–1870*, 1983) 'Their present difficulty is that they are not a party.' (source E) Referring to all the sources, and to your wider knowledge, consider the aptness of these views.
4 Generally the leading figures amongst the Peelites were free traders, were opposed to religious intolerance and bigotry, disliked Palmerston's chauvinistic foreign policy and took a pragmatic view of the need to reform and modernise the institutions of the state. Given these views, and the political experience of 1846, which political party would they be likely to merge with, why was any merger 'put on ice' until after 1850, and why could Derby still have realistic hopes of a reunion of the Conservative forces as late as 1859? You will need to do some wider research to complete this task.

The realignment of the parties

The Conservative ministry Derby formed in February 1852 was always going to be weak. The failure of attempts to persuade Palmerston to join and take the Leadership of the Commons from Disraeli left Derby with an unconvincing and unknown Cabinet. Disraeli was leader of the House and, reluctantly and full of misgivings, Chancellor of the Exchequer. His personal doubts were widely shared.

Although Russell wanted to eject the minority Conservative government as soon as possible, Lord Aberdeen, for the Peelites, persuaded him to allow vital legislation through before forcing the test of a General Election.

The ambiguous views of Derby and Disraeli on the future of protectionism destroyed any chance of a reconciliation between the Conservative factions which would end the political instability. Both implied different policies in their parliamentary statements, whilst Cabinet colleagues were critical of Disraeli's address to his Buckinghamshire electors which hinted at compensation for agriculture but was discreetly silent on protection. This uncertainty, and the revival of the old Protestant 'Church in danger' cry, damaged the government with potential Peelite defectors.

IDENTIFY 'LITTLE BEN' AND 'HIS COBDEN'. THE AMBIVALENT STANCE OF THE CONSERVATIVE LEADERSHIP ON THE FREE TRADE ISSUE MADE REUNION WITH THE PEELITES IMPOSSIBLE, BUT THE CARTOONIST IS A LITTLE UNFAIR IN IMPLYING THAT DISRAELI WAS THE MORE RELUCTANT OF THE TWO PARTY LEADERS (DERBY IS ALREADY SWIMMING IN THE 'FREE TRADE SEA').

TALKING POINT

Why was the protectionist policy so difficult for the Conservatives to abandon despite its political unpopularity?

now go in like a man – you'll find it so Bracing –

Oh! after the First Plunge It's so nice !

FREE TRADE

A DIP IN THE FREE TRADE SEA.

"THERE, TAKE OFF HIS COAT LIKE A GOOD LITTLE BEN, AND COME TO HIS COBDEN."

TALKING POINT

'At once the necessity of Lord Derby and his curse.' Discuss Gladstone's comment on Disraeli's position in the Conservative Party at this time.

Although the Conservatives were the only party to gain seats at the General Election, they remained in a minority with the Peelites holding the balance. Existing contacts between Russell and Graham were widened to include Aberdeen and the younger Peelites. Most were prepared to consider an accommodation with the Whigs, except Gladstone, still a Conservative at heart, who urged caution. Increasingly, however, he regarded Disraeli, the vilifier of Peel, as the real obstacle to Conservative reunion.

After the election, the Conservatives swiftly abandoned protectionism. Disraeli's budget, postponed until after the General Election, was now crucial to the government's survival. He planned to compensate the agricultural interest for losses inflicted by free trade, and to extend the liability to payment of income tax. These proposals provoked Peelite hostility, because Peel's fiscal principles were being undermined, and Irish opposition, the proposed extension of income tax to Ireland alienating a group whose support ministers desperately needed. The budget was, as Macaulay put it, 'nothing but taking money out of the pockets of people in towns and putting it in the pockets of the growers of malt.'

A reduction in the malt duty was one of the main concessions to agriculturists.

The budget was systematically demolished by Gladstone, the closing stages of the debate climaxing as a thunderstorm rattled round the Houses of Parliament. Disraeli's own speech did not impress. When the House finally divided, the government was defeated 305–286. Gladstone's speech and the vote had ended any remaining prospect of Conservative reunion. A few days later Gladstone was mobbed by drunken Tory MPs at the Carlton Club and although Derby still hoped to recapture him for the Conservatives it is unlikely that the backbenchers would have allowed themselves to be led by the man who had destroyed their government in December 1852.

The logical outcome, to which the centre politicians and the Court had been working, was a coalition of Whigs and Peelites. Disraeli could assert that 'England does not love Coalitions' but the new government with Aberdeen as Premier, Gladstone as Chancellor of the Exchequer, Russell at the Foreign Office, and Palmerston, despite royal misgivings, at the Home Office, contained almost all the men of ability and ambition in the Commons apart from Disraeli. Although there were some tensions between the members of the Cabinet, this was a relatively

A STRUGGLE BETWEEN DUTY AND INCLINATION.

GALLANT LITTLE JOHN TAKING LEAVE OF HIS PET TO SERVE HIS COUNTRY.

Gladstone extended Peel's free trade policies with further duty changes and the promise of a staged reduction of income tax towards abolition within seven years.

DESPITE THE DOUBTS OF SOME OF HIS COLLEAGUES, RUSSELL WAS DETERMINED TO PRESS ON WITH PARLIAMENTARY REFORM. HIS EAGERNESS FORCED PALMERSTON INTO A BRIEF TACTICAL RESIGNATION AT THE END OF 1853. THE OUTBREAK OF THE CRIMEAN WAR MEANT THE ABANDONMENT OF THE BILL.

successful and harmonious administration until it ran into the crisis that became the debacle of the Crimean War. The highlight was undoubtedly Gladstone's first great budget in 1853, but the Trevelyan Northcote Commission, which reported in 1854, laid the foundations for civil service reform, and Gladstone's Universities Bill of 1854 was the first of the institutional reforms that he was to be associated with.

The coalition was the beginning of the realignment of parties. No Peelite who served in it ever sat again in a Conservative Cabinet and they discovered that they had more in common with the Whigs and the Radicals than perhaps they had believed. It was an essential stage on the liberal-conservative journey towards Gladstone's Liberal Party.

LORD ABERDEEN WAS THE SENIOR PEELITE. HIS DIPLOMATIC EXPERIENCE HAD COMMENCED WITH CASTLEREAGH AT THE CONGRESS OF VIENNA. HE HAD BEEN FOREIGN SECRETARY UNDER BOTH WELLINGTON AND PEEL (1828–30, 1841–46). HE LACKED THE ALL-ROUND ABILITIES OF PEEL, AND THE PARLIAMENTARY SKILL OF RUSSELL AND DERBY, WAS A POOR SPEAKER AND, ALTHOUGH SUFFICIENTLY CONCILIATORY TO PRESIDE OVER A PEACETIME COALITION, DID NOT POSSESS THE DECISIVENESS NEEDED IN WARTIME OR THE PUBLIC POPULARITY TO PROVIDE LEADERSHIP IN A CRISIS.

11.1 The emergence of Lord Palmerston – the unexpected Prime Minister

HENRY JOHN TEMPLE, 3RD VISCOUNT PALMERSTON – BORN 1784, EDUCATED AT HARROW AND EDINBURGH AND CAMBRIDGE UNIVERSITIES. AT EDINBURGH HE BECAME FAMILIAR WITH THE NEW ECONOMIC THEORIES OF FREE TRADE. MP FROM 1807 FOR THE POCKET BOROUGH OF NEWPORT ON THE ISLE OF WIGHT. AS AN IRISH PEER, PALMERSTON SPENT HIS POLITICAL CAREER IN THE HOUSE OF COMMONS.

Political allegiance

The Tory: Secretary at War 1809–28. A junior administrative post in which he displayed industriousness and efficiency, but little flair.

The Canningite: entered Canning's Cabinet, 1827. Resigned from Wellington's in 1828.

The Whig: Foreign Secretary 1830–34, 1835–41 (protected by Melbourne, brother of Lady Cowper, his long-standing mistress and eventual wife), 1846–51 (in spite of the hostility of Russell, the Whig elite and the court), Home Secretary 1852–55 (Aberdeen coalition), Prime Minister 1855–58, 1859–65 (coalition renewed – the first *Liberal* government). Throughout his long tenure as Foreign Secretary, Palmerston was never accepted by the great Whig families, and in 1852 Derby seriously considered that Palmerston could lead the Conservatives to victory.

A political late developer

Lady Malmesbury on one of Palmerston's early parliamentary performances, March 1810:
Harry spoke extremely well on the Army Estimates. On such subjects where clearness & perspicacity are the requisite & time is given for preparation, he will always succeed, but where opinions are to be given & effect to be produced by spontaneous eloquence I doubt it. He is reserved & so very cautious, so singularly so for a young man, so afraid of Committing himself even in common life and conversation with his most intimate friends, that it will throw a coldness & want of effect on such speeches of his.

Talking Point

'It has been said that he was constant only in the retention of office ... that his one principle was that of the Vicar of Bray.' (*The Times*, obituary of Palmerston, 18 October 1865.)
Explain this comment, and why it could be made.

THERE'S ALWAYS SOMETHING.

"I'M VERY SORRY, PALMERSTON, THAT YOU CANNOT AGREE WITH YOUR FELLOW SERVANTS; BUT AS I DON'T FEEL INCLINED TO PART WITH JOHN, YOU MUST GO, OF COURSE."

The Court view

Victoria and Albert were glad to find an excuse to dismiss Palmerston in 1851 and did their best to find somebody else to be Prime Minister in 1855. They disliked his anti-Austrian foreign policy and the cavalier way in which he failed to inform them of events or send them copies of dispatches.

TALKING POINT

'the most English Minister that ever presided over the foreign affairs of this country' (*Morning Advertiser*, December 1851).

What do you think this means, and how would it contribute to Palmerston's popularity?

Personal Popularity

● Palmerston was one of the first politicians to 'manage' the press. He regularly leaked information to the Morning Post and wrote articles for it. Other newspapers were also fed stories and, from 1855, The Times, previously hostile, came round to supporting the government.

● A well-cultivated flippancy coupled with his known love of racing, rumours that he attended illegal prize fights, and the behaviour which gained him the nickname of 'Lord Cupid', gave him a wider popularity. His geniality in old age erased the memory of 'Lord Pumice stone' whose meticulous standards had so upset the Foreign Office clerks in the 1830s.

● His visits to Manchester, Leeds and Bradford in the 1860s were personal triumphs.

NOW FOR IT !

A Set-to between "Pam, the Downing Street Pet," and "The Russian Spider."

The Public perception, 1855

PALMERSTON, PRIZE FIGHTER AND PRIME MINISTER, WITH MR PUNCH AS HIS SECOND, PREPARES TO TAKE ON TSAR ALEXANDER II.

The Palmerston years

The Crimean War revealed the growing power of the press. Uncensored reports from the Crimea in *The Times* created a sensation. J.T. Delane, the editor, abandoned his support for Aberdeen, and his paper's revelations contributed to a growing tide of indignation and disillusion with the government.

The coalition had seemed powerless to halt the stumble into war, and proved incompetent to manage it. Gladstone's staged abolition of income tax was an instant casualty – it had to be doubled in his 1854 Budget. More seriously, reports of conditions endured by British troops in the Crimea and the failure of the British and French to get a decisive result focused public criticism on the War Office and its head, the Duke of Newcastle. In January 1855 the radical MP J.A. Roebuck successfully moved for a Committee of Inquiry to be set up to look into the conduct of the war. Aberdeen resigned.

Although there were failings at the War Office, much of the criticism was unfair. The price was being paid for years of neglect of the armed forces by economising governments backed by the tax-paying public.

To Disraeli's dismay, Derby refused the Queen's offer of the premiership after ascertaining that Palmerston would not join without the Peelites, and that Gladstone's conditions were unacceptable. Derby was probably right. There is no evidence that an inexperienced minority Conservative administration would have managed the war better than Palmerston.

Both Victoria and Albert wanted to keep Palmerston out of the premiership, but there was no alternative. Russell's early resignation from the coalition in 1854 to escape the collective disgrace made him unacceptable to former colleagues. No government could survive without Palmerston, and, as Home Secretary, he had escaped incrimination in the Crimean disaster, although he had pressed for the extension of the war into the Crimea in 1854. Public opinion also believed, perhaps correctly, that if he had been Foreign Secretary war might have been avoided. The Court had to accept the popular view.

Aberdeen persuaded Gladstone and the remaining Peelites to stay in office despite their antipathy towards Palmerston, but they resigned after three weeks when he agreed to grant Roebuck his Committee of Inquiry.

Despite the credit of winning the war, Palmerston's parliamentary position was insecure. Russell remained hostile, the Peelites were unreliable, the Radicals were opposed to his conservatism and international belligerence, and the Conservatives, in opposition, were the largest party in the Commons. On 3 March 1857 these elements coalesced to defeat Palmerston on Cobden's motion censuring the government's high-handed Chinese policy. The subsequent General Election was a triumph for the Prime Minister. His supporters were strengthened in the Commons, and his great critics, Bright and Cobden, lost their seats. Instability was not removed, however. In February 1858, responding to Napoleon III's concern that an assassination attempt on him had been planned from England, Palmerston introduced legislation to control the activities of political exiles. For once Palmerston misjudged the temper of the House. An amendment moved by the Radical MP Milner-Gibson, and seconded by Bright, won Disraeli's support, and the government was defeated by 19 votes.

Bright was returned for Birmingham at a by-election later in 1857. Cobden was out of the House until the 1859 General Election.

Another minority Conservative administration was succeeded by a General Election (1859) in which the Party again increased its seats but still failed to achieve a Commons majority. On 6 June 1859 274 opposition MPs met in Willis's Rooms. Palmerston helped Russell onto the platform. Bright offered the support of the Radicals. Sidney Herbert represented the Peelites who, despite reduced numbers, still had talent to offer. Their purpose was simple – to create a stable majority to keep the Conservatives out of office and a progressive government in. Only later did the meeting gain its significance as marking the formation of the Liberal Party.

Gladstone was the only notable absentee from that meeting. He still preferred Derby to Palmerston and he had been tempted by offers of office in both 1858 and 1859 as Derby tried to bolster his ministry. When the new Parliament met, the combined opposition moved a 'no confidence' motion against the Conservative government, Gladstone voted against it. Other political and personal pressures, however, were pushing him unwillingly towards Palmerston, and when the Queen reluctantly accepted her second Palmerston administration Gladstone was there as Chancellor of the Exchequer. With Russell as Foreign Secretary, the surviving Peelites back in harness, a Cabinet place for the Radical Milner-Gibson, and the Whigs well represented, the realignment of parties foreshadowed in 1852 had finally come about. Cobden, offered the Presidency of the Board of Trade, had excluded himself but was kept busy negotiating his free trade treaty with France. Bright was the only leading figure not invited to serve, but his attacks on the aristocracy were too recent to be forgotten.

See page 277 for a discussion of Gladstone's motives in 1859.

Marking time – Palmerston's second ministry, 1859–65

We now live in anti-reforming times. All improvements have to be urged in apologetic, almost in supplicatory tones. I sometimes reflect how much less liberal, as to domestic policy, in any true sense of the word, is this Government than Sir Robert Peel's; and how much the tone of Ultra-Toryism prevails among a large portion of the Liberal party.

W. E. Gladstone to Sir James Graham, 1860.

Oh, there is really nothing to be done. We cannot go on adding to the Statue Book *ad infinitum*. Perhaps we may have a little law reform, or bankruptcy reform; but we cannot go on legislating for ever.

Lord Palmerston in conversation with G. J. Goschen on the Queen's speech of 1864.

Gladstone as Chancellor

Gladstone was the driving force in domestic policy. His budgets of 1860 and 1861 delivered major fiscal reform to complete the work begun by Peel twenty years before, and Cobden's free trade treaty with France (1860) was, Gladstone believed, the first step in extending the free trade message into the wider world.

TALKING POINT

What impression do these comments give of Palmerston's second ministry? Comment on Gladstone's perception with reference to Palmerston's opinion and the actual domestic policies followed.

By political precedent the House of Lords left money bills (the Budget) to the House of Commons.

Gladstone's earnestness provoked conflict with the Prime Minister, but he was the only minister who could stand up to Palmerston and get his own way. He also proved his ability to get his own way in Parliament. When the House of Lords rejected Gladstone's proposed abolition of duties on paper, he threatened to resign, and raised the spectre of a constitutional crisis. He then incorporated the measure into the 1861 Budget where it was safe from amendment by the Lords.

Palmerston the practical reformer

On the one side, he was serious, intellectual, even theoretical: militantly progressive and humane; scientific and modern to an extent rarely realised. He 'got up all the sanitary questions and *believes* in them' ...

J. Vincent, *The Formation of the Liberal Party 1857–1868,* 1966.

At the Home Office (1852–55), Palmerston extended the scope of the factory legislation and was well informed on public health matters. His two governments continued the uncontroversial public health reforms; his first government prepared the Newcastle Commission to enquire into elementary education, his second introduced the Revised Code of 1862 ('Payment by Results') in response to its findings and recommendations. The Poor Law was reformed in 1865. In 1860, despite his personal distaste for parliamentary reform, he allowed Russell to introduce a Reform Bill since party unity required it.

Palmerston's conservative reputation

It has been suggested by the historian E.D. Steele that Palmerston was seeking to educate the country in class cohesion to ensure a peaceful transition to an enlarged electorate which would not lead to the immediate destruction of aristocratic government. This is a large claim but it is probably true to say that Palmerston's aim was to hold society together and to make humane and useful improvements which did not threaten the foundations of social and political stability. He was never totally negative but,

It can only be suggested that Palmerston saw clearly, as we cannot, the resistances operating in the Parliamentary system he knew, and felt them to be too much for him.

J. Vincent, *The Formation of the Liberal Party 1857–1868*, 1966.

TALKING POINT

Was Palmerston the right Prime Minister for a period of conservatism and domestic calm presiding over a necessary period of stability and consolidation, or was he an old man, obsessed by fears of franchise extension and his laissez faire beliefs, fighting a rearguard action to delay much needed reforms?

FOCUS

11.2 Explaining Palmerston's dominance

Political opponents made the mistake of under-estimating him.

Palmerston Prime Minister! What a hoax! The aged charlatan has at length attained the great object of his long and unscrupulous ambition.

John Bright in 1855.

[Palmerston] seems now the inevitable man, and tho' he is really an impostor, utterly exhausted, and at best only ginger beer and not champagne, and now an old painted Pantaloon, very deaf, very blind, and with false teeth, which would fall out of his mouth when speaking, if he did not hesitate and halt so in his talk – he is a name which the country resolves to associate with energy, wisdom, and eloquence, and will until he has tried and failed ...

Benjamin Disraeli to Lady Londonderry, 2 February 1855.

How wrong they were:

P's popularity is wonderful – strange to say, the whole turns on his name. There seems to be no measure, no principle, no cry, to influence men's minds and determine elections; it is simply, 'Were you, or were you not? are you, or are you not, for Palmerston?'

Lord Shaftesbury, Palmerston's son-in-law, writing in his diary during the 1857 General Election.

In both 1857 and 1865 Palmerston, as Prime Minister, increased his parliamentary majority. In 1859 he won as leader of the opposition.

Consider the following points which may explain the dominance of Lord Palmerston at this time:

● Palmerston got the credit for winning the Crimean War.

● He was a supremely professional politician with unequalled administrative experience.

Friend and enemy alike bore witness to his mastery over Parliament in his second ministry, and there lay his real achievement.

J. Vincent, *The Formation of the Liberal Party 1857–1868*, 1966.

● The meeting in Willis's Rooms in 1859 gave his government the stable majority in the Commons that had been lacking since 1846.

● There was no controversial legislation in the period 1859–65. Palmerston's known opposition to parliamentary Reform was tolerated. After 1859 Gladstonian finance satisfied the Radicals, whilst Palmerston's resistance to his Chancellor's plans kept the Whigs happy.

● 'Radicalism is out of fashion' (Palmerston to Brand, the Chief Whip, in 1862). A prime minister with these opinions paralysed the Conservative Party – there was nothing for them to oppose.

● He had accepted the 1832 Reform Act but further Parliamentary reform was anathema to him.

● 'Can it be expected that men who murder their children to get £9 to spend on drink will not sell their vote for whatever they can get for it?' (to Aberdeen, 1854). He

> *£9 to spend on drink* – a reference to life insurance policies

feared that working class voters would be controlled by the Trade Unions.

● Even the Church was safe in the hands of a premier who looked to the Conservative churchman Lord Shaftesbury, his son-in-law, for advice on Church appointments.

● A patriotic foreign policy was used to 'distract the mind of the people from internal improvement.' (Disraeli in 1862)

● Derby's tactics were to wait for the government coalition to split up, or for the elderly Palmerston to die.

TALKING POINT

To what extent was Palmerston's dominance due to his own personal strengths, and to what extent was it due to the weaknesses, or hesitations, of his opponents?

REVIEW

Whatever happened to the Conservative Party?

Danish Duchies crisis – see pages 227–8.

In 1864 294 Conservatives voted against the Palmerston ministry at the end of the censure debate on the government's handling of the Danish Duchies crisis. The Party was the largest organised political grouping in the House of Commons throughout the mid-Victorian period but only formed two short-lived minority governments. The purpose of this Review is to consider the factors that made the Conservatives so ineffective.

Problems facing the Conservative Party, 1845–64

● The inability to offer a credible alternative government – after the 1845 split the Protectionists were mocked as 'the Conservative Party with most of the brains knocked out.'
● The political disadvantages of a protectionist policy which was hard to abandon.
● The hostility felt towards Disraeli by the Peelites.
● The antipathy between Gladstone and Disraeli.
● Derby's pessimism.
● The pre-eminence of Palmerston.
● The Conservatives had no distinctive policies once they had abandoned protection.
● Despite their solid base in the English counties and the smaller rural boroughs, the Conservatives had to win seats in the larger English boroughs and the hostile districts dominated by 'the field of coal' if they were to obtain a parliamentary majority, but their reputation as the party of the landed interest made that very difficult.
● Lack of organisation, and of an alternative programme from which to challenge the in-built Whig/ Peelite/Liberal majority.

Lord Derby's view

The following sources reveal the feelings of the Conservative leader in this period:

Source A

I have known as long ago as 1845 that I was playing a losing game: I said so then: I thought I was left high and dry forever: the tide has risen once, high enough to float me again, which was more than I expected: it will never do so again: the game is lost, but I think it ought to be played and I will play it out to the last.

Lord Derby to Lord Stanley (his son), 28 December 1852.

Source B

In short he [Palmerston] has been a Conservative Minister working with Radical tools and keeping up a show of Liberalism in his foreign policy which nine in ten of the House of Commons care nothing about. That a Conservative party should have held together at all in such circumstances is rather to be wondered at, than that there should be apathy and indifference when there is nothing to be fought for by the bulk of the party.

Lord Derby to Lord Malmesbury, 15 December 1856.

Source C

Our game must be purely defensive, and we must be ready to support the moderate portion of the Cabinet, and watch for every opportunity of widening the breach between them and the Rads.

Lord Derby to Benjamin Disraeli after the 1865 Election.

Source D

A purely Conservative Government is all but an impossibility until upon Palmerston's death ... Gladstone tries his hand with a Radical Government and alarms the middle classes.

Lord Derby to Benjamin Disraeli, 4 August 1865.

Essay

Using the material in this Review and elsewhere in the chapter, and your wider knowledge, consider the reasons given above for the frustrating of the Conservative Party in this period, and use them as the basis for a response to this question:

To what extent was Conservative political weakness in the period 1846–65 a consequence of the pre-eminence of Lord Palmerston?

12 Gladstone, Disraeli and the Second Reform Act

PREVIEW

Parliamentary reform – a dead issue?

Source A

PUNCH, 12 MARCH 1859

IN THE WINTER OF 1858–59 BRIGHT MADE A SERIES OF MAJOR SPEECHES IN AN ATTEMPT TO CREATE FRESH PUBLIC PRESSURE FOR PARLIAMENTARY REFORM. DISRAELI HAD PRESENTED A CONSERVATIVE REFORM BILL TO THE COMMONS IN FEBRUARY 1859; RUSSELL HAD BEEN TRYING TO BRING IN A NEW REFORM BILL SINCE 1850.

Parliamentary reform – the background

What impression does this source convey of the attitude of politicians and the public to parliamentary reform at this time?

Russell's Reform Bills (1852, 1854) had both been withdrawn, as they went too far for the Whigs, but not far enough for the Radicals. At the same time, as Bright was to discover, public apathy on the issue of reform was almost universal. Disraeli's Reform Bill (1859) was a political tactic designed to gain party advantage by increasing the number of potential Conservative voters in the counties, and by a redistribution of seats. It was defeated by a combination of dissatisfied Radicals, anxious Whigs and Russell, who wanted the credit if any measure was to be passed. The Radicals were tempted into Palmerston's Liberal coalition at the Willis's Room meeting by the promise of an early Reform Bill. Palmerston was unhappy about this, but allowed Russell his Bill in 1860. Despite the support of Bright, and to Palmerston's great relief, it was greeted by 'profound indifference in the House and in the country' (*The Greville Memoirs*, volume 7).

TALKING POINT

Referring back to the agitations of the first half of the century, how far would you agree that prosperity made political agitation unlikely.

Reform was removed from the political agenda for the remaining years of Palmerston's life. All parties, however, recognised that when the Prime Minister finally left the scene the issue would have to be settled. Meanwhile other forces were at work in society which made the prospect of a working class electorate less alarming, and in May 1864 Gladstone made his much misunderstood and misinterpreted statement in support of an extended franchise, which gave the question a totally new emphasis.

12.1 Disraeli: the opportunistic 'outsider'; Gladstone: the troubled 'insider'

DISRAELI WAS THE 'OUTSIDER' AMONGST NINETEENTH CENTURY CONSERVATIVE LEADERS. PEEL'S FATHER HAD BEEN A COTTON MANUFACTURER BUT THE FAMILY HAD JOINED THE LANDED GENTRY AND PEEL HAD BEEN EDUCATED AT HARROW AND OXFORD. DERBY WAS AN EARL, AND DISRAELI'S SUCCESSOR, LORD SALISBURY, WAS A MARQUIS. DISRAELI'S FLAMBOYANT APPEARANCE, JEWISH ANCESTRY AND NOVEL-WRITING WERE ALL HANDICAPS TO A SUCCESSFUL POLITICAL CAREER.

REVIEWING GLADSTONE'S BOOK *THE STATE IN ITS RELATION TO THE CHURCH* (1838), MACAULAY MARKED HIM AS 'THE RISING HOPE OF THOSE STERN AND UNBENDING TORIES'. HE HAD ALL THE ADVANTAGES DISRAELI LACKED – WEALTH, EDUCATION AT ETON AND OXFORD, MARRIAGE INTO THE ARISTOCRACY, AND ALL THE RIGHT CONTACTS. YET HIS CAREER WAS AS UNPREDICTABLE AS DISRAELI'S AS HE MOVED ACROSS PARTY BOUNDARIES TO EMERGE AS A LIBERAL PRIME MINISTER IN 1868.

Both men became Premier for the first time in 1868. Compare and contrast their reactions.

Disraeli to a friend – 'Yes, I have climbed to the top of the greasy pole.'

Gladstone, writing in his diary on his birthday, 29 December 1868 – 'This birthday opens my 60th year. I descend the hill of life. It would be a truer figure to say I ascend a steepening path with a burden ever gathering weight. The Almighty seems to sustain and spare me for some purpose of his own deeply unworthy as I know myself to be. Glory be to his name.'

TALKING POINT

What differences do these short comments reveal in the character and outlook of the two men?

Working from the Index, construct parallel career lines for the two men up to 1865. Compare and contrast their achievements.

This cartoon appeared in *Punch* on 4 April 1845. Place it in its context, and explain why and how Disraeli had overthrown the 'giant' a year later

YOUNG GULLIVER AND THE BRODNIGNAG MINISTER

DISRAELI PURCHASED THE HUGHENDEN ESTATE IN 1848 WITH THE ASSISTANCE OF LORD GEORGE BENTINCK AND THE PORTLAND FAMILY. IT GAVE HIM THE COUNTRY SEAT THE LEADER OF THE CONSERVATIVES IN THE COMMONS NEEDED BUT HE DID NOT FOLLOW THE 'RURAL PURSUITS' OF SHOOTING, FARMING, GARDENING, AND 'IMPROVING' HIS ESTATE, PREFERRING HIS 'GOOD LIBRARY' AND 'IN FINE WEATHER ... WALKING ABOUT THE NEIGHBOURHOOD.'

HAWARDEN CASTLE, THE NORTH WALES HOME OF HIS WIFE'S FAMILY, BECAME GLADSTONE'S ESCAPE FROM LONDON AND POLITICS. IT REMAINED A FAMILY HOME, OFF THE CIRCUIT OF POLITICAL HOUSE PARTIES. IN 1860 HE WAS ABLE TO MOVE HIS BOOKS INTO THE NEWLY BUILT LIBRARY AND WORKING ROOM.

The Debt to Sir Robert Peel

In the Board of Trade Gladstone discovered ... an absorbing fascination with the details of administration ...

The implications of this realization of the beauty, joy, and technical satisfaction of department work were profound for Gladstone's general approach to politics. For it launched him on that life-long passionate effort of 'working the institutions of the country', and of explaining and defending the details of administration in the Commons ... By 1845 time spent on 'business' was counted with study and devotion as time spent in a Godly way ... The diary is a continual witness to the influence of Peel ... This on a speech in 1848, 'Peel was gratified and that was enough for me.'

H.C.G. Matthew, *Gladstone 1809–1874*, 1986.

Gladstone remarked to the editor of the *Quarterly Review* in 1856:

There is a policy going a-begging; the general policy that Sir Robert Peel in 1841 took office to support – the policy of peace abroad, of economy, of financial equilibrium, of steady resistance to abuses, and promotion of practical improvements at home, with a disinclination to questions of reform gratuitously raised.

TALKING POINT

Both men owed something to Peel, and both learnt from his success. Starting from the sources in this section consider the contribution made by Peel, directly and inadvertently, to the political careers of Gladstone and Disraeli.

Examining the Evidence

Gladstone and Disraeli: principles and motives

Source A

The Tamworth Manifesto of 1834 was an attempt to construct a party without principles: its basis therefore was necessarily latitudinarianism; and its inevitable consequence has been Political Infidelity ... There was indeed considerable shouting about what they called Conservative principles; but the awkward question which naturally arose, what will you conserve? The prerogatives of the Crown, provided they are not exercised; the independence of the House of Lords, provided it is not asserted; the Ecclesiastical estate provided it is regulated by a commission of laymen. Everything in short that is established, as long as it is a phrase and not a fact ... Conservatism discards Prescription, shrinks from Principle, disavows Progress; having rejected all respect for Antiquity, it offers no redress for the Present, and makes no preparation for the Future.

Benjamin Disraeli, *Coningsby*, 1844.

Source B

The office of leader of the Conservative party in the H[ouse] of C[ommons] at the present day, is to uphold the aristocratic settlement of this country. That is the only question at stake, however manifold may be the forms which it assumes in public discussion, and however various the knowledge and the labour which it requires.

Benjamin Disraeli to Lord Stanley, 26 December, 1848.

Source C

There is certainly a very prevalent impression that Disraeli has no well-defined opinions of his own; but is content to adopt and defend any which may be popular with the Conservative party at the time.

Derby, Disraeli and the Conservative Party – the Political Journals of Lord Stanley 1849–69, edited by J. Vincent, 1978.

Source D

Lord Stanley writing in his journal, 6 May 1866, as the Conservatives planned their response to the Liberal Reform Bill.

Long conference with Disraeli: but we do not agree: he is eager to turn out the government ... I soon saw that to discuss the possibility of a compromise with him would be labour lost ... It is after all natural and perhaps inevitable in his position he should feel as he does. To suppose that he can see Gladstone's success with pleasure would be absurd: and it is only human nature that he should look more to a personal triumph over a rival, than to the permanent effect of what he does on the party or principle which he represents.

Derby, Disraeli and the Conservative Party – the Political Journals of Lord Stanley 1849–69, edited by J. Vincent, 1978.

Talking Point

'We are here for fame', Disraeli remarked to Bright. 'I feel like a man under a burden', Gladstone recorded in his diary, 31 December 1868. Was there more to Disraeli's politics than his flippant remark suggests, and, was 'duty' Gladstone's sole driving force?

This Lord Stanley was the son of Lord Derby, the Conservative leader. He was more sympathetic to Disraeli than most on the Conservative side and served as his Foreign Secretary in 1868 and 1874–78. He eventually joined the Liberals and became a member of Gladstone's second Cabinet.

1. Consult sources A and B. What is Disraeli's perception of the role of a Conservative Party and its leader? How does it fit into the tradition of Liverpool and Peel?
2. 'I am Disraeli the adventurer', he told Derby in 1849. His reputation was that of an unprincipled opportunist who was prepared to ally with Palmerston, Bright, the Irish and even Gladstone if that would give the Conservatives a stable majority. To what extent do these sources support that charge?
3. Referring to the sources above, and Focus 12.1, and using your wider knowledge, how far, and why, had Disraeli, a destructive force in the 1840s, become a constructive one in the 1850s and 1860s?

Gladstone had supported Italian nationalism ever since his visit to the political prisoners in Naples during 1850. In the summer of 1859 the Kingdom of Piedmont, assisted by France, seemed on the verge of uniting Northern Italy and driving the Austrians back over the Alps.

1. Compare source E with the historian's comment in source G. In what ways does Matthew modify and qualify Gladstone's explanation?

2. How reliable and helpful is source F in helping us to understand Gladstone's decision?

3. Gladstone was always a more pragmatic politician than his explanations and justifications suggest. In 1859 'His duty and his interest were coincident and clear' (P. Magnus, *Gladstone* (1954)). Referring to the sources, what was 'his duty'? and, using your wider knowledge, explain 'his interest'.

Source E

Gladstone had consistently opposed Palmerston's foreign policy throughout the 1850s. It was only pressure from his fellow Peelites and his distaste for Disraeli that prevented him from seriously considering Derby's offer in 1858. Why, then, did he agree to join Palmerston in 1859?

I felt sure that in finance there was still much useful work to be done. I was desirous to co-operate in settling the question of the franchise ... My friends were enlisted, or I knew would enlist ... And the overwhelming interest ... of the Italian question, ... joined to my entire mistrust of the former government [Derby's] in relation to it, led me to decide without one moment's hesitation.

Source F

I greatly felt being turned out of office [in 1855], I saw great things to do. I longed to do them. I am losing the best years of my life out of my natural service.

W.E. Gladstone in conversation with Samuel Wilberforce in 1857.

Source G

Always reluctant to admit the role of ambition in politics, Gladstone was none the less aware of his abilities and their lack of application since 1855; his entry to Palmerston's Cabinet ... thus involved no great moral choice ... It was the hard-headed response of an able politician with a programme for action, invited to join a Cabinet at the outset of its formation ... it is hard to see Italy as more than a convenient issue on which to combine with the Whigs ... This is not to say that Gladstone was using the Italian question deceitfully: he undoubtedly believed in the policy to which ... he contributed, but he can hardly have seen Italy as the basis for a government ... But, to last, a peace-time government must offer ... a substantial programme of domestic legislation. This Gladstone could provide. There was 'a policy going a-begging', already prepared in some detail ... A Prime Minister whose chief interest was bound to be in the area of foreign policy could have advantages for a Chancellor of the Exchequer with his own programme of legislation ...

H.C.G. Matthew, *Gladstone 1809–1874*, 1986.

FOCUS

12.2   Gladstone – politics and religion

It is impossible to understand Gladstone without appreciating the centrality of religion in his life. For a short time he had contemplated the Church as a career, but his father's lack of enthusiasm had stifled that. Instead Gladstone saw the world, and politics, as his sphere of religious action. His meticulously kept diary reveals the centrality of religion to Gladstone, and reflects his methodical approach to life. Here is a typical entry. ➡

17 April 1848

Monday St Martin's 8 a.m. The Gospel at prayers in mg: evg prayers this week: with Avrillon – H.S. and Latin with Willy. Visited Soup Kitchen with C. & M. Wrote to Wm. Gladstone – Dr Harington – Dr. Richards – Haddan – Woolcombe – Fraser & Tayleur – Dowbiggin – Lyttleton – Scotts – Griffiths – Amery. Saw Scotts – Ld Ashley – H. of C. 4–7 and 10–12. Spoke on Copper ores. read Sterling – Hodgkins L. to Cobden – Watson's Appeal to the Laity.

Gladstone Diaries, volume 4, 1848–1854.

TALKING POINT

Many politicians have kept diaries. In the 19th century, political diarists included Lord Ashley and Disraeli's friend and Foreign Secretary, Lord Derby (son of the Conservative Prime Minister). Consult the extracts from Derby's diary, written when he was Lord Stanley, on page 276.

1   Consider the reasons why politicians keep diaries.
2   How is Derby's diary different from Gladstone's in content and purpose?
3   Discuss the value to historians of diaries, and the dangers inherent in using them as historical evidence.

In *The State in its Relations with the Church* (1838), Gladstone argued for the restoration of all the privileges of the established Anglican Church and a reaffirmation of the link between Church and State. Although his views had begun to change by 1845, he felt impelled to resign over Maynooth. He remained a high church Anglican, opposed to divorce law reform and the removal of religious tests at the universities, but argued that the State could no longer be trusted to protect the Church which should, therefore, be given greater autonomy. A tolerant approach based on religious liberty, together with an acceptance of Christian diversity, made possible his future political links with Nonconformism.

If the State had forfeited its religious role it still had a responsibility to pursue social justice and to exercise morality in its foreign relations. This moral purpose of the state allowed Gladstone to take up causes and 'missions'. His commitment to financial and fiscal reform in the 1850s and 1860s was, in this sense, a mission. Its wider purpose was to achieve social justice and to encourage individual moral and political responsibility.

TALKING POINT

Can morality ever provide the basis for effective political action, or are politicians inevitably driven by expediency?

The Second Reform Act – a political manoeuvre?

The Liberal Party and reform

Palmerston died on 18 October 1865 and Russell, who had been elevated to the House of Lords in 1861 as Earl Russell, became Premier once again, with Gladstone as Leader of the Commons. Russell wanted to crown his political career with a new Reform Act. Gladstone, who was to prepare the Bill, had already established his credentials by speaking out in a previous reform debate:

> I venture to say that every man who is not presumably incapacitated by some consideration of personal unfitness or political danger, is morally entitled to come within the pale of the constitution.
>
> W.E. Gladstone in the debate on Baines's Reform Bill, 11 May 1864.

However much Gladstone qualified this statement the impression remained amongst his colleagues and the reformers that he anticipated a very wide extension of the franchise. For the first time he became a popular political figure.

> God knows I have not courted them. I hope I do not rest on them. I pray I may turn them to account for good. It is, however, impossible not to love the people from whom such manifestations come.
>
> Gladstone commenting in his diary on his reception during a successful tour of Lancashire in October 1864.

As Chancellor of the Exchequer Gladstone received delegations of working men, including representatives of the New Model Unions. There had always been a working class élite of well paid craftsmen who strictly maintained the distinction between themselves and the rest of the working class. Increasingly this group was indicating its acceptance of the industrial and capitalist system. Gladstone was impressed by his contact with the new trade union leaders, and recognised that they were responsible men at the head of responsible organisations, not dangerous agitators seeking to overturn the established order.

Gladstone was also receptive to the arguments of the Radicals, in particular John Bright, who held up the example of Rochdale to indicate how a large section of 'respectable' society was disenfranchised:

> We now come to the Rochdale District Co-operative Corn Mill Society, which does a large business. It has a capital of £60,000 and turns over £164,000 per annum. It has also a committee of eleven, but neither the president, nor treasurer, nor secretary, nor any of this committee has a borough vote ... Then there is the Rochdale Co-operative Manufacturing Society, which has more than 1,500 members or shareholders, and a capital of £109,000 ... This society is also managed by a committee of eleven, of whom three have borough votes, and two have county votes. But of these five voters only one ... is a 'working man' in the usual sense ...
>
> John Bright, debate on the second reading of the 1866 Reform Bill, 23 April 1866.

Gladstone remarked that Rochdale 'has probably done more than any other town in making good to practical minds a case for some enfranchisement of the working class.'

JOHN BRIGHT WAS THE LEADING BRITISH SUPPORTER OF THE NORTH IN THE AMERICAN CIVIL WAR. FOR HIM IT WAS A CONFLICT BETWEEN DEMOCRACY (THE UNION) AND ARISTOCRACY (THE CONFEDERACY) IN WHICH THE ABOLITION OF SLAVERY WAS CENTRAL. HIS ATTITUDE BEGAN TO LESSEN WORKING CLASS HOSTILITY TOWARDS HIM, AND ENABLED HIM TO MAKE CONTACT WITH THE NEW TRADE UNION LEADERS. THE SOLIDARITY AND DISCIPLINE SHOWN BY THE LANCASHIRE COTTON WORKERS DURING THE COTTON FAMINE MADE AN IMPRESSION ON BOTH DERBY AND GLADSTONE. IT GAVE BRIGHT THE MASS FOLLOWING HE HAD FAILED TO OBTAIN IN 1859. AFTER THE DEFEAT OF THE LIBERAL REFORM BILL OF 1866 BRIGHT KEPT THE ISSUE ALIVE AT A SUCCESSION OF GREAT REFORM DEMONSTRATIONS IN THE MAJOR INDUSTRIAL CITIES IN THE AUTUMN OF 1866.

TALKING POINT

What factor prominent in the crisis of 1830–32 is missing here?

The Destruction of the Liberal Reform Bill, 1866

Gladstone's Reform Bill was presented to the House of Commons on 12 March 1866. It proposed a £7 rental qualification in the boroughs – low enough to increase the working class vote, but high enough to prevent a working class majority. The county occupation franchise was to be reduced from £50 to £14. The Bill would have enfranchised about 400,000 new voters, of whom half would have been working men. The measure was restricted to franchise extension. Bright and the Radicals wanted a redistribution of seats, but ministers did not want to complicate their Bill and needed the support of Whig MPs sitting for small boroughs.

During the next few months Gladstone lost control of the parliamentary Party. His high-handed leadership style caused resentment but, more seriously, some feared that Bright was the real driving force behind the legislation. Derby and Disraeli knew that they had to defeat the Bill to prevent Gladstone gaining the ascendancy in the House of Commons and the Liberals from acquiring electoral advantage. 'No matter how you modify the bill, it is still theirs, and not ours, and will give them the control of the boroughs for half-a-dozen years to come.' (Disraeli in conversation with Stanley).

Disraeli sensed that the divisions within the Liberal Party would give the Conservatives the opportunity of smashing the Liberals. He deliberately refused to take the lead in attacking the government's proposals, leaving that to the Whig rebels with whom he made a secret agreement.

Bright was making a biblical reference to David who, when escaping from Saul, hid in the cave of Adullam, where 'every one who was discontented, gathered to him' (1 Samuel 22:2).

PUNCH, OR THE LONDON CHARIVARI.—January 20, 1866.

LOWER AWAY THERE
LOWER AWAY

THE OFFICIOUS PASSENGER.

Lord John. " EXCUSE ME, FRIEND BRIGHT, BUT DO YOU COMMAND THIS SHIP, OR DO I ! "

The leader of the rebel Whigs was Robert Lowe. He was no apologist for the aristocracy, but he feared the onset of democracy following his political experiences in Australia. If anything Lowe was a meritocrat, arguing that ability would be swamped by a mass of corrupt working class voters prepared to sell out to the highest bidder, or to vote for their own narrow class interests. He feared that political power would go to the demagogues who could make the most extravagant electoral promises. Bright nicknamed Lowe's group the Adullamites.

On 27 April the government's majority was cut to 5 on an amendment that a redistribution of seats should accompany the Franchise Bill. As the government should have commanded a majority of 65, this was a major humiliation, and the Cabinet initially considered resignation before giving way. Two months later the government was defeated when Lord Dunkellin's motion to substitute a rating qualification for the proposed rental qualification in the boroughs was carried by a majority of nine. Dunkellin was an Adullamite and 48 Liberals voted with the opposition. Disraeli did not speak in the debate.

The Conservatives and the Adullamites wanted to defeat the Bill, not amend it. Gladstone urged Russell to dissolve Parliament and call a General Election, but the elderly Prime Minister had had enough. His government resigned. The Adullamites had achieved their objective.

A Conservative interlude

Derby now became Prime Minister for the third time. The Adullamites expected places in his Cabinet, but neither Derby nor Disraeli wanted them, even if that meant forming another minority government. Reform seemed to have been abandoned. The new government made no pledges and Gladstone and Russell quietly left for the Continent.

The Reform League was London-based with a working-class membership. Its programme included manhood suffrage and the secret ballot.

The Reform Union was based in the North West with a middle-class membership. Its programme included household suffrage, the secret ballot and redistribution.

The situation was not so simple, however. The Liberals had created a demand for parliamentary reform which could not be ignored. The Reform League and the Reform Union organised demonstrations, and in London the Reform League planned a protest meeting in Hyde Park. The Home Secretary closed the park and prohibited the gathering. The leadership obeyed but the crowds broke into the Park. With police and troops powerless, Spencer Walpole, the Home Secretary, had to accept the Reform League's offer to restore order. Throughout the autumn Bright attended a series of demonstrations in the industrial cities of the North and the Midlands. Reform was kept alive, and the main agitation remained 'respectable'.

Examining the Evidence

A Conservative conversion

Source A

I am coming reluctantly to the conclusion that we shall have to deal with the question of Reform.

Lord Derby to Benjamin Disraeli, 16 September 1866.

Source B

I agree with you that the Reform question requires very mature consideration ... but I think the general feeling is that we cannot escape doing something. The Queen spoke to me about it the other day. She said she is very anxious to see it all settled ... On the other hand the violence of Bright's language is, I think, in our favour: not in favour of resisting all Reform, for which I believe there is a genuine demand *now,* however it may have been excited, but in favour of the acceptance of a moderate and Conservative measure ...

Lord Derby to Benjamin Disraeli, 27 September 1866.

Source C

'POLITICAL ECONOMY', *PUNCH*, DECEMBER 1, 1866.

plurality of voting – the 'fancy franchises' (see below) proposed by the Conservatives to create extra votes for the social groups which tended to support them

Source D

Of all possible Hares to start I do not know a better than the extension of Household Suffrage, *coupled with plurality of voting*.

Lord Derby to Benjamin Disraeli, 22nd December 1866.

1 Explain 'The Old '59' banner in source C.
2 From the evidence of these sources, who seems to be pressing for a Conservative Reform Bill, and why?
3 Why might the cartoonist (source C) be surprised if he read source D?

LIKE THE OTHER REFORMERS, BRIGHT WAS NEVER A DEMOCRAT. HE WANTED AN EXTENSION OF THE FRANCHISE, BUT ONE THAT WOULD EXCLUDE THE 'RESIDUUM' (THOSE WITH NO REAL STAKE IN SOCIETY).

WHOM OR WHAT DOES 'FRANKENSTEIN' REPRESENT, AND WHY MIGHT BRIGHT SEEM ALARMED?

Lord Cranborne, the leader of the Conservative opposition to Disraeli in 1867, eventually succeeded him as leader of the party and (as Lord Salisbury) was Prime Minister 1885–86, 1886–92, 1895–1902.

PUNCH OR THE LONDON CHARIVARI.—September 8, 1866.

THE BRUMMAGEM FRANKENSTEIN.

John Bright. "I HAVE NO FE—FE—FEAR OF MA—MANHOOD SUFFRAGE!"—*Mr. Bright's Speech at Birmingham.*

Disraeli's triumph – the Conservative Reform Bill in the Commons

Although Derby had started the 'hare' of household suffrage, the Cabinet was too divided to take such a radical step. The agreed intention was to appoint a committee of inquiry with legislation following in 1868. The debate on the government's proposals began on 11 February 1867. Disraeli quickly realised that something more dramatic was necessary if the Conservatives were to retain the initiative and keep control of the Commons. Three days later, without consulting his Cabinet colleagues, he committed the government to the immediate introduction of a Reform Bill. Despite the misgivings of three of its members, Lord Carnarvon, Lord Cranborne and General Peel, the Cabinet decided to prepare a bill to bring in household suffrage.

The Bill was to be introduced on 25 February. Cranborne, having calculated the probable effects of household suffrage, persuaded Derby to recall the Cabinet, and the Bill was changed to a £6 rating franchise in the boroughs. The 'Ten Minute Bill', so called because it had been drafted at great speed, was clearly inadequate and likely to be defeated, giving the initiative back to Gladstone and the Liberals. Disraeli's own soundings amongst Conservative backbenchers indicated considerable support for household suffrage – with a qualification of three years' residence and personal payment of rates – especially if this could be a final settlement.

The Cabinet, meeting on 2 March, took the decision to support a household suffrage bill after all. Cranborne, Peel and Carnarvon resigned but the Party united behind the Cabinet in favour of what seemed to be an attainable policy. Disraeli was recognised as a leader capable of handling the emergency and coping with Gladstone. Thus, Disraeli's bold action left the Cabinet rebels isolated.

The Conservative Bill proposed household suffrage for the boroughs with personal payment of rates and a two year residence qualification as safeguards. The county occupation franchise would be reduced from £50 to £15, and 15 seats would be redistributed. The conservative element in the electorate was to be bolstered by the 'fancy franchises' which the Bill proposed. These would have enfranchised middle class voters who were not householders (in particular sons living at home), and gained a second vote for many existing electors. These extra votes would have gone to graduates, those who paid direct taxes and holders of accounts with Savings Banks.

Gladstone, however, was concerned that the Bill would be amended into manhood suffrage, with no safeguards, as the minority Conservative government could be forced to accept Radical amendments as the price of staying in office. He hoped to replace the household suffrage proposals with a £5 rating qualification based on personal payment. The franchise would be widened by making all occupants of houses rated at this level pay their own rates. With these proposals, he hoped to bring Liberals, Adullamites and Conservative rebels together in alliance to defeat Disraeli.

PUNCH, OR THE LONDON CHARIVARI—March 16, 1867.

DERBY & CO

REFORM

THE HONEST POTBOY.

Derby (*aside*). "DON'T FROTH IT UP THIS TIME, BEN. GOOD MEASURE—THE INSPECTORS HAVE THEIR EYE ON US."

Personal payment of rates as a voting qualification became a crucial safeguard. Large numbers of working class householders compounded for their rates – paying them as a part of the rent. Personal payment of rates would put a financial cost on gaining the vote, and was therefore a disincentive that would prevent the boroughs being swamped by working class votes. A long residence qualification would also reduce the electorate as the working class was highly mobile.

NAME THE 'HONEST POTBOY' AND THE 'INSPECTORS'. WHAT QUALIFICATIONS DID THEY HAVE TO INSPECT, AND HOW DID THE 'POTBOY' GIVE 'GOOD MEASURE'?

The 'Tea Room revolt' disrupted his plans. About 50 Liberal MPs, some alienated by Gladstone's authoritarianism, others wanting a quick settlement and preferring a concession on household suffrage to facing the spectre of manhood suffrage, declared their unwillingness to vote with him.

On 12 April Gladstone's amendment was defeated by 21 votes. Forty five Liberals voted with the government. It was a triumph for Disraeli and a humiliating defeat for Gladstone – 'a smash perhaps without example', he wrote in his diary. He even contemplated abandoning the leadership of the Party. For the first time Disraeli was in an unassailable position as the brilliant leader who had destroyed his Party's leading opponent. His backbenchers scented a great victory. Their confidence enabled Disraeli to make the necessary concessions to the Radicals to get the Bill through without losing Conservative support, and without having to concede any amendments supported by Gladstone.

The two year residence qualification was the first 'safeguard' to be sacrificed by Disraeli; on 2 May an amendment to a one year qualification was accepted. The £10 lodger was next enfranchised, and on 17 May Disraeli unexpectedly agreed to Hodgkinson's amendment – this solved the problem of the compounding by effectively abolishing it and making all householders direct ratepayers. The evidence would suggest that Disraeli did this to forestall an amendment from Gladstone due to be debated that evening.

When the Act finally received royal assent it was very different to the original Bill. It gave full household suffrage in the boroughs, though not in

TALKING POINT

Historians have debated the significance of 6 May in hastening the rapid radicalisation of the Reform Bill. How far did this orderly and well managed protest warn Conservative backbenchers of the dangers inherent in a moderate and unacceptable measure, and prepare them to accept the removal of the safeguards?

ON 6 MAY 1867 THE REFORM LEAGUE LEADERSHIP DEFIED A GOVERNMENT PROHIBITION OF DEMONSTRATIONS IN HYDE PARK. BETWEEN 100,000 AND 150,000 PEOPLE ENTERED THE PARK DESPITE THE DISCREET PRESENCE OF POLICE AND TROOPS. *THE TIMES* COMMENTED THAT THE REFORM LEAGUE LEADERS APPEARED TO BE 'THE ACTUAL GOVERNMENT OF THE COUNTRY'. SPENCER WALPOLE, THE HOME SECRETARY, RESIGNED.

the county seats. Before the Bill left the Commons, dual voting and the 'fancy franchises' had been abandoned and the county occupation franchise had been lowered.

All of this was a price worth paying if the Conservatives could control the redistribution of seats and turn it to their political advantage. Disraeli's aim was to preserve the small rural boroughs whilst redrawing urban boundaries to take in new suburbs and other growth areas, and so exclude these potential areas of Liberal / Radical support from the more Conservative county seats. A Liberal redistribution in 1866 could have been disastrous for the Conservatives, so in 1867, despite some defeats, Disraeli capitalised on the opportunity to defend his Party's position. A large increase in the Liberal vote in the urban boroughs was no great concession if traditional Conservative control of the rural areas could be re-asserted and extended to redress the balance in the House of Commons that had left that Party in a minority since 1846.

PUNCH, OR THE LONDON CHARIVARI.—MAY 25, 1867.

THE DERBY, 1867. DIZZY WINS WITH "REFORM BILL."

MR. PUNCH. "DON'T BE TOO SURE; WAIT TILL HE'S *WEIGHED.*"

TALKING POINT

Punch cartoons are an important source for the political history of the 19th century. They have been used to provide contemporary comment for this account of the events surrounding the passage of the Second Reform Act.
How helpful have they been, and what can the political cartoon add to our understanding of past events?

IDENTIFY THE OUTPACED 'JOCKEYS'. IN THE LIGHT OF LATER EVENTS, HOW APPROPRIATE WAS MR PUNCH'S NOTE OF CAUTION?

Examining the Evidence

The Second Reform Act: myths and realities

The paradox of 1867 is that a Conservative government was responsible for a more radical measure of parliamentary reform than the Liberal Bill they helped defeat in 1866. Myths were invented and perpetuated by the participants to explain this U-turn.

Creating the myths

Source A

I had to prepare the mind of the country, and to educate – if it be not arrogant to use such a phrase – to educate our party. It is a large party, and requires its attention to be called to questions of this kind with some pressure. I had to prepare the mind of Parliament and the country on this question of Reform. This was not only the concurrence of Lord Derby, but of my colleagues.

Speech made by Disraeli in Edinburgh, November 1887.

Source B

... thankful ... to say that we [had] had that which, perhaps, may be called the highest triumph of a party ... to see [our] opponents themselves compelled to be the organs of giving effect to [our] principles and fulfilling [our] wishes (*cheers*).

Speech made by Gladstone in Ormskirk, 19 December 1867.

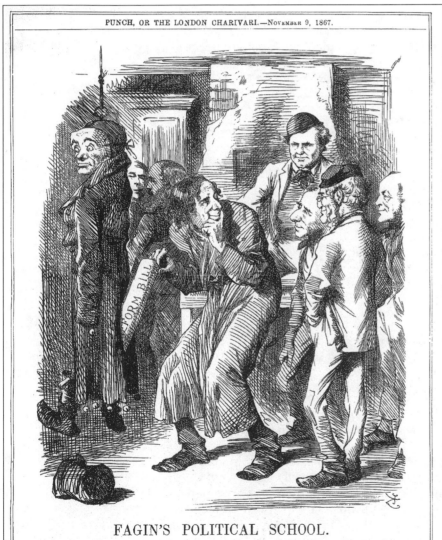

PUNCH, OR THE LONDON CHARIVARI.—November 9, 1867.

FAGIN'S POLITICAL SCHOOL.

"Now, mark this; because these are things which you may not have heard in any speech which has been made in the city of Edinburgh. (*Laughter and cheers*.) I had—if it be not arrogant to use such a phrase—*to educate our party*. It is a large party, and requires its attention to be called to questions of this kind with some pressure. I had to prepare the mind of Parliament and the country on this question of Reform."—Mr. Disraeli's *Speech at the Edinburgh Banquet*.

 Source C

PUNCH, 9 NOVEMBER 1867

Source D
Lord Cranborne, the leading Conservative critic of the Reform Bill, wrote an article in the *Quarterly Review*, November 1867, with the title 'The Conservative Surrender':
The dullest of their antagonists perfectly understands that they have not yielded to argument or sentiment; that the apostles of reform who have the real credit of their conversion are the mobs who beat down the palings of Hyde Park, or went out marching with bands and banners in the towns of the North.

As the wind blows, so will they point. Any minister who takes it as his first principle that he will not be 'ousted', renounces all pretensions to independence. He becomes the slave of the majority of the House of Commons. He is a leader in no other sense but that in which the first horse in a team is called a leader: he is the first to be driven.

1 Identify the dummy and Fagin in source C, and 'the mobs' in source D.
2 Explain *Punch*'s response to Disraeli's 'educating' of his party.
3 Compare and contrast the views of *Punch*, Disraeli, Gladstone and Cranborne on the motives and actions of ministers during 1867.

Derby and Disraeli explain themselves
Source E
Disraeli explains his decision to accept Hodgkinson's amendment.
I tried to get up some debate, or, rather, I waited for it, for I could do no more, but it was impossible ... I waited until the question was put, when, having resolved everything in my mind, I felt that the critical moment had arrived, and when, without in the slightest degree receding from our principle and position of a rating and residential franchise, we might take a step which would destroy the present agitation and extinguish Gladstone and Co. I therefore accepted the spirit of H's amendment.

Benjamin Disraeli to Gathorne Hardy, 18 May 1867.

Source F
... talk with Lord D. whom I find bent on remaining in power at whatever cost, and ready to make the largest concessions with that object.

Lord Stanley's diary, 10 March 1867.

Lord D – Lord Derby, Stanley's father and the Prime Minister.

Source G
I did not intend for a third time to be made a mere stop-gap until it would suit the convenience of the Liberal party to forget their dissensions and bring forward a measure which would oust us from office and replace them there: I determined that I would take such a course as would convert, if possible, an existing minority into a practical majority. As our political opponents had failed in carrying a measure, the carrying of which was of vital importance to the interests of the country, and the postpone-ment of which, added to the public inconvenience and embarrassment year after year, and the agitation for which was standing in the way of every measure of practical improvement and ... legislation. I felt it to be my duty to undertake this difficult task ... to endeavour towards the close of my political career to settle one great and important question ...

Lord Derby in the House of Lords, 1867.

4 Using your wider knowledge comment on Disraeli's claim that he had not 'in the slightest degree' receded 'from our principle and position of a rating and residential franchise.'

5 In what ways, and for what reasons, might source E be a better explanation of Disraeli's concerns than source A?

6 How far do sources E, F and G support the contemporary accusation that both men were determined 'to retain office at the sacrifice of principle, conviction or consistency'?

The historians and the myths

Source H

Gladstone's role in the great reform battles of 1866 and 1867 was strange. Throughout his views on the substance of the question were moderate and consistent and the popular hero-worship of him as a zealous reformer was almost a misunderstanding. His leadership in Parliament ... was in many ways disastrous ... Yet it was his great weight as a man of high principle, allied to his remarkable gifts of intellect and speech, that ultimately gave him the power to dominate, even in failure, the course of events.

E.J. Feuchtwanger, *Gladstone*, 1975.

Source I

Tory backbenchers were bounced by Disraeli into a Reform Act which bore virtually no relation to their government's bill ... Few supported it on its merits, but ... they could reflect that their party had brought off a tactical coup of the first magnitude. It was a triumph of expediency over both principle and rational calculation. Suggestions that the Act encapsulated Disraeli's version of a Tory democracy to which he must now educate his followers may be discounted ... He was never a democrat and his overwhelming concern for Toryism was to make it, for the first time since 1846, a party of stable government. His success in 1867 rested on the two talents in which he was pre-eminent: parliamentary management and the ability to think more quickly on his feet than his opponents.

E. Evans, *The Forging of the Modern State*, 1983.

Source J

The Reform Bill of 1867 survived because a majority of the members of both Houses of Parliament dared not throw it out. They did not want it, they did not like it, they feared what it might do, but they passed it. For the first time in the Second Reform period a majority of members felt an imperative need to make a settlement.

Disraeli led his country gentlemen to accept anything as long as they appeared to be winning.

F.B. Smith, *The Making of the Second Reform Bill*, 1966.

Source K

The final shape of the 1867 Reform Act owed little to the Conservatives' political assumptions and much to their calculations of party advantage.

R. Stewart, *The Foundation of the Conservative Party 1830–1867*, 1978.

Source L

... if Reform was a gamble taken in the interests of Party expediency, what was it that transformed the harmless flutters of the 'fifties and early 'sixties into the relentless game of brag which began in February and ended in August 1867? The Act went far beyond anything which had been desired before 1866. It was surely the presence of the Reform League which stopped the players crying off as they had done so often in the past ...

R. Harrison, *Before the Socialists*, 1965.

Source M

The action ... was a battle within the political classes to sustain, support and achieve power.

M. Cowling, *1867: Disraeli, Gladstone and Revolution*, 1967.

Source N

Derby and Disraeli and their followers, in 1867, did not determine to trust the people, or to put their faith in a Conservative democracy. They did what they felt they had to do, to satisfy the popular agitation, reconcile the upper strata of the working classes to the established political system, and 'dish the Whigs'.

P. Smith, *Disraelian Conservatism and Social Reform*, 1967.

---

7 How does source L differ in its interpretation from that of the other historians? This view of 1867 has been dismissed as 'wrongheaded', but what are its strengths?
8 Reconsider the 'myths' ushered in by Gladstone and Disraeli in sources A and B with reference to the opinions voiced in sources H, I, J, K, L, M and N.
9 'The crisis of the Second Reform Bill was a desperate gamble to win a tactical victory and party advantage'. Discuss this view, referring to the evidence and opinions you have read and your wider knowledge of events.

TALKING POINT

Disraeli was educating his party; his recognition that working class conservatism existed was rewarded in 1874. Tory Democracy was a reality.
Gladstone manipulated a Conservative government desperate to retain office at any cost. In 1868 the new electorate voted for the man who was really responsible for the substance of the Reform Act. Gladstone was swept into the premiership.
These are the potent myths on which political parties built their identity.

● Why do political parties need myths?
● How are they created?
● What dangers do they pose for the historian?

> **The Second Reform Act**
>
> **The Franchise**
>
> *Boroughs*
> Adult male householders after one year's residence.
> Lodgers paying at least £10 a year, after one year's residence.
> *Counties*
> £12 rating qualification.
> Owners of land with annual value of £5 (or occupiers with a lease of at least 60 years).
> Qualifications as established in 1832.
>
> The Redistribution
>
> *England and Wales*
> 52 borough seats abolished.
> 11 new borough constituencies created – 2 with 2 members, 9 with 1.
> Birmingham, Leeds, Manchester and Liverpool given a third MP; two boroughs upgraded from 1 to 2 MPs.
> 25 seats reallocated to the counties.
> University of London graduates to elect an MP.
>
> *Scotland (separate Act)*
> No seats abolished.
> Glasgow given a third member.
> 5 extra seats for Scottish counties and universities.
> 1 new parliamentary borough created.
> *Ireland (separate Act)*
> Borough franchise reduced to £4 householder, county franchise remained £12. There was no redistribution.

EXAMINING THE EVIDENCE

1867 – Staging post on the road to mass politics?

Source A

The eighteen years that followed the Reform Act of 1867 were particularly important in British history, because they were the years in which the nation accustomed itself to the notion of democracy.

H.J. Hanham, *Elections and Party Management – Politics in the time of Disraeli and Gladstone*, 1959.

Optimists

Source B

No doubt we are making a great experiment and 'taking a leap in the dark', but I have the greatest confidence in the sound sense of my fellow-countrymen, and I entertain a strong hope that the extended franchise which we are now conferring upon them will be the means of placing the institutions of this country on a firmer basis, and that the passing of this measure will tend to increase the loyalty and contentment of a great portion of Her Majesty's subjects.

Lord Derby in the House of Lords.

Source C

Disraeli, speaking at the Merchant Taylor's banquet, 11 June 1867.

It is said we are on the verge of a great democratic change. My Lords and gentlemen, believe me the elements of democracy do not exist in England (*cheers*). England is a country of classes, and the change impending in the country will only make those classes more united, more content, more complete and more cordial (*cheers*).

Morning Post, 12 June 1867.

1 Neither Derby nor Disraeli thought in terms of 'democracy'. Why do you think that was, and how did they expect society to benefit from the Reform Act?

Pessimists

Source D

Robert Lowe feared that 'the principle of numbers' would prevail over 'wealth and intellect.'

Once give working men the votes, and the machinery is ready to launch those votes in one compact mass upon the institutions and property of this country.

Robert Lowe, *Speeches and Letters on Reform*, 1867.

Source E

All is new & changed & large and, I fear I must say, in some respects *dark*.

G. Glyn, Liberal Chief Whip, to Gladstone.

Gladstone was able to adapt to the new political realities more readily than most other politicians. He addressed mass meetings at which shorthand reporters sat next to the platform and gave him a national audience by printing his speeches in full in the next day's newspapers. Similarly, the first working class MPs, Thomas Burt and Alexander Macdonald, were elected as Liberals in 1874. It became increasingly clear that such working-class Liberals were working within the system, rather than looking to overthrow it.

2 'a leap in the dark' (Derby); 'All is ... in some respects dark' (Glyn). Why were politicians of all parties apprehensive in 1867? To what extent were their fears removed by 1874?

Organisation

The parties met the challenge of the new urban electorate in different ways. Conservative organisation came from the centre under the direct control of the Party leadership. On the Liberal side it grew from the grass roots as a direct challenge to the parliamentary leadership.

The Conservatives

In 1870 John Gorst was appointed as Conservative Party agent by Disraeli. He probably believed his leader's Tory democracy rhetoric and recognised that the new working class Conservative vote had to be organised and managed. With Disraeli's support, the Party organisation was brought under one roof at Conservative Central Office. The Central Press Board was acquired to provide a news agency service for the provincial Conservative press. As secretary of the National Union of Conservative and Constitutional Associations from 1872 Gorst controlled the main propaganda mouthpiece of the Party leadership. Gorst saved the National Union from collapse and directed it to carry Conservative principles to the working man through local associations affiliated to it. Disraeli's choice of the Union's annual conference at the Crystal Palace for a major policy speech in June 1872 marked the leadership's acceptance of an organisation that was theirs to control and which made no demands on them. An effective organisation which ensured that there were Conservative candidates standing in every winnable seat made a major contribution to the 1874 electoral success.

The Liberals

The National Liberal Federation, founded in 1877, emerged from the success of the Birmingham Liberal Association in distributing the Liberal vote to ensure that the city's three MPs were Liberal, and that the School Board and the Council were controlled by the Party. Its technique gave a semblance of democracy and shared decision making, but the real power lay in the hands of a small committee at the apex of the organisational pyramid. The Association became the vehicle of the Birmingham radical, Joseph Chamberlain. When he sought to extend the Birmingham method to other constituencies in 1877 he was only partially concerned about organisation. His main purpose was to challenge the Party leadership and to win for the Federation a share in the formation of Party policy. Although Gladstone attended the inaugural meeting it is not surprising that the more conservative elements within the Liberal Party viewed the Federation with some suspicion.

TALKING POINT

In an attempt to assist Conservative candidates in the largest boroughs, where three MPs were returned (the big cities, which were natural Liberal strongholds), electors had only two votes each. Comment on how effective this regulation would be in achieving its aim, and consider how Liberal Party strategists could help secure victory for all three of their candidates.

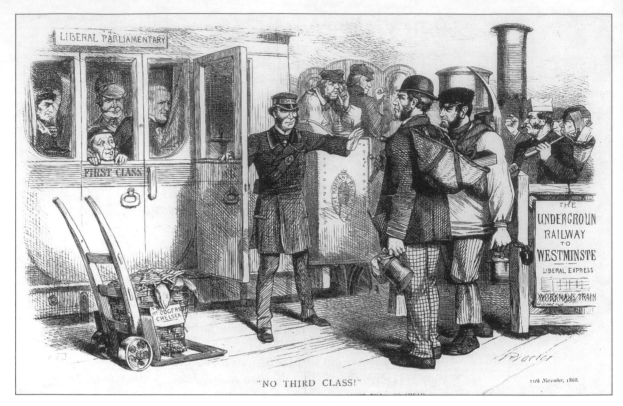

LIBERAL PARLIAMENTARY

FIRST CLASS

THE
UNDERGROUN
RAILWAY
TO
WESTMINSTE
LIBERAL EXPRESS

WORKMANS TRAIN

"NO THIRD CLASS!"

11th November, 1868.

REVIEW

Referring to this chapter, and using your wider knowledge, consider these comments on the 1867 Reform Act:
- An inevitable step towards full democracy
- A triumph and a defeat for the working class
- An episode in the battle between the Parties for power at Westminster

Discuss the appropriateness of each, examine the contradictions they suggest and explain which, if any, you find the most apt.

WHO ARE THE DRIVER AND THE FIREMAN ON THE 'RAMPANT RADICAL'? THIS CARTOON APPEARED DURING THE 1868 GENERAL ELECTION. WHAT IS IT SUGGESTING ABOUT THE RELATIONSHIP BETWEEN THE LIBERAL PARTY AND THE WORKING MAN?

13 Gladstone and Disraeli, 1868–80 – The Domestic Arena

PREVIEW

Source A

A BAD EXAMPLE.

'A BAD EXAMPLE', *PUNCH*, 10 AUGUST 1878.

Source B

Lord Granville in a letter to Queen Victoria, 14 April 1880.

Lord Beaconsfield and Mr Gladstone are men of extraordinary ability; they dislike each other more than is common among public men. Of no other politician would Lord Beaconsfield have said in public that his conduct was worse than the Bulgarian atrocities. He has the power of saying in two words that which drives a person of Mr Gladstone's peculiar temperament into a great state of excitement.

TALKING POINT

What indication is there that Gladstone and Disraeli were beginning to fulfil the role of national political leaders in an age of mass politics?

1 How did *Punch* see Gladstone and Disraeli in 1878?
2 What, according to Granville, had complicated political disagreements?

The 1868 General Election

The election was Gladstone's triumph. If Disraeli had seized and retained the initiative in 1867, dominating the reform crisis, Gladstone retrieved it in 1868, reuniting his party in the process. He had become leader on Russell's resignation despite his unacceptability to the Whig elite. He was imposed on them because of his administrative reputation and the mass following he had acquired in the country during the 1860s. 'I am become', he wrote to A.H. Gordon in 1864, 'for the first time a popular character.' In 1866 and 1867 it was his name that was emblazoned on the banners carried at reform meetings and demonstrations.

An outburst of Fenian violence in Britain during 1867 had heightened public awareness of the Irish question. Gladstone capitalised on this by astutely proposing the disestablishment of the Church of Ireland as the first stage in the settlement of that country's problems. This left the Conservatives defending an institution whose continued existence could hardly be justified, whilst the simple directness of the policy drew the Liberals together.

Whig landowners with Irish estates, alarmed by the prospect of land reform, were happy with the principle of disestablishment. It fitted their convictions that the Church should be subordinate to the State and that Ireland should be treated fairly. Radical politicians from both the middle and working classes welcomed the attack on privilege implicit in the campaign against the Irish Church, whilst the Nonconformists acclaimed the new leader who had adopted their long advocated solution for the Irish problem. Some even deluded themselves that Gladstone might proceed from Irish to English disestablishment. Irish and Catholic voters were also attracted by the programme.

With Liberal opinion united behind him, Gladstone's leadership of the opposition took on a new assurance. Church Rates abolition was carried with his backing, he defeated the government and got his resolutions on the state of the Irish Church through the Commons, whilst his bill to suspend all Irish Church patronage had to be thrown out by the Conservative majority in the Lords.

The dissolution of parliament was delayed until the new electoral registers were prepared. Once the election campaign began, in the autumn of 1868, it was less a question of whether the Liberals would retain their majority than its size.

The previous Liberal majority of about 70 was extended to 112. Disraeli set a new precedent by resigning immediately instead of waiting for the meeting of the new parliament and a 'No confidence' vote. His fortunes plunged to a new depth of ineffectiveness as Gladstone rose to meet the challenge of the premiership.

There is a fuller discussion of the background to Gladstone's policy and of his broader purpose in Chapter 15.

TALKING POINT

Why was Gladstone's initial 'mission ... to pacify the Liberal Party', and how successful was he?

TALKING POINT

Gladstone began a careful cultivation of leading Nonconformist ministers at this time. Why was he an unlikely Nonconformist hero, why did he become one and why were those who hoped he would disestablish the Church of England deceiving themselves?

However, the Conservatives did well in Lancashire – suggesting that they could win urban seats among the new electorate. Gladstone's defeat in South West Lancashire was particularly satisfying.

THE RISING TIDE.

Mrs. Gamp. "O YOU BAD, WICKED BOY! I S'POSE YOU'LL BE FOR A WASHIN' AWAY *THAT* CHURCH NEXT!"

WHAT IS GLADSTONE ABOUT TO DO? WHAT CHURCH IS MRS GAMP POINTING TO? WHAT IS SHE IMPLYING ABOUT GLADSTONE'S INTENTIONS? HOW REALISTIC IS THIS CARTOON AS A COMMENT ON GLADSTONE'S POLICIES AT THIS TIME?

FOCUS

13.1 The 'Gladstonian' Liberal Party

Talk of the Liberal Party? Why it consists of Mr G. After him it will disappear and all will be chaos.

John Morley in conversation in 1891.

TALKING POINT

'He [Gladstone] stood at once for the serious aristocracy, the High Churchmen, the industrialists, the cheap press and radical agitation, the provincial towns, Dissent, and the working class. So quickly did he evolve, that differing impressions of him, mutually exclusive in the long run, but all favourable, were co-existent in the minds of great classes, and Gladstone obtained the support of the general interest he looked for, from a party which was a confederation of all classes, each acting in its own interests.' (K. Vincent, *The Formation of the Liberal Party 1857–1868*, 1966) How, by 1868, had Gladstone won the sympathy of the business community, radical working class reformers and the Nonconformists without sacrificing the 'serious aristocracy' and the High Churchmen?
Using the material in this Focus, chart the strengths and weaknesses of the Gladstonian Liberal Party.

Nonconformists were 'the backbone of British Liberalism', wrote Gladstone in *The Nineteenth Century* in 1877. Gladstone, the High Churchman, became the focal point of their political attention. For many Nonconformists, their ultimate aim was to see the disestablishment of the Church of England. The events of the 1870s, however, taught them that Nonconformity was not strong enough to make a political impact on its own. As part of the Liberal Party, they might achieve some of their objectives. By 1880, noted the Rev. John Guinnes Rogers, they had become 'Liberals first, Nonconformists afterwards.'

By 1880, 24 per cent of Liberal MPs were nonconformists.

The 'Celtic fringe', Scotland and Wales, helped to give Gladstone his majority in 1892.

The Welsh had a clear national identity moulded by a shared religious nonconformity, language and cultural heritage, and hostility to an alien Anglican landlord class. Stuart Rendel, MP for Montgomeryshire from 1880, became leader of the Welsh group and provided Welsh MPs with a programme for Wales to be achieved through the Liberal Party. Scottish nationalism was a less potent force but the fact that Gladstone sat for a Scottish constituency from 1880 reinforced allegiance to his Party.

Labour leaders displayed a willingness to work with the Liberal Party that surprised party managers in 1868. The Reform League backed the Gladstonian campaign and the Liberals funded lecturers the League sent into working class areas. There was no demand at this time for a separate Labour Party. The working class 'elite' enfranchised in 1867 still had too much in common with the middle classes to challenge them, and the 'enemy' was still the land-owning aristocrat rather than the middle class employer. The first working men to enter Parliament did so as Gladstonian Liberals.

dstone succeeded in imposing unity on coalition of interest and pressure groups t made up the Liberal Party. In 1868, 1880 d after 1885 he produced the great moral e behind which all could march thus sking the divisive tendency of individual ses and aims. In his view the purpose of Party transcended all sectional interests. Gladstone's aims were conservative; to reserve the political balance between the ropertied and the masses; to maintain ow expenditure and low taxation; to re-stablish the authority of central executive government; to safeguard the doctrinal heritage of the Church of England from ttack; to secure stability and the rule of aw in Ireland; . . . to demonstrate to the nlarged electorate that its proper function was the age-old one of checking orruption and extravagance in overnment, rather than the disreputable ne of using its voting muscle to press for ectional gain . . .

J.P. Parry, *Democracy and Religion – Gladstone and the Liberal Party 1867–1875*, 1986.

'Section Men' or 'Faddists'
The pressure groups concentrated on single issues, imitating the Anti-Corn Law League in the methods they used. There was cross-membership, and links into the interest groups, particularly Nonconformity. They could put pressure on MPs at election time by requiring pledges. Usually they were reluctant to accept the compromises that might have enabled a Liberal government to deliver practical and workable reforms.

The United Kingdom Alliance – founded 1853, campaigned for legislation to end the sale of alcohol. Appreciating that a national ban was unlikely the Alliance's main aim was to get its Permissive Bill through Parliament to enable ratepayers to vote for local prohibition.

The Liberation Society – founded 1844 as the Anti-State Church Association with the aim of disestablishing the Church of England. In 1871 the Nonconformists mustered 96 votes in the Commons for a disestablishment motion, but the whole Liberal front bench, led by Gladstone, was against them.

The National Education League emerged in Birmingham in 1869. It demanded national, free and secular elementary education. Its link with Nonconformity, and its leadership of their opposition to the 1870 Education Act made it a potent divisive force during Gladstone's first ministry.

Examining the Evidence

What did Gladstone's Liberal Party stand for?

Source A

Talking Point

Since Gladstone did not invent the Liberal Party, nor did it cease to exist with his retirement how correct is it to label Liberalism 'Gladstonian'? Was his contribution a particular leadership style and image? Or was it a policy and philosophy?

PUNCH, OR THE LONDON CHARIVARI.—December 13, 1879.

THE COLOSSUS OF WORDS.

WHAT, ACCORDING TO *PUNCH*, DID GLADSTONIAN LIBERALISM STAND FOR? COMMENT ON THE SUITABILITY OF THIS IMAGE IN DECEMBER 1879 (REFER TO PAGES 336-338 IN CHAPTER 14).

Source B

John Stuart Mill published *On Liberty* in 1859. He was a Liberal MP 1865–68.

The ... most cogent reason for restricting the interference of government is the great evil of adding unnecessarily to its power.

A Government cannot have too much of the kind of activity which does not impede, but aids and stimulates, individual exertion and development. The mischief begins when instead of calling forth the activity and powers of individuals and bodies it substitutes its own activity for theirs; when, instead of informing, advising, and upon occasion, denouncing, it makes them work in fetters, or bids them stand aside and does their work instead of them ...

Source C
Gladstone, writing in 1897 to the authors of a proposed series of *Essays on Liberalism.*

I regard the design formed by you and your friends with sincere interest, and in particular wish well to all the efforts you may make on behalf of individual freedom and independence as opposed to what is termed collectivism.

Source D
Politically, Gladstone's view was consistent. For the previous two decades he had seem politics and policies from the perspective of the Treasury. As Chancellor of the Exchequer he had been the codifier, legislator, and guardian of the canons of Peelite finance. Under his suzerainty the Treasury had become the guarantor of a 'minimalist' State.

No industrial economy can have existed in which the State played a smaller role than that of the United Kingdom in the 1860s . .

There were always ... substantial qualifications both in Gladstone's mind and in the minds of most mid-Victorians to the view that minimal 'interference' was the best government. It is probably the case that, although the minimalist State was achieved in Victorian Britain in the fullest form compatible with the social requirements of an industrialised population, none the less, in these qualifications were contained the assumptions which were to lead to its gradual disintegration ... Though many of the measures of Gladstone's first administration prepared the ground for future developments, these were not intentionally pursued, at least at Cabinet level ...

H.C.G. Matthew, *Gladstone 1809–1874*, 1986.

---

1 What do you understand by 'collectivism' (Source C) and 'minimalist' State' (source D)?
2 Consult sources B and C. Explain, and comment on, Mill's and Gladstone's view of the role of the State.
3 Examine the domestic legislation of Gladstone's first Ministry (1868–74) in the light of sources A, B, C and D:
a To what extent was its focus the freeing of the individual, and in what ways was the activity of the State extended?
b Discuss the view that there was little difference between Liberals and Conservatives in the principles of domestic legislation, 1868–80.

TALKING POINT

Gladstone's political opponents denounced him as a dangerous radical and demagogue, but he was really a conservative in politics and outlook. Comment on, and explain, this paradox.

13.2 'Gladstonian Liberalism' and 'Tory Democracy' – A decade of reform?

LIBERALS

Modernising the State

1870 Entry to the Civil Service was to be by public competitive examination. Only the Foreign Office was excluded.
1871 Abolition of purchase of commissions in the Army.
1872–73 Cardwell masterminds major reforms in the organisation and equipping of the army to remove the deficiencies highlighted during the Crimean War and by the Franco-Prussian War.
1873 Judicature Act rationalises the Law Courts.

Completion of Civil Equality

1871 Abolition of religious tests at Oxford and Cambridge for teaching fellows. Gladstone was reluctant to concede this reform.

Education

1870 Education Act:
1 School Boards could be set up in districts where school places were inadequate.
2 They were to provide elementary education.
3 Elected by ratepayers they could raise a school rate to finance their activities.
4 Pupils were to pay fees.
5 Boards had to pay the fees for children whose parents were too poor, even if they wished to attend Church Schools.
6 Religious teaching in Board Schools were restricted to simple Bible instruction. .

The Drink Question

1872 Licensing Act restricted opening hours and increased the powers of magistrates.

Social Reform

1871 Local Government Act set up the Local Government Board under a Minister with responsibility for health and Poor Law administration. A succession of lightweight and ineffective Ministers, and of governments eager to cut expenditure, ensured that this did not initiate a period of social reform.
1872 Local authorities compelled to appoint medical officers of health who were required to send detailed reports to the Local Government Board.

Labour Laws

1871 Trade Union Act legalised trade unions and gave their funds the same protection as Friendly Societies.
The Criminal Law Amendment Act reiterated the prohibition of picketing in the 1825 Trade Union Act. This legislation followed from the Royal Commission set up by the Derby government in 1867.
1872 Mines Act strengthened safety regulations and included arrangements for the weighing of coal to ensure proper wage payments.

Electoral Reform

1872 Ballot Act gave electors the protection of the secret ballot. This was a logical consequence of the 2nd Reform Act, and a concession to Bright which Gladstone did not like.

CONSERVATIVES

Education

1876 Sandon's Education Act made elementary education compulsory, but Conservative motives were political – to preserve voluntary Church schools and prevent the spread of School Boards into rural areas – rather than educational.

The Drink Question

1874 Licensing Act modified the 1872 Act by extending opening hours and reducing magistrates' powers. Many Conservatives were as concerned about the drink problem as the Liberals, although few were members of the United Kingdom Alliance.

Social Reform

1875 Artisan's Dwelling Act gave councils powers to undertake slum clearance. It was, noted Disraeli, 'our chief measure', but there was no compulsion and the legislation was largely ignored.

The Public Health Act was a major consolidating measure but there were no new principles in it. The Adulteration Act introduced regulations to control food abuse but local authorities were not required to appoint a public analyst.

The Friendly Societies Act set up a register but registration and regulation was voluntary.

The Agricultural Holdings Act was an attempt to give tenants the benefit of improvements they had made when farms changed hands.

1876 River Pollution Act lacked effective definitions and enforcement procedures.

The Merchant Shipping Act aimed to prevent the use of unseaworthy ships by shipowners, but without compulsion was ineffective. The Liberal Act of 1871 had been equally weak.

Labour Laws

1874 Factory Act further reduced hours of work but not to the full demand of the nine-hour day.

1875 Criminal Law Amendment Act repealed; the Conspiracy and Protection of Property Act legalised peaceful picketing.

The Employers and Workmen's Act removed the grievance of the Masters and Servants Act which made breach of contract a criminal offence.

1878 Factory Act was a consolidating measure.

TALKING POINT

Which government's legislation would appear to have most benefited the working class?

Gladstone's first ministry – the collapse of the Liberal coalition

GLADSTONE'S FIRST CABINET HAD BEEN, LORD KIMBERLY NOTED IN 1873, 'WONDERFULLY HARMONIOUS DURING OUR FOUR YEARS OF OFFICE AND POWER.' WHIGS PREDOMINATED; EIGHT OF THE FIFTEEN SAT IN THE HOUSE OF LORDS BUT JOHN BRIGHT'S APPOINTMENT AS PRESIDENT OF THE BOARD OF TRADE SHOWED THAT THE RADICALS AND NONCONFORMISTS HAD NOT BEEN FORGOTTEN. EDWARD CARDWELL, AT THE WAR OFFICE, WAS THE LAST OF GLADSTONE'S PEELITE COLLEAGUES. ROBERT LOWE, THE ADULLAMITE OF 1866–67, BECAME CHANCELLOR OF THE EXCHEQUER.

The government's record was impressive. Its reforms ranged from a Peelite concern for sound administration and government, to a Liberal challenge to the privileges of the aristocratic elite in favour of talent and ability; from Gladstone's honest attempt to conciliate Irish opinion to a major innovation in educational policy which recognised the failure of voluntarism to provide an all-embracing system of elementary schools. In foreign affairs Gladstone's unpopular concern with international law and morality contrasted with the aggressive populism of Palmerston.

Unfortunately the reform processes opened the divisions within the Liberal Party since the Government could not satisfy the aspirations and interests of all sections within it. Its Irish policies failed to win the confidence of the Irish, whilst alarming Whig landowners who feared the extension of the principles of the 1870 Land Act to England. Gladstone himself reluctantly agreed to the removal of religious tests at Oxford and the secret ballot.

The Education Act of 1870 unleashed a storm of vociferous protest from the government's Nonconformist supporters. By the late 1860s it was generally agreed that voluntary provision of elementary education for the masses was failing to meet the national need. The Reform Act (1867) and the rising spectre of German industrial competition gave added urgency. In Birmingham the National Education League proposed a national system of compulsory and free elementary schools from which the churches were

Voluntarism – that elementary schools should be provided by the churches and education societies, not by the State.

excluded; teaching would be entirely secular. The Anglican response was the National Education Union which sought to preserve the place of religious teaching.

The Nonconformist sense of betrayal stemmed from perceived threats to religious equality and freedom inherent in the Education Bill. They feared that denominational education, largely Anglican education, would be supported from the proposed school rate. The Cowper–Temple clause amended the Bill to exclude denominational religious teaching from new schools maintained by the School Boards. Proposals that School Boards could make grants to denominational schools were abandoned but, undetected by the Bill's opponents, clause 25 crept into law. This required School Boards to pay the school fees of pauper children at a school of their parents' choice, including the denominational schools. The government carried its Bill, but, as its critics regretfully pointed out, with the help of Conservative votes.

Nonconformist militants now demanded the exclusion of religious teaching from the schools as the only guarantee of religious liberty. The Central Nonconformist Committee and the National Education League organised a national opposition. School Board elections, and School Boards themselves, became battlegrounds. Liberal election candidates were asked to pledge themselves to the amendment of the Act to satisfy Nonconformist views, or forfeit Nonconformist support. This was one factor contributing to a series of by-election losses as the Ministry entered its declining years.

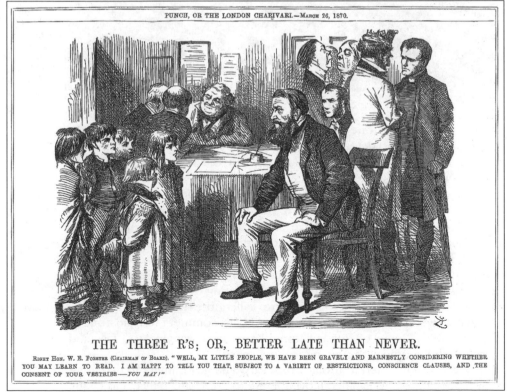

PUNCH, OR THE LONDON CHARIVARI.—March 26, 1870.

THE THREE R's; OR, BETTER LATE THAN NEVER.

Right Hon. W. E. Forster (Chairman of Board). "WELL, MY LITTLE PEOPLE, WE HAVE BEEN GRAVELY AND EARNESTLY CONSIDERING WHETHER YOU MAY LEARN TO READ. I AM HAPPY TO TELL YOU THAT, SUBJECT TO A VARIETY OF RESTRICTIONS, CONSCIENCE CLAUSES, AND THE CONSENT OF YOUR VESTRIES——*YOU MAY!*"

PUNCH'S COMMENT ON THE RELIGIOUS CONTROVERSIES SURROUNDING THE EDUCATION BILL. W.E. FORSTER, THE MINISTER RESPONSIBLE FOR THE BILL, WAS A NONCONFORMIST.

Temperance and trade union legislation also failed to satisfy the aspirations of the Ministry's supporters. The first attempt to legislate on drink had to be abandoned in 1871; the second got through Parliament but was unacceptable to the United Kingdom Alliance since there was to be no local veto. The trade unions had a wish to protect both workmen and employers from intimidation. Legal decisions on picketing and breach of contract after 1872 clearly defined the limitations on trade union activity and gave the Conservatives the opportunity to angle for discontented trade unionist votes.

TALKING POINT

Reconsider the weaknesses of the Gladstonian Liberal Party. To what extent was this government undermined by its attempts to reform and solve national problems?

Gladstone and the 1874 General Election

GALLANT CONDUCT OF THE POLICE.——HEROIC ATTACK UPON THE LITTLE MATCHMAKERS AND MATCHSELLERS ON THE THAMES EMBANKMENT.

LIBERAL MORALE WAS FURTHER UNDERMINED BY LOWE'S INCOMPETENCE AS CHANCELLOR OF THE EXCHEQUER. THE OPPOSITION TO HIS ATTEMPT TO TAX MATCHES IN 1871 SWUNG PUBLIC OPINION AGAINST THE GOVERNMENT IN AN EMOTIVE CAMPAIGN THAT EXPLOITED THE POVERTY OF THE MATCHMAKER AND MATCHSELLER. THE CHARGE OF HEARTLESSNESS WAS ADDED TO THE MINISTRY'S OTHER FAILINGS.

In March 1873 Gladstone tried to resign following the defeat of his Irish University Bill. The determined opposition of the Catholic Church in Ireland swung the Irish Catholic MPs against the measure. There were enough Whig rebels to ensure a majority of three for the Bill's opponents. Disraeli refused to form a Conservative administration since neither he nor his colleagues wanted to form yet another minority government. Disraeli could appear conservative and 'safe' whilst giving the Liberals more time to display their ineffectiveness and internal divisions

Outside Parliament the Radicals were beginning to put pressure on the leadership. Joseph Chamberlain advocated a programme of 'Free Church, Free Land, Free Schools and Free Labour', writing to Charles Dilke of the need to smash 'the whited sepulchre called the Liberal Party.' Whig misgivings were reflected in the Duke of Argyll's comment to Gladstone in January 1874: 'Some of our tail joints have been wagging too fast and alarming the people with their radical nonsense.'

Gladstone attempted to revitalise the Party and government in two ways. First he reshuffled his cabinet. moving Lowe to the Home Office and taking

There is more about the Irish University Bill on page 346.

PUNCH, OR THE LONDON CHARIVARI—August 9, 1873.

FRANCHISE FOR HODGE

GREAT AUTUMN MANŒUVRE.

Hodge. "LOR-A-MASSY, MR-ASTER! BE OI TO BE A 'POWER IN T' STE-ATE'? WHAT BE OI TO GET
BY THA-AT?"
Mr. G. "THAT, MY GOOD FRIEND, IS A MERE DETAIL. THE QUESTION IS, WHAT AM I TO GET
BY IT!!"

"In the Debate as to giving a vote to the Agricultural Labourer, Mr. FORSTER read a letter from the PREMIER, who declared that such extension;
of franchise was just and politic, and could not long be avoided. The question was thus taken up by Government, which much needs a 'good cry.'"

the Exchequer himself. Bright, who had resigned in 1870, was brought back as a pledge of good faith to the Nonconformists. It was more difficult to find the 'positive force to carry us forward as a body' (Gladstone to Bright, 14 August 1873).

Gladstone's return to the Exchequer was significant. He hoped that a financial policy of rigid economy leading to the eventual abolition of income tax would reunite the Party and attract those voters who had shown their disillusionment with the Liberals in recent by-elections. Unfortunately neither Cardwell nor Goschen were prepared to sanction the military and naval spending cuts Gladstone believed necessary. A cabinet crisis loomed. The Conservatives were also promoting doubts about the legality of Gladstone's position as Prime Minister and Chancellor of the Exchequer.

The decision to dissolve Parliament was totally unexpected, but to Gladstone it seemed advantageous:

> This day I thought of dissolution. Told Bright of it. In evening at dinner told Granville and Wolverton. All seemed to approve. My first thought of it was an escape from a difficulty. I saw on reflection that it was the best thing in itself.
>
> Gladstone's Diary, 20 January 1874.

Gladstone was gambling. He hoped to restore party unity, to win back public confidence and to rally the party around himself. If the electorate responded to his tax proposals, the resistance of the military spending departments would have been circumvented without a disastrous Cabinet crisis. In the event the divisions within the party proved to be less deep than anticipated, but the electorate was not tempted by the promise of lower taxes. The Prime Minister had misread the temper of the times.

On appointment to office MPs had to seek re-election in their constituencies. Liberal lawyers argued that, since Gladstone was already Prime Minister, that requirement did not apply. The Conservatives disagreed.

TALKING POINT

Why was abolition of income tax unlikely to tempt the voters enfranchised in 1867?

Examining the Evidence

The 1874 Election

1874 was a disaster for the Liberals. Their great majority of 1868 was converted into a minority of 52. what had gone wrong?

Source A

A Nonconformist revolt?

... for a Liberal Ministry to extend and enlarge at the public cost machinery constructed on a principle so vicious – to create new facilities at the public expense for maintaining it – to involve the nation still more deeply in the policy of sustaining sectarian religious teachers out of rates and taxes – this was contrary to all that we had a right to anticipate. ('Hear, hear,' and cheers.) It is a retrograde policy. (Hear, hear.) It is a policy which has secured for the Government, the enthusiastic approbation of Conservatives – (hear, hear) – but it is a policy which relieves Nonconformists from their old allegiance to the Liberal Party – ('hear, hear,' and loud cheers) and which requires us so to organise our political power as to prevent the Liberal party from ever inflicting a similar injury again on the principles of religious equality. (Renewed cheers.)

R.W. Dale, *The Politics of Nonconformity*, 1871.

R.W. Dale, a leading Birmingham Nonconformist minister, was a prominent member of the national Education League and campaigner against the Education Act.

Source B

PUNCH, OR THE LONDON CHARIVARI.—February 21, 1874.

BEER
BALLOT

NATIONAL SPRING MEETING. 1874.
THE FINAL HEAT.

HOW DOES *PUNCH* EXPLAIN THE ELECTION RESULT?

Talking Point

These sources present an unbalanced view of the 1874 election. What else is needed to reach a balanced conclusion?

1. What did Gladstone mean by 'a torrent of beer and gin' and 'the action of the Education Act'?

2. What was significant about the 'Ballot' (source B)?

3. What does source A tell us about the changing relationship between the Nonconformists, the Liberal Party and Gladstone?

4. Referring to these sources, and your broader knowledge of the period, discuss the reasons why the Liberals lost their majority in 1874.

Source C

Gladstone explains the result to his brother. February 1874.

We have been borne down in a torrent of gin and beer. Next to this has been the action of the Education Act of 1870, and the subsequent controversies. Many of the Roman Catholics have voted against us because we are not denominational; and many of the dissenters have at least abstained from voting because we are. Doubtless there have been other minor agencies; but these are the chief ones ...

The 1874 Election – the historical perspective

Although the National Education League had actively intervened in by-elections after 1870, Chamberlain used Bright's re-entry into the Cabinet as an excuse to suspend its campaign in the autumn of 1873. Chamberlain wanted a broader platform and programme from which to launch his own political ambitions. The 'Nonconformist Revolt' petered out because large numbers rejected militancy and were satisfied by candidates who promised to support the repeal of clause 25. Loyalty to Gladstone was still a powerful factor and the Liberal vote held up well in constituencies where Nonconformity was strong. It is an indication of Nonconformist weakness as a political force that they failed to dislodge W.E. Forster, the Minister responsible for the Education Act, in Bradford.

The shift of the drink trade to the Conservative side was not as immediate as Gladstone suggested. Much depended on local conditions and candidates from both parties were quizzed by publicans. Licensing legislation was not a Liberal monopoly and the 1872 Act had been supported from both sides. Historians would now discount the importance of the drink issue in 1874, and although they agree that there was a drift to Conservatism amongst publicans and brewers it was much slower than earlier writers implied,

> It was not so much the Gladstone government as the temperance movement and the gradual identification of the Liberal Party with the United Kingdom Alliance which finally drove the publicans into the Conservative camp.
>
> H.J. Hanham, *Elections and Party Management – Politics in the Time of Disraeli and Gladstone*, 1959.

> Far more important in explaining the change is the shifting allegiance of wealthy dissenters and of the propertied and educated classes in general. ... fears for the security of property were more important than the licensing question in weakening the Liberal Party, and received proportionately more attention in Disraeli's two famous speeches of 1872.
>
> B. Harrison, *Drink and the Victorians*, 1971.

> Abstentions on the 'left' of the party ... probably bear relatively little responsibility for the election defeat – which must rest squarely on those from the 'right' who retracted their support.
>
> J.P. Parry, *Democracy and Religion – Gladstone and the Liberal Party 1867–1875*, 1986.

Parry argues that the Whigs distrusted Gladstone's high churchmanship. Many on the right of the party were alarmed by the strident Nonconformist demand for disestablishment and were concerned at the National Education League's campaign for secular education in Board Schools. They feared that Gladstone would concede control of elementary education in Ireland to the Catholic Church to win votes if the election resulted in a 'hung' parliament.

Gladstone admitted in a reflective letter to the Queen that:

In and about the Metropolis there certainly appears to have been also a change of political sentiment in the shape of dislike to the Government ...

It was this movement of opinion in the new suburban areas that Disraeli appealed to. In 1874 the Conservatives won nineteen seats in London, Middlesex and Surrey. In 1865 they had only won two. Gladstone fought the election on a fiscal policy that was an outdated return to the Peelite policies followed since the 1840s. He never made that mistake again.

Examining the evidence

Disraeli and the Conservative revival

In 1868 Disraeli failed the only test of political leadership that mattered – he lost a general election. He was blamed for a Reform Act that had apparently given the electoral advantage to the Liberals. Ill-health, and a realisation that there was little the opposition could do about Irish church and land reform, led to him making infrequent appearances in the Commons. The old antipathy to his background and distrust of his flexible policies re-surfaced. A proposal that Lord Salisbury, who as Lord Cranborne had been his most vociferous Conservative opponent in 1867, should become leader of the party in the Lords, was a direct challenge to the party leader's authority. In January 1872 serious consideration was given to a plan to move the liberal-conservative Lord Derby into the party leadership.

1872 saw Disraeli once again taking the lead in the Commons. Two major public speeches followed which reasserted his position and silenced his critics.

Source A

The Conservative programme – extract from Disraeli's speech in Manchester, 3 April 1872.

...The Conservative Party are accused of having no programme of policy. If by a programme is meant a plan to despoil churches and plunder landlords, I admit we have no programme. If by a programme is meant a policy which assails or menaces every institution and every interest, every class and every calling in the country, then I admit we have no programme. But if to have a policy with distinct ends...be a becoming programme for a political party, then, I contend, we have an adequate programme...

The programme of the Conservative Party is to maintain the Constitution of the country ... The Constitution of England is not merely a Constitution in State, it is a Constitution in Church and State ...

Source B

Social reform – extract from the Manchester speech.

... in attempting to legislate upon social matters the great object is to be practical – to have before us some distinct aims and some distinct means by which they can be accomplished.

... I think that public attention as regards these matters ought to be concentrated upon sanitary legislation. That is a wide subject, and, if properly treated, comprises almost every consideration which has just claim upon legislative interference. Pure air, pure water, the inspection of unhealthy habitations, the adulteration of food, these and many kindred matters may be legitimately dealt with by the Legislature ... It is impossible to overrate the importance of the subject. After all, the first consideration of a minister should be the health of the people ...

Source C

The Conservative Party and the Empire – extract from his speech to the National Union of Conservative Associations at the Crystal Palace, 24 June 1872.

... there is another and second great object of the Tory Party. If the first is to maintain the institutions of the country, the second is ... to uphold the Empire of England. If you look to the history of this country since the advent of Liberalism ... you will find that there has been no effort so continuous, so subtle, supported by so much energy, and carried on with so much ability and acumen, as the attempt of Liberalism to effect the disintegration of the Empire of England.

Source D

'THE CONSERVATIVE PROGRAMME', *PUNCH*, 6 JULY 1872.

Source E

... in 1872 and 1873 Disraeli was able to do something that no Conservative leader had done since Peel: to present the party as having not only a distinctive colour and style, but also a broad-based appeal on the one hand to the working class, on the other – and this was much more important – to the forces of property everywhere, not simply the landed interest, as a bulwark against the harassing, disturbing, restless legislation of the Liberals. At the same time – and perhaps this was even more significant – he boldly staked the claim of the Conservatives to be 'the patriotic party', something that could never be established while Palmerston lived.

R. Blake, *The Conservative Party from Peel to Churchill,* 1970.

Source F

It was Disraeli's concern, as a general election became imminent, to present an essentially negative and quietist front adapted to appeal to those elements of the middle classes which were seeking a refuge from Radicals, and 'democracy'.

Smith, *Disraelian Conservatism and Social Reform,* 1967.

1   Referring to sources A, B and C what seem to be new elements in the Conservative programme, and what would Liverpool and Peel have found familiar?
2   Comment on *Punch*'s (source D) view of the Crystal Palace speech.
3   Referring to source C and to Chapter 14 explain what the Liberals had done, or had failed to do, that enabled Disraeli to claim the Conservatives as 'the patriotic party'.
4   Disraeli later asserted that it was not the job of an opposition to devise programmes and policies. What contradictions suggested in sources E and F made it essential there should be no commitments to legislation and reform? Explain your opinion.

The 1872 speeches did not provide a programme, but they pointed in a direction and gave a sense of purpose that had previously been lacking. To the negative defence of the constitution and attacks on the 'harassing' legislation of the Liberals were added the positive, but ill-defined, elements of imperialism and social reform. For a Party seeking to attract the propertied classes from the Liberals there was no place for a social reform programme. It would deter potential Conservative voters who wanted a respite from change and hoped to see the working class controlled not rewarded at their expense as tax- and rate-payers.

By being negative the Conservatives exploited the swing against the Liberals. The positive Conservative contribution to their victory lay not in policy but in organisation. Party organisation helped to give the Conservatives the crucial advantage in England where they needed a majority to counter-balance Liberal seats in Wales and Scotland. The successes in the larger English boroughs suggested that the Conservative working man did exist although there was a price to be paid for his support:

TALKING POINT

Disraeli was always strong on rhetoric and vision, but weak on detail. In the collected edition of his speeches the two from 1872 take up 45 pages; references to social questions and the Empire occupy a small proportion of them. Defence of the constitution, of the monarchy, of the Church, are the core themes.
Was there a new departure, or was it the old Conservative Party with some additions to attract new voters from the middle and working classes?

The Conservatives won 44 seats in boroughs with a population of more than 50,000 – an increase of 19 on 1868.

The elections in Lancashire have largely hinged upon 2 questions – the 9 Hours bill and the demands of the Trade Unionists. On both these points – every candidate for a borough constituency has had to promise compliance ...

W.R. Callender, successful Conservative candidate for Manchester, 1874.

How to satisfy these aspirations whilst retaining and exploiting the middle class drift to conservatism was the challenge facing the Conservatives in office.

Examining the evidence

Conservatives and social reform

Talking point

'The social reform measures of the Conservative Government were of varying quality and efficacy, but it would be safe to say on balance they did a great deal more good than harm.' (R. Blake, *Disraeli*, 1966)
'The impact of the legislation of 1874–6 on the condition of the people was doubtless beneficial, but it was hardly resounding.' (P. Smith, *Disraelian Conservatism and Social Reform*, 1967)
Review the legislation in the Focus on page 303 with these assessments in mind. What were the deficiencies of the Conservative legislation, and what nineteenth century values did they continue to reflect?

This period of Conservative social reform raises these questions:

1   Are the reforms evidence of Disraeli's concern for the working classes and of Tory Democracy in action?
2   Are they evidence of Disraeli's belief in 'one nation'?
3   Was there anything uniquely conservative about them?
4   How serious were Disraeli, and his Cabinet, about these social questions?

Source A
Disraeli's election address, *The Times*, 26 January 1874.
Gentlemen, I have endeavoured, and, if returned to Parliament, I shall ... continue to endeavour, to propose or support all measures calculated to improve the condition of the people of this Kingdom. But I do not think this great end is advanced by incessant and harassing legislation. The English people are governed by their customs as much as by their laws, and there is nothing they more dislike than unnecessary restraint and meddling interference in their affairs. Generally speaking, I should say of the Administration of the last five years that it would have been better for us all if there had been a little more energy in our foreign policy and a little less in our domestic legislation.

Source B

Richard Cross describes Disraeli's first Cabinet meeting.

From all his speeches, I had quite expected that his mind was full of legislative schemes, but such did not prove to be the case; on the contrary, he had to entirely rely on the various suggestions of his colleagues, and as they themselves had only just come into office, and that ... there was some difficulty in framing the Queen's Speech.

R.A. Cross, A Political History, 1903.

RICHARD CROSS WAS AN UNLIKELY CHOICE AS HOME SECRETARY. HE HAD HAD NO PREVIOUS MINISTERIAL EXPERIENCE. HIS APPOINTMENT REFLECTED THE IMPORTANCE OF LANCASHIRE TO THE CONSERVATIVES (HE WAS ONE OF THE LOCAL LEADERS) AND THE INFLUENCE OF LORD DERBY. HIS CAUTIOUS AND PRAGMATIC OUTLOOK SUITED A CABINET OF RELUCTANT REFORMERS. NEVER AN INNOVATOR, HE SUCCESSFULLY SUPERVISED THE WORK OF OTHERS.

Source C

FUN.—JUNE 13, 1874.

A SLOW CAB-INET.

Mrs. Britannia:—"COME, DO WAKE UP, AND MOVE ON, OR I MUST GET OUT AND DISCHARGE YOU."

'A SLOW CAB-INET', *PUNCH*, 13 JUNE 1874.

Source D

Disraeli speaking in the Commons at the end of the 1875 session.

... it has been a Session in which, as a Ministry, we were called upon to perform that ceremony ... 'redeeming your pledges'. During the five years that we spent in Opposition we endeavoured to impress upon the country our sincere convictions that the time had arrived when political change was no longer required, when the distribution of political power was no longer the problem to solve in this country, but that its intelligence and energy should be directed to the improvement and elevation of the condition of the people. (Cheers.) ... Well, then, when we had acceded to power it became our first duty . ... you bring into practice that policy ...

1 Consult sources A and D. What had this government done to redeem its pledges by the end of 1875?
2 How does source B suggest that Disraeli did not place great importance on social reform issues?
3 Consult sources B and C, then refer to source A. How do they help to explain the rush of legislation in 1875?
4 Compare source D with source B. How honest was Disraeli in 1875, and what 'myth' was he helping to create?

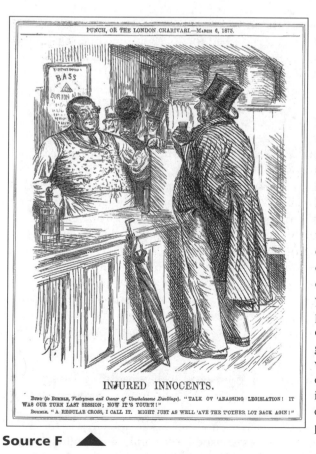

'INJURED INNOCENTS', *PUNCH*, 6 MARCH 1875.

EXPLAIN 'ARASSING LEGISLATION' AND 'A REGULAR CROSS'; WHAT JUSTIFICATION DID 'BUNG' AND 'BUMBLE' HAVE FOR THEIR COMPLAINTS?

Source F ▲

Source E

Disraeli speaking during the debate on the Artisans' Dwelling Bill, 1875.

...permissive legislation is the characteristic of a free people. It is easy to adopt compulsory legislation when you have to deal with those who only exist to obey; but in a free country, and especially in a country like England, you must trust to persuasion and example as the two great elements, if you wish to effect any considerable change in the manners and customs of the people.

Source G

Disraeli comments on government legislation in a letter to Queen Victoria in July 1875.

... they will greatly content the mass of the people; and reduce the materials for social agitation.

Sir George Elliot, the greatest employer of labour in your Majesty's dominions, assured Mr Disraeli ... that a very great and benevolent change had come over the feelings of the working classes; perceiving as they do, that the object of all the measures of the present Ministry is really to elevate their condition and mitigate their lot.

---

5 Consult source E. How is this view likely to limit the scope of Conservative social reform, and how far does it differ from those of J.S. Mill and Gladstone on pages 300–301?

6 What other motive for social reform is suggested by sources G?

7 Referring to all the sources and using your wider knowledge comment on each of the four questions that opened this Examining the Evidence section.

Source H

... Not until 1872 did he [Disraeli] seriously attempt to make political capital out of support for the improvement of the social condition of the people ... but he understood the need for caution to reconcile its pursuit with the interests and prejudices of his existing and potential followers of the propertied classes, and knew that the emphasis of the Conservative platform must like rather on the furtherance of the common cause of all classes than on the special promotion of the welfare of one ...

The government of 1874–80 was responsible for one of the most notable instalments of social reform of the century ... To some extent, these achievements were the product of a deliberate intention to use social improvement as a means of gaining working-class favour. But very largely they were semi-enforced responses to problems which ministers could not ignore, shaped principally by the results of formal inquiry, the pressure of public opinion, and the promptings of the civil service. They implemented no programme and embodied no philosophy. Nearly all were cautious and limited, and some were weak and ineffectual ... Only the labour laws of 1875 went substantially beyond what the immediate situation demanded ... as a whole, the measures ... form an impressive corpus of work ... but what they symbolise is less Conservative zeal for social reform than Conservative empiricism in the face of concrete problems.

P. Smith, *Disraelian Conservatism and Social Reform*, 1967.

Source I

His [Disraeli's] motives were hard-nosed as well as romantic. He feared for the future of the race, if the slums were to continue to breed teeming new generations with inferior bodies, minds and morals. He was acutely afraid of revolutionary societies and plots, and he was anxious to win the assent of the working class to the established economic and political order, without making concessions which might actually damage the position and resources of his propertied supporters ... To this end, he sought to remove unnecessary grievances and to restore and sustain the state of harmony between rich and poor, employer and employee, which he held to be the natural state of society. The social reform programme of 1874–6 was a sustained gesture in that direction ...

J.K. Walton, *Disraeli*, 1990.

8 In what ways do these historians qualify the view that Disraeli's second Ministry was a great social reform government? How do they interpret Disraeli's role?

9 **Essay**
'Disraeli's domestic policy during his second ministry was designed more to appeal to the voters than to secure social improvements.' How far would you agree with this statement?

Comment

The credit for most of the practical details rests with Cross. The other ministers responsible for domestic departments were largely ineffective. After 1876 Disraeli's attention was diverted into foreign and imperial affairs which he found much more congenial.

The great difficulty was the possible cost of social reform. A government hoping to win the propertied classes to its side could not be seen to be increasing taxes and rates. In their early years of government the Conservatives matched the Liberals in the savagery with which expenditure was slashed.

It is significant that the most successful pieces of legislation were the labour law reforms of 1875. Disraeli backed Cross in his willingness to adopt the proposals of the minority report from the 1874 Royal Commission on Trade Unions against the misgivings of the rest of the Cabinet. The two acts gave the trade unions everything they had demanded before the general election, but even here there was a fair degree of agreement with the Liberals who had been considering similar proposals in 1873. The Conservatives did not reap the political reward Disraeli had anticipated. By removing a point of difference between the Liberal leadership and their working class followers, the legislation contributed to that party's reunion.

TALKING POINT

Using examples from the politicians you have studied (e.g. Liverpool, O'Connell, Peel, Disraeli) discuss the criteria that could be used to measure political success or failure.

REVIEW

Disraeli – lucky opportunist or political failure?

Disraeli's influence reaches out to the modern Conservative Party:

Social policy is not socialism. It is a cheap slur or perhaps a muddled mind to try and connect the two. We Conservatives have possessed a social policy ever since Disraeli, more than a century ago.

Edward Heath, quoted in *The Guardian*, 25 May 1989.

Yet Disraeli was an outsider who reached the premiership, in spite of the political system, as the consequence of a series of accidents. He made his own political creed which was not based on inherited values and attitudes – 'all my opinions ... have been the result of reading and thought.'

His opponents only saw the unprincipled opportunist whilst his friends frequently doubted the firmness of his political opinions. To what extent was he a cynical charlatan deviously working out a powerful sense of personal ambition?

In a *History Today* article (October 1981) John Vincent asked 'Was Disraeli a failure?'

In this review section, you should be referring back to the sections on Disraeli's early career and forward to Chapter 14 on the foreign and imperial policies of his 1874–80 administration.

The myth of the Conservative hero emerged soon after Disraeli's death in 1881. The Primrose League, founded in 1883, adopted his 'one nation' slogan and provided many activists for the Party in the age of mass politics.

The successes of the Conservative hero	The failures of political judgement or miscalculation
Masterminding the miracle of 1867.	The electoral disaster of 1868 tarnished that.
He gave the party an aura of social concern.	After the 1875 session he opted for domestic peace, and turned to foreign and imperial affairs. The reform record was not used in the 1880 election campaign.
He provided the rhetoric of imperialism, and ensured that the Palmerston mantle fell to the Conservatives.	Imperialism turned sour with his government's failure to control its officials in India and South Africa.
Between 1875 and 1878 he showed that Britain could not be ignored by the European powers. The Congress of Berlin was his triumph.	Britain did not possess the military strength to force her view on the great powers. His bluff from a weak position was not challenged.
With his encouragement Gorst created an effective party organisation.	He let it fall into disuse and decay after 1874. Gorst resigned.
He created a party that had a style and rhetoric that and distinguished it from the Liberals – a party of stability and moderation.	As party leader he only won one election – 1874, and then only because of Liberal disunity. He expected to win in 1880.
He recognised that the Conservatives needed to appeal to the middle classes and to a proportion of the working class.	He never understood the urban middle class, and ignored their MPs; he wanted working class votes, but feared the policies that might imply. His party remained aristocratic and 'conservative'.

1 Political success, or political failure? Write a political obituary for Disraeli.
2 Comment on these contrasting views of Disraeli's political career:
a successful but unprincipled 'adventurer'
b 'blatant careerist'
c failure whose reputation was saved by the party's need for a 'hero' figure.

14 Foreign and Imperial Affairs in the Age of Gladstone and Disraeli

PREVIEW

Differing Approaches

Source A

Although Disraeli was elevated to the peerage as Earl of Beaconsfield in 1876, he is referred to throughout as Disraeli. His political opponents attacked his foreign and imperial policies as 'Beaconsfieldism'.

PUNCH, OR THE LONDON CHARIVARI.—MARCH 27, 1880.

THE CHOICE OF HERCULES.

THIS CARTOON APPEARED AFTER THE DISSOLUTION OF PARLIAMENT IN MARCH 1880.

Source B
Gladstone speaking in Edinburgh during his Midlothian Campaign, November 1879.

... the great duty of a government, especially in foreign affairs, is to soothe and tranquillise the minds of the people, not to set up false phantoms of glory which delude them into calamity, not to flatter their infirmities by leading them to believe that they are better than the rest of the world, and so to encourage the baleful spirit of domination; but to proceed upon a principle that recognises the sisterhood and equality of nations, the absolute equality of public right among them; above all, to endeavour to produce and to maintain a temper so calm and so deliberate in the public opinion of the country, that none shall be able to disturb it. But the conduct of the present government [Disraeli's 2nd Ministry] has been exactly the reverse. Their business has been to appeal to pride and to passion, to stir up those very feelings which every wise man ought to endeavour to allay

Gladstonianism – Putting Morality in Foreign Policy, 1868–1874

Gladstone had always been bitterly opposed to what he regarded as Palmerston's deliberately aggressive and provocative stance towards foreign states, and his readiness to exploit nationalist xenophobia for political purposes. His had been the most telling speech against the Foreign Secretary during the Don Pacifico debate (1851), and he had voted against Palmerston's government in the censure motions of 1856 and 1858. He wanted to inaugurate a new era in international relations through a return to conference diplomacy and the general acceptance of a code of international law which would enable the nations to settle disputes peaceably.

Lord Clarendon was Gladstone's first Foreign Secretary. He was followed, in July 1870, by Lord Granville. The relationship between Gladstone and Granville was especially close and this gave the Prime Minister some influence over policy. Gladstone's approach was outlined in an article published in 1870:

Certain it is that a new law of nations is gradually taking hold of the mind, and coming to sway the practice, of the world; a law which recognises independence, which frowns on aggression, which favours the pacific, not the bloody settlement of disputes, which aims at permanent and not temporary adjustment; above all, which recognises, as a tribunal of paramount authority, the general judgement of civilised mankind. It has censured the aggression of France; it will censure, if need arise, the greed of Germany. It is hard for all nations to go astray. Their ecumenical council sits above the partial passions of those, who are misled by interest, and disturbed by quarrel. The greatest triumph of our time, a triumph in a region loftier that that of electricity or steam, will be the enthronement of this idea of Public Right, as the governing ideal of European policy.

Gladstone in an article, 'Germany, France and England', published anonymously in the *Edinburgh Review*, October 1870.

TALKING POINT

What are the dangers for historians in using the speeches of politicians as evidence for the politics of their time?

1 How does Gladstone's view of foreign policy seem to differ from that adopted by the government?
2 What is *Punch* suggesting about the nature of the coming electoral contest and the likely issues?

TALKING POINT

During the 1874 election campaign, Disraeli complained that the Gladstone government had neglected British interests and damaged the Empire. In what way might the tone of Gladstone's language add substance to this charge?

An Opportunist in Action – Disraeli and Foreign Policy

On 17 November 1875 Disraeli persuaded his Cabinet to authorise the purchase the Suez Canal shares put on the market by the bankrupt Khedive of Egypt. It was his personal triumph, managed, against the misgivings of his colleagues, with speed and secrecy to prevent the shares falling into the hands of the French. Britain's 44 per cent of the Canal Company shares was not the controlling interest Disraeli boasted of, but a crucial investment in a seaway dominated by British traffic to India and Australasia. It was the grand gesture that Disraeli excelled at, a clear assertion of British power and imperial greatness, a purchase, he told the Commons, 'necessary to maintain the Empire.'

PUNCH, OR THE LONDON CHARIVARI.—FEBRUARY 26, 1876.

THE LION'S SHARE.

"GARE À QUI LA TOUCHE!"

WHAT, ACCORDING TO *PUNCH*, WAS THE SIGNIFICANCE OF THE SUEZ CANAL SHARE PURCHASE?

Disraeli's diplomatic interventions displayed the same qualities. Foreign policy was the most important task for the statesman, and after 1875 it almost exclusively occupied his attention. His 1872 speeches had not, however, suggested the direction of future Conservative policy. Lord Blake has suggested that when Disraeli 'took office in 1874 it is doubtful whether he had any clear ideas on foreign policy other than doing something ... to reassert Britain's power in Europe' (*Disraeli*, 1966) Others have seen his purpose as simply 'the need ... to maintain the British Empire and the prestige of England throughout the world' (R. Millman, *Britain and the Eastern Question 1875–1878*, 1979). Certainly he wanted to escape from the diplomatic isolation inherited from the Liberals, and to reverse the alleged inactivity of the previous six years. He wanted Britain to play the independent role in European affairs that her interests demanded. Initially he 'set his sights on the disruption of the Dreikaiserbund' which seemed to allow Germany, Austria-Hungary and Russia to dominate European affairs without consulting the other European powers.

TALKING POINT

Both Disraeli and Gladstone were interventionists in European and international affairs. Why, then, did they find agreement on foreign policy impossible?

FOCUS

14.1 A Changing World – Background to Foreign and Imperial Policies after 1870

The New Realities

1860: Italy was united, a process completed by completed by the occupation of Rome in 1870. Italy offered no economic or political challenge to Britain.

1865: The American Civil War ended. High wartime tariffs were never relaxed; a state united from Pacific to Atlantic, from Mexico to Canada, was likely to become a serious economic rival.

1871: The declaration of the German Empire at Versailles completed the unification of Germany. The balance of power in Europe was broken. France had suffered the humiliation of defeat, Austria-Hungary was subordinate to Germany whilst Russia was turning to expansion in Asia. The old equilibrium on which foreign policy had been based since 1815 was overthrown.

The Imperial Challenge

In times past ... we did what we pleased, where we pleased, and as we pleased. The whole of heathendom ... was our inheritance, and the salt sea our peculiar possession. All that has changed. Europe has overflowed into Africa, Asia, America, Australasia and the Pacific. At every turn we are confronted with the gunboats, the sea lairs, or the colonies of jealous and eager rivals ... The world is filling up around us. ...Europe ... throws off ever increasing swarms to settle in other continents ... we now find every ocean highway furrowed by European ironclads, while over many a colonial frontier frowns the cannon of Continental rivals.

Pall Mall Gazette, 4 February 1885.

TALKING POINT

Referring to the evidence in this Focus, consider the view that the British imperialism of the last quarter of the nineteenth century was a defensive reaction to new uncertainties and challenges. Was Britain really in decline?

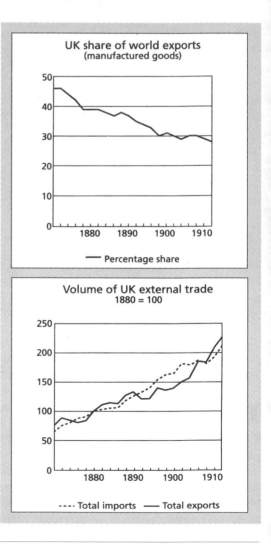

The Commercial Challenge

Referring to the statistics in this focus, account for the concerns reflected in this cartoon from 1896. Free Trade, the doctrine of Britain's economic primacy in the mid-nineteenth century, reached its international apogee with the commercial treaty Cobden negotiated with the French in 1860. The developing economies of Europe and the United States were protected behind high tariff barriers. British traders and manufacturers found themselves facing intense competition in world markets which they had previously dominated, and in which the foreigner had acquired an unfair advantage.

The Fair Trade League (1881) was both a response to the challenge and a demand for political action. Few politicians, however, were willing to question Free Trade orthodoxy.

Economic indicators, 1875-1913

	% of world production		
	Steel	Pig Iron	Sulphuric Acid
	1875–79	**1875–79**	**1878**
Great Britain	35.9	46.0	46.2
Germany	16.6	12.7	8.6
USA	26.6	15.6	13.8
	1910–13	**1910–13**	**1913**
Great Britain	10.3	13.9	13.0
Germany	22.7	21.0	20.3
USA	42.3	40.2	27.1

PUNCH, OR THE LONDON CHARIVARI—September 5, 1896.

CAUGHT NAPPING!

THERE WAS AN OLD LADY AS I'VE HEARD TELL, | SHE WENT TO MARKET ON A MARKET DAY | BY CAME A PEDLAR—GERMAN—AND STOUT,
SHE WENT TO MARKET HER GOODS FOR TO SELL, | AND SHE FELL ASLEEP ON THE WORLD'S HIGHWAY. | AND HE CUT HER PETTICOATS ALL ROUND ABOUT.

14.2 The Russian Dimension – the Eastern Question and India

THE CYPRUS CONVENTION, 1878, GAVE BRITAIN AN ADVISORY ROLE IN THE DEFENCE OF THE OTTOMAN EMPIRE'S FRONTIER IN ARMENIA. RUSSIAN PENETRATION HERE WOULD THREATEN THE IMPERIAL COMMUNICATION ROUTES TO INDIA. THE TURKS HAD TO BE GIVEN A DEFENSIBLE FRONTIER TO KEEP RUSSIA AWAY FROM THE PERSIAN GULF. INDIA ITSELF SEEMED AT RISK AS THE RUSSIANS EXTENDED THEIR EMPIRE IN CENTRAL ASIA AND BUILT STRATEGIC RAILWAYS. CONTROL OF AFGHANISTAN SEEMED ESSENTIAL TO PROTECT THE 'JEWEL IN THE CROWN'.

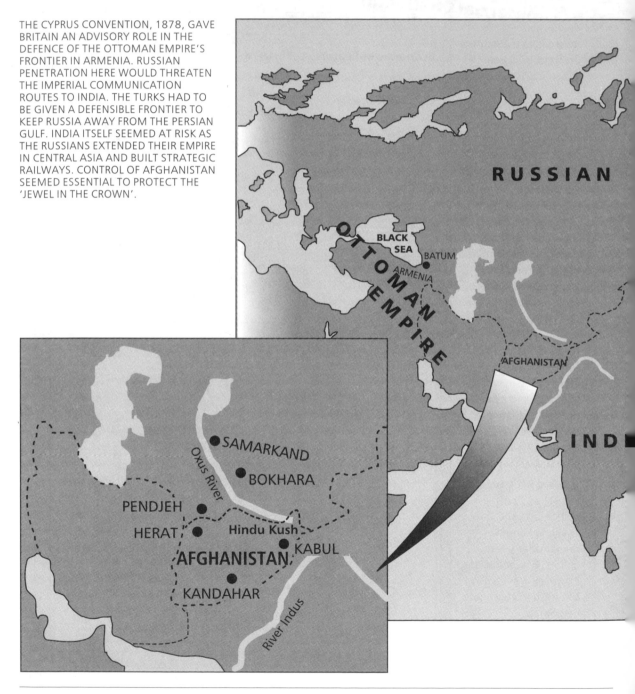

Russia is profoundly distrusted, and not without reason. She is profoundly disliked, and not without reason also.

The Times, 8 February 1878.

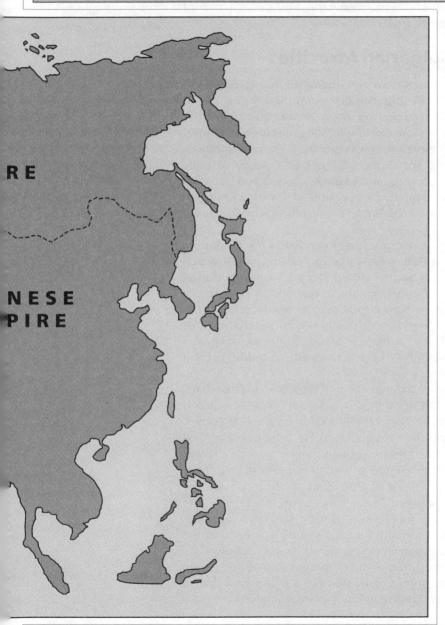

RE

NESE
PIRE

Suspicion of Russia and her intentions towards the declining Ottoman Empire had been a constant thread running through foreign policy. Distrust was compounded by a popular aversion which equated all things Russian with tyranny, epitomised by the crushing of Polish liberties and rebellions in 1831 and 1863.

Castlereagh, Canning and Palmerston all had to face the Russian threat to Constantinople. The Crimean War (1854–56) had been fought to preserve the territorial integrity and independence of the Ottoman Empire against Russian pressure and aggression. The neutralisation of the Black Sea, renounced by Russia in 1871, served two purposes. It protected Constantinople from Russian attack, and removed a potential threat to British naval pre-eminence in the eastern Mediterranean. The 'Crimean Policy' of propping up Turkey assumed that the Porte could reform itself and the system of government it imposed on the European peoples in the Balkans. Palmerston had maintained this view since the 1830s. During the crisis of 1875–8 Disraeli was the last British minister to follow the old Palmerstonian policy.

The work of Castlereagh, Canning and Palmerston is discussed in Chapter 9.

Britain and the Eastern Question, 1875–78

The British government reluctantly accepted the Andrassy Note (December 1875) because the Turks requested it. Disraeli was concerned that Britain had not been consulted by Austria-Hungary, Germany and Russia before the Note had been published, had no sympathy with Balkan nationalism and was unhappy about possible parallels with the British position in Ireland. Britain's rejection of the Berlin Memorandum (May 1876) was much more explicit, and was accompanied by the dispatch of the fleet to Besika Bay, just outside the Dardanelles.

The Impact of the Bulgarian Atrocities

Rumours of the violent suppression of the Bulgarian revolt began to circulate early in May 1876. On 23 June the first confirmed report of the massacres and atrocities appeared in the *Daily News*. Misled by the Foreign Office and its officials in Constantinople, the government assured MPs and the Queen that the reports were exaggerated. These assurances did not satisfy those amongst the Nonconformist and Anglo-Catholic communities who were becoming increasingly concerned at the immorality of a British policy which, by its support for the Ottoman Empire, seemed to be sanctioning the horrors inflicted on the Bulgarian Christian communities.

Nevertheless, when the parliamentary session ended at the beginning of August there was no sign of that great surge in public opinion which was to stir Gladstone into action and to curtail Disraeli's options during the rest of 1876 and into 1877. Gladstone's initial response in the debate of 31 July had disappointed those who hoped that he would provide the political leadership needed if government policy was to be changed. At end of August, however, influenced by W.T. Stead, Nonconformist and radical editor of the *Northern Echo*, there was a rash of public protest meetings.

On 29 August Gladstone wrote to Granville that he was 'in half, perhaps a little more than half, a mind to write a pamphlet'. *The Bulgarian Horrors and the Question of the East* rapidly sold over 200,000 copies. Remembered for its plea that the Turks should be expelled 'bag and baggage' 'from the province they have desolated and profaned', it was wrongly assumed that Gladstone wanted to sweep the Ottoman Empire out of Europe. In fact he argued for a settlement of the crisis by the Concert of Europe which he believed Disraeli was trying to disrupt. The anti-atrocity campaign gathered momentum during the early autumn. Whilst Gladstone advocated alliance with Russia, Disraeli, worried that the atrocities would encourage Russian intervention to protect fellow slavs and Orthodox Christians, warned her of the consequences of any action that might threaten Constantinople. Constantinople was the vital British interest, the fate of the Ottoman Empire in Europe was immaterial.

TALKING POINT

'British obsession with the Eastern Question stemmed from ancient habit rather than clear thought.' (R. Blake, *Disraeli*, 1966)
As you work through this section, consider this view, and discuss its appropriateness.

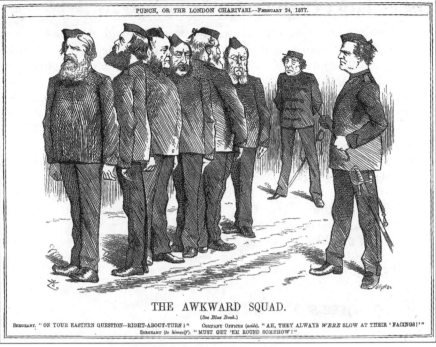

PUNCH, OR THE LONDON CHARIVARI—February 24, 1877.

THE AWKWARD SQUAD.
(See Blue Book.)

Sergeant. "ON YOUR EASTERN QUESTION—RIGHT-ABOUT-TURN!"　Company Officer (aside). "AH, THEY ALWAYS WERE SLOW AT THEIR 'FACINGS!'"
Sergeant (to himself). "MUST GET 'EM ROUND SOMEHOW!"

The Russo-Turkish War, 1877–78

Salisbury was undermined by the Turcophile British ambassador at Constantinople, Sir Henry Elliot.

Derby proposed that the great powers should meet in Constantinople (January 1877) to force a settlement on the Turks. Salisbury, chosen as the British representative, believed that agreement with the Russians was essential. He was ignored by the Turks who refused to accept he truly represented a government which had sent a fleet (it appeared) to sustain them, and he was accused of being manipulated by the Panslavist Russian ambassador Ignatiev. Confident that they could rely on British support in a crisis the Turks rejected the Conference's demands.

Exasperated by Turkish prevarication, Russia finally declared war in April 1877. the state of public opinion and Cabinet divisions ensured that Disraeli could not take the steps to deter Russia that both he and the Queen felt were necessary.

Disraeli directed foreign policy, ignoring his foreign secretary, schemed for an alliance with Austria, proposed military action, and the movement of ships to Gallipoli as a warning to the Russians. Derby responded by working with the Russian ambassador, Shuvalov, to prevent the war he believed Disraeli was intent on provoking.

After their capture of Plevna (December 1877), the Russians advanced rapidly towards the Straits and Constantinople. Parliament was recalled to provide a vote of credits (£6 million) as a mild warning to Russia. On 21 January 1878 the fleet was ordered to Constantinople. Derby and Carnarvon resigned. The order was cancelled and Derby withdrew his resignation. Neither Britain nor Russia wanted to fight but suspicions grew as the Russians refused armistices and rushed on to Constantinople. Growing anxieties about Russian intentions moved Salisbury closer to Disraeli and away from Derby.

The Treaty of San Stefano

The terms of the treaty between the Russians and the Turks were published on 23 March 1878. They were unacceptable to both Austria-Hungary and Britain. It was feared that the proposed 'Big' Bulgaria, with access to the Aegean Sea and the Mediterranean, and in which Bulgars would be a minority, would become a Russian satellite. Although Turkey in Europe survived it was so truncated that Constantinople had become undefendable. In the East Russian gains in Armenia threatened the Persian Gulf.

On 27 March the Cabinet agreed to pressurise Russia into submitting the whole treaty to a European Congress. The reserves were called up and a contingent of Indian troops moved to Malta. Derby finally resigned. The cabinet was a united at last. Public opinion was swinging in the government's favour. In Salisbury Disraeli had a foreign secretary who had a clear purpose and the ability to see it through. An exhausted Russia was not in a position to call Britain's bluff – the threat of war was enough to force a climb down.

The Congress of Berlin

The Congress (July 1878) was Disraeli's great triumph. Britain was no longer isolated, and the crisis had sufficiently strained relations between Russia, Austria-Hungary and Germany for Disraeli to feel that their alliance was damaged beyond repair. Most of the contentious issues were resolved before the Congress met in preliminary negotiations between Salisbury, the Russians and the Austrians, although Disraeli was able to make his opinion felt as the Treaty was finalised.

The 'Big' Bulgaria of San Stefano was split into three parts to give the Ottoman Empire a defensible frontier in the Balkan Mountains. Salisbury also negotiated the 'Cyprus Convention' directly with Constantinople. As a result, Britain acquired Cyprus as a naval base in return for providing military advisors to assist the Turks in their defence of Armenia against possible Russian attack. The Turks promised reforms in the administration of their Asiatic territories.

It was, claimed Disraeli, 'peace with honour.' Constantinople had been saved, Turkey in Europe preserved and Britain had gained Cyprus.

But did Constantinople really matter any more? In 1882 Gladstone's second government occupied Egypt, and firmly focused British attention on direct control of the Canal. Gladstone had condemned the Cyprus Convention. He withdrew the military advisors in 1880, but did not return the island to the Ottoman Empire. Cyprus was never developed into the Eastern Mediterranean naval base that Salisbury had envisaged. Relations with the Ottoman Empire were irrevocably soured. Balkan nationalism, despite Disraeli's fears, proved a better obstacle to Russian expansionism than the Ottoman Empire. When Eastern Rumelia merged with Bulgaria in 1885 there was no opposition from Britain.

TALKING POINT

'The commonest error in politics is sticking to the carcasses of dead policies.' (Lord Salisbury to Lord Lytton, March 1877). What do you think he meant, and, in the context of this crisis, was he right?

Examining the Evidence

British Aims and Objectives

Source A

Extract from Disraeli's 'Memorandum on his Eastern Policy' to Queen Victoria, 16 May 1876.

Mr Disraeli fears that we are being drawn step by step, into participating in a scheme, which must end very soon in the disintegration of Turkey.

Though we may not be able to resist the decision of the three Military Empires, he does not think that we ought to sanction or approve, their proposals.

It is almost a mockery for them to talk of a desire, that the Powers should 'act in concert' and then exclude France, Italy, and England from their deliberations, and ask us by telegraph to say yes or not to propositions, which we have never heard discussed.

Moreover it is asking us to sanction them in putting a knife to the throat of Turkey, whether we like it or not.

Source B

Report of Disraeli's comments to Lord Barrington, October 1876.

England might take Egypt and so secure our highway to India. But ... If the Russians had Constantinople, they could at any time march their Army to the mouth of the Nile, and then what would be the use of our holding Egypt? Not even the command of the sea could help us under such circumstances. People who talk in this manner must be utterly ignorant of geography. Our strength is on the sea. Constantinople is the Key to India, and not Egypt and the Suez Canal.

G.E. Buckle, *The Life of Benjamin Disraeli, Vol. 6*, 1920.

Source C

Lord Salisbury criticises government policy in a letter to Lord Lytton (Viceroy of India), 15 June 1877.

... On your view that Turkey is sustainable, and that Russia is the real danger of the future, the old Crimean policy should have been clearly avowed and followed from the first. The view which after two years study of the subject commends itself as the true one in my mind, differs from this. The Russian power appears to me feeble: and I do not think any protection could have set the Turk upon his legs again. I would have devoted my whole effort to securing the waterway to India – by the acquisition of Egypt or Crete: and would in no way have discouraged the obliteration of Turkey ...

Source D

... He [Disraeli] wished to preserve as much of Turkey as he could, stop the Russians entering Constantinople, break up the Dreikaiserbund, if possible without war, though he did not flinch at war if there was no alternative. He succeeded in his object, despite the divisions of the Cabinet, despite the opposition of Derby ... despite the deep divisions in the country, despite Gladstone and despite his own bad health.

... judged by the criteria of tactical skill and achievement of objectives, Disraeli's foreign policy was an undoubted success.

R. Blake, *Disraeli*, 1966.

TALKING POINT

Too often foreign policy was influenced by a poor knowledge of basic geography, and by a use of maps with too small a scale. How significant were these failings in explaining British policy 1875–78, and towards Russian expansion into Asia?

1 What, according to sources A and B, appear to be the aims of, and justification for, Disraeli's policy in the Balkans, 1875–78?

2 Consult sources B and C. What differences in policy and opinion do they suggest existed in Cabinet by 1877? Using your wider knowledge, explain Salisbury's priorities.

Source E

The Congress of Berlin was in a way a fitting climax to the career of the Prime Minister. From the beginning of the Eastern crisis he had fought for his image of the greatness of Britain ... If he and Salisbury had not exactly brought back peace with honour they had secured peace with prestige...

R. Millman, *Britain and the Eastern Question*, 1979.

Source F

Beaconsfield's empty role at Berlin aptly symbolised the speciousness of his ultimate achievement in foreign affairs. Turkey-in-Europe was saved; but more of it could have been saved at the Constantinople Conference ... and more of it still at the time of the Berlin Memorandum. The division of the two Bulgarias in any case lasted only until 1884. Otherwise nothing substantial was achieved except perhaps to please the 'national' public. Above all, the re-imposition of a Palmerstonian European credit was not attained. Berlin, far from inaugurating a new era of concert politics, in fact inaugurated, in 1879, the first of the alliances – the Austo-German alliance – which indicated definitively the direction in which the post-concert system of Europe would ... find its logical expression

R. Shannon, *The Crisis of Imperialism: 1865–1915*, 1974.

---

3 Compare and contrast the views of the historians in sources D, E and F.

4 Essay

'A strategic retreat brilliantly concealed by ... the propagandist effect of 'Peace with Honour' and the spoils won through the Cyprus Convention ...' (R.W. Seton-Watson, *Gladstone, Disraeli and the Eastern Question*, 1935); 'an undoubted success', or merely 'peace with prestige'? Discuss Disraeli's handling of the Eastern crisis, and his achievement, using your wider knowledge and referring to the sources.

Disraeli and Imperialism

Disraeli's motives in appropriating the imperial theme in his 1872 speeches have been much debated. Those who accuse him of political opportunism can point to a letter written to Lord Malmesbury in 1852:

these wretched colonies will all be independent, too, in a few years, and are a millstone round our necks.

He also described the self-governing North American colonies as 'deadweights' in 1866. On other occasions he had extolled the benefits Britain gained from her Empire, in particular from the possession of India. It was the grand sweep of ideas that enthused Disraeli, not the details of colonial and imperial policy. For him the Empire was important because it reflected and enhanced the power and greatness of the country, and was a visible expression of that power.

The day is coming ... when the question of the balance of power cannot be confined to Europe alone ... Remember always that England, though she is bound to Europe by tradition, by affection, by great similarity of habits ... is not a mere power of the Old World. Her geographical position, her laws, her language and religion, connect her as much with the New World as the Old...

Speech at Aylesbury, 1859.

TALKING POINT

'...it was the part the possession of empire could play in assisting Great Britain's role in world affairs that interested him [Disraeli] most ...' (C.C. Eldridge, *England's Mission*, 1973). Consider this view after you have worked through the section on the imperial policies of this government.

This theme was reiterated in his Crystal Palace speech of 1872 when he denounced those

> ... who ... looked upon the Colonies of England, looked even upon our connection with India, as a burden upon this country, viewing everything in a financial aspect, and totally ignoring those moral and political considerations which make nations great ... no Minister in this country will do his duty who neglects any opportunity of reconstructing as much as possible our Colonial Empire, and of responding to those distant sympathies which may become the source of incalculable strength ... to this land...

When Disraeli formed his government in 1874 there was no imperial policy. Disraeli left the details and decisions to Lord Carnarvon, the Colonial Secretary. Liberal initiatives were followed through in West Africa, Fiji and South East Asia. Like their predecessors the government continued to resist pressure from trading, religious and humanitarian interests for intervention and expansion. In 1879, however, it was Disraeli's imperialism that aroused the ire of Gladstone in his Midlothian campaign.

PUNCH, OR THE LONDON CHARIVARI.—April 15, 1876.

"NEW CROWNS FOR OLD ONES!"

(ALADDIN *adapted.*)

IN 1876 DISRAELI SUCCUMBED TO ROYAL PRESSURE BY GUIDING THE ROYAL TITLES ACT THROUGH PARLIAMENT, ENABLING VICTORIA TO ASSUME THE TITLE 'EMPRESS OF INDIA'. IT WAS THE KIND OF FLAMBOYANT GESTURE THE PRIME MINISTER ENJOYED, IT FLATTERED THE QUEEN AND IT WAS AN ASSERTION OF THE BRITISH POSITION IN INDIA TO COUNTER RUSSIAN AMBITIONS IN CENTRAL ASIA.

EXAMINING THE EVIDENCE

The Case of Afghanistan: Imperialism by Accident

Disraeli's return from the Berlin Congress marked the high point of his government's popularity. After the summer of 1878 the government's fortunes declined, a decline marked by disasters in South Africa and Afghanistan.

Afghanistan: What went wrong?

Lord Lytton had been appointed Viceroy of India in 1876 with instructions to persuade the Amir of Afghanistan to accept a permanent British agent at Kabul. Salisbury believed that the Liberal policy of 'masterly inactivity' had encouraged the Russian expansion that had reached the frontiers of Afghanistan by 1874.

Source A

... I have no doubt whatever, as to our course; we must completely and unflinchingly, support Lytton. We chose him for this very kind of business. Had it been a routine age, we might have made what might be called more prudent selection, but we fore-saw what would occur, and indeed what was occurring; and we wanted a man of ambition, imagination, some vanity, and much will – and we have got him.

Disraeli to Lord Salisbury, 1 April 1877.

Source B

I have read with some alarm the Viceroy's telegram. It appears that Lord Lytton could not have been kept *au fait* to the communications that have taken place, and are taking place, between HM's government and that of Russia, on the subject of Afghanistan ...

If Lord Lytton has ventured on these steps with full acquaintance with our relations with Russia on the subject of Afghanistan, he has committed a grave error; if he has been left in ignorance of them, our responsibility is extreme.

Disraeli to Lord Cranbrook, 12 September 1878.

Lord Cranbrook became Secretary of State for India when Salisbury moved to the Foreign Office in 1878.

Source C

I have read all your documents ... Lytton grapples with his subject and grasps it like a man. I always thought very highly of his abilities, but this specimen of them elevates my estimate. With his general policy I agree, in great measure – but the all-important question, which disturbs me, immediately arises – is he acquainted with the negotiations now going on with Russia?

Disraeli to Lord Cranbrook, 13 September 1878.

TALKING POINT

The government did not seek these imperial adventures which drained financial and military resources when these were needed to persuade the Russians to fulfil the terms of the Treaty of Berlin.

The Indian border was the longest land frontier in the British Empire. The map on p. 324–5 suggests some of the problems, real and imaginary, that were anticipated.

In 1878 a Russian mission appeared at Kabul, but the British approach had been rebuffed. The Cabinet supported Lytton's decision to send an uninvited British mission. What did they fail to inform him of?

Source D

Under these circumstances, when you and the Viceroy agree, I shall, as a general rule, always wish to support you.

... there are occasions when prudence is not wisdom. And this is one. There are times for action. We must control, and even create events.

... what we want at this present moment, is to prove our ascendancy in Afghanistan, and, to accomplish that, we must not stick at trifles ...

Disraeli to Lord Cranbrook, 22 September 1878.

Source E

... I am not satisfied with the position, as nothing could justify Lytton's course except he was prepared to act, and was in a situation which justified the responsibility of disobeying the orders of H M Government.

He was told to wait until we had received the answer from Russia. I was very strong on this ... He disobeyed us. I was assured by Lord Salisbury that, under no circumstances, was the Khyber Pass to be attempted. Nothing would have induced me to consent to such a step. He was told to send the Mission by Kandahar. He has sent it by the Khyber, and received a snub, which it may cost us much to wipe away.

When Viceroys and Commanders-in-chief disobey orders, they ought to be sure of success in their mutiny. Lytton, by disobeying orders, has only secured insult and failure.

Disraeli to Lord Cranbrook, 26 September 1878.

Following diplomatic pressure the Russians withdrew from Kabul, but Lytton persisted in his plan to install a British mission. Disregarding advice from London he provocatively and unsuccessfully attempted to send a British force through the Khyber Pass.

A punitive expedition had to be dispatched. After a successful campaign the Amir agreed to a British mission taking up residence in Kabul. In September 1879 mutinous Afghan troops massacred all its members.

1 Why, according to Disraeli in source A, was Lytton a good appointment?
2 Outline the nature of Disraeli's concerns and anxieties about Lytton's activities using sources B, C, D and E.
3 Comment on the implications of the last paragraph in source E.
4 Using the evidence of the sources, comment on the view that the government's imperial policies were created and driven by its officials, not by Disraeli and the Cabinet.

Events in South Africa followed the same pattern. The officials on the spot acted independently of each other and of the Colonial Office. The Colonial Secretary, Lord Carnarvon, hoped to consolidate British control by federating the two Boer republics (the Transvaal and the Orange Free State) and the two crown colonies (Natal and Cape Colony) within the empire. Unfortunately, the Transvaal was hastily annexed to save it from a Zulu onslaught and Britain was plunged into the Zulu war. The annihilation of a British force at Ishandlawana in January 1879 helped destroy the prestige the government had won for its successful resolution of the Eastern crisis in 1878.

Source F

In fact Disraeli's reputation for following an aggressive 'forward' policy was totally undeserved. The outcome was rather a product of the weakness of the Prime Minister than of any determined policy on his part.

C. C. Eldridge, *England's Mission*, 1973.

Source G

The blame [for the situation in Afghanistan] can be ... apportioned between Cranbrook's slackness and Lytton's 'gaudy vanity'. Apart from the initial error of appointing the Viceroy, Disraeli cannot be held seriously responsible. Perhaps, ... he ought to have made sure that the men on the spot were fully apprised of the limits within which the Government expected them to work. But this would have required much interference, whereas Disraeli believed in leaving departmental ministers to get on with their job .... The truth was that, in an era of slow communications and an ill co-ordinated governmental machine, it was not at all easy to control those high officers of state ...

R. Blake, *Disraeli,* 1966.

5 Referring to all the sources, and to your wider knowledge, comment on Eldridge's judgement in source F, discussing the extent to which Disraeli was responsible for his government's Imperialist policies and reputation.

After the 1874 election defeat Gladstone only stayed on as leader for the 1874 session. In 1875 he retired to devote himself to theological and classical studies. An awkward dual leadership, Lord Granville in the Lords and Lord Hartington in the Commons, ensued. Both men were Whigs and found it difficult to respond to the 'new' radicalism represented by Joseph Chamberlain. More seriously, Gladstone's re-entry to active politics from 1876 embarrassed both men and compromised their position.

Gladstone's Return – the Atrocity Agitation, the Midlothian Campaign

PUNCH, OR THE LONDON CHARIVARI.—MAY 26, 1877.

"WOODMAN, SPARE THAT TREE!"

LORD BEACONSFIELD *sings*—

" WOODMAN, SPARE THAT TREE ! | THE ASIAN MYSTERIE,
I LOVE IT, EVERY BOUGH; | THAT IT HAS LIVED TILL NOW !"

WHAT COMMENT IS BEING MADE HERE ON THE RESPECTIVE VIEW OF GLADSTONE AND THE NEWLY ENNOBLED DISRAELI?

Opponents accused Gladstone of hypocritically joining the anti-atrocity campaign to strike down a successful political adversary. The Liberal myth stressed his 'instinct for right timing', and the moral basis for his intervention. In fact Gladstone's pamphlet, *The Bulgarian Horrors and the Question of the East*, came late in the agitation and up to its publication he had scarcely spoken on the Bulgarian issue. Gladstone was motivated less by horror at the atrocities than by the realisation that he and a great mass movement were in a state of moral rapport. In August 1876 he wrote to Granville:

> Good ends can rarely be attained in politics without passion, and there is now, the first time for a good many years, a righteous passion.

Here was an opportunity to regain the leadership of the masses lost in 1874. Through the pamphlet Gladstone successfully articulated the public mood.

> that there was a strong element of opportunism ... is obvious. It was not the opportunism, however, of one who watches events and waits for the moment to intervene. It was the opportunism of a very belated enlightenment, of one standing absent-mindedly at a bus stop, and then having to scramble hurriedly to catch the bus which has almost passed by.
>
> R. Shannon, *Gladstone and the Bulgarian Agitation 1876*, 1975.

In May 1877 he could only get Party support for one of five resolutions critical of government policy.

Gladstone resisted demands that he should lead the agitation although his prominence was obvious. In the House of Commons, however, he failed to convince either the leadership or the parliamentary party as a whole.

Gladstone and the Liberal Party

The agitation built up a real empathy between the different groups involved in the campaign. At its core were the Nonconformists. They came to view Gladstone as the spokesman for their concept of public morality, whilst he appreciated their political and moral commitment. This, with the support the agitation received from trade unionists and the working class, helped to convince Gladstone of the virtue of the masses against the classes. The agitation was strongest in the provinces and, with the exception of the High Church element, the Church of England was untouched by it.

The failure to win the parliamentary party was one reason for Gladstone's decision to attend the inaugural meeting of the National Liberal Federation in June 1877. Joseph Chamberlain hoped to radicalise the Party through the Federation and to oust the Whig leadership. He needed Gladstone and Gladstone needed the platform that the Federation offered. Both had different purposes, but Chamberlain agreed to back Gladstone on the Eastern Question, hoping that the elderly political leader would provide the momentum needed to secure radical control of the Party.

Hartington had declined an invitation from Chamberlain and both he and Granville were unenthusiastic about Gladstone's attendance.

The Midlothian Campaign

Gladstone refused to fight his Greenwich constituency at the next general election. Many constituencies would have welcomed him, but he accepted the invitation of Lord Rosebery to contest the Scottish seat of Midlothian. It was an old-fashioned constituency with a small electorate of just over 3,000, in which influence and deference would play an important part. The Rosebery influence, as the largest Liberal landowner, would be thrown behind a Gladstone candidature.

The first Midlothian Campaign (November–December 1879) was Gladstone's introduction to the seat, but it also provided a wider platform. He spoke with the authority of a former Prime Minister, as the greatest Liberal figure of the day, not only to his future constituents but also to the entire electorate.

> The Midlothian Campaign ... had little to do with winning the Edinburghshire seat. It had everything to do with establishing Gladstonianism as the dominant force in Liberal politics and in winning the unknown and unpredictable new electorate in the boroughs. It was essentially a campaign not in or for Midlothian, but from Midlothian.
>
> H.C.G. Matthew, *The Gladstone Diaries, Vol. IX, 1875–1880*, 1986.

Gladstone was appealing directly to the national electorate, by-passing the party leadership and the machine Chamberlain was creating. The widely reported extra-parliamentary speech gave Gladstone the freedom to set his own programme and to influence voters' decisions.

Gladstone's parents were both Scottish, although he was born in Liverpool. His personal inclinations favoured a Scottish seat.

DEPARTURE OF MR. GLADSTONE FROM WEST CALDER.

GLADSTONE'S JOURNEY NORTH WAS A TRIUMPHAL PROGRESS. IMPROMPTU SPEECHES WERE MADE AT EVERY STATION. THERE WERE SIX MAJOR SPEECHES IN THE CONSTITUENCY AND MANY LESSER ONES. HE WAS RECEIVED WITH TREMENDOUS ENTHUSIASM IN EDINBURGH AND ALL THE SMALL TOWNS. HE REPEATEDLY STATED THAT HE HOPED FOR A MAJORITY HARTINGTON/GRANVILLE GOVERNMENT AT THE NEXT GENERAL ELECTION, BUT HIS POPULARITY AND BEHAVIOUR WERE MAKING THEIR POSITION UNTENABLE.

EXAMINING THE EVIDENCE

The Gladstonian Case Against Beaconsfieldism

Source A

With one party, her first care is held to be the care of her own children within her own shores, the redress of wrongs, the improvement of laws and institutions. Against this homespun doctrine, the present Government appears to set up territorial aggrandisement, large establishments, and the accumulation of a multitude of fictitious interests abroad ... and since the available store of national time and attention is a fixed quantity, there ensues that comparative remissness in domestic affairs, which is too conclusively shown by the beggarly returns of our legislation, the aggravation of our burdens, and the fast growing arrears of business.

With the one party, the great duty and honour and charge of our transmarine Colonial Empire is, to rear up free congenital communities...

... It is the administrative connection, and the shadow of political subordination, which chiefly give them value in the sight of the party, who are striving to cajole or drive us into Imperialism.

... Especially is it inexpedient to acquire possessions which, like Cyprus, never can become truly British, because they have acquired indelibly an ethnical nature of their own. In them we remain as masters and as foreigners.

W.E. Gladstone, 'England's Mission' in *The Nineteenth Century, Vol. IV*, 1878.

Source B

... now let us look at what have been their spontaneous acts. They have annexed in Africa the Transvaal territory, inhabited by a free European, Christian, republican community ... We have made war upon the Zulus. We have ... become responsible for their territory. ... Sir Bartle Frere ... has announced in South Africa that it will be necessary for us to extend our dominions until we reach the Portuguese frontier to the north.

... In Europe we have annexed the island of Cyprus ... We have assumed jointly with France the virtual government of Egypt. ... We ... have undertaken to make ourselves responsible for the good government of Turkey in Asia ... we have undertaken to defend the Armenian frontier of Turkey against Russia ...

... we have, by the most wanton invasion of Afghanistan, broken that country into pieces, made it a miserable ruin ...

Gladstone's first Midlothian speech, Edinburgh, 25 November 1879.

Source C

I will tell you what I think to be the right principles of foreign policy ... The first ... is to foster the strength of the empire by just legislation and economy at home, thereby producing two of the great elements of national power – namely, wealth ... and union and contentment ... and to reserve the strength of the empire, to reserve the expenditure of that strength, for great and worthy occasions abroad ... My second principle is ... its aim ought to be to preserve to the nations of the world ... the blessings of peace.

... the third sound principle is ... to strive to cultivate and maintain ... what is called the concert of Europe; to keep the powers of Europe in union together. Because ... you neutralise and fetter and bind up the selfish aims of each ...

My fourth principle is – that you should avoid needless and entangling engagements ...

My fifth principle is ... to acknowledge the equal rights of all nations ...

And the sixth is ... the foreign policy of England should always be inspired by the love of freedom ...

Gladstone's third Midlothian speech, West Calder, 27 November 1879.

---

1 Consult source A:
How does Gladstone distinguish between the Liberal and the Conservative view of Empire and 'England's Mission'?
2 Consult source B:
Comment on Gladstone's use of the phrase 'their spontaneous acts', and the effectiveness of his tone and language.
3 Consult source C:
Explain Gladstone's 'right principles of foreign policy'. In what ways had they been subverted by 'Beaconsfieldism'?
4 Consult all three sources. Using your wider knowledge, comment on the fairness and accuracy of Gladstone's case against the Conservative government.

The Reluctant Imperialists – Gladstone's 2nd Ministry, 1880–85

TALKING POINT

'There is no place for high moral principles in foreign affairs. The national interest alone should guide policy.' Starting from Gladstone's Midlothian opinions, and the imperial and foreign policies of his second government, consider this view.

The Boers acknowledged British suzerainty, but even this was abandoned in 1884.

Gladstone's indictment of Beaconsfieldism did not mean that he was anti-Empire or an isolationist in foreign affairs. Rather, he differed from Disraeli on when, where and how interventions to resolve international crises should take place. For Gladstone the appropriate avenue was co-operative action by the powers through the Concert of Europe. His criticism of Disraeli's handling of the Eastern crisis was that Britain appeared to be acting alone without mobilising the Concert – in fact, at times, working against it.

Gladstone's priority was to reverse the policies he had condemned. This was easily accomplished in Afghanistan. The British troops sent into the country in 1879 were swiftly withdrawn once a stable and friendly regime had been established in Kabul.

South Africa proved more difficult. The Liberals had favoured federation and Gladstone was persuaded that this was still achievable. The Transvaal Boers, having expected an immediate grant of independence, reacted angrily. The defeat of a small British force at Majuba Hill (1881) confirmed a change of policy forced by the urgency of the Irish crisis. The decision was unpopular but jingoistic protests were ignored and the Boers retrieved their independence in the Convention of Pretoria (1891).

The Turkish failure to reform the administration of their Asiatic territories provided the excuse to abandon the commitment to defend Armenia from Russian attack. Gladstone would have surrendered Cyprus, but the state of public opinion after the South African retreat made that impossible. His insistence that the great powers should compel the Turks to implement the Balkan boundary changes further alienated the Porte and alarmed the other powers. Bismarck's renewal of the Dreikaiserbund in 1881, the isolation of France and her transformation into a jealous opponent after 1882 meant that Britain was without allies and influence in Europe.

Blundering into Empire – the Egyptian Predicament

The construction of the Suez Canal gave Egypt a new strategic and financial importance. In 1879 Britain and France had set up the Dual Control to manage the finances of the bankrupt Egyptian government and to protect the interests of the Canal investors. Salisbury was also determined to control French influence in a country which was now a vital link in the imperial communications network.

Preoccupied with Ireland, the Liberal Cabinet was caught unawares by events in Egypt. A nationalist movement led by Colonel Arabi was provoked by the continual European interference in Egypt's internal affairs. The country collapsed into chaos, and in February 1882 Arabi took over power. Gladstone was not averse to intervention to restore order, but he believed that this was the responsibility of the Sultan, as Egypt's overlord, or, failing that, of the Concert. Joint intervention by Britain and France, acting as agents of the Concert was an acceptable alternative.

Within the Cabinet Hartington, Secretary of State for India, pressed for intervention, by Britain alone if necessary, to protect the Canal.

By July 1882, with Gladstone, Bright, Chamberlain and Dilke all on the verge of resignation, the Cabinet was on the point of breaking up. Hartington was becoming more insistent as first the Turks and then the French rejected Gladstone's interpretation of their responsibilities. The ultimatum eventually sent to Arabi came from Britain alone and it was the Royal Navy that bombarded Alexandria when he remained defiant. The French withdrawal, the unilateral British intervention and the routing of Arabi's forces at the battle of Tel-el-Kebir left Britain in sole control of Egypt and the Canal.

Gladstone agreed to intervention to save his Irish Arrears Bill. John Bright was the only Minister to resign.

There was no clear agreement on the purpose of the occupation. Gladstone's hope that once self-government had been restored the British could withdraw was unrealistic. The Canal had to be secure, and 'order' depended on the presence of British forces and British officials. Hartington, the Queen and Lord Northbrook, who replaced Hartington at the India Office at the end of 1882, pressed for an indefinite occupation. Withdrawal would create a vacuum in which other European powers, especially France, would meddle. the Liberal government had occupied Egypt by accident, and once there did not know what to do, but they could not afford to take risks with the imperial lifeline.

The Consequences of Occupation

Occupation presented the government with two unforeseen problems:
1   How to manage Egypt's finances and its international debts?
2   How to respond to the Mahdi's challenge to Egyptian authority in the Sudan?

Both were complicated by the government's ambivalent attitude to the occupation and Gladstone's moral conscience.

The Mahdi: religious leader of the Sudanese revolt.

His insistence that the occupation was only temporary, and that all the great powers should be involved in the management of Egyptian finances, gave the French the opportunity to embarrass Britain, and allowed Bismarck to gain colonial concessions to satisfy German claims in West Africa and elsewhere. The Berlin Conference (1884) was the price Britain had to pay for Egypt. Britain was left dependent on the goodwill of the other powers on the debt management commission to counter the obstruction of a jealous France.

By 1882 the Sudanese revolt against Egyptian rule had confined Egyptian forces to a few garrisons. Britain recommended a withdrawal. Egypt could not afford to continue the war, and the Mahdi presented no threat to the British in Egypt.

In November 1883 an Egyptian army commanded by a British general was massacred. Public opinion was being whipped into a frenzy by the *Pall Mall Gazette's* campaign against the revival of slavery in the Sudan. General Charles Gordon, with previous successful experience of combating the Sudanese slave traders, was the public choice to resolve the crisis. Slowly and reluctantly the Cabinet agreed to send Gordon to manage the evacuation of the remaining Egyptian troops. His orders were muddled; once established

The Conservatives did not renew the forward policy in Afghanistan, and, despite their assault on Gladstone's policy in 1885, did not reverse the decision to evacuate the Sudan. Salisbury was in charge of foreign affairs for much of the next 15 years, but the liberal foreign secretaries (Lord Rosebery 1886, 1892–94 and Lord Kimberley 1894–95) shared his outlook and there was no repeat of the differences between the parties that had characterised the Disraeli/Gladstone years.

in Khartoum he bombarded the Cabinet with advice and failed to organise an evacuation. By the spring of 1884 he was cut off. The Cabinet prevaricated. Gladstone, alarmed by talk of annexation, was reluctant to send a relieving force to rescue Gordon. When a relief column was eventually dispatched it was too late. On 5 February 1885 the news reached London that Khartoum had fallen and that Gordon was dead. The Queen publicly rebuked her Prime Minister in an un-ciphered telegram. Feelings ran high. The 'GOM' (Grand Old Man') became the 'MOG' ('Murderer of Gordon'). For a time the Cabinet, which survived a Commons censure motion by only 14 votes, responded to the jingoistic surge of opinion by ordering General Wolseley to advance into the Sudan. There was talk of annexation.

By April, however, the government had returned to its preferred policy of withdrawal, using a renewed Russian threat to Afghanistan as their justification. Gladstone's remarkably swift response to the Penjedh Incident, and the urgent request to Parliament for emergency credits, diverted attention from the Sudanese disaster and persuaded the Russians to accept a viable and stable frontier with Afghanistan.

It would be wrong to accuse Gladstone's Cabinet of hypocrisy in its Egyptian policy. Ministers had blundered into Egypt with no clear objectives. Gradually the realisation dawned that an early evacuation was impossible but the alternative of declaring a British protectorate was unpalatable to Gladstone and the Liberals in the Cabinet, although Hartington and the Whigs would have welcomed it. For Ministers preoccupied with Ireland (1881–82) and the reform crisis (1884), Egypt and its problems were an unwelcome and unnecessary complication. Gladstone's conscience created more difficulties, and the final acceptance of the French scheme for the international financial management was to restrict Britain's freedom of action in Egypt and internationally until the end of the century.

REVIEW

There is little to be said in favour of Gladstone's handling of foreign and colonial affairs from 1880 to 1885. However laudable his basic intentions and fundamental principles – and they were on the whole a good deal more laudable than Disraeli's – his attempts to apply them ... were marked by almost continuous incompetence, administrative inefficiency and at times almost wilful self-deception. It was impossible to take seriously a prime minister who thought Arabi a villain but the Mahdi a patriot; who abandoned the Transvaal but occupied Egypt ... who had proclaimed in 1878 that Russia had been doing God's work but in 1885 that it was doing the Devil's ...

Though Gladstone indeed believed 'the sentiment of Empire was innate in every Briton', and though, whereas Disraeli merely acquired Cyprus, Gladstone acquired Egypt, the simple view prevailed: under Disraeli and the Conservatives England had been great; under Gladstone England had been humiliated.

L.C.B. Seaman, *Victorian England*, 1973.

Essay

How true was it that England had been 'great' under Disraeli and the Conservatives, but 'humiliated' under the Liberals? Refer fully to the foreign and imperial policies of the period 1868–85 to illustrate your answer.

TALKING POINT

Examine the view that, despite the rhetoric of the Midlothian Campaign, there was more continuity than change in imperial and foreign policies after 1880.

LEARNING RESOURCE CENTRE
THOMAS ROTHERHAM COLLEGE
MOORGATE ROAD
ROTHERHAM S60 2BE
0709 828603

15 Gladstone, Parnell and the Irish Question, 1868–93

PREVIEW

Defining the Question

Source A

Disraeli speaking in the House of Commons in 1844.

> Let them consider Ireland ... they will see a teeming population ... created solely by agriculture, with none of those sources of wealth which are developed with civilization; and sustained consequently upon the lowest conceivable diet, so that in case of failure they had no other means of subsistence upon which they could fall back. That dense population in extreme distress inhabited an island where there was an established church which was not their church; and a territorial aristocracy, the richest of whom lived in distant capitals. Thus they had a starving population, an absentee aristocracy, and an alien church, and, in addition, the weakest executive in the world. That was the Irish question. ... What then was the duty of an English minister? To effect by his policy all those changes which a revolution would do by force. That was the Irish question in its integrity ...

Source B

> The tired old witticism that every time the English came within sight of solving the Irish question the Irish changed the question, contains ... a small grain of truth submerged in a vast sea of misconception. The Irish did not change the question ... The 'national demand' ... remained in essence what Wolfe Tone had declared it to be as long ago as 1791, 'to break the connection with England, the never-failing source of all our political evils'. It is true ... that men differed in the nineteenth century ... about how complete the break should be, or more precisely, perhaps, about how far the full separatist ideal was practicable. But ... they were emphatic that the first step towards real independence was to recover for Irishmen the right to control their own affairs.
>
> F. S. L. Lyons, *Ireland Since the Famine*, 1973.

1 How, and with what success, had English ministers tried to solve Disraeli's 'Irish question' before the 1860s?
2 What, according to source B, would make it difficult for any British politician to solve the 'question'?

Fenianism and the Revival of the Revolutionary Tradition

Following the political upheavals of the 1840s, Ireland experienced a period of relative calm. Politically the tenant farmers remained susceptible to landlord influence, although they did achieve some parliamentary representation. However, by the 1860s bodies such as the Irish Republican Brotherhood (1858) and the American-based Fenian Brotherhood were plotting for immediate and violent revolution against British rule. Although the Fenian insurrection collapsed in 1867, the issue of Ireland was back on the political agenda.

THE EXECUTION OF THOSE WHO TOOK PART IN THE ATTACK ON THE POLICE VAN IN MANCHESTER TO FREE FELLOW FENIANS GAVE THE IRB ITS MARTYRS, BUT OUTBREAKS OF FENIAN VIOLENCE IN BRITAIN HAD A WIDER SIGNIFICANCE. PUBLIC OPINION, LONG INDIFFERENT TO IRISH ISSUES, WAS FORCED TO RECOGNISE THAT REAL PROBLEMS EXISTED. GLADSTONE SEIZED THE OPPORTUNITY TO PRESS FOR CONCILIATORY POLICIES TO REMOVE IRISH GRIEVANCES.

Examining the Evidence

Gladstone and Ireland, 1868–1874 – the Making of Policy

Source A

Ireland, Ireland! that cloud in the West, that coming storm, the minister of God's retribution upon cruel and inveterate and but half-atoned injustice! Ireland forces upon us these great social and great religious questions – God grant that we may have courage – to look them in the face and to work through them.

W.E. Gladstone writing to Catherine Gladstone in 1845.

1 Gladstone used the Irish issue to unite the Liberals and to defeat the Conservatives in 1868. What other motives are suggested in sources A, B, D and E?
2 Consult sources C and D, and refer to Chapter 6. To what extent was Gladstone reviving Peelite solutions to the Irish Question?

Source B

To this great country the state of Ireland after seven hundred years of our tutelage is in my opinion so long as it continues, an intolerable disgrace, and a danger so absolutely transcending all others, that I call it the only real danger of the noble empire of the Queen.

W.E. Gladstone in a letter to Queen Victoria, 1870.

Source C

The Church of Ireland ... is but one of a group of questions. There is the Church of Ireland, there is the land of Ireland, there is the education of Ireland; there are many subjects, all of which depend on one greater than them all; they are all so many branches from one trunk, and that trunk is the tree of what is called the Protestant ascendancy ... We therefore aim at the destruction of that system of ascendancy which, though it has been crippled and curtailed by former measures, yet still must be allowed to exist. It is still there like a tall tree of noxious growth, lifting its head to heaven and darkening and poisoning the land so far as its shadow can extend; it is still there, Gentlemen, and now at length the day has come when, as we hope, the axe has been laid at the root of that tree, and it nods and quivers from its root to its base.

Election speech at Wigan, *The Times*, 24 October 1868.

Source D

... our purpose & duty is to endeavour to draw a line between the Fenians & the people of Ireland, & to make the people of Ireland indisposed to cross it.

W.E. Gladstone in a letter to General Grey, Queen Victoria's private secretary, 1869

TALKING POINT

Gladstone's 'mission' was to 'pacify' Ireland. Why might that make it impossible for him to 'satisfy' Ireland?

Gladstone visited Ireland for the first time in 1877.

Source E

England must for her own safety hold Ireland, come what may, and it is her duty to leave no remedial measures untried.

Lord Kimberley, Lord Privy Seal in Gladstone's Cabinet, writing in his Journal, 14 December 1869.

Gladstone aimed to preserve the Union by making it more acceptable to the Irish. Unfortunately his understanding of the Question came from books, and the implicit assumption that only an Englishman could solve the Question and understand how Irish grievances could be redressed rankled. Gladstone's policy was fatally flawed and doomed to fail in its primary purpose, despite his obvious mastery of the detail of the proposals. There was no appreciation of the deeper problems and no recognition of the existence of a genuine sense of Irish nationality. Irish grievances were viewed from the British political context, not from an Irish perspective.

FOCUS

15.1 The Failure of a Mission – Gladstone's Irish Policy 1868–74

"Church of Ireland"

1869 Disestablishment of the Church of Ireland

Background

The general election had given Gladstone a clear mandate. A Liberal majority of 118 assured its easy passage through the Commons although the Lords proved difficult. A compromise was reached since neither the Queen, who disliked the Bill, nor the Conservative leadership, relished a conflict with Gladstone's popular majority.

Legislation

- All legal connection between the Church of Ireland and the State ended.
- The property of the Church was confiscated.
- Churches and burial grounds in use in 1869 were returned to the new Church.
- The life interests of clergymen, school teachers and officials of the old Church were protected.
- State grants to the Irish Presbyterian Church and to the Catholics ended.
- The Temporalities Commission was established to manage the surplus income for the benefit of the people of Ireland.

Impact

SUCCESS – immediate objective achieved. Disestablishment was, however, a largely symbolic recognition of the vulnerability of Protestant ascendancy. It did nothing to remove real and pressing grievances.

"Education of Ireland"

1873 University Bill

Background

Religion complicated education in Ireland. The Catholic bishops wanted denominational education at all levels, but state support for Catholic education would have been unacceptable to a Protestant House of Commons. A Report of 1870 which recommended denominational control of primary education was quickly shelved. The bishops wanted the endowment of a Catholic University to enable Catholics to study for a degree in a denominational environment.

Legislation

The Bill proposed a federal university of Dublin; all existing Irish colleges, Protestant, Catholic, or non-denominational, would be affiliated to the new institution which would organise teaching and examining. To prevent controversy, some subjects – theology, moral philosophy and history – would be excluded from the curriculum.

Impact

FAILURE – the Catholic bishops rejecting mixed education opposed the Bill. They broke the alliance with the Liberals, and 35 Irish MPs were persuaded to vote against the second reading. The Bill was defeated, although it was probably unworkable. Gladstone was perceived to be anti-Catholic, a distrust that was intensified by his later attack on the doctrine of 'papal infallibility'.

"Land of Ireland"

1870 Land Act

Background

This was much more controversial. Resignations were anticipated in a Cabinet of landowners opposed to the restriction of property rights. Bright demanded an extensive land purchase scheme to remove the landlord from the Irish countryside. Gladstone wished to strengthen and preserve the influence of the landlords whilst giving the tenants greater security and encouragement to improve their holdings. He had no intention of conceding the tenant demand for the '3 Fs' – fair rents, fixity of tenure, and free sale of the tenant's interest – but he wanted to reduce evictions and give tenants compensation where they had improved the farm.

Legislation

– Ulster tenant custom, which allowed the tenant to sell his interest in his holding to an incoming tenant and required the landlord to compensate the tenant for improvements he had made, was legalised in the districts where it operated. Elsewhere tenants were to receive compensation for improvements when giving up a farm, and compensation for 'disturbance' if evicted for any reason except non-payment of rent. Tenants who wished to buy had to find 1/3 of the purchase price, the state providing 2/3s repayable at 5 per cent over 35 years.

Impact

FAILURE – the tenants were not pacified and Gladstone was forced to re-introduce coercion in 1871. Few tenants benefitted from the Act. If Ulster tenant custom was claimed, the case had to be proved in the courts – landlords had the upper hand. Compensation was a 'tax' to deter evictions but the landlord only had to raise the rent and he could then evict without any penalty. Few tenants had the resources to take advantage of the land purchase scheme. Historians of the land question have argued that Gladstone's 1870 Act dealt with the wrong issues. Rent rises were not excessive before 1870, larger tenant farmers were prosperous, eviction rates were low and improvements were often made by landlord and tenant in co-operation. The legislation worsened landlord/tenant relations and discouraged landlord improvements since the Act assumed that they were always made by the tenant.

TALKING POINT

'The objective of the first government, of attempting to remove the Protestant ascendancy, would, if achieved, pacify Ireland by leaving no major grievance. The problem of this strategy was that its measures, dramatic though they seemed at the time, were too modest and too slow.' (H.C.G. Matthew, *Gladstone Diaries, vol. X*, 1991) How fair is this assessment of the failure of Gladstone's policies 1868–74?

The Origins of the Home Rule Movement

The formation of the Home Rule League in 1873 emphasised the extent of Gladstone's failure to conciliate two key groups in Irish society – the farmers and the Catholic Church. The League was preceded by the Home Government Association (1870) which brought Irish Protestants, angered by disestablishment and fearful for the future of Protestant Ascendancy, Irish Liberals dissatisfied by the Land Act, moderate nationalists and some Fenians into an uneasy alliance. Led by Isaac Butt, the Association campaigned for Home Rule for Ireland within a federal United Kingdom.

The character of the Home Government Association began to change. Gradually the Protestant element withdrew and it became more strongly Catholic. The Church welcomed an active Home Rule party which would defend Catholic interests at Westminster. Increasingly the Association's by-election candidates supported tenant grievances against the Land Act and landlords. Transformed into the Home Rule League, approved by the priesthood and tolerated by the Fenians, it was clearly a popular and nationalist organisation although its programme remained federalist and its methods constitutional.

In 1868 the Liberals had won 66 seats in Ireland. Unprepared for Gladstone's 'snap' election in 1874 the Home Rule League, benefitting from the secret ballot which freed tenants from landlord influence, could still claim 59 Members elected on its programme. Only 10 Gladstonian Liberals survived. Gladstone's failure to 'satisfy' Ireland was very clear.

Isaac Butt (1813–79), a Conservative and Protestant, won the confidence of the nationalists and Fenians as the defence lawyer at the trials of Fenians in 1865–67. A federal United Kingdom in which Ireland would have local self-government was his preferred solution to the problem.

The Home Rule Confederation of Great Britain rapidly became a Fenian front organisation. Parnell's election as President in 1877, replacing Butt, indicated that the Fenian leadership recognised him as the future leader of the constitutional movement.

Charles Stewart Parnell – the Making of a Nationalist Leader

Parnell, elected MP for Co. Meath in 1876, soon found himself associating with a small group of Home Rule members who had begun obstructing government business to focus attention on Irish issues. Butt's ineffective public condemnation of the tactic reflected his loss of control. These activities, and Parnell's powerful language, attracted the attention of the Fenians. If British rule could not be overthrown by revolution perhaps this ambitious and outspoken young MP could make constitutionalism work. The election of the moderate William Shaw as leader after Butt's death in 1879 suggested that it was not time for him to take over. Parnell was willing to make concessions to the more extreme nationalist factions but he recognised that the party lacked a wide popular appeal and the charismatic leadership that O'Connell had been able to give. In 1879 it was

CHARLES STEWART PARNELL (1846-1891) WAS A STRANGE FIGURE TO BECOME THE LEADER OF IRISH NATIONALISM. PARNELL BELIEVED THAT HIS CLASS, THE ANGLO-IRISH PROTESTANT GENTRY, HAD A CRUCIAL PART TO PLAY IN THE SOLUTION OF THE IRISH QUESTION, AND THAT IN A HOME RULE IRELAND THEY WOULD STILL BE THE NATURAL GOVERNING CLASS.

still not clear whether Parnell could provide the latter, but the revival of the land question as the agricultural economy sank into depression offered an opportunity for him to seize the leadership of the mass movement.

Parnell and the Land War

A series of bad seasons in the late 1870s and falling prices for all agricultural products aggravated tenant insecurity. Potato crop failures 1878, 1879 raised the spectre of the Great Famine in the west of the country. Tenants demanded an easing of rents as the depression worsened and evictions increased from 463 in 1877 to 2,110 in 1880. In April 1879 the land agitation was launched in Mayo with the ex-Fenian Michael Davitt as organiser.

Parnell was a constitutionalist whose ultimate aim was Home Rule. But he needed to maintain alliances with more extreme groups such as the IRB. Davitt was able to arrange meetings between Parnell and John Devoy, the representative of the American Fenian organisation, Clan na Gael. The Americans could provide funding and moral support in the struggle. Parnell attended his first land agitation meeting at Westport in June 1879 and became President of the National Land League in the autumn. In January 1880 he departed for a fund-raising tour of the United States.

Michael Davitt had bitter memories of eviction during the Great Famine. Self-educated, he joined the Fenians in 1865 and was imprisoned for his activities in 1870. In 1877, he was released and soon resumed his activities in the Irish countryside.

TALKING POINT

The Land League was a temporary deviation from the Home Rule path. The challenge was to ensure that the farmers' support for Parnell, the Land League president, was transformed into support for the nationalist leader.
How could active involvement with the Land League benefit Parnell politically in Ireland?

PROPAGANDA–CONSIDER THE IMPACT OF THIS ON IRISH AMERICANS WITH VIVID MEMORIES OF THE GREAT FAMINE.

Balancing the demands of Clan na Gael and the land agitation presented Parnell with a difficult challenge. The rhetoric expected in his American speeches differed greatly from that of a constitutional leader, whilst his view of the land question differed markedly from Davitt's. The latter wanted land nationalisation, Parnell wished to see a peasant proprietorship with fair compensation for the landowners to remove the tensions in Irish society which prevented them from taking their natural leadership role. The tide of the land agitation carried Parnell into the 1880 General Election. Although his supporters only won 24 seats that was enough, in a poorly attended Party meeting, to give him the chairmanship with 23 votes to Shaw's 18. Could he manage the disparate forces massing behind him?

Gladstone's Second Land Act, 1881

The severity of the Irish crisis took Gladstone and his Cabinet by surprise. As the land war intensified in the autumn of 1880 the Chief Secretary, W.E. Forster, demanded the recall of parliament, a Coercion Bill and the suspension of Habeas Corpus. Parnell and other leaders were arrested, but the case against them collapsed. Divisions in the Liberal cabinet made the passage of legislation to alleviate the situation difficult. When it did emerge, the generosity of the Land Bill presented Parnell with a dilemma. Reluctantly acknowledging that his 1870 Act had failed, Gladstone followed the recommendation of the Bessborough Commission in conceding the '3 Fs' - 'Fair rent', 'Fixity of tenure' and 'Free sale of the Tenant's interest'. Parnell could neither afford to oppose it nor seem too welcoming. Amendments were moved during the committee stage but the Irish leader engineered his supension from the House to miss the third reading vote.

Despite serious limitations – leaseholders and those already in arrears with rent payments were excluded from its benefits – the Land Act split the Land League and eventually broke it. In the short term it left Parnell with a tricky decision. Many tenants wanted to go to the Land Courts; his American backers wanted continued resistance. His solution was to 'test the Act' – send selected cases to the new Courts to 'test' their impartiality. He hoped this would restrain the tenants, give him breathing space with the moderates, and satisfy the Irish-Americans. To Gladstone it seemed the Irish leader was deliberately seeking to destroy the Act. A vicious public exchange of views led to Parnell's arrest and imprisonment in October 1881. This was actually a blessing for Parnell, as he could pose as the victim of Gladstone's coercion and he was also absent from the violent break up of the Land League.

An attempt to provide some immediate relief for evicted tenants, the Compensation for Disturbance Bill, was lost in the Lords, October 1880.

The Coercion Bill preceded the Land Bill through Parliament. The obstructive tactics of the Irish MPs forced Gladstone to modify the rules of the House to curtail debate.

Land Act, 1881

'Fair rents' – Tenants could submit their rent for arbitration by Land Courts.

'Fixity of tenure' – If the tenant paid the judicial rent he could not be evicted.

'Free sale of the tenant's interest' – When a farmer left a tenancy he could get a fair price for any improvements from the incoming tenant.

Examining the Evidence

The Political Purpose of the Land Act

Source A

The immediate necessity for Mr. Gladstone's land bill was a condition of things in Ireland which bordered on social anarchy. This was largely, if not entirely, the deliberately planned work of the Land League.... [The Land Act was] a concession to the tenants to detach them from the League.

Michael Davitt, *The Fall of Feudalism in Ireland*, 1904.

Source B

The Bill was intended to castrate the Land League by attracting the Irish tenants into Courts and a Land Commission appointed by the Westminster Parliament ... which would reduce their rents .... The metropolitan parliament would thus be seen to be offering a boon which the Land League could not match.

H.C.G. Matthew, *The Gladstone Diaries, Vol. X*, 1990.

Source C

... the Land Act of 1881 was not solely, nor perhaps primarily, concerned with long-term agricultural goals. It was an attempt to cut the ground from beneath the Land League .... It was put forward, as has been well said, 'less as an economic policy than as a political stroke.'

F.S.L. Lyons, *Charles Stewart Parnell*, 1977, quoting B. Solow, *The Land Question and the Irish Economy 1870–1903*, 1971.

Source D

Politically it is a fortunate thing for me that I have been arrested as the movement is breaking fast and all will be quiet in a few months, when I shall be released.

Parnell in a letter to Katharine O'Shea on his first day in Kilmainham Jail.

Referring to these sources, and to your wider knowledge, comment on the motives behind the 1881 Land Act and its success as 'a political stroke'.

The 'Kilmainham Treaty'

Imprisonment saved Parnell from the wreck of the Land League. Realising that the Land Act would break the League, his actions in the autumn of 1881 almost suggest that he was deliberately provoking the government into ordering his arrest. Parnell and his colleagues issued the 'No Rent Manifesto' from Kilmainham Jail but it was a gesture, at least on Parnell's part, to satisfy the extremists and the Irish-Americans. Despite the propaganda, prison life was easy and Parnell was insulated from the violent terminal struggle of the Land League, posing as the victim of coercion and Gladstone's vindictiveness. By the spring of 1882 personal and political reasons demanded compromise with the government and an early release. His and Katharine O'Shea's first child was born in 1882 whilst the chaos in the countryside threatened his authority within the nationalist movement.

Katharine O'Shea had become Parnell's mistress during 1880. When her husband, Captain O'Shea, learnt of the liaison is unclear.

The Cabinet was alarmed by the failure of the authorities to control the disturbances. Despite Forster's misgivings secret and informal negotiations were opened with Parnell through Captain O'Shea. There was no formal arrangement, but the 'Kilmainham Treaty' satisfied the needs of both Parnell and the government. In return for an extension of the Land Act's protection to tenants in arrears and to leaseholders, the Irish leader agreed to end the agitation and obstruction. For its part, the Cabinet conceded that coercion would not be renewed. There were also vague assurances that the Irish MPs would give general support to government reforms. Both the Viceroy, Lord Cowper, and Forster, the Chief Secretary, resigned. The Phoenix Park Murders, 6 May 1882, saved Parnell from his critics on the nationalist side. The sincerity of his Commons statement denouncing the assassinations won him the sympathy of the House, whilst the inevitable renewal of coercion, which he opposed, safeguarded his reputation in Ireland and America. Parnell got the credit for the government's promised Arrears Act, as well as for the Land Courts which were now delivering substantial rent reductions.

The new Chief Secretary, Lord Frederick Cavendish, and the Permanent Under Secretary, T.H. Burke, were murdered whilst walking in Phoenix Park, Dublin.

EXAMINING THE EVIDENCE

Assessing the 'Treaty'

Source A

The Kilmainham treaty ... was a great victory for Mr. Parnell. All the forces of the empire had been pitted against him, and he had beaten the empire. The terms of the Government are sufficient proof of this. ... the failure of coercion was acknowledged frankly and unreservedly. The completeness of the confession involved the sacrifice of the men chiefly responsible for coercion ....

T.P. O'Connor, *The Parnell Movement*, 1887.

Source B

... concessions were obtained on the condition that the forces which compelled Mr. Gladstone to change his policy were to be disbanded, while the movement that had given Mr. Parnell his position and power was to disappear. ... The price was too great, and the terms were so obnoxious to the league sentiment in Ireland and America that had not the Phoenix Park catastrophe intervened ... Mr. Parnell's leadership would have trembled in the balance. ... English rule in Ireland had never been so shaken and demoralized since 1798 as it was in 1881–2, nor had Castle rule ever been so fiercely and effectively assaulted. ... The country was absolutely ungovernable, while an organization ... stood behind Mr. Parnell's lead, with abundant friends and ample power to keep the struggle going until the whole system of anti-national administration would fall to pieces and necessitate a radical and fundamental change. Looked at from the point of view of the

1 Explain 'the sacrifice of the men chiefly responsible for coercion' (source A) and 'Dublin-Castle' (source B).

2 'Victory' or a 'political defeat'? Account for these contrasting views of the 'Kilmainham Treaty'.

policy and purpose of the Land League, to destroy landlordism and to demoralize Dublin-Castle rule so as to force a settlement of the agrarian and national problems on radical but rational lines, the Kilmainham treaty was a victory for those menaced institutions and a political defeat of the forces led by Mr. Parnell.

M. Davitt, *The Fall of Feudalism in Ireland*, 1904.

The National League – Parnell's Party

Following early release from prison, Parnell founded the National League in October 1882. He laid down its agenda, 'National Self-Government' first and 'Land Law Reform' second, and behind a democratic facade he controlled policy and selected the parliamentary candidates. It was the moderate non-revolutionary organisation he wanted to lead. With funds available to support its MPs when resident in London, the National League was able to enforce loyalty and party discipline. Candidates had to pledge to act in a constitutional and parliamentary way, and to follow the party line on all political questions.

The National League became the focus of Irish, Catholic and nationalist opinion:

● The tenant farmers remained loyal to the leader who had won the Land Act, and to an organisation that promised peasant ownership of the land.
● The Catholic hierarchy endorsed the League because it was non-revolutionary and respected the political role of the clergy - even though it was led by a Protestant.
● The Catholic middle class could support a non-violent constitutional party.
● The Fenians were won over by Parnell's rhetoric and reputation.

There were tensions. How could a Catholic nation be led by a Protestant? The problem of the protestant north, and the role of protestants elsewhere in Ireland, was ignored. Protestant tenants had benefitted from land reform and would welcome land ownership but the more nationalist the League became the more Protestant Ireland distanced itself from it.

By-elections were won consistently after 1882. The Third Reform Act, 1884, treated the Irish franchise on an equality with the rest of Britain. The electorate increased from 4.4 to 16 per cent of the population but this merely increased rural support for the League and had only a marginal effect on the number of winnable seats. In 1885 the League won 85 seats including 17 in Ulster.

Having now achieved status as a constitutional politician, Parnell now received overtures from both sides in return for his support in parliament. Joseph Chamberlain proposed a Central Board scheme.This offered a measure of self-government, but fell far short of the Irish parliament which Parnell envisaged. The scheme was, in any case, rejected by Chamberlain's Liberal cabinet colleagues.

Rejecting Chamberlain, Parnell was tempted by an offer from Lord Randolph Churchill. Acting independently of the Conservative Party leadership, he hinted that a Conservative government might not renew coercion if the Home Rule MPs voted with the opposition against the Liberal budget. Alliance with the Conservatives was attractive. Their control of the

TALKING POINT

Could the National League ever become a national party?

TALKING POINT

Parnell, a conservative landowner leading a party representing peasant farmers and the catholic clergy. Chamberlain, the leader of English urban radicalism who wanted to exclude the churches from education. What made an alliance unlikely?

Lords would guarantee the success of any Irish legislation and a judicious vote with the Conservatives would neatly dissociate Parnell from Liberal failures. Following the Liberal defeat and resignation in June 1885, the new Conservative Cabinet did not renew coercion and the first really effective Land Purchase Act (Ashbourne's Act) was passed. Lord Carnarvon, the Conservative Lord Lieutenant, met Parnell secretly to discuss home rule. Salisbury, the Premier, knew of this, the Cabinet did not.

As the autumn general election approached Parnell had to advise Nationalist electors in mainland constituencies how to use their votes. Neither Salisbury nor Gladstone were willing to make home rule commitment. The instruction to vote for Conservative candidates was intended to reduce the expected Liberal majority. In the short term, the result was better than Parnell could have expected.

Carnarvon had tried to federate South Africa during his period as Colonial Secretary 1874-1878.

PUNCH, OR THE LONDON CHARIVARI—October 24, 1885.

THE IRISH "VAMPIRE."

Liberals	335
Conservatives	249
Home Rulers	86

The Nationalists won 85 seats in Ireland and one in Liverpool.

PARNELL, DEPICTED AS A VAMPIRE, PREYS ON A SLEEPING IRELAND. SUCH CARTOONS SHOW THE DEMONISING OF PARNELL.

EXAMINING THE EVIDENCE

Gladstone and Home Rule – 'an old man in a hurry'?

On 17 December 1885 the press reported Gladstone's conversion to home rule. The 'story' was leaked by Herbert Gladstone, a convinced home ruler, who believed that only his father could solve the problem. The 'Hawarden Kite' took the political world by surprise since Gladstone had deliberately avoided a statement during the election campaign.

Source A
Gladstone to W.E. Forster (Chief Secretary), 12 April 1882.

In truth I should say (differing perhaps from many), that for the Ireland of today, the first question is the rectification of the relations between

TALKING POINT

Assess the significance of the election result for the political parties, for Parnell and for home rule

Gladstone's political motives for adopting the home rule policy are discussed in Chapter 16.

landlord and tenant, which happily is going on; the next is to relieve Great Britain from the enormous weight of the government of Ireland unaided by the people, and from the hopeless contradiction in which we stand while we give a parliamentary representation, hardly effective for anything but mischief without the local institutions of self-government which it pre-supposes, and on which alone it can have a sound and healthy basis.

Source B

A Memorandum read by Gladstone to Lord Hartington, 7 August 1885.

> Had party been agreed, and other circs favourable, on the Central Board Scheme, I shd have been ready to offer myself at the Dissolution on that basis.

Hartington had opposed Chamberlain's Central Board scheme and was totally against any concession to the nationalists.

Source C

Gladstone's 'Address to the Electors of Midlothian, September 17, 1885'.

> Down to this hour Ireland has continued greatly in arrear both of England and Scotland, with respect to those powers of local self-government which associate the people, in act and feeling, with the law, and which lie at the root, as I believe, of political stability, of the harmony of classes, and of national strength.
>
> ... In my opinion, not for the first time delivered, the limit is clear, within which any desires of Ireland, constitutionally ascertained, may, and beyond which they cannot, receive the assent of Parliament. To maintain the supremacy of the Crown, the unity of the Empire, and all the authority of Parliament necessary for the conservation of that unity, is the first duty of every representative of the people. Subject to this governing principle, every grant to portions of the country of enlarged powers for the management of their own affairs is in my view, not a source of danger, but a means of averting it, and is in the nature of a new guarantee for increase cohesion, happiness, and strength.

Source D

Gladstone to Lord Rosebery, 13 November 1885. Rosebery had been pressing for a clear statement on Irish policy.

> ... my final and paramount reason is, that the production at this time of a plan by me would not only be injurious, but would destroy all reasonable hopes of its adoption. Such a plan, proposed by the leader of the liberal party, is so certain to have the opposition of the tories *en bloc*, that every computation must be founded on this anticipation. This opposition, and the appeals with which it will be accompanied, will render the carrying of the measure difficult even by a united liberal party; hopeless or most difficult, should there be serious defections.
>
> Mr. Parnell is apprehensive of the opposition of the House of Lords. That idea weighs little with me. I have to think of something nearer and more formidable. The idea of constituting a legislature for Ireland, whenever seriously and responsibly proposed, will cause a mighty heave in the body politic. It will be as difficult to carry the liberal party and the two British nations in favour of a legislature for Ireland, as it was easy to carry them in the case of Irish disestablishment.

Source E

Gladstone to Lord Hartington, 17 December 1885. This was an attempt at reassurance; Hartington had already made it clear that he was opposed to home rule.

> I consider that Ireland has now spoken; and that an effort ought to be made *by the Government* without delay to meet her demands for the management by an Irish legislative body of Irish as distinct from Imperial affairs.
>
> Only a government can do it and a Tory Government can do it more easily and safely than any other.

Source F

Gladstone to A.J. Balfour, 20 December 1885.

> On reflection I think that what I said to you ... may have amounted to the conveyance of a hope that the Government would take a strong and early decision in the Irish question. ... I think it will be a public calamity if this great subject should fall into the lines of party conflict.
>
> I feel sure that the question can only be dealt with by a Government, & I desire specially on grounds of public policy that it should be dealt with by the *present* Government. If therefore they bring in a proposal for settling the whole question of the future Government of Ireland, my desire will be, reserving of course necessary freedom, to treat it in the same spirit in which I have endeavoured to proceed with respect to Afghanistan & ... to the Balkan peninsula. You are at liberty ... to mention this to Lord Salisbury.

TALKING POINT

Could the Irish Question have only been solved by the bipartisan approach Gladstone seemed to suggest?

Balfour was Salisbury's nephew and President of the Local Government Board in his uncle's administration. Gladstone had met and conversed with him at Eaton Hall three days previously.

1   With reference to the extracts and to your knowledge, explain what is meant by the following phrases in the context of the events 1882–85: 'rectification of the relations between landlord and tenant' (source A) 'Central Board Scheme' (source B) 'I consider that Ireland has now spoken' (source E).
2   Referring to sources A, B, C and E, comment on the view that Gladstone was converted to home rule in the autumn of 1885.
3   Lord Randolph Churchill was to accuse Gladstone of being 'an old man in a hurry', desperately bidding for Irish support. To what extent does this evidence counter that charge?

The First Home Rule Bill, 1886

The 'Hawarden Kite' upset Gladstone's calculations. Salisbury had had no intention of splitting the Conservative Party over home rule, and the Cabinet took the decision to reintroduce coercion before the 'kite' was flown. Herbert Gladstone's indiscretion informed them that an incoming Gladstone government would be hampered by the Irish alliance and that home rule would destroy Liberal unity. Hartington had made it plain that he, for one, would not join a home rule Liberal administration although he agreed to impartially 'examine' any proposals. Gladstone had clearly expected a majority Liberal government which would give him time to educate public opinion, Cabinet colleagues and backbenchers before

The amendment was moved by Chamberlain's lieutenant Jesse Collings, and supported by Chamberlain and the radicals.

The Land Purchase Bill

Intended to win over the Irish landlords, it was objected to on principle by some Liberals who were reluctant to 'buy out' their political opponents. Others were alarmed by the cost.

The Home Rule Bill

Intended to satisfy and pacify the Irish while preserving the Union.
● An Irish parliament in Dublin would be responsible for Irish affairs. The Irish Executive would have full legislative powers and the ability to raise taxes for Irish matters.
● Responsibility for defence, foreign relations and customs would be retained in Westminster.
● The Irish was to contribute 1/15 of the UK budget for Imperial purposes.
● The Irish government would ultimately have responsibility for the Royal Irish Constabulary.
● Irish representation at Westminister would cease.

introducing legislation. The balance in the new House of Commons removed that option. On 26 January 1886 the Conservative government was defeated on an amendment to the Queen's Speech. Cleverly Gladstone ensured that this was not on an Irish issue but on small-holdings for agricultural labourers. With the Conservatives now committed to coercion, the Parnellites had no alternative but to vote with the Liberals although Gladstone had made no promises on Irish policy. Only eighteen Liberals, including Hartington, voted to save the government. By the end of January Gladstone was forming his third ministry.

For Gladstone, only one issue mattered. He consult neither his colleagues nor the views of the Irish. Confronted by Chamberlain in Cabinet on 13 March he was forced to admit that he was planning an independent Irish legislature. Chamberlain's resignation was inevitable, although it was delayed until 26 March when full details of the scheme were revealed to the Cabinet. He was accompanied by G.O. Trevelyan, the Scottish Secretary.

The 1886 scheme contained two major bills.

Despite an enthusiastic response in Ireland and America, Parnell was less happy about the proposals. The loss of control over customs was a serious blow but his main concern was the size of the Irish contribution to the imperial budget. After failing to extract concessions, he still had to recommend acceptance of the Bill in principle. The fate of the Bill rested with the dissident Liberals. Hartington and his supporters were irreconcileable. Before the second reading Chamberlain met a group of wavering and anti-home rule Liberals in a Commons committee room. He read them a letter from John Bright in which the veteran radical announced his intention of

PUNCH, OR THE LONDON CHARIVARI.—April 3, 1886.

"SET DOWN TWO, AND CARRY ONE." (P)

Anxious Parent. "IT'S MY ONLY CHANCE. CAN'T GET ACROSS SAFELY WITH BOTH OF 'EM."

'SET DOWN TWO, AND CARRY ONE', *PUNCH*, 3 APRIL 1886. THIS SUGGESTS THE POLITICAL DIFFICULTIES OF GLADSTONE IN TRYING TO GET THE HOME RULE PACKAGE THROUGH THE HOUSE. THE LAND BILL HAD TO BE ABANDONED.

voting against the second reading. That convinced enough waverers to ensure the Bill's defeat on 8 June by 343 votes to 313 – 93 Liberals voted in the majority.

This defeat, and the Liberal disaster in the subsequent general election, meant that the real challenge had been evaded. Throughout the crisis

Gladstone and Parnell had remained silent on the role of the House of Lords. The inbuilt Conservative and unionist majority there would have ensured the Home Rule Bill's defeat, as it did Gladstone's second Bill in 1893. Until the powers of the House of Lords were limited, until there was the public desire to see them restricted, Home Rule, despite the rhetoric of both Gladstone and Parnell, was unattainable.

Examining the Evidence

The Ulster Problem

Source A

Speech by Lord Randolph Churchill in Ulster Hall, Belfast, February 1886.

If the political parties and political leaders, not only Parliamentary but local, should be so utterly lost to every feeling and dictate of honour and courage as to hand over coldly, and for the sake of purchasing a short and illusory Parliamentary tranquillity, the lives and liberties of the Loyalists of Ireland to their hereditary and most bitter foes, make no doubt on this point – Ulster will not be a consenting party; Ulster at the proper moment will resort to the supreme arbitrament of force; Ulster will fight, Ulster will be right; Ulster will emerge from the struggle victorious, because all that Ulster represents to us Britons will command the sympathy and support of an enormous section of our British community.

RANDOLPH CHURCHILL ALMOST SEEMED TO BE ADVOCATING EXTRA-PARLIAMENTARY ACTIVITY TO PRESERVE THE UNION.

Source B

Gladstone, introducing the Home Rule Bill, 8 April 1886.

I cannot conceal the conviction that the voice of Ireland, as a whole, is at this moment clearly and Constitutionally spoken. I cannot say it is otherwise when five-sixths of its lawfully chosen Representatives are of one mind in this matter ... Certainly, Sir, I cannot allow it to be said that a Protestant minority in Ulster, or elsewhere, is to rule the question at large for Ireland.

Source C

Joseph Chamberlain, House of Commons, 9 April 1886.

... Ireland is not a homogeneous community ... it consists of two nations ... it is a nation which comprises two races and two religions ... I certainly might say a good deal in favour of the Protestant population. In Ulster they are prosperous and industrious and enterprizing, and in Ulster they have rivalled the peaceful activity of Glasgow, or Manchester, and of Birmingham. If you are going to carry this scheme in the face of the opposition of one-fifth of the population of Ireland ... and if ... they should feel their interests so much compromised that they resist your decision, how are you going to enforce it? Are you going to apply coercion to the loyal and law-abiding population while you taunt us with a desire and intention, which do not in fact exist, to apply it to those who have not always been loyal or law-abiding?

Source D

Parnell comments on the Ulster question during the 2nd reading debate, 7 June 1886.

... the ... Member for West Birmingham (Mr. Chamberlain) has claimed for Ulster ... a separate Legislature .... the opponents of this Bill have been compelled to seek refuge in the north-east corner of Ulster, consisting of three counties. Here again comes in the difficulty that, instead of protecting the majority of the Protestants of Ireland by constituting a Legislature in the north-east corner of Ulster you would abandon the majority of the Protestants of Ireland to their fate under a Dublin Parliament. Seven-twelfths of the Protestants ... live outside these three counties in the north-east corner of Ulster ... So that, whichever way you put it, you must give up the idea of protecting the Protestants either as a body or as a majority by the establishment of a separate Legislature, either in Ulster or in any portion of Ulster. No, Sir, we cannot give up a single Irishman. ... We want, Sir, all creeds and all classes in Ireland. We cannot consent to look upon a single Irishman as not belonging to us.

1 Compare and explain the different uses of electoral and population statistics in sources B, C and D.
2 Remembering the intended audience discuss the language and tone of sources A and C. What can be learnt about the prejudices of the writers or speakers?
3 Referring to the sources, categorise and explain the fears and concerns of the unionists and protestant critics of home rule.
4 Using the evidence of all the sources, discuss the view that politicians on all sides minimised the likelihood of Ulster/protestant resistance in 1886.

Parnell 1886–1891 – Zenith and Nadir

The years after the defeat of the Home Rule Bill were not easy. Parnell had to convince Liberal MPs and English voters that the Irish could safely be entrusted with their own parliament. At the same time he had to retain the loyalty of the Irish without committing himself to statements and policies that would alienate his uneasy English allies. The worsening agricultural depression made this doubly difficult. Evictions began to increase and rural disorder spread as tenants even finding it impossible to pay the judicial rents fixed by the land courts after 1881.

On selected estates tenants were advised to offer a reduced but realistic rent to the landlord; if he refused, the money was paid into a fund to finance the scheme and support evicted tenants. This was the campaign in which Parnell's leading lieutenants played a crucial role. Parnell remained aloof.

Parnell was reluctant to abandon the drive for home rule. He spent less and less time in the Commons, preferring to nurse his ill-health at the Eltham home of his mistress, Katharine O'Shea. This self-imposed remoteness suited his personality but it was to undermine his position with MPs and the tenant farmers in the crisis of 1890–91. Yet the harshness and violence of the Conservative government's response to the rural disorder gave the Irish leader the propaganda lever he needed to reawaken Liberal and nonconformist consciences. His reputation was further enhanced by the clumsy attempts of his political enemies, encouraged by Chamberlain, to discredit him. In the spring of 1887, *The Times* published a series of articles which included letters, allegedly signed by Parnell, condoning the Phoenix Park murders. The case against Parnell collapsed when Richard Pigott, an unemployed journalist, confessed that he had forged the crucial evidence.

By the end of 1889 Parnell's position seemed unassailable. He had been invited to Hawarden, and regularly shared platforms with leading Liberals. As long as Gladstone remained their leader they were committed to home rule, and the increasing unpopularity of the Conservative government suggested that there would be a majority Liberal administration after the next general election. Then, on 24 December 1889, Captain O'Shea petitioned for a divorce because of his wife's adultery with Parnell. Parnell's cool confidence convinced MPs that O'Shea would be bought off before the suit reached the court. The case was undefended when it was heard in November 1890. Parnell wanted the divorce so that he could marry Katharine. Unfortunately, soundings at the National Liberal Federation Conference suggested the Liberals would suffer politically if Parnell retained the leadership of the Irish party. The Party's commitment to home rule was not challenged, but continued alliance with a party led led by an adulterer was. Nonconformist morality had been offended.

TALKING POINT

Parnell rejected advice to retire temporarily from active politics, marry and then to return to party leadership once the scandal had been forgotten. How far, and why, did Parnell destroy everything he had built during the 1880s?

The Conclusion

... notwithstanding the splendid services rendered by Mr. Parnell to his country, his continuance at the present moment in the leadership would be productive of consequences disastrous in the highest degree to the cause of Ireland... would render my retention of the leadership of the Liberal Party, based as it has been mainly upon the prosecution of the Irish cause, almost a nullity.

Gladstone writing to John Morley, 24 November 1890. This appeared in
The Pall Mall Gazette on 26 November.

The publication of Gladstone's letter fatally undermined Parnell's position. After being rejected by the majority of his party, Parnell took his fight for political survival to Ireland. Contesting three violent by-elections (all lost by the Parnellite candidates) during 1891, he denounced all that he had achieved. The priests were against him, the bishops's condemnation of the Protestant adulterer had swiftly followed the decision of the MPs, his leading lieutenants were amongst his opponents and the farmers rejected him because he had ceased to lead during the Plan of Campaign. Exhausted by the struggle, he returned to Katherine, now his wife, in October 1891, a sick and dying man. He left his party weak and divided, but with a large majority clinging to the fundamental policy of the Liberal alliance.

In 1892 Gladstone, pledged to home rule, formed his fourth administration, this time with a parliamentary majority. His second Home Rule Bill, 1893, retained Irish representation at Westminster. A Commons majority was never going to be enough, and the Unionists overwhelmingly defeated the Bill in the Lords. After his resignation in 1894 his successor, Lord Rosebery, stressed that home rule was no longer the first priority for the Liberal Party or any future Liberal ministry.

TALKING POINT

Discuss the view that home rule was unattainable until the powers of the House of Lords had been restricted.

REVIEW

Charles Stewart Parnell – a Flawed Leader?

The Myth

- A traitor to his country! replied Dante. A traitor, an adulterer! The priests were right to abandon him. The priests were always the true friends of Ireland. ....
Mr Casey, freeing his arms from his holders, suddenly bowed his head on his hands with a sob of pain. - Poor Parnell! he cried loudly. My dead king!

James Joyce,
A Portrait of the Artist as a Young Man, 1916.

TALKING POINT

Who, according to the 'myth', was responsible for the fall of Parnell? The 'myth' placed him in the revolutionary tradition that ran through the Fenians to the Easter Rebellion of 1916. Did this reflect Parnell's role and intentions?

THE IRISH HORSE AND HIS MASTER (?)

Mr. Punch. "LEAVE HIM ALONE, JOHN; HE'S SAFE TO COME A CROPPER!"

MR PUNCH WARNS JOHN BULL TO HAVE NOTHING TO DO WITH PARNELL. WHAT DOES THE CARTOON SUGGEST ABOUT BRITISH ATTITUDES TO THE 'IRISH QUESTION'?

Hypothesis A

... uncompromising emphasis on constitutional action seemed to be justified by results ... In the realm of positive achievement his [Parnell's] principal successes were – the Land Act of 1881; the creation of a 'third force' in the House of Commons by the forging of a disciplined, pledge-bound parliamentary party; the inclusion of Ireland in the Reform Act of 1884 without loss of numerical representation in terms of parliamentary seats; the development, through the Irish National League, of constituency organisation ... which habituated the people to some of the forms of democratic self-government; the bringing of Home Rule on to the centre of the stage at Westminster; and the involvement of the Liberal party in the cause of Ireland.

F.S.L. Lyons, *Charles Stewart Parnell*, 1977.

Hypothesis B

Parnell's great flaw, of course, remains. The O'Shea liaison was reckless in the extreme. But it can now be seen in a different light. Too often in the years after 1882, when he might have fought actively for his ideal, Parnell lingered in Eltham. He saw the problem – that of sectarian division in the Irish people. He early grasped the nature of this problem in the South; belatedly he appreciated its full significance in the North. But he intervened only fitfully before his last great fight. He surrendered, not the leadership, but much of the initiative, to inferior hands. There are excuses: an overwhelming disgust with terrorism is one, and illness is another. But in the end it must be said that by his own lights he was inadequate.

P. Bew, *C.S. Parnell*, 1980.

TALKING POINT

Consider Hypothesis A and Hypothesis B. In the light of these comments, and drawing on your wider reading, assess Parnell's successes and failures.

Essay "'Poor fellow! poor fellow! it was a terrible tragedy. I do believe firmly that if these divorce proceedings had not taken place there would be a Parliament in Ireland to-day.'" (Gladstone in an interview he gave to R.B. O'Brien for his *Life of Charles Stewart Parnell 1846–1891*, 1898)

Comment on Gladstone's opinion. To what extent does the divorce explain the failure of the Liberal Party to enact a Home Rule Bill by 1894?

16 Liberal Decline and Conservative Ascendancy, 1880–1900

PREVIEW

The Electoral Evidence

The Liberal victory in 1880 suggested that Disraeli's 1874–80 ministry had been a temporary interruption in the Liberal/Whig political dominance since 1846. Yet by 1900 the Conservatives and their allies had become the natural party of government, with the Liberals a disorganised and ineffective opposition.

Election	Cons.	Lib. Unionists	Labour	Libs	Home Rulers
1880	238			353	61
1885 (Nov.)	249			335	86
1886 (July)	316	78		191	85
1892	268	47		274	81
1895	341	70		177	82
1900	334	68		186	82
1906	156		52	379	83

Governments 1880–1905		
	Party	Prime Minister
1880–85 (June)	Liberal	Gladstone
1885–86 (January)	Conservative	Lord Salisbury
1886–86 (July)	Liberal	Gladstone
1886–92 (June)	Conservative	Lord Salisbury
1892–94 (March)	Liberal	Gladstone
1894–95	Liberal	Lord Rosebery
1895–1902	Conservative/Unionist	Lord Salisbury
1902–05	Conservative/Unionist	A.J. Balfour

Compare this table with the one on page 252. What, in both periods, seems responsible for the monopoly of government by one political party?

Cabinet Making the Second Time – Gladstone in 1880

Gladstone was credited with the Liberal electoral victory, but he was not the leader of the party. Throughout the campaign he had insisted that he was subordinate to Hartington and Granville. It was, he wrote to Lord Acton, his '*last* general election',

A decisive accession of the Liberal Party to office without me ... is what I hope and pray.

The result made this position untenable. No Liberal government could survive without him. Victoria tried to avoid the inevitable, and on Disraeli's advice sent for Hartington. He indicated that she would have to offer the premiership to Gladstone. The Queen prevaricated, requesting Hartington to ask Gladstone whether he was willing to serve in a lesser capacity. Gladstone declined. Granville and Hartington then persuaded a distraught Victoria that she had no alternative.

The Whigs had found Gladstone's methods in Midlothian highly distasteful but they willingly joined his new cabinet. Gladstone himself took the Chancellorship of the Exchequer, whilst different radical sections were represented by Sir William Harcourt (Home Secretary), W.E. Forster (Chief Secretary for Ireland), and John Bright (Chancellor of the Duchy of Lancaster). Gladstone was reluctant to bring the 'new' Radicals into his cabinet. Neither Joseph Chamberlain nor Sir Charles Dilke had held junior office, and Gladstone believed that to be an essential first step to the Cabinet. Dilke's outspoken republicanism made him unacceptable to the Queen but the two co-operated to force one into the cabinet. Chamberlain exaggerated the contribution of the National Liberal Federation to the electoral victory. Unable to test these claims, and advised its President would be a greater menace on the backbenches, Gladstone offered him the Presidency of the Board of Trade with a cabinet seat. Dilke, out-manoeuvred by his colleague, had to be content with an under-secretaryship at the Foreign Office, although he later entered the Cabinet as President of the Local Government Board (1882).

Granville went back to the Foreign Office, Hartington was Secretary of State for India, Lord Spencer Lord President of the Council, the Duke of Argyll Lord Privy Seal, Lord Northbrook First Lord of the Admiralty and Lord Kimberley Secretary for the Colonies.

CABINET-MAKING.

HEAD CARPENTER. "I HOPE YOUR MAJESTY LIKES THE NEW CABINET. IT'S BEEN HARD WORK—SUCH A QUANTITY OF MATERIAL!"
THE QUEEN. "I SEE MOST OF IT IS WELL SEASONED—LET US HOPE THE NEW WOOD WILL STAND WELL!"

'CABINET MAKING', *PUNCH*, MAY 8, 1880.

WHO WAS THE 'NEW WOOD' AND WHY MIGHT THERE BE DOUBTS ABOUT ITS SEASONING? WOULD THE QUEEN LIKE THE NEW CABINET?

FOCUS

16.1
Parliamentary Reform in the 1880s – Politicians and the Political Context

> **In the 1880s, there were three important reform measures:**
>
> **1.** The Corrupt Practices Act 1883
> **2.** The Third Reform Act – franchise extension – 1884
> **3.** The Redistribution Act 1885.

The Corrupt Practices Act, 1883

The Ballot Act (1872) had not stopped bribery and corruption. In 1880 at least 4,000 Macclesfield electors accepted payments – some from both sides. The Corrupt Practices Act set a limit on expenditure and prohibited treating and bribery of the electorate. Expenditure was to be accounted for by an election agent. Penalties ranged from fines to imprisonment and expulsion from the Commons.

The Reform Crisis – Timescale

December 1883 – Cabinet crisis as Hartington is forced to accept franchise extension as the main measure for the 1884 session.
10 July 1884 – Reform Bill defeated in the Lords.
Summer/autumn 1884 – Chamberlain's anti-Peers campaign.
October 1884 – Reform Bill reintroduced in the Commons.
19 November 1884 – First meeting between Gladstone, Northcote and Salisbury to agree a compromise.

The Third Reform Acts

1 Reform Act, 1884: Household suffrage and the lodge franchise extended to the Counties.
2 Redistribution Act, 1885:
● Boroughs with a population of less than 15,000 lost their MPs; those with less than 50,000 lost one member; Macclesfield and Sandwich were disfranchised for corruption.
● 142 seats were re-distributed mainly into single member constituencies. Large urban areas were divided into divisions (e.g. Birmingham 7, Leeds 5, Liverpool 9) as were the counties (e.g. Cheshire 8, Lancashire 23, Somerset 7, Yorkshire 26).
● 24 boroughs retained two members.

TALKING POINT

'... the Third Reform Bill was a *major question* in British politics; it is worthy of attention precisely because the Third Reform Bill was not the occasion of a major crisis.' (A. Jones, *The Politics of Reform 1884*, 1972)
In what sense was the Third Reform Bill a 'major question' in British politics, and how was a 'major crisis' avoided?

Gladstone had resisted Chamberlain's demands that reform should be an early ministerial priority. By 1883 the government needed a domestic success to satisfy its radical critics, and, perhaps, the 'People's William' wished to restore his waning popularity in the country and his authority over his subordinates. The House of Lords defeat of the Reform Bill took him by surprise ('What a suicidal act of the Lords!'). Although he was critical of Chamberlain's assault on the privileges of that House he exploited his colleague's extremism to encourage royal mediation. After discussions, the Conservatives agreed to franchise extension provided it was followed by a Redistribution Bill. 'His still un-rivalled parliamentary skill, great political cunning, detachment from all factions combined with his undiminished hold on the party in the country, had enabled him to bring to fruition a matter that was ripe for treatment.' (E.J. Feuchtwanger, *Gladstone*, 1975)

Hartington opposed household suffrage for Ireland, arguing that it could only strengthen Parnell's position and lead to home rule. Isolated in the Cabinet on the issue, he could not afford to resign since that would throw Gladstone into the arms of the Radicals. He shared the Whig misgivings that the first household suffrage election would benefit the Radicals and leave Chamberlain to manage the redistribution in the new parliament. Hartington had pressed for a Redistribution Bill to accompany franchise extension.

Chamberlain needed a radical measure to restore reforming credentials damaged by three disappointing and frustrating years in office. He had campaigned for franchise extension during 1883. He looked forward to a radicalised House of Commons managing the redistribution after a general election on the new registers. Chamberlain questioned the powers and privileges of the Upper House in speeches that were condemned by the Queen and Hartington and rebuked by Gladstone. Although he liked to pose as Gladstone's lieutenant on domestic issues, he was outmanoeuvred by the Premier who exploited his radical speeches to persuade Queen and opposition of the need for compromise. The settlement left Chamberlain isolated in a Cabinet which had decisively rejected a 'Peers against People' general election.

Lord Salisbury was the insecure co-leader of a demoralised and divided party when the crisis began. He did not fear the extension of the franchise to the agricultural labourers but opposed the Franchise Bill because minority interests would be swamped by the new mass electorate. A redistribution was essential. Chamberlain's assault on the Lords did not alarm him; alone amongst the Conservative leadership he was prepared to face the challenge of a general election to defend the privileges of that House. Forced into compromise by his colleagues he took the lead, surprising Gladstone by his lack of respect for tradition during the redistribution negotiations. It was Salisbury who pressed for new single-member constituencies.

TALKING POINT

If there was no popular demand for parliamentary reform in 1884, why did it become the crucial political issue of that year? Comment on the similarities and differences between 1832, 1867 and 1884.

FOCUS

16.2 The Impact of Reform

The franchise was still not based simply on residence, it was far from universal, and a host of franchise and related registration eccentricities remained.

N. Blewett, 'The Franchise in the United Kingdom 1885–1918' in *Past & Present*, December 1965.

Parliamentary Electors in the UK

1866	1,364,000
1869	2,445,000
1883	3,152,000
1885	5,708,000
1911	7,904,000

By 1911 40 per cent of all adult males were not on the electoral register.

The complexities of the registration and the residential qualification disfranchised many working men.

Plural voting continued. There were about 500,000 plural voters in 1911.

The household and occupation franchises accounted for 84 per cent of all electors in 1911, but there were five other voting qualifications.

Domestic servants resident with employers and sons living with parents had no vote.

No women had the vote.

The Redistribution Act did ensure that, for the first time, representation of different regions was related to population. For example, London's MPs increased from 22 to 59. Ireland was the exception. It remained over-represented at Westminster compared to the other parts of the United Kingdom because Parnell was too powerful to be offended.

The Political Implications of Reform

They may periodically return to office, but they will have place not power. If I were a Tory I would poison Salisbury's rum and water. If he had been in the pay of the caucus what more could he have done to destroy his party and give up everything for which it has hitherto existed?

How accurate was Chamberlain's assessment of the likely effects of the redistribution for the Conservative Party?

Both Chamberlain and the Whigs were concerned at the loss of the small two-member boroughs where a Whig and a Radical and been run in harness although it was believed that the Whigs would be more damaged.

Chamberlain seized the opportunity to launch a campaign to win the new rural voters for radicalism. This became the 'unauthorised programme'.

Salisbury viewed the redistribution as a means of protecting Tory landowners from the new electorate by drawing boundaries to separate urban and rural areas.

The Conservatives benefitted from the splitting of previously radical cities into several divisions. They soon dominated the suburban middle class constituencies.

The Corrupt Practices Act and the intricacies of the registration meant that organisation was essential. Professional agents became more important, but the restrictions on expenditure required an increase in voluntary work by party activists.

The Irish Nationalists never won fewer than 81 Irish seats on the wider franchise. The over-representation of Ireland at Westminster allowed them to hold the balance in 1885, 1892 and 1910.

TALKING POINT

Britain was still not a democracy after 1884, but there was no widespread demand for further parliamentary reform. How can this be explained?

TALKING POINT

A triumph for Gladstone, an opportunity for Chamberlain, a successful defence of party interests by Salisbury. Who gained most from the Third Reform Act?

Gladstone's Second Ministry, 1880–85: Successes against the Odds?

P.W. Clayden, radical Nonconformist journalist and National Liberal Federation activist, identified the tasks facing a Liberal government in 1880:

> England under Lord Beaconsfield has been led back from prosperous to unprosperous days, from peace and plenty to privation and war; from assured self-government to personal rule. The effort to shake herself free may be a supreme one, but it will certainly result in restoring the country to honest and economical finance, to domestic legislation ruled by desire for the people's welfare, and to a foreign policy based on truth, humanity and justice'.
>
> P.W. Clayden, *England under Lord Beaconsfield*, 1880.

TALKING POINT
Explain Clayden's priorities for a Liberal government. To what extent had they been achieved by 1885?

Gladstone would have accepted Clayden's agenda. His decision to combine the Premiership with the Exchequer enabled him to start on the national finances. In his 1880 Budget he abolished the Malt Tax, a longstanding agricultural grievance, and increased income tax by 1d. Unlike 1868 there were no agreed policy objectives. It was assumed that the Ministry would extend household suffrage to the counties, but Gladstone was reluctant to introduce a measure that would require an early general election. Chamberlain, in particular, found this enforced delay frustrating.

Ireland dominated from 1880 until the passage of the Arrears Act in 1882. The 1881 Land Act restored peace to the Irish countryside but the cost to the government had been great – disputes in Cabinet, the breakdown of parliamentary business, the resignations of the Duke of Argyll in 1881 and of W.E. Forster and Lord Cowper in 1882. Nevertheless, the crisis had been well handled. Gladstone revealed all his old parliamentary skills in managing the passage of the Land Act and his political judgement in devising a measure that disabled the Land League. South Africa, 1880–1881, and Egypt provided imperial distractions. Egypt, in one form or another, disrupted government from 1881 until after the withdrawal from the Sudan in 1885. Like Ireland it split the Cabinet and provoked a resignation – Bright in 1882. Gladstone's management of the crisis, however, lacked the deftness and assurance he displayed in resolving the Irish difficulty.

Ireland, Egypt, the Bradlaugh affair, the disruption of Commons business by the Fourth Party and the Irish merely emphasised the Cabinet's lack of adequate planning. No real attempt was made to use parliamentary time effectively and each session was marked by the abandonment of legislation. Gladstone's own assumption that he would only remain in office long enough to deal with the legacy of Beaconsfieldism left Ministers without a sense of direction and long-term purpose.

Gladstone's constant talk of retirement was unsettling but he always seemed able to find an excuse to remain. With Beaconsfieldism finally laid to rest in 1881, he had to stay on to deal with Irish land. In 1882 he gave up the Exchequer but postponed retirement because of Egypt. A year later he

The Egyptian and Sudan crises are covered in Chapter 14 pages 339–341, Ireland in Chapter 15 pages 343–362.

CHARLES BRADLAUGH, RADICAL, ATHEIST, ADVOCATE OF BIRTH CONTROL, WAS ELECTED MP FOR NORTHAMPTON IN 1880. GLADSTONE DEPLORED HIS VIEWS BUT RESPECTED HIS RIGHT TO HOLD THEM AND TO TAKE HIS SEAT. A SELECT COMMITTEE REJECTED BRADLAUGH'S REQUEST THAT HE SHOULD BE ALLOWED TO AFFIRM RATHER THAN TAKE THE OATH REQUIRED FROM MPS. POINTING TO THE HYPOCRISY, HE THEN PREPARED TO TAKE THE OATH. OPPOSITION TO THIS WAS ORCHESTRATED BY THE FOURTH PARTY. THE LIBERALS WERE DIVIDED. BRADLAUGH'S ATHEISM WAS UNACCEPTABLE TO THE MAJORITY, BUT LIBERALS HAD CAMPAIGNED FOR CIVIL AND RELIGIOUS EQUALITY. BRADLAUGH WAS EXPELLED AND RE-ELECTED THREE TIMES; IN 1883 THE GOVERNMENT'S AFFIRMATION BILL WAS DEFEATED DESPITE THE WHOLE-HEARTED SUPPORT IT RECEIVED FROM GLADSTONE. THE BRADLAUGH AFFAIR WAS AN ADDED DISTRACTION, AND ANOTHER ISSUE WHICH THE PREMIER'S OPPONENTS COULD EXPLOIT AGAINST HIM.

THE MEMBERS OF THE FOURTH PARTY WERE LORD RANDOLPH CHURCHILL, SIR HENRY DRUMMOND WOLFF, JOHN GORST AND A.J. BALFOUR. THEY INDULGED IN OBSTRUCTION AND VITUPERATIVE ATTACKS ON GLADSTONE LEADING THE ATTACK ON BRADLAUGH PARTLY TO EMBARRASS HIM. ENCOURAGED BY DISRAELI, THEIR REAL TARGET WAS SIR STAFFORD NORTHCOTE,

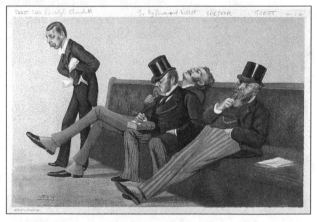

CONSERVATIVE LEADER IN THE COMMONS. HE WAS OVERAWED BY GLADSTONE AND INCLINED TO CONSTRUCT A CENTRE COALITION WITH THE WHIGS. AFTER DISRAELI'S DEATH IN 1881, THEY BACKED SALISBURY IN THE CONTEST FOR THE LEADERSHIP OF THE PARTY. TOGETHER WITH THE IRISH THEIR TACTICS HELPED TO MAKE THE HOUSE OF COMMONS UNMANAGEABLE UNTIL THE PROCEDURAL CHANGES OF 1881.

agreed to remain to pilot the Franchise and Redistribution Bills through the Commons. In truth neither Whigs nor Radicals wanted him to go. Hartington believed that the Whigs needed Gladstone to restrain the Radicals. Chamberlain and Dilke knew that the Liberals could only form a government which included the Whigs. Perhaps Gladstone's talk of retirement was a deliberate ploy to control his ambitious and argumentative colleagues. Ministers were reluctant to commit themselves to long term policies because of the uncertainty, and their frequent quarrels justified Gladstone's retention of the leadership as the indispensable preserver of Liberal unity.

Examining the Evidence

Whigs and Radicals – Competing Principles?

The Protagonists

THE MARQUESS OF HARTINGTON, BORN 1833, HEIR TO THE DUKE OF DEVONSHIRE, ENTERED PARLIAMENT AGED 24, JUNIOR MINISTER AT 30, IN THE CABINET AT 33. HIS FAMILY HAD IMPECCABLE WHIG CREDENTIALS. HE HAD SHARED THE PARTY LEADERSHIP WITH GRANVILLE, 1875–80, AND WAS GENERALLY ACKNOWLEDGED AS GLADSTONE'S LIKELY SUCCESSOR.

Source A
The 'strength' of Liberalism

It is ... more meaningful to regard the Liberal party as an organism, constantly evolving out of the tensions between conflicting forces, but with no fixed, ultimate objective ... The crucial question in Liberal politics was where to find the common ground on which contending sections, each claiming to embody 'Liberal principles' and perhaps having little sympathy with the aims of others, yet each needing the support of the others if there were to be any chance of gaining power and carrying any measures at all, could agree to co-operate for immediate political purposes.

... it was necessary for 'Liberalism' to remain vague if the Liberals were to remain a viable force in politics. the absence of any precise definition of 'Liberalism' was potentially a great source of strength, for it enabled the party to embrace a wide diversity of opinions which, while making a certain degree of disunity almost unavoidable, acted at the same time as a powerful influence against disintegration.

T.A. Jenkins, *Gladstone, Whiggery and the Liberal Party 1874–1886*, 1988.

TALKING POINT

To what extent does this view of the Liberal Party concidence with those discussed in Chapter 13?

Source B
Lord Hartington explains the role of the Whigs within the Liberal Party in a speech at Accrington, 1883.

I admit that the Whigs are not the leaders in a popular movement, but the Whigs have been able, as I think, to the great advantage of the Country, to direct, and guide, and moderate those popular movements. They have formed a connecting link between the advance party and those classes which, possessing property, power and influence, are naturally averse to change, and I think I may claim that it is greatly owing to their guidance and to their action that the great and beneficial changes which have been made in the direction of popular reform in this Country, have been made not by the shock of revolutionary agitation, but by the calm and peaceful process of constitutional acts.

TALKING POINT

Refer back to Chapter 5. How similar is Hartington's view to that of the Whigs of the 1830s?

JOSEPH CHAMBERLAIN, BORN 1836, SUCCESSFUL BUSINESSMAN AND ORGANISER OF BIRMINGHAM LIBERALISM. LED NONCONFORMIST CAMPAIGN AGAINST THE 1870 EDUCATION ACT; CREATOR OF THE NATIONAL LIBERAL FEDERATION. FORCED HIMSELF INTO THE CABINET 1880. HE BELIEVED THAT THE POLITICAL FUTURE LAY WITH THE RADICALS.

Source C

The Radical Programme

A series of articles appeared in the *Fortnightly Review* during 1883 which were re-published in 1885, as 'The Radical Programme', with a Foreword by Chamberlain. Its proposals became the core of the 'unauthorised programme' on which Chamberlain fought the 1885 election.

Local government reform: elected country councils to replace the administration of rural areas by the gentry and magistrates.

'Free land': councils to have compulsory purchase powers to acquire smallholdings and allotments for agricultural labourers.

'Free schools': free elementary education.

'Free churches': disestablishment of the Church of England and the Church of Scotland.

A new graduated income tax and taxes on the unearned increment from land.

Restrictions on the powers of slum landlords to encourage clearance and rebuilding.

Payment of MPs.

Reform of the House of Lords.

Its unifying theme was an assault on a privileged and selfish class of landlords.

Source D

But then I ask, what ransom will property pay for the security which it enjoys? What substitute will it find for the natural rights which have ceased to be recognised? Society is banded together in order to protect itself against the instincts of those of its members who would make very short work of private ownership if they were left alone. That is all very well, but I maintain that society owes these men something more than mere toleration in return for the restrictions which it places upon their liberty of action.

Chamberlain's speech at Birmingham, 5 January 1885.

TALKING POINT

Was Chamberlain a 'problem' because he was challenging the assumptions on which the Liberal Party rested by demanding a clear radical programme?

Source E

I believe that the great difficulty with which we have to deal is the excessive inequality in the distribution of riches ... It is not our duty, it is not our wish, to pull down and abase the rich, although I do not think that the excessive aggregation of wealth in a few hands is any advantage to anybody; but our object is to raise the general condition of the people.

Chamberlain's speech at Hull, 5 August 1885.

Source F

... despite an instinctive temptation in times of crisis to challenge the Liberal coalition with some new political line-up, Chamberlain had shown ... a sound aversion to casting himself into the rain-swept terrain beyond the Gladstonian umbrella.

... Chamberlain wanted to work with Hartington, he told Harcourt [in September 1885], and 'I do not think he will find me exacting.'

... Chamberlain was not renouncing his ambition ultimately to control Liberalism by eliminating 'whiggery'. For the immediate future, however, he was skirmishing for greater Radical influence over Liberalism's traditional elite.

R. Jay, *Joseph Chamberlain: a Political Study*, 1981.

---

1 Chamberlain's Radical Programme was an attempt to counter emerging socialist ideas. What, if anything, was new about the Radical Programme, who was it likely to appeal to? Refer to sources D and E and your wider knowledge.
2 To what extent did the Whig/Radical confrontation contribute to the weakness of Gladstone's Second Ministry?

Gladstone's Second Ministry – a Review

In May 1885 the Cabinet discussed and rejected Chamberlain's Irish Central Board scheme. The Crimes Act was to be renewed without any remedial legislation. On 20 May Dilke and Chamberlain submitted their resignations to a Prime Minister who had earlier received similar letters from Hartington and Selbourne because of the decision to withdraw from the Sudan. Gladstone prevaricated whilst Churchill negotiated the alliance of Irish Nationalists and Conservatives that challenged the government's budget proposals on 8 June. The absence of a significant number of Liberal Members contributed to defeat by 12 votes. The Cabinet seized the opportunity to escape from the difficulties of office by resigning.

Essay

Consider these two assessments of Gladstone's second Ministry:

'What was exceptional about the 1880 government was the extent of unforeseen problems and events that beset its course ... Gladstone dealt with these matters with his great mastery of detail and powers of work, marred by his lack of proportion and impulsiveness; he did it with a team of able but very disparate men.'

E.J. Feuchtwanger, *Gladstone*, 1973.

A ministry of all the troubles with few achievements to its credit.

NEAB Advanced Level question.

You will need to refer to Chapters 14 and 15 to complete this task.

In your essay preparation, you will need to explain 'unforeseen problems' and 'all the troubles'.
Examine Gladstone's handling of the crises.
Ireland was a 'trouble' but did the Land Act provide a short-term solution? The Reform Act was an achievement but is this counter-balanced by the mishandling of imperial affairs, particularly Egypt and the Sudan?
What 'troubles' were there in the Cabinet? To what extent was Gladstone a destabilizing factor?

Joseph Chamberlain and the 'Unauthorised Programme'

CHAMBERLAIN OFFERED SOLUTIONS FOR THE PROBLEM OF SLUM HOUSING BOTH IN 'THE RADICAL PROGRAMME' AND IN THE 'UNAUTHORISED PROGRAMME'. ECONOMIC DIFFICULTIES, UNEMPLOYMENT AND SQUALID LIVING CONDITIONS SEEMED TO PROVIDE FERTILE GROUND FOR THE GROWTH OF THE SOCIALIST IDEOLOGY HE WAS TRYING TO COMBAT.

Although the eventual political crisis stemmed from the Irish Question, and Gladstone's search for a solution, Ireland was not a significant issue during the election campaign.

Chamberlain, rebuffed by the Parnell and the nationalist press, abandoned his Central Board Scheme and devoted his attention to the 'unauthorised programme' which he believed would win the election for the Liberals. He hoped to reunite the Radicals and to reconstruct the Party around a programme that would supersede the 'fads' and 'causes' that had driven Liberalism.

The 'unauthorised programme' is outlined on page 371.

There was nothing new in the 'unauthorised programme', there was nothing 'socialist' about it despite the language used by Chamberlain and the abuse of his opponents. Hartington and other Whig leaders took great exception to Chamberlain's tone, to his attacks on privilege, wealth and the landlord class. Hartington tried to stop Chamberlain imposing the programme on the Party, but it was not intended as a direct assault on the Whigs. Chamberlain was prepared to accept Hartington's leadership in the short term provided he had the freedom to implement the Radical Programme. The heated exchanges, however, convinced Gladstone that he had to remain leader to hold the Party together. Neither side could afford the odium of denying their venerable leader, nor could either group survive without him.

Chamberlain even failed to unite the Radicals, many of whom preferred Gladstone's moral leadership to the complexities and controversies of Chamberlain's programme. Dilke and other Chamberlain supporters quickly realised that the 'unauthorised programme' was a vote-loser in urban areas. The attack on slum landlords was overshadowed by the sectarianism of 'free schools' and 'free churches' which alarmed more voters than they attracted and frightened Liberal churchmen. Chamberlain blamed the Whigs for his failure, but there was no 'urban cow' to woo the working man and Nonconformity was too narrow a base to win the new constituencies.

Gladstone attributed Liberal losses to 'Fair Trade + Parnell + Church + Chamberlain.' The great Radical's reputation for political leadership and electoral foresight was shattered by the collapse of the 'programme'. Chamberlain's weakened position in the Party enabled Gladstone to ignore his claims for high office when he formed his Third Ministry, relegating him to the backwater of the Local Government Board.

'Three acres and a cow' – the promise of the 'Unauthorised Programme' to the newly enfranchised agricultural labourers.

TALKING POINT

Explain, and comment on, Gladstone's assessment of the election result.

EXAMINING THE EVIDENCE

The Liberal Party and Home Rule: Motives and Purposes

Source A

The [Home Rule] bill was ... meant to unite the Liberal party by committing it to the principle of home rule and to prepare it for further protracted struggle in which there would only be one possible leader.

All that in the end can be said about Gladstone's short-term political motives, is that he wished to recapture control of his party, control which he had had to share with powerful colleagues in 1880–85 ... he did not dislike Hartington ... Home rule need not have been meant to make Chamberlain a pariah, but it could not have failed to make him either that or a subordinate.

A.B. Cooke and J. Vincent, *The Governing Passion: Cabinet Government and Party Politics in Britain 1885–86*, 1974.

Source B

Home Rule was not only good for Ireland; it was good in itself, and by espousing it Liberalism would do itself good ... Parnell ... offered Gladstone the possibility of double advantages: on the one hand Home Rule and reconciliation with Ireland would be seen as the ultimate consummation of Gladstone's career and an inevitable fulfilment of the central point and purpose of Liberal politics; on the other hand Liberalism ... would be saved from losing its soul to Chamberlain, the man Gladstone had come to see rather as a potential second Beaconsfield, a power for political debauchery, instilling base passions of class jealousy.

Home Rule ... would ... keep Liberalism trimmed and in balance to avoid being swamped in the 'jingo' and 'constructionist' tides ...

R. Shannon, *The Crisis of Imperialism 1865–1915*, 1974.

TALKING POINT

How completely can we understand the motives of people in the past? What makes it difficult to reach final conclusions?
Consider the view that the Home Rule crisis was more about control of the Liberal Party than it was about Ireland.

Source C

[Chamberlain] Having absorbed the lesson of 1880 ... had no intention of allowing the Grand Old Man to lead the party off on another crusade, and thus forget the real business of radical politics. Since the 1885 election had confirmed that he could not dominate the party Chamberlain had sought a short cut by co-operating with Hartington and the Whig elements to topple Gladstone. The basis for a Hartington–Chamberlain government existed in their common dislike of Gladstone's supine and unpatriotic foreign policy; within such a government Chamberlain believed that Hartington, lacking Gladstone's influence with the radicals, would be obliged to allow him to determine the pace of domestic reform. This prospect of an alternative Liberal ministry posed a dilemma for Gladstone from which he escaped successfully by seizing the initiative over Home Rule. The joint withdrawal of Hartington and Chamberlain was a logical consequence in that it reflected their common failure to ditch Gladstone, and Chamberlain's inability to win control of the radical forces.

M. Pugh, *The Making of Modern British Politics 1867–1939*, 1982.

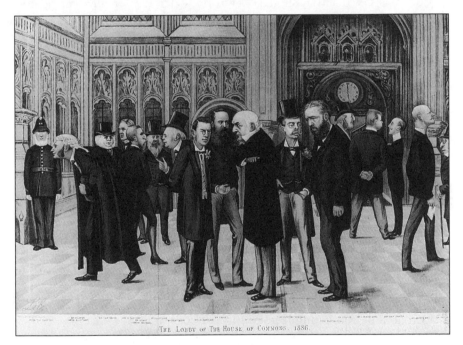

THE LOBBY OF THE HOUSE OF COMMONS. 1886.

KEY FIGURES IN THE HOME RULE CRISIS ARE AT THE CENTRE: CHAMBERLAIN (WITH HIS MONOCLE AND ORCHID BUTTON-HOLE), PARNELL, GLADSTONE, CHURCHILL AND HARTINGTON. HOW MIGHT THIS BE A MISLEADING PIECE OF EVIDENCE?

The Liberal Party Split

Apart from Home Rule, there was no reason why the Liberal Party should have broken up in 1886. Whigs and Liberals agreed that remedial legislation was needed for Ireland, the difference was over its extent. Although there had been a steady drift of Whigs and conservative Liberals away from the Party Radical pressure was not sufficient to drive Hartington out. As Gladstone's acknowledged successor he had too much to lose by precipitate action. T.A. Jenkins has shown that the anti-Home Rulers came from all sections of the Liberal Party – it was not a Whig exodus.

Lords Spencer, Ripon, Kimberley and Granville maintained the Whig presence in Gladstone's third cabinet.

Gladstone bears a major responsibility for the split. He tried to win Hartington over at the end of 1885 but was prepared to carry on without him. Chamberlain entered the Cabinet with misgivings. Gladstone's off-handedness, and his attempt to reduce the salary of Chamberlain's under-secretary, Jesse Collings, were insensitive. His refusal to consult with and to conciliate the Radical leader reflected Gladstone's inability to handle difficult colleagues. Underestimating Chamberlain's positive qualities, disliking his 'constructionism' and deploring his overt ambition Gladstone welcomed his resignation.

Chamberlain, however, was not ready to be conciliated. Believing Home Rule to be inexpedient and unpopular with the electorate he calculated that he would be better placed as a possible future leader outside the Cabinet rather than remaining on the inside to modify a politically dangerous policy.

The split contributed to the electoral disaster of July 1886. Liberal abstentions and an exceptionally large number of uncontested seats merely emphasises the Party's disarray. The Liberal Unionists survived because Salisbury insisted that they should not be opposed by Conservative candidates. Chamberlain retained control of his Birmingham power base but he had been forced out of the leadership of 'the party of progress' by the 'Grand Old Man' whose longevity continued to frustrate the younger man's hopes.

Gladstone had hoped to cut Colling's salary by £300 as part of an economy drive.

The Liberals 1886–1900 – a Summary

The breakdown of the 'Round Table' talks on reunion between leading Gladstonians and Chamberlain, February 1887, confirmed the split. Harsh Conservative coercion policies began to consolidate support for Home Rule in the Party. Parnell's vindication in 1889 merely strengthened a by-election tide already flowing in the Liberals' favour. The divorce scandal discredited both Parnell and the policy. The Liberal revival stuttered and the Irish Nationalists held the balance in the Parliament elected in 1892. Home Rule had to be given priority. Its slow passage through the Commons, 1893, to inevitable defeat in the Lords, prevented any other legislation being considered. During 1894 and 1895, numerous Liberal bills were lost in the Upper House. 'Filling up the cup', deliberately sending measures to be rejected by the Lords to unite the country against their powers, was punished in the 1895 Election. Internal squabbles were exacerbated by conflicting reactions to the Boer War, 1899.

Gladstone – a Leadership Liability?

Gladstone's position was unassailable after 1886 but, out of sympathy with changing social and political values, and intending resignation once Home Rule had been carried, he did not appreciate the necessity to develop policies for the future. Colleagues and followers who pressed for additional commitments were ignored. Old age increased his egotism and ill-health his aloofness. This was a negative form of leadership.

TALKING POINT

To what extent was the 1886 crisis a significant landmark in the decline of the Liberal Party?

Home Rule – political 'albatross'?

Home Rule did not appeal to the broader English electorate. It seemed to pander to an obstreperous racial and religious minority. The divorce scandal undermined Gladstone's claim that it was a morally superior cause.

... or source of unity?

The majority of radical MPs accepted the policy as the price of driving the Whigs out and reconstructing the Party. Unfortunately it was reconstructed on Gladstonian principles, with a focus on the single great moral issue as a temporary answer to the difficulty of prioritising other claims. The underlying sources of conflict were not removed.

A more radical party?

A radicalised Party adopted Home Rule to clear the Irish obstruction to further reform. The National Liberal Federation Conferences drew up annual programmes – all the old radical and nonconformist demands – culminating in the Newcastle Programme of 1891. The defection of Chamberlain, however, deprived the radicals of a leader who could have provided discipline and purpose. A more radical party became a more sectionalist party with Nonconformist, Welsh and temperance lobbies pressurising the leadership for priority. Rosebery's government was overwhelmed by these quarrels and disputes. In 1895 the Welsh threatened to secede if disestablishment of the Church of Wales was abandoned in favour of the local veto of the United Kingdom Alliance.

TALKING POINT

'A backward-looking 'product of panic' rather than a constructive attempt to provide a positive alternative to Home Rule and solutions to contemporary social and political problems.' What was missing from the Newcastle Programme? To what extent would it unite the Party and attract broader support?

The Newcastle Programme 1891

Parnell's disgrace in 1890 caused many to question the Irish priority. The Newcastle Programme was a concession to this feeling in outlining other policy areas. It received only a half-hearted endorsement from Gladstone. The main features of the Programme were as follows:

- Home Rule
- disestablishment in Wales and Scotland
- local veto on sale of alcohol
- land reform
- elected parish and district councils
- public control of denominational schools
- employers' liability to compensate for injuries at work
- reform of the registration system
- ending of plural voting.

Gladstone's Legacy

Gladstone's resignation, March 1894, came as a relief. The defeat of Home Rule, the Cabinet's refusal to fight an election on the powers of the Upper House, his dismay at Rosebery's foreign policy and his lone opposition to increased naval expenditure suggested that his brand of Liberalism had lost its relevance. Unfortunately, Gladstone had not prepared the way for a successor. Lord Rosebery was the Queen's choice. Clashes with a jealous Sir William Harcourt soured Rosebery's premiership and leadership until he resigned in 1896. Harcourt provided an impossible leader and was eventually replaced by the quiet and inoffensive Sir Henry Campbell-Bannerman in 1898.

There was no policy to follow Home Rule. The Party was split by disputes over priorities in the 1894–95 session – Rosebery unsuccessfully tried to make reform of the House of Lords the next great uniting question. Ministers welcomed defeat in 1895 (over a minor military supply issue). The Party had apparently lost the will to govern. It collapsed into disarray as old-fashioned Radicals, Liberal Imperialists and the 'New' Liberals debated the best ways to face the challenges of socialism and the new century.

Home Rule remained part of the Liberal programme, but it was now the demand of one section, waiting, like the rest, for the resolution of the problem of the House of Lords. The Unionists claimed to be the national party condemning the Liberals as a 'mongrel political combination of teetotallers, Irish revolutionists, Welsh demagogues, Small Englanders, English separatists, and general uprooters of all that is national and good' (Conservative pamphlet, 1895).

The 1892–5 government had its successes. The Parish Councils Act (1894) extended democratic local government. Other legislation reduced the hours of workers in royal ordnance factories and the railways. Harcourt's introduction of death duties in 1894 was a first tentative step towards a policy of wealth redistribution.

The 'New Liberalism' and the Party's relationship with socialism and the Labour movement is covered in Chapter 17.

---

1 Consider these influences on Gladstone and find examples from his political career to illustrate them.
   – an acceptance of moral certainties rooted in religious belief;
   – an unambiguous belief in the value of free trade and individualism;
   – a concern to preserve the existing social order;
   – political ambition;
   – Peelite pragmatism.

2 Gladstone became increasingly more aloof and detached from those whom he led:
   – He believed in aristocracy and the leadership role the Whigs had to play in the Liberal Party. His sympathies were with them but he was not a Whig. They distrusted him.
   – He shared many aspirations with the Nonconformists, but as a High Churchman found their more extreme demands difficult to accommodate.
   – His background was Liverpool commerce and finance but, as a Flintshire landowner, he had little in common with the middle classes that formed the backbone of the later Liberal Party.
   – He praised the 'moral virtue' of the masses but did not understand the needs of the working class and deplored the materialism that was attracting them by the end of his career.

   Discuss Gladstone's strengths and weaknesses as a party leader and explain his success as leader of the Liberals.

PUNCH, 28 MAY 1898.

GLADSTONE ENTERED THE HOUSE OF COMMONS AT THE 1832 GENERAL ELECTION; HE LAST SPOKE IN 1894, FINALLY RETIRING AT THE 1895 ELECTION.

TALKING POINT

Discuss Gladstone's
contribution to the
development of Liberalism
during the nineteenth
century.
To what extent was he
responsible for the Party's
decline?

Lord Salisbury, the Liberal Unionists and Conservative Ascendancy

The Political Context

Conservative political dominance was caused by two things – Ireland and the redistribution of seats in 1885. In Ireland Salisbury discovered an issue 'where his desires, the interests of his party, and the prejudices of the country came together powerfully' (P. Marsh, *The Discipline of Popular Government: Lord Salisbury's Domestic Statecraft 1884–1902*, 1978). The new one-member constituencies enabled the Conservative Party to benefit from the increasing conservatism of the properted middle classes. Careful drawing of boundaries separated rural from mining and industrial county seats, and created 'class' constituencies in the larger cities. The effect was most marked in London – in 1865 no Conservative MPs were elected in London; in 1900, over 50 were returned.

In Leeds the Conservatives regularly won two of the five seats, and in Sheffield three. 'Villa' Toryism helped the Conservatives to their majorities in 1886, 1895 and 1900; in 1892 it gave them their majority in England. Traditionally the Conservatives had been the party of the shires, but in 1885 the Liberals won more county seats than the Conservatives. They compensated in the boroughs.

TALKING POINT

Was there really a
'Conservative ascendancy'?
What problem of the British
electoral system is
highlighted here?
Comment on the
'uncontested seats'.

% of the votes cast for Conservative/Unionist and Liberals					
	Conservative % vote	seats won	Liberal % vote	seats won	uncontested seats
1892	47.0	314	45.1	272	63
1895	49.1	411	45.7	177	189
1900	51.5	402	44.6	184	243
1906	43.6	157	49.0	401	114

Few businessmen reached high office. W.H. Smith, Leader of the House of Commons (1887–91), C.T. Ritchie, a member of Salisbury's second and third cabinets, and George Goschen, Chancellor of the Exchequer (1887–92) were amongst the exceptions. Entering politics later in life than landed gentlemen, businessmen did not have the time or the inclination to build a political career. Cabinets were still dominated by the landed class. However, Salisbury rewarded influential middle-class supporters with honours and peerages – the first Prime Minister to do so on a large scale.

The Leadership of Lord Salisbury

Salisbury was a pessimist, seeking to lead a party of resistance to delay the democratic changes and attacks on property that he feared in the aftermath of franchise extension. He viewed the Conservative Party and the House of Lords as the last defences of the established order. The Liberal failures to win an overall majority in 1892 justified his use of the

House of Lords veto to block Liberal legislation, 1892–95. Salisbury's were not great reform ministries although the preoccupation with Ireland (1886–92) and with imperial affairs (Boer War 1899–1902) left little parliamentary time for constructive activity. Nevertheless, enough was done to give an impression of cautious progressivism. His own reputation rested on his assured handling of international affairs. He combined the Foreign Office with the Premiership, 1885–86, 1887–92, 1895–1900.

A party of resistance had to be well organised under the firm control of the leadership. Salisbury presided over a significant development in the Conservative party machine. The National Union of Conservative Associations built up an extensive branch network but the work of 'Captain' R.W.E. Middleton, principal agent from 1885, was more important. Under his supervision, professional agents were appointed in many constituencies and regional offices were established. The National Liberal Federation made louder political noises at its conferences but the quietly efficient work of Middleton was more electorally valuable.

Consolidating Authority – Salisbury's Challenges

After the 1886 Election two pressing difficulties faced Salisbury – the unpredictable behaviour of Lord Randolph Churchill, and the need to accommodate his Liberal Unionist allies.

The Ejection of Lord Randolph

Through the Fourth Party, Churchill had helped to force Salisbury's leadership on the Party. By cultivating the National Union of Conservative Associations and adopting a rabble-rousing form of Tory Democracy at its annual conferences in 1883 and 1884, he forced his way into the Party's inner councils. His reward was the India Office in Salisbury's caretaker administration and then the Exchequer and Leader of the House of Commons in his second.

Salisbury found Churchill's attempts to commit the government to a sweeping programme distasteful and disliked Churchill's insubordination. Churchill's mistake was to overestimate his own indispensability. Proposed budget cuts for the armed forces were unacceptable to Salisbury and the rest of the Cabinet. Churchill's letter of explanation was not intended as a resignation but Salisbury chose to interpret it as such. Defence was the wrong issue on which to challenge the Prime Minister's authority – the Party backed him, not Churchill. The Whig banker George Goschen accepted the Chancellorship, becoming the first Liberal Unionist to join the government.

The Muzzling of Joseph Chamberlain

The Conservative government could not afford to alienate its Liberal Unionist allies. Salisbury offered Hartington the Premiership in 1886 and in 1887 but Chamberlain's likely hostility made a formal coalition unthinkable. Although his personal following was small (12 MPs in 1886)

SALISBURY'S ACHIEVEMENT WAS TO PROVIDE MIDDLE CLASS CONSERVATIVES WITH THE ARISTOCRATIC LEADERSHIP THEY CRAVED FOR BUT SO VERY RARELY FOUND. HE LED HIS PARTY IN FIVE ELECTIONS AND, WITH HIS ALLIES, WON MAJORITIES IN THREE. THE REALIGNMENT OF PARTIES INTO THE UNIONIST COALITION DID NOT LESSEN HIS OWN POLITICAL CONTROL OR WEAKEN HIS PRINCIPLES.

Foreign and imperial affairs are covered in Chapter 17.

CHURCHILL ENVISAGED AN ALLIANCE BETWEEN HIMSELF AND CHAMBERLAIN WHICH WOULD DELIVER SUBSTANTIAL MEASURES OF SOCIAL REFORM.

Churchill's political career was finished. Salisbury could safely ignore him and his health rapidly broke down.

his presence was evidence that Liberal Unionism was not the refuge of the Liberal right wing. Churchill's promise of social reform was crucial for Chamberlain's continued support. It is significant that the abortive talks on Liberal reunion followed Churchill's resignation.

To retain his radical credentials, Chamberlain had to demonstrate influence over policy. By 1892 he could assure his followers that 'The Tory party is not what it was' and assert that the 'Unauthorised Programme' had been implemented by the Conservatives. Irish policy – land purchase, the adjustment of judicial rents and help for distressed districts – met Chamberlain's criteria, although his vote against the proscription of the National League in 1887 reminded ministers that he could not be taken for granted. Local government reform (1888), the Allotments Act (1887), the Smallholdings Act (1892) and free elementary education (1891) satisfied aspects of the 1885 programme.

Initially isolated in parliament, challenged in Birmingham by the National Liberal Federation, he was courted by the Conservatives. During 1888 he established close relations with Balfour, Chief Secretary for Ireland until 1891 and then Leader of the House of Commons. Balfour provided the link with Salisbury, his uncle. Hartington's elevation to the peerage as Duke of Devonshire (1891) left Chamberlain as leader of the Liberal Unionists in the Commons. There was close co-operation in the 1892 Election campaign from which Chamberlain emerged strengthened. The West Midlands went against the national trend with five Unionist gains and only two losses.

The coalition ministry was formed before the 1895 Election. Devonshire, Lord President of the Council, was part of the leading quartet but Salisbury, Balfour and Chamberlain were the key figures. Conservative MPs resented the elevation of Liberal Unionists, especially after the election gave the Conservatives an overall majority. They distrusted Chamberlain for his nonconformity and his radicalism.

Balfour, Salisbury, Chamberlain and Devonshire became the leaders of an alliance that was fast becoming a coalition. Once Home Rule had been defeated Chamberlain pressed for an ambitious social reform programme. Salisbury rebuffed his approaches but conceded that a coalition government should have clear reform policies. Although the Workmen's Compensation Act was passed in 1897 and a Royal Commission appointed to examine old age pensions, Chamberlain's reforming influence was negligible. His choice of the Colonial Secretaryship in 1895 (Salisbury offered him every major domestic post) was a recognition that social reform was a low priority for Conservative MPs. Imperialism, the Empire, was a field where he could raise rather than risk his reputation.

Conservative Ascendancy – the Reform Record

Irish policy occupied much parliamentary time but social reform could not be ignored if the Liberal Unionists were to be conciliated. This was, however, a period of unimaginative policies that ended in stagnation. Salisbury was not a reformer and feared the attack on the rights of property that social reform implied. He was concerned about working class housing and intervened in educational issues. His administrations believed in 'laissez faire', opposed the extension of State activity, and in Goschen had a Chancellor of the Exchequer (1877–92) who cut taxes and followed impeccable Gladstonian principles.

A party of resistance could not provide a reforming government. A party that aspired to represent the middle class and to unite all natural conservatives would not pay for social reform. The Unionists did not win elections on their record in office and the by-election losses after 1886 and again after 1895 would suggest that the electorate was not impressed. 1900 was a snap election called when the South African War seemed to be reaching a victorious climax. Liberal advances were repulsed by a patriotic vote against a party that was divided over the war and could be accused of being pro-Boer.

Juggler Joe and his vanishing programme

JOE THE JUGGLER
MARVELLOUS PERFORMANCES!!
SLEIGHT OF HAND!
CONJURING!
LIGHTNING CHANGES!!
VARIED PROGRAMMES

THE VERY LATEST PROGRAMME
DOMESTIC QUESTIONS
POOR LAW REFORM!
OLD AGE PENSIONS
CHEAP AND EASY TRANSFER OF LAND!
IMPROVEMENT OF THE DWELLINGS OF THE POOR!
EXTENSION OF SMALL HOLDINGS
EMPLOYERS LIABILITY
8 HOURS LABOUR IN MINES
Printed in BIRMINGHAM

JUGGLER: 'I will now proceed, ladies and gentlemen, to roll up this extensive programme into a ball, and the Old Party will swallow it without the slightest difficulty.'
OLD PARTY: 'Look here! I say! I'm not going to swallow all that!'
JUGGLER (aside): 'Alright, my Lord! You sit tight. You've only got to pretend. I'll manage all the vanishing business.'

IDENTIFY THE 'OLD PARTY' AND COMMENT ON THE USE OF THE PHRASE 'JUGGLER JOE'.

TALKING POINT

Should historians talk of Unionist Ascendancy rather than Conservative Ascendancy in this period?

CONSERVATIVES' REFORM MEASURES

Allotments Acts 1887, 1890 Smallholding Act 1892	Gave local authorities powers to purchase land for letting at economic rents.
The Local Government Act 1888	The administration of county affairs by the landed gentry as magistrates in Quarter Sessions ended. Democratically elected Country Councils were formed, and County Borough Councils for large urban areas. The London County Council was to administer the London area, although the City was excluded.
Education Act 1891	Elementary education (compulsory since 1875) was made free. This was a longstanding Chamberlain objective, but Salisbury's purpose was to protect the struggling denominational schools from School Board competition. In 1896 the Conservatives failed in an attempt to replace School Boards by County Councils.
Workmen's Compensation Act 1897	Another Chamberlain objective, but the Act did not satisfy all his aspirations and did not protect all workers.
Old Age Pensions	A commission of inquiry buried them amidst concerns about cost and the impact on individual thrift of a state scheme.

16.3 Constructive Unionism – 'killing home rule with kindness'?

By adopting home rule Gladstone had made it impossible for his Conservative and Liberal Unionist successors and opponents to ignore the Irish Question. It was a measure of Parnell's achievement that his success forced the Conservatives to devise an alternative strategy.

Constructive Unionism – The Achievement

Land Purchase

This was the heart of Conservative policy and was its great success. Its purpose was to undermine the nationalist movement by removing peasant discontent. The land purchase policy was designed to derail the home rule movement. It would also protect the landowners from the expropriation of estates, without compensation, expected from a nationalist parliament.

1885 Ashbourne's Act allowed tenants to borrow the whole purchase price for their farm with repayment over forty-nine years.

1888, 1891, 1896 Acts refined the policy.

1903 Wyndham's Land Purchase Act offered landlords prepare to sell entire estates a 12% cash bonus, and purchasing tenants were tempted with reduced interest rates and sixty-eight and a half years to pay. The Treasury bore the full cost. Over 200,000 sales followed Wyndham's Act.

Land Act, 1887

Allowed tenants reviews of judicial rents previously set in the land courts, and brought leaseholders under the protection of the 1881 Land Act. This was the price the Conservatives had to pay to win Liberal Unionist support for coercion. 1887 was the year of the Plan of Campaign.

Local Government Reform

Ireland had been excluded from the 1888 Local Government Act, despite Salisbury's agreement that reform was necessary. The 1898 Irish Local Government Act extended elected county councils, urban district and rural district councils to Ireland. It finally destroyed the political influence of the landowners and Protestants in southern Ireland. Power was transferred to the Roman Catholic majority.

Removing Distress and Disadvantage

1891 Congested Districts Board formed as part of the 1891 Land Act. A 'congested district' was one in which the majority of the population were always close to starvation. All were in the far west of Ireland. The Board encouraged the construction of light railways, promoted the fishing industry, gave farmers expert advice, consolidated holdings and improved them for new owners. the success of the Board was praised by the Nationalists and Balfour always considered it one of his greatest Irish achievements.

1899 The Department of Agriculture and Technical Instruction was set up to encourage farmers to innovate and to adopt co-operative marketing methods.

TALKING POINT

'... contrary to popular belief, it was the Conservative party, not Gladstone, that came closest to solving the Irish problem in the late nineteenth century.' (A.B. Cooke, *The Ashbourne Papers*, 1974)

Assess the strengths and weaknesses of this view. How valid is it?

Motives and Purposes

Source A

I agree with Buller, as you cannot govern the Irish as anybody else, by severity alone; but I think that he is fundamentally wrong in believing that conciliation and severity must go together. The severity must come first. They must 'take a licking' before conciliation will do them any good.

Salisbury to Hicks Beach, Chief Secretary 1886–7, 28 February 1887.

Source B

Balfour comments on his task when taking over the Chief Secretaryship, 1887.

Cromwell failed because he relied solely upon repressive measures. That mistake I shall not imitate. I shall be as relentless as Cromwell in enforcing obedience to the law, but, at the same time, I shall be as radical as any reformer in redressing grievances, and especially in removing every cause of complaint in regard to the land. It is on the twofold aspect of my policy that I rely for success. Hitherto English governments ... have either been all for repression or all for reform. I am for both: repression as stern as Cromwell; reform as thorough as Mr Parnell or anyone else can desire.

Source C

What then was Balfourism? In terms of Ireland, until the 1890s it hardly got beyond being a law and order policy against class war ... to the Chief Secretary, the proof of his success ... was that out of 1614 imprisoned under the Crimes Act, only 80 were convicted again. His constructive reforms were too late and aspired to too little to be the core of his Irish strategy. This is not to say that Balfour doubted that these reforms could have a beneficial effect or event that kindness would eventually kill home rule. Nonetheless his priorities unmistakably lay elsewhere. As a progressive policy, Balfourism is only comprehensible in the context of British politics.

A. Gailey, 'Failure and the Making of the New Ireland' in D G Boyce (ed.), *The Revolution in Ireland*, 1988.

1 Compare and contrast the tone and the approach to Irish policy in sources A and B.
2 Most Tories wanted 'firmness', Liberal Unionists expected some conciliation to justify their support for a Conservative government, public opinion swung behind Parnell by 1889 – How were all these pressures reflected in the Unionist Irish policy to 1892; were political pressures in England the driving force?
3 Referring to all the sources, and to your wider knowledge, to what extent did Balfour initiate a 'settled and consistent' (F.S.L. Lyons, *Ireland since the Famine*, 1971) reform policy?

Constructive Unionism – a Failed Policy?

If the aim was to kill home rule with kindness then constructive unionism failed.

● It did not transform opinion in Ireland. Nationalists remained suspicious of   policies which threatened to undermine home rule; Unionists opposed moderation because it was a concession to the home rule agitation. William O'Brien's United Irish League co-operated with the Dunraven Land Commission; fellow Nationalists forced him to withdraw. When Lord Dunraven began to consider devolution, the Unionist uproar threatened the survival of the government and forced Wyndham's resignation as Chief Secretary in 1905.

● The Home Rule Party was not weakened. In 1900 it reunited under the leadership of the Parnellite John Redmond.

● Nationalism was strengthened by a Gaelic and cultural revival which emphasised Irish distinctiveness.

● The government failed to win over the Catholic Church with higher education concessions. By 1904 the hierarchy saw home rule as the only way to achieve their educational objectives.

● Neither Salisbury nor Balfour understood or appreciated the reality of Irish nationalism. This blinkered view ensured the failure of a policy which hoped to eradicate the home rule movement.

REVIEW

Why was there a Conservative Ascendancy?

Take each statement and assess its importance in explaining why the Conservatives dominated the political stage from 1886–1905. What other developments could be seen as important, and why?

The Conservative ascendancy came about for a number of reasons, many of which were related. Among reasons cited by contemporaries and historians are the following:

● The effect of the Home Rule policy on the Liberal Party. It was not a policy which attracted English support.

● After 1894, the Liberals were divided over policy and lacked firm leadership. The divisions were deepened by the Boer War. They ceased to be a credible party of government.

● Salisbury led a broad-based coalition united by hostility to Home Rule. His administrations were cautiously progressive in domestic and Irish affairs, and showed sound common sense in foreign policy.

● The Conservative Party became an alliance of wealth and title, a Peelite party of natural conservatives. The Party machine was reorganised and benefitted from the influx of middle-class wealth.

● The Liberals neglected the concerns of their natural supporters among the working class. Neither party offered reforms to attract the working class voter, but no alternative existed to challenge for their support. The franchise reforms of the 1880s benefitted the Conservatives more than the Liberals.

TALKING POINT

How far was Conservative ascendancy based on 'negative' rather than 'positive' reasons? To what extent did that make it vulnerable?

LEARNING RESOURCE CENTRE
THOMAS ROTHERHAM COLLEGE
MOORGATE ROAD
ROTHERHAM S60 2BE
TEL. 0709 828606

17 Imperialism and Labour: Challenges to the Old Certainties, 1885–1906

PREVIEW

Source A

"BLOODY SUNDAY": THE LIFE GUARDS HOLDING TRAFALGAR SQUARE. (*See p. 166.*)

ON BLOODY SUNDAY, NOVEMBER 1887, POLICE AND SOLDIERS HAD TO DISPERSE PROCESSIONS MARCHING TO TRAFALGAR SQUARE FOR A BANNED PUBLIC MEETING. THE SOCIAL DEMOCRATIC FEDERATION, FOUNDED BY THE MARXIST H.M. HYNDMAN, WAS INVOLVED.

1 What conclusions might be drawn about popular attitudes from sources A and B?
2 How valid would these conclusions be?
3 What was the political significance of events like those shown in source A occurring in London, and affecting the West End?

Source B ▼

NEWS OF THE RELIEF OF MAFEKING, BESIEGED SINCE THE BEGINNING OF THE BOER WAR AT THE END OF 1899, BECAME AN EXCUSE FOR CELEBRATION.

Focus

17.1 Britain and the 'New Imperialism'

The last twenty years of the nine-teenth century witnessed the 'scramble for Africa'. In the Pacific, Asia and China the great powers disputed over territory and spheres of influence. Informal empire was in decline as powerful rivals challenged British pre-eminence. The occupation of Egypt and the Boer War were consequences of a need to exert direct control to protect vital interests in key locations rather than continued dependence on informal mechanisms.

In Africa alone, Britain acquired Egypt (1882), Somaliland, Bechuanaland and Nigeria (1884–5), the Rhodesias (1889), Kenya, Zanzibar, Uganda and Nyasaland (1890s), the Transvaal and the Orange Free State (1900).

Source A

Notions of pegging out colonial estates for posterity hardly entered into British calculations until the late Eighteen nineties, when it was almost too late to affect the outcome ... Imperialism in the wide sense of empire for empire's sake was not their motive. Their territorial claims were made not for the sake of African empire or commerce as such. They were little more than by-products of an enforced search for better security in the Mediterranean and the East. It was not the pomps or profits of governing Africa which moved the ruling elite, but the cold rules for national security handed on from Pitt, Palmerston and Disraeli.

If the papers left by the policy-makers are to be believed, they moved into Africa, not to build a new African empire, but to protect the old empire in India. What decided when and where they would go forward was their traditional conception of world strategy.

R. Robinson and J. Gallagher, *Africa and the Victorians*, 1961.

Talking Point

In the 1880s 80 per cent of trade passing through the Suez Canal was British. Is it possible to separate the economic and the strategic motives for imperial expansion as Robinson and Gallagher implied?

BRAND LOYALTY – THE MINGLING OF IMPERIAL THEMES WITH PRODUCT PROMOTION WAS ONE VISIBLE WAY IN WHICH IMPERIALISM PENETRATED POPULAR CULTURE, ALTHOUGH HISTORIANS QUESTION WHETHER THE WORKING CLASS WAS EVER DEEPLY IMPERIALISTIC.

The historians' view: differing interpretations

Source B

The history of British foreign and colonial policy in the 1890s sometimes took strange and unpredictable turns. But there was a kind of consistency about it. Very rarely did it stray beyond the boundaries set, on the one hand, by a concept of the 'national interest' which had as its central imperative the preservation of Britain's capacity to trade and invest as freely and as widely as possible, especially in the developing countries; and on the other hand, by the prevalent apprehensions of the time about the threats to that capacity from other nations. Within these very broad bounds, policy varied considerably, according to how the chemistry of each separate situation was mixed: how valuable the 'national interest' there was, or might become; how far it was threatened; what extraneous pressures were there (especially from private financial interests) to affect policy; and – most important in the over-stretched 'nineties' – the means the government had in its hands to deal with it, and its preoccupations elsewhere.

B. Porter, *The Lion's Share*, 1975

Source C

We have questioned the widespread and long-standing assumption linking the 'triumph of industry' to imperialist expansion, and have emphasised instead the role of finance and services ... The representatives of British industry were less wealthy than their counterparts in the City, made their money in ways that did not meet the approval of their social superiors, and exercised only limited political influence at national level ... The international order that was erected on the basis of free trade and the gold standard served the purposes of finance and services rather better than it did those of manufacturing: the increasing scale of multilateral trade relations gave the City opportunities and commitments that extended far beyond the distribution of British manufactures. Moreover, where a choice had to be made, policy invariably favoured finance over manufacturing ... the manufacturing lobby always put its case, but it rarely got its way ...

... it is apparent that an important segment of the non-industrial business elite consisted of gentlemen who moved in the same circles and shared the same values as those who had their hands on the levers of power – and often managed their investments too.

P.J. Cain and A.G. Hopkins, *British Imperialism: Innovation and Expansion 1688–1914*, 1993.

Cain and Hopkins have developed the concept of 'gentlemanly capitalism', focusing on the banking and financial services sectors as the driving force behind imperial expansion. The northern industrialists lacked the social and political contracts that London financiers were able to exploit.

TALKING POINT

What are the similarities and differences between these interpretations of the motives behind imperialism?

EXAMINING THE EVIDENCE

The Boer War (1899–1902) – Whose War?

The Background and the Issues

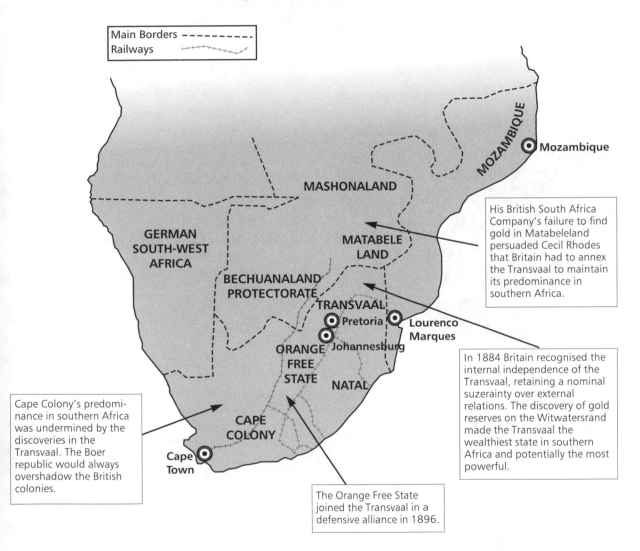

Main Borders ----------
Railways ┼┼┼┼┼┼┼

MOZAMBIQUE

Mozambique

MASHONALAND

His British South Africa Company's failure to find gold in Matabeleland persuaded Cecil Rhodes that Britain had to annex the Transvaal to maintain its predominance in southern Africa.

GERMAN SOUTH-WEST AFRICA

MATABELE LAND

BECHUANALAND PROTECTORATE

TRANSVAAL

Pretoria

Lourenco Marques

ORANGE FREE STATE

Johannesburg

NATAL

In 1884 Britain recognised the internal independence of the Transvaal, retaining a nominal suzerainty over external relations. The discovery of gold reserves on the Witwatersrand made the Transvaal the wealthiest state in southern Africa and potentially the most powerful.

Cape Colony's predominance in southern Africa was undermined by the discoveries in the Transvaal. The Boer republic would always overshadow the British colonies.

CAPE COLONY

Cape Town

The Orange Free State joined the Transvaal in a defensive alliance in 1896.

His British South Africa Company's failure to find gold in Matabeleland persuaded Cecil Rhodes that Britain had to annex the Transvaal to maintain its predominance in southern Africa. In 1884 Britain recognised the internal independence of the Transvaal retaining a nominal suzerainty over external relations. The discovery of gold reserves on the Witwatersrand made the Transvaal the wealthiest state in southern Africa and potentially the most powerful.

The construction of a railway to the coast at Lorenco Marques, in Portuguese territory, freed the Transvaal from British supervision of its trade. Kruger was able to build up the military strength of the republic.

The influx of immigrants (Uitlanders) to the Rand goldfields threatened to destabilise the Transvaal. The Uitlanders' grievances were exploited by Rhodes, Milner and the British government to force concessions out of Kruger. They complained about excessive taxation, the Transvaal government's dynamite monopoly and control of rail freight charges, and the denial of the franchise and civil rights.

DURING 1895 RHODES WAS PLOTTING TO PROVOKE A UITLANDER RISING WHICH WOULD JUSTIFY BRITISH INTERVENTION. UNFORTUNATELY THE UITLANDERS DID NOT REBEL, BUT ON 29 DECEMBER 1895 DR JAMESON LED A FORCE OF 500 COLONIAL TROOPS INTO THE TRANSVAAL. WITHOUT THE JUSTIFICATION OF A 'SPONTANEOUS' REBELLION THIS BECAME A HOSTILE ACT AGAINST A PEACEFUL STATE. CHAMBERLAIN ASTUTELY ESCAPED ANY BLAME, BUT TO THE BOERS AND THE OUTSIDE WORLD BRITAIN WAS IMPLICATED IN A SQUALID LITTLE CONSPIRACY.

The Personalities

CECIL RHODES, CAPITALIST AND IMPERIALIST, WANTED TO INCORPORATE THE TRANSVAAL WITHIN THE EMPIRE TO PRESERVE BRITISH PREDOMINANCE IN SOUTH AFRICA. AS PREMIER OF CAPE COLONY HE COULD INFLUENCE BRITISH GOVERNMENT POLICY AND THROUGH HIS BRITISH SOUTH AFRICA COMPANY HE HAD THE MEANS TO ACT INDEPENDENTLY. THE FIASCO OF THE JAMESON RAID DESTROYED HIS CREDIBILITY AND FORCED HIM TO RESIGN HIS PREMIERSHIP.

KRUGER'S POSITION AS PRESIDENT OF THE TRANSVAAL WAS STRENGTHENED BY THE JAMESON RAID. THE GERMAN EMPEROR SENT A CONGRATULATORY TELEGRAM, THE ORANGE FREE STATE SIGNED A DEFENSIVE ALLIANCE AND MANY MEMBERS OF THE CAPE DUTCH COMMUNITY OPENLY DISPLAYED THEIR SYMPATHY. AFTER MILNER'S REJECTION OF THE CONCESSIONS OFFERED AT BLOEMFONTEIN (JUNE 1899) KRUGER PREPARED FOR WAR. HIS ULTIMATUM TO THE BRITISH GOVERNMENT AND THE BOER INVASION OF CAPE COLONY (OCTOBER 1899) SAVED CHAMBERLAIN FROM HAVING TO JUSTIFY A WAR TO THE BRITISH PUBLIC.

SIR ALFRED MILNER, ADMINISTRATOR AND IMPERIALIST, WAS APPOINTED HIGH COMMISSIONER AT THE CAPE IN 1897. CONVINCED THAT WAR AND ANNEXATION WERE ONLY THE SOLUTION TO THE TRANSVAAL PROBLEM, HE SET OUT TO DELIBERATELY PROVOKE A CONFRONTATION AND TO MANIPULATE PUBLIC AND POLITICAL OPINION IN BRITAIN.

Source A

Two of the conclusions from Lord Selbourne's Colonial Office Memorandum on South Africa, 26 March 1896.

1 If we can succeed in uniting all South Africa into a Confederacy on the model of the Dominion of Canada and under the British Flag, the probability is that the Confederacy will not become a United States of South Africa.

2 If South Africa remains as now a congeries of separate States, partly British Colonies and partly Republics, it will inevitably amalgamate itself into a United States of South Africa.

Source B

Milner's dispatch of 4 May 1899 stressed the political instability of the Transvaal and the urgent need for British intervention to support the Uitlanders.

The spectacle of thousands of British subjects kept permanently in the position of helots, constantly chafing under undoubted grievances, and calling vainly to her majesty's government for redress, does steadily undermine the influence and reputation of Great Britain and the respect for the British government within the queen's dominions. A certain section of the press ... preaches openly and constantly the doctrine of a republic embracing all South Africa and supports it by menacing references to the armaments of the Transvaal, its alliance with the Orange Free State, and the active sympathy it would receive in case of war from a section of her majesty's subjects ...

I can see nothing that will put a stop to this mischievous propaganda but some striking proof of the intention of her majesty's government not to be ousted from its position in South Africa. And the best proof alike of its power and its justice would be to obtain for the Uitlanders ... a fair share in the government of the country which owes everything to their exertions.

Source C

Chamberlain's Cabinet Memorandum, 6 September 1899, 'The South African Situation'.

What is now at stake is the position of Great Britain in South Africa – and with it the estimate formed of our power and influence in our Colonies and throughout the world ...

... the Dutch in South Africa desire, if it be possible, to get rid altogether of the connection with Great Britain... and to substitute a United States of South Africa which ... would be mainly under Dutch influence ... it would probably have died out as a hopeless impossibility but for the evidence of successful resistance to British supremacy by the south African Republic [Transvaal]. The existence of a purely Dutch Republic ... flouting successfully British control and interference, is answerable for all the racial animosities which have become so formidable a factor in the South African situation.

1 Explain, and comment on, the use of the following expressions:
'United States of South Africa' (sources A and C)
'British subjects kept permanently in the position of helots' (source B)

2 Consult source B. To what extent were the Uitlanders and their grievances at the centre of the crisis in South Africa?

3 In what ways do sources A, B and C agree in their assessment of what was at stake in southern Africa?

4 Here are a series of statements about the causes of the Boer War:
'It was Chamberlain's war. He wanted to assert Britain's predominance in southern Africa.'
'It was Milner's war. The men on the spot dragged a reluctant cabinet into a confrontation they wanted to avoid.'
'It was a capitalist war to win control of the goldfields for the randlords.'
Referring to the sources, and using your wider knowledge, write an essay reviewing the causes of the Boer War and commenting on the validity of these statements.

Foreign Policy 1885–1905: Adjusting to New Realities

Salisbury and the myth of 'splendid isolation'

Until persuaded to give up the Foreign Office in 1900, Salisbury combined it with the Premiership for all but the early months of his second ministry. Lords Rosebery and Kimberley, Liberal Foreign Secretaries 1886, 1892–95, gave foreign policy a continuity that had not existed in the Gladstone/Disraeli years.

The policy of 'splendid isolation' is associated with Salisbury's tenure of the Foreign Office, but he was not an isolationist. In 1885 his condemnation of the outgoing Gladstone administration was scathing.

They have at least achieved their long desired 'Concert of Europe'. They have succeeded in uniting the continent of Europe – against England.

Salisbury merely sought to avoid commitments that would entangle Britain in any future continental conflict, but as soon as he entered the Foreign Office in 1885 serious approaches were being made to Berlin. Bismarck rebuffed him. Four years later Salisbury rejected Bismarck's advances because they would commit Britain against France in Europe. By then Salisbury had ended Britain's isolation through the Mediterranean Agreements (March and December 1887) with Italy and Austria.

The Agreements were anti-Russian because the powers agreed to consult to maintain stability in the Balkans and the independence of Turkey, including freedom of navigation at the Straits. They were anti-French because they bolstered Britain's position in the Eastern Mediterranean and Egypt. The secret Agreements were not formal treaties and were not laid before Parliament, but were closer to a peace-time alliance with Great Powers than anything since the Quadruple Alliance (1815).

By the 1890s Europe was divided into two alliances: 1882 Bismarck's anti-French Triple Alliance of Germany, Austro-Hungary and Italy; 1894 the Franco-Russian Alliance, anti-German in Europe but threatening British interests in the Mediterranean and China.

Salisbury had achieved his objective. Britain was no longer isolated and was indirectly linked to Germany and the Triple Alliance. Although Britain gained concessions from Germany in East Africa in return for the use of Heligoland as a North Sea naval base in 1890, Salisbury could not obtain from either Bismarck or his successors the anti-Russian alliance that Britain really wanted as tension rose in China and Persia. For his part Salisbury was not prepared to give Germany guarantees against France. The failure to renew the Mediterranean Agreements in 1897 marked the end of Salisbury's alignment with the Triple Alliance. It also marked a final shift in policy from Constantinople to Cairo as the control point on the route to India.

The Naval Aspects of Foreign Policy

During the nineteenth century Britain's worldwide naval supremacy had never been seriously challenged. The Naval Defence Act (1889) recognised that times were changing with its promise that a two-power standard would be maintained. Both political parties upheld the policy. Gladstone resigned from the premiership in 1894 because his Liberal cabinet insisted on a large increase in expenditure on ship construction.

Country	Battleships in 1883	Battleships in 1897 (plus those building)
Britain	38	62
France	19	36
Germany	11	12
Russia	3	18
Italy	7	12
USA	0	11
Japan	0	7

IN 1897, THE PRESENCE OF OVER 165 BRITISH WARSHIPS AT THE SPITHEAD NAVAL REVIEW, INCLUDING 21 FIRST CLASS BATTLESHIPS AND 54 CRUISERS DEMONSTRATED THE IMMENSE SIZE AND FIGHTING STRENGTH OF THE ROYAL NAVY.
WHAT DOES THE CHART SUGGEST ABOUT THE TWO-POWER STANDARD?

Germany's First Navy Law (1897) added a new dimension. In Britain the German building programme was seen as the first stage in preparations for war against Great Britain. Maintaining a two-power standard had been prohibitively expensive; a three-power standard was unthinkable. The alternative was to reduce worldwide commitments to allow the concentration of capital ships in the North Sea. Agreement with the United States (1901), alliance with Japan (1902) and the 'entente' with France (1904) all made naval consolidation easier and less dangerous. Britain maintained its lead in naval technology by launching HMS *Dreadnought* in 1904. All older battleships were instantly obsolete, but only the most wealthy states could compete in the resultant arms race.

The Search for an Ally 1897–1905

In 1898 Salisbury was able to force the French to recognise British control of the Sudan (the Fashoda Incident) without the assistance of an ally. The Boer War once again revealed the dangers of isolation, with only Germany preventing the formation of an anti-British continental league. The 1901 Hay–Pauncefote Treaty finally conceded naval supremacy in the Americas to the United States. Approaches to Russia and Germany both failed, but in 1902 the Anglo-Japanese alliance was signed.

TALKING POINT

In what sense was the abandonment of Constantinople a significant change in British foreign policy?

Two-power standard: Britain's naval strength would be maintained at twice the level of the next two most powerful naval powers. In 1889 this was aimed at France and Russia.

TALKING POINT

Consider the view that railway construction in Europe, and from Europe into Asia, had undermined the significance of sea power, and therefore Britain's global influence.

Alliance with Japan against Russia was a natural consequence of British concerns at Russian ambitions in the Far East and in China. Although the allies were committed to support each other if one was attacked by two opponents, its terms were limited to the Far East where the extra naval support against Russia was needed. By giving added security to British interests in China, the alliance freed Britain from having to consider commitments in Europe and, to that extent, reinforced isolation. After the Russo-Japanese War (1903–05) the treaty was renewed and extended. The success of the alliance, and the destruction of the Russian Far Eastern Fleet at the battle of Tsushima, resolved the naval problem – allowing ships to be redeployed to home waters.

As concern with German activities – the Navy Laws, lack of co-operation in China, trade rivalry and railways construction in the Turkish Empire – intensified public opinion and the government became more responsive to approaches from France. The Russo-Japanese War quickened the process – neither Britain nor France wanted to be dragged into the conflict by their ally. The 'Entente' (1904) was designed to eliminate an enemy rather than to make an ally. It settled outstanding colonial disputes over Egypt and Morocco and, by easing tension in the Mediterranean, met the criteria of allowing naval consolidation in home waters. It took German suspicions and mistakes to make it into something more significant.

When the Balfour government resigned at the end of 1905, Britain was no longer isolated, France was a friend and a contact with Russia but German enmity was becoming more apparent.

The Challenge from Labour

The Socialist Strand

Karl Marx wrote *Das Kapital* in London. Although his writings were based on his observations of the British social and political scene, the proletarian revolution he predicted did not materialise. In 1884 the Marxist influenced old-Etonian and Cambridge graduate H. M. Hyndman founded the Social Democratic Federation. The SDF was never clear about priorities or methods, but its leaders seized the opportunities presented by the economic problems of the mid-1880s by assuming the leadership of the London unemployment demonstrations, 1886–7. The SDF achieved some notoriety but its membership was never large. Hyndman's autocratic behaviour forced the early departure of prominent activists like John Burns, Eleanor Marx, Tom Mann and the artist William Morris who founded the Socialist League. The SDF's most significant contribution to the emerging labour movement lay less in ideology than in the early training it provided for young working class militants.

The members of the Fabian Society (1884) had an inflated view of their importance. They were not revolutionaries. Their socialism was practical and pragmatic. An unjust and inefficient capitalist society contained the seeds of its own evolution in its responses to the pressures for change. Increasing state intervention and municipal enterprise would gradually move society to socialism. The Fabians, therefore, sought to inform those

Ill-health forced Salisbury to resign from the Foreign Office in 1900. Lord Lansdowne, his successor, was inclined to agree with Chamberlain and Balfour that Britain needed an ally if her worldwide interests were to be adequately safeguarded. Salisbury retained his misgivings about formal commitments.

TALKING POINT

In what sense, if at all, had there been a 'diplomatic revolution' by 1905?

John Burns proved a magnetic leader during the 1886–7 demonstrations and the Dockers' Strike of 1889. Elected to Parliament in 1892 he was the first working man to enter the Cabinet, as a Liberal, in 1905.

Tom Mann began working in a pit at the age of 9. He joined the SDF 1885, was a leader of the Dockers' Strike, and secretary of the Independent Labour Party in 1893.

The Fabian Society's most famous publication, *Fabian Essays*, sold 27,000 copies in the two years after its publication in 1887. Fabians claimed some influence over the 'Progressive Alliance' that dominated the London County Council after 1889.

Talking Point

The 1867 and 1884 Reform Acts increased the number of working class voters. Why was it 1900 before a distinct organisation to elect men sympathetic to the labour movement to Parliament emerged?

Although total membership rose to about 1,500,000 in 1892 and to just over 2,000,000 by 1900, the majority of the workforce remained outside the unions.

Before 1889 trade unions tended to represent skilled workers and craftsmen. The powerful miners' organisations were an important exception. In 1889 the London Dock Strike and the successful negotiation of an eight-hour day in the London gasworks by Will Thorne, leader of the new General Labourers Union, encouraged the rapid growth of unions for the unskilled – the 'new unionism' – although their memberships declined swiftly when faced by the challenges of economic depression and employer resistance.

who were in power and had influence. A political party to represent the interests of the working class was unnecessary.

Working Men and Politics

It would be wrong to assume that there was a socially cohesive working class. The Tyneside blastfurnaceman earning £2 to 3 a week had little in common with the Wiltshire farm labourer on 14 shillings or the casual labourer struggling to survive in the London slums. Labour leaders were generally uninterested in the impoverished slum populations.

> It is the skilled artisan, the trade unionist, the member of the friendly society, the young workman who reads and thinks who are the recruits to the army of socialism.
>
> Ramsey MacDonald, 1911.

In the last quarter of the century the majority of these politically aware working men were Gladstonians. Only after 1895, with the Liberal Party an ineffective opposition, did the political context change in favour of those who wanted separate representation for the working class in Parliament.

Electoral reform did not enable working men to enter Parliament. Although the MPs property qualifications had been abolished in 1858 they were still unpaid; the costs of managing a constituency were beyond a working man. Only sponsorship by a Trade Union could provide the necessary funding.

The Trade Union Strand

In 1871, the Trades Union Congress set up a Parliamentary Committee to review legislative proposals likely to affect trade unionists. The Committee willingly accepted political dependence on the Liberals. Its secretary from 1875 to 1890 was Henry Broadhurst, former stonemason and Liberal MP. He was one of a small group of Lib-Lab MPs, most returned for mining constituencies, who took the Liberal whip but acted independently on labour questions. Numbers were never large, eleven in 1898, but they formed a distinct group within the Liberal Party – working class trade unionists with a special interest in labour questions.

The TUC resisted demands that it support the return of independent working men to Parliament. In 1899, when the TUC voted to convene a meeting of representatives from groups interested in increasing the number of 'Labour members' in Parliament, it was for sound practical, not ideological reasons. The unfavourable economic conditions of the mid-1890s had strengthened the position of the employers. For example, the engineering employers organised themselves to defeat union resistance to new working practices in the 1897 lock-out. Black-leg labour organisations flourished and union rights were increasingly challenged in the courts. *Lyons* v *Wilkins* (1896) cast serious doubts on the legality of picketing. With the Liberals powerless after 1895, the unions could only safeguard their members' interests by getting suitable men into Parliament.

The Independent Labour Party

Keir Hardie's experiences in Mid-Lanark, and his success at West Ham in 1892, taught him that independent representation of labour in Parliament was both necessary and possible. The Independent Labour Party, founded in Bradford in 1893, aimed to convert working men to socialism and to wean the unions from their dependence on the Liberal Party. It was more successful in its 'missionary' work than in winning the unions to the 'labour alliance' of socialists and trade unionists that Hardie envisaged – it never secured the mass support it needed. All twenty-eight ILP candidates, including Hardie, were defeated in the 1895 General Election. An independent labour political party needed the money and the numbers that only the trade unions could deliver.

KEIR HARDIE, SCOTTISH MINERS' LEADER, FAILED TO SECURE THE BACKING OF THE LOCAL LIBERAL ASSOCIATION FOR HIS CANDIDATURE FOR THE MID-LANARK BY-ELECTION IN 1888. FIGHTING ON AN INDEPENDENT LABOUR PLATFORM HE CAME BOTTOM OF THE POLL. IN 1892 HE WON WEST HAM AS AN INDEPENDENT LABOUR CANDIDATE.

The Failure of the Liberal Party

In 1893 the Southampton Liberal Council rejected Ramsey MacDonald as one of its candidates.

> Just at the time when your Liberal Council plunged you into your difficulties you were hearing of similar things in scores of other constituencies throughout the country ... In deference to such overwhelming evidence you had to make up your minds that local Liberal Associations had cast themselves adrift from the forward movement in politics, and that the decision of the Southampton Liberal Council was but part of a national policy which is compelling what was once the advanced wing of Liberalism to sever itself from an old alliance and form itself into an independent Labour party ...
>
> Ramsey MacDonald to the Southampton Labour Electoral Association, 16 July 1893. He had applied for membership of the ILP the previous day.

MacDonald's letter reflected the feelings of many politically active working men. Local Liberal Associations consistently failed to endorse working class candidates. This alienated key activists.

The Liberal Party found it increasingly difficult to devise a social reform programme that would satisfy the demands of its working class supporters. The industrialists and businessmen who financed and dominated the party organisation were opposed to any form of graduated taxation and to any interference with industrial freedoms. In 1889, 1890 and 1891 the annual conference of the National Liberal Federation rejected proposals that the eight-hour day should be added to its programme. Here was evidence that the interests of the working class could not be secured through a Liberal Party that apparently danced to the tune of its capitalist backers.

TALKING POINT

Discuss the implications for the Liberal Party and the labour movement of MacDonald's conclusion.

The meeting convened by the TUC met in London on 27 February 1900. Representatives from trade unions, the ILP, the SDF and the Fabian Society attended.

AT FIRST RAMSEY MACDONALD WAS THE LRC'S UNPAID SECRETARY. TOGETHER WITH KEIR HARDIE, HE WAS RESPONSIBLE FOR THE EARLY DEVELOPMENT OF THE LRC AND FOR ITS SUCCESSES AT THE 1906 ELECTION.

In 1900 the Taff Vale Railway Company had sued the Amalgamated Society of Railway Servants to recover losses incurred during a strike. The judgement in favour of the Company in the House of Lords enabled it to proceed against the Union for damages. In December the Company was awarded £23,000 and costs.

Herbert conducted the secret negotiations with MacDonald that led to the 1903 agreement that the LRC and the Liberal Party would not put up official candidates against each other. In 1906 the LRC won 29 seats, 24 in straight fights with the Conservatives.

Examining the Evidence

The Labour Representation Committee, the Trade Unions and the Liberal Party, 1900–06

Source A
Extracts from the Agenda of the meeting of 27 February 1900.

1 OBJECT OF THE CONFERENCE.
A resolution in favour of working-class opinion being represented in the House of Commons by men sympathetic with the aims and demands of the labour movement.

2 LABOUR MEMBERS IN THE HOUSE OF COMMONS.
A resolution in favour of establishing a distinct Labour Group in Parliament who should have their own Whips and agree upon their policy, which must embrace a readiness to co-operate with any party which ... may be engaged in promoting legislation in the direct interest of labour, and be equally ready to associate themselves with any party in opposing measures having an opposite tendency.

'Report of the Conference on Labour Representation', 1900.

Source B
An extract from the Taff Vale judgement, House of Lords, 1901.
Has the Legislature authorised the creation of numerous bodies of men capable of owning great wealth and of acting by agents with absolutely no responsibility for the wrongs they may do to other persons by the use of that wealth and the employment of those agents? In my opinion Parliament has done nothing of the kind. I cannot find anything in the acts of 1871 and 1876 ... to warrant or suggest such a notion ...

... I have no doubt whatever that a trade union, whether registered or unregistered, may be sued in a representative action if the persons selected as defendants be persons who, from their position, may be taken fairly to represent the body.

Source C
Jesse Herbert to Herbert Gladstone (Liberal Chief Whip), 6 March 1903.
The LRC can directly influence the votes of nearly a million men. They will have a fighting fund of £100,000 ... their members are mainly men who have hitherto voted with the Liberal Party. Should they be advised to vote against Liberal candidates, and ... should they act as advised, the Liberal Party would suffer defeat not only in those constituencies where LRC candidates fought, but also in almost every borough, and in many of the Divisions of Lancashire and Yorkshire. this would be the inevitable result of unfriendly actions towards the LRC candidates. They would be defeated, but so also should we be defeated.

1 Explain the significance of the resolutions in Source A.
2 In what ways does Source B threaten the status of trade unions?
3 'The LRC needed the agreement MacDonald negotiated in 1903 far more than the Liberal Party.'
   Comment on this view, referring to the sources, and your broader knowledge of the period.
4 Referring to all the sources and your wider knowledge prepare and write this essay:
   Despite the franchise extensions of 1867 and 1884, why was it 1906 before a Labour Party took its seats in the House of Commons?

Balfour's Premiership, 1902–05: an Undeserved Failure?

A.J. BALFOUR SUCCEEDED HIS UNCLE, LORD SALISBURY, AS PRIME MINISTER IN JULY 1902. RECOGNISING THE NEW POSITION IN WHICH BRITAIN FOUND ITSELF AT THE BEGINNING OF THE TWENTIETH CENTURY, HE POSSESSED THE VISION TO DEVISE THE DEFENCE AND FOREIGN POLICIES THAT WOULD SECURE HER WORLD ROLE. UNFORTUNATELY HE FAILED TO APPRECIATE THE MORE IMMEDIATE CONCERNS OF BRITISH ELECTORS. HIS POLITICAL SHORTSIGHTEDNESS DIRECTLY CONTRIBUTED TO THE ELECTION DISASTER OF 1906 AS HIS GOVERNMENT'S POLICIES ALIENATED SECTIONS OF ITS SUPPORTERS.

Balfour inherited a strong administration with a large Commons majority. Chamberlain had worked closely with him since 1895 and there was no reason to expect that good relations would not continue. However, by the autumn of 1902–03 both Chamberlain and Devonshire had left the government and by-elections were being consistently lost. When he finally resigned in December 1905 electoral defeat was expected. What was surprising was the scale of that defeat.

In the 'khaki' election (1900) the Unionists had been swept back into office on a tide of patriotic fervour as the British occupied Pretoria and the war seemed won. It dragged on for another two years. The Boers resorted to guerrilla tactics, the British to harsh measures to starve them into surrender. Farms, crops and livestock were systematically destroyed. Salisbury remained in office until the peace was finally signed at Vereeniging in May 1902 but it was

Public opinion was shocked by reports of the 'concentration camps' in which non-combatant Boer women and children were placed.

Chinese labourers were contracted for a fixed term of years, lived in compounds which they could only leave on 48–hour permits, could own no property, had no legal rights, worked a 60-hour week for 2 shillings an hour, were disciplined by their employer and could not bring their families.

Campbell-Bannerman's condemnation of 'methods of barbarism' that was remembered. The Unionists were blamed for the military inadequacies which had turned the war into a long drawn-out struggle. The cost to the British taxpayer and the cost in lives hardly seemed worthwhile when the only winners were the wealthy mineowners on the Rand. Public disillusionment with the imperial ideal could only damage the imperialist party.

Another issue which upset important sections of public opinion was that of Chinese 'slave' labour. Faced by an acute labour shortage, the South African mineowners persuaded Milner to pressurise the government into sanctioning the employment of indentured Chinese labourers. In 1904 ministers reluctantly gave way.

They failed to anticipate the political storm the decision provoked. Chinese 'slavery' became an emotive issue around which the Liberals rallied a strange alliance of outraged Nonconformists and trade unionists. For trade unionists and the LRC it was a betrayal of the men who had fought in the Boer War. Jobs that could have been made available to British emigrants were going to cheaper 'slave' labour to satisfy the greed of the mineowners. The moral conscience of Nonconformity was shocked at the prospect of hundreds of men herded together in the workers' compounds and at the 'nameless practices' that would result. It all seemed to confirm the suspicion that the Boer War had been for the benefit of a few Rand mineowners.

Achievements of Balfour's Administration

The successes of Balfour's administration were but the government was accident-prone and Balfour's political judgement flawed. Although he tried to be constructive, the policies pursued tended to offend certain sections of his support. For example, Wyndham's Land Act (1903) finally resolved the bitter Irish land question but Wyndham, the Irish Chief Secretary, was forced to resign in 1905 when it was learnt that a senior official in Dublin had been negotiating on the possibilities of devolution. This showed the limits of 'constructive unionism'.

The Boer War humiliated Britain. The farmers of the two republics had defied the might of the world's greatest imperial power for three years, inflicting damaging defeats in the early months of the conflict. The changing international environment and military and naval developments made fresh defence thinking imperative, but it was the failures of the Boer War that gave Balfour the co-operation he needed for reforms to be implemented.

The Committee of Imperial Defence emerged in December 1902 as a forum in which politicians with military and naval professionals could plan strategy. Balfour, as Prime Minister, was a constant attender at its meetings. The difficult task of army reform was left to the Liberals after 1906. At the Admiralty, however, the First Sea Lord, John Fisher, initiated a vigorous review of naval practice and strategy. Officer training and education was revolutionised, the worldwide deployment of the fleet was revised, the reserve fleet was re-organised and the construction of the new 'Dreadnought' class of battleships commenced.

Failure in South Africa intensified the 'national efficiency' debate – that

Britain was in decline because its people were inadequately educated and physically incapable of maintaining Britain's role as a world power. Protagonists argued the merits of conscription and increased state intervention to reduce poverty and to improve education and health. Balfour's Education Act was partly a response to these concerns.

Education reform was essential but Salisbury, conscious of the need to hold the Conservative and Unionist coalition together and of the view of his Nonconformist allies, had been unwilling to act. Both Balfour and the Duke of Devonshire, the responsible minister, wanted a major legislative achievement. In 1899 the Board of Education had been set up to co-ordinate elementary and secondary education. Many School Boards were too small and were riven by sectarian rivalry. Some of the larger School Boards provided secondary education for able pupils but the Cockerton Judgement (1901) stated that School Boards could only legally use the school rate for elementary education.

The Education Bill set out to resolve these two problems. It created a third. Chamberlain warned Balfour that if the proposed local education authorities were required to support denominational schools (mainly Anglican) out of the rates the votes of Nonconformist Liberal Unionists would be lost. Balfour ignored him, opposing a compromise that would have made rate-support for voluntary schools optional. Despite a furious Nonconformist campaign, the Bill became law unamended.

Intense Nonconformist fury at the 'Church on the rates' and the assault on religious freedom gave the broken Liberal Party a traditional issue around which it could rally. By-elections were lost, leading Nonconformist ministers adopted a new political role, many Nonconformists refused to pay their rates, and in Wales County Councils denied rate aid to voluntary schools.

The support of denominational (mostly Anglican) schools on the rates provided an issue around which the Nonconformist Liberal Party could rally. By-elections were lost by the government and nonconformist ministers adopted a new political role. Many nonconformists refused to pay their rates and councils in Wales denied rate aid to voluntary schools.

The Nonconformist conscience was also offended by the passage of the 1904 Licensing Act. There was widespread agreement that a reduction in the number of public houses was desirable. However, the Act provided for compensation to be paid to the publicans. The Nonconformist temperance lobby condemned the Act as a 'brewer's Bill' in which the drink trade was given a public endowment.

Through its actions and omissions the government upset many of the interest groups on whose electoral support it depended. The Education and Licensing Acts offended the sensibilities and consciences of those middle class Nonconformist Liberal-Unionists who had followed Chamberlain in 1886. Chinese 'slavery' angered the working class whilst the government's refusal to consider legislation to reverse the Taff Vale Judgement drove the Trade Unions to the LRC. The overriding issue in 1906, however, was free trade. Tariff reform split the Unionists and exposed the inadequacies of Balfour's leadership style.

The 1902 Education Act
School Boards were abolished.

Responsibility for education was taken over by County Borough and County Councils (local education authorities).

The new authorities were responsible for both elementary and secondary education.

Denominational schools were to receive support from the rates.

TALKING POINT

Discuss the view that Balfour was an effective Prime Minister as policy-maker, but a failure as a politician.

EXAMINING THE EVIDENCE

Chamberlain, Imperialism and Tariff Reform

Chamberlain's choice of the Colonial Office in 1895 was surprising but he aimed to make it the powerhouse of the ministry, and the Unionists a party of imperial reform. Unforrtunately the Treasury did not share Chamberlain's vision. The necessary investment and expenditure was never forthcoming. Businessmen were reluctant to follow where Chamberlain led. His broader vision of imperial federation met with a cool response from the premiers attending the Colonial Conference in 1897. The proposed Imperial *Zollverein* was unenthusiastically received, a suggested Imperial Council rejected as an infringement on colonial independence whilst proposals for imperial defence contributions were ignored. All favoured closer imperial union but none were prepared to sacrifice money or autonomy in its pursuit.

Chamberlain's protectionist message was popular in areas which were experiencing severe competition from overseas industries, such as the steel, iron and engineering industries. Yet most working people were more concerned with the idea of the 'dear loaf' which the Liberals, and particularly Herbert Asquith, suggested would be the result of any system of tariff reform. It was this that was thought to make Chamberlain's scheme a vote loser in the 1906 General Election.

Zollverein – a customs union which would make the Empire a free trade zone protected by tariffs. Customs duties provided a large proportion of colonial revenues whilst they safeguarded infant industries which would be unable to complete against unfettered British imports.

Source A
Chamberlain speaking in 1895.

Great Britain, is the centre of a vaster Empire than the world has ever seen, owns great possessions in every part of the globe, and many of these possessions are still almost unexplored, entirely undeveloped. What would a great landlord do in a similar case with a great estate? If he had the money he would expend some of it at any rate in improving the properly.

Source B
Extract from Chamberlain's speech in Birmingham, 13 May 1898.

All the powerful States of Europe have made alliances, and as long as we keep outside these alliances, as long as we are envied by all, and suspected by all, and as long as we have interests which at one time or another conflict with the interests of all, we are liable to be confronted at any moment with a combination of Great Powers ... We stand alone ... What is the first duty of a Government under these circumstances? ... to draw all parts of the Empire closer together ...

TALKING POINT

The Dominions sent 60,000 men to fight in South Africa. Why would this encourage Chamberlain?

Source C
Chamberlain's speech at Birmingham, 15 May 1903, launching the debate on economic policy.

... the question of trade and commerce is of the greatest importance. Unless that is satisfactorily settled, I for one do not believe in a continued union of the Empire.

... I say that it is the business of British tradesmen to do everything they can, even at some present sacrifice, to keep the trade of the Colonies with Great Britain, to increase the trade and promote it, even if in so doing we lessen ... the trade with our foreign competitors.

... You want an Empire ... They [the people of the Empire] have two alternatives before them. They may maintain ... in all its severity, the interpretation ... which has been placed upon the doctrine of Free Trade by a small remnant of Little Englanders of the Manchester School ... although it is repudiated by every other nation, and by all your own colonies. In that case, they will be absolutely precluded from giving any kind of preference or favour to any of their colonies abroad ... The second ... is that we should insist that we will not be bound by any purely technical definition of Free Trade...

1 Study sources A and B. What attitude towards Empire do they reflect?
2 Source C is an extract from the speech in which Chamberlain launched the policy debate. In what ways was he challenging free trade economics and how effectively did he justify that challenge?
3 'Chamberlain's tariff reform proposals were the main reason for the Conservative defeat in 1906.' Discuss this view with reference to the sources and the relevant sections in this chapter.

TALKING POINT
Chamberlain also promised that tariff reform would enable the Conservatives to repel the challenge from socialism – how was that possible?

TALKING POINT
Would imperial preference and protection have really solved the problems some British industries faced at the beginning of the twentieth century?

17.2 Joseph Chamberlain – 'destructive force and disappointed man'?

Although he continued to represent West Birmingham in Parliament until his death in 1914, Chamberlain's political career ended in 1906 when he suffered an incapacitating stroke.

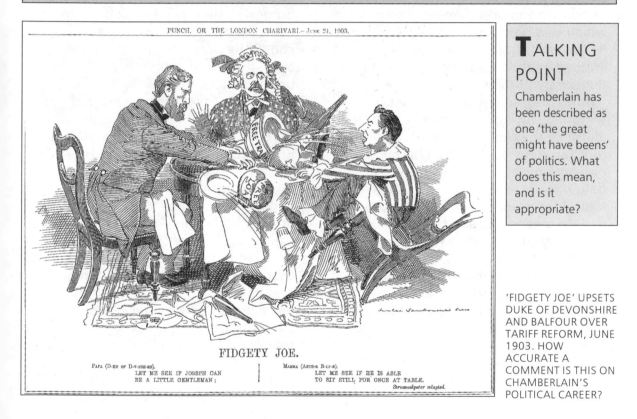

PUNCH, OR THE LONDON CHARIVARI.—June 24, 1903.

FIDGETY JOE.

PAPA (D-KE OF D-V-NSH-RE).
LET ME SEE IF JOSEPH CAN
BE A LITTLE GENTLEMAN ;

MAMMA (ARTH-R B-LF-R).
LET ME SEE IF HE IS ABLE
TO SIT STILL FOR ONCE AT TABLE.
Struwelpeter adapted.

TALKING
POINT

Chamberlain has been described as one 'the great might have beens' of politics. What does this mean, and is it appropriate?

'FIDGETY JOE' UPSETS DUKE OF DEVONSHIRE AND BALFOUR OVER TARIFF REFORM, JUNE 1903. HOW ACCURATE A COMMENT IS THIS ON CHAMBERLAIN'S POLITICAL CAREER?

Chamberlain has the unenviable distinction of shattering the Liberal Party in 1886, and then of repeating the process with the Conservatives after 1903. Despite a leading role in national politics for over thirty years, it is easy to dismiss Chamberlain as a disappointing politician who failed to live up to his promise. He held no major office, although he gave the Colonial Office (1895–1903) great prestige, was responsible for no major domestic reform and threw himself into two great campaigns (for the 'Unauthorised Programme' and tariff reform) which failed to win the support of the electorate.

Source A

... interpretations of Chamberlain's politics ... are all inclined to undervalue his sheer originality and creativity as a political actor. His personal dynamism; an urge to 'get things done', and to associate himself with great constructive achievements; the restless pursuit of domination over men and events which was both a personal need and, he believed, the precondition for imposing rational solutions upon contemporary problems ...

Ultimately, so typical a product of the Victorian city, and so eloquent an articulator of the central political questions that taxed his generation, Chamberlain proved a misfit, unable to accommodate himself entirely to the main ideological forms in terms of which party debate proceeded, and incapable of operating successfully with the institutional structures available.

... He may have merited much of the bad press he received; assessed against the great objectives of Radicalism and imperialism he espoused ... his career was a failure.

R. Jay, *Joseph Chamberlain: a Political Study*, 1981.

Essay

'In retrospect, it is easy to dismiss Chamberlain as a destructive force and a disappointed man. But ... he was creative and successful for much of his life.' (David Cannadine reviewing P. Marsh, *Joseph Chamberlain: Entrepreneur in Politics* in *The Observer*, 22 May 1994).

Research the career of Joseph Chamberlain, commenting on Cannadine's contrasting of 'destructive force', 'disappointed man' with 'creative and successful'.

Source B

... his experience in industry enabled him to present fresh responses to many of the questions, old and new, with which the political leaders of Britain were confronted ... He widened the range of the questions, as much on overseas matters as on domestic. He escalated debate on how the powers of the state should be used to meet the needs of an industrial economy and urban society.

... social vision became blurred and his constructive capacity for these purposes lessened as he moved from Birmingham town council ... His domestic initiatives in Gladstone's ministry accomplished little. The Radical programme was ill-judged and an electoral failure ... In a curious way the Unionist alliance sharpened the cost-accounting tools Chamberlain used so well as mayor of Birmingham, and helped him work out self-financing schemes of social insurance ... Even so, his social accountancy reached its limits with the enactment of the workmen's compensation for industrial accidents. His social prescriptions as a tariff reformer were timorous and vague.

... From one perspective, tariff reform was a scheme for general self-financing of social reform, to be paid largely by the working class consumer for his own benefit.

... his most substantial achievements were in the city of his adoption ...

P. Marsh, *Joseph Chamberlain: Entrepreneur in Politics*, 1994.

The Liberal Party and the 1906 General Election

General Election 1900 (the 'Khaki' election)

Conservatives and Unionists	402
Liberals	184
Irish Nationalists	82
Labour Representation Committee	2

In 1900 the Liberal Party, split between Liberal Imperialists and pro-Boers with Campbell-Bannerman unsuccessfully trying to hold the balance, was incapable of fighting an election against the prevailing patriotic mood. The party organisation collapsed and 152 English, Welsh and Scottish seats were left uncontested.

General Election 1906

Conservatives	157
Liberals	401
Irish Nationalists	83
Labour	29

Liberal organisation was much improved. Only five Conservatives were unopposed by a Liberal or LRC candidate. The Liberals had a majority over all other parties, and were not dependent on the Irish as in 1892.

An analysis of the votes cast for each party modifies the 'disaster' of these elections for the main parties:

	1900	1906
	\% vote	
Cons./Unionist	51.5	43.6
Liberal	44.6	49.0

The 'New' Liberals

The 1890s saw a reinterpretation of Liberal philosophy to accommodate policies of state intervention to ensure a minimum standard of living for all citizens. The persistence of economic difficulties, evidence that poverty was not being eliminated, and political developments that implied greater social and class division prompted a search for solutions. The individualism of the old Liberalism provided no answers. Sweeping social reforms funded by graduated taxation became an enlightened means of promoting the 'common interest' and removing class conflict. The individual was to be freed from external restrictions on his personal liberty.

The intelligentsia and young politicians of the 'new' Liberalism had little influence over the party leaders but powerful organs of Liberal opinion supported them. The radical editors of the *Manchester Guardian*, the *Daily Chronicle*, the *Westminster Gazette* and the *Daily News* willingly gave the new radicals public platforms. P.F. Clarke has argued (*Lancashire and the New Liberalism*, 1971) that in Lancashire at least progressivism enabled the Liberals to adapt successfully to a new age of class politics.

SIR HENRY CAMPBELL-BANNERMAN BECAME LEADER OF THE PARTY IN 1898, A TEMPORARY ARRANGEMENT UNTIL ASQUITH WAS READY TO TAKE OVER. BY 1905 THE PARTY WAS FIRMLY UNITED BEHIND CAMPBELL-BANNERMAN. HE EASILY DEFEATED AN ATTEMPT BY THE LIBERAL IMPERIALISTS TO MOVE HIM TO THE LORDS LEAVING THE LEADERSHIP IN THE COMMONS WITH ASQUITH.

Historians and the Election

Source A

...1906 represented a reversion to 1880. ... The Liberals were again swept in on a tide of reaction against the policies and conduct of their Conservative opponents, not of enthusiasm for the policies that they ... had to offer ... The mood of the campaign was deliberately and essentially negative and marked the culmination of the strategy followed by the leaders since 1901 of blurring over the disagreements within the party and concentrating on rallying a majority of resentment against the initiatives and innovations of the Unionists.

D.A. Hamer, *Liberal Politics in the Age of Gladstone and Rosebery*, 1972.

Source B

It was quite clear what the Liberals were against. They were against Tariff reform: against high arms expenditure: against Chinese 'slavery': against the 1902 Education Act, and so on. The liberals had even promised not to introduce a Home Rule Bill ... But what were the Liberals for?

G.R. Searle, *The Liberal Party: Triumph and Disintegration, 1886–1929*, 1992.

Source C

... this change [to the 'new' Liberalism] was somewhat obscured by the aftermath of the south African War ... After 1902 Liberal rhetoric was diverted towards such tempting targets as education, 'Chinese Slavery' and free trade, and propaganda took the negative line of reversing Toryism. This inevitable attempt to exploit the government's difficulties culminated in the revivalist campaign of 1906. However, this obscures the underlying trend. Examination of the 1906 campaign material shows the general commitment of candidates to old age pensions, graduated taxation, poor law and land reform ...

M. Pugh, *The Making of Modern British Politics 1867–1939*, 1982.

H.H. ASQUITH WAS ONE OF THE LEADING LIBERAL IMPERIALISTS, BUT HE PLAYED A MAJOR ROLE IN THE UNITING OF THE LIBERALS AFTER 1902. RECOGNISING THE OPPORTUNITY PRESENTED BY TARIFF REFORM, HE ASSIDUOUSLY FOLLOWED CHAMBERLAIN AROUND THE COUNTRY, SPEAKING IN EVERY CITY VISITED BY THE TARIFF REFORMER DURING 1903. THE OFFER OF THE EXCHEQUER IN CAMPBELL-BANNERMAN'S GOVERNMENT ENDED ANY POSSIBILITY OF REBELLION BY THE LIBERAL IMPERIALISTS.

REVIEW TASK

The 1906 General Election raises many questions:

● Did the record of Balfour's administration (1902–05) deserve this verdict of the electorate?
● Was this an election that the Conservatives lost rather than the Liberals won?
● Did the 'New' Liberalism count for anything in 1906?
● In the circumstances of 1906, did the 1903 agreement save the LRC from possible disaster?

As shown by the extracts from these historians, the 1906 General Election raises many questions. Prepare notes from the sources and your wider reading, then answer one of the following essay questions:
'Considered as a verdict on the work of Balfour's ministry the overwhelming Conservative defeat in the election of 1906 was undeserved.' Discuss this opinion.
'The Liberals benefited from a fortunate combination of circumstances which allowed them to unite in the defence of shared ideologies.' Comment on this explanation for the Liberal landslide of 1906.

Despite the omens and
fears, why had Britain
escaped the revolution
many had predicted?
'Politicians were not
obsessed by a fear of
democracy; they were
playing a party political
game in which party
advantage was the aim.'
How far do the careers of
the politicians listed in this
Review support this view?

REVIEW

The Frustrating of Democracy?

Conventionally, textbooks on nineteenth century Britain end in August 1914 rather than with the General Election of 1906. The election was fought over issues that would not have been out of place for much of the previous sixty years. After 1906 things began to change. For the first time there was a strong working class presence in the House of Commons. The Liberal government could not ignore the implications of that, nor could they neglect the new ideas being generated within their own ranks. Admittedly the social reforms they eventually embarked on owed much to nineteenth century precedents and to the administrative structure that had been built up, but there was a definite departure from Gladstonian principles of limited state intervention and rigid economy.

No leading nineteenth century politician was a democrat. Liverpool, Grey, Peel, Russell, Palmerston, Gladstone, Disraeli and Salisbury had all attempted to prevent or control political change. Viewing the century from the vantage point of 1906 it could be argued that they had been successful. Successive extensions of the franchise had been absorbed without the feared democratic excesses. Universal manhood suffrage had not been conceded. With a few exceptions, cabinet ministers still came from the same small elite. The powers of the House of Lords were still intact. The presence of Labour MPs in the House of Commons and the arrival of class politics might seem alarming but the new Members accepted the institution to which they had been elected and were willing to work through and not against it.

Index

Page numbers in bold denote major section/chapter devoted to subject